POLITICS AND MARKETS IN THE WAKE OF THE ASIAN CRISIS

This book is a challenging volume by distinguished, leading scholars of East Asian political economy. It provides a distinct alternative to simplistic accounts of the Asian crisis which generally swing between an emphasis on convergence imposed by global economic forces and the resurrection of the special patterns of East Asian economic governance. The authors argue that global forces and domestic structures are engendering new forms of economic and political regulation in East Asia. While these signal the death knell of the developmental state, this in itself does not presuppose a convergence towards a standard model of global capitalism. The arguments in this book will contribute significantly to the construction of a new research agenda for comparative political economy at the dawn of a new century.

Politics and Markets in the Wake of the Asian Crisis covers a range of East Asian countries including the People's Republic of China, South Korea, Indonesia, Thailand and Malaysia. All the studies are linked together by a common endeavour to explore the dynamic interaction between global economic forces and domestic structures. The book is at the cutting edge of the study of East Asian political economy, and is distinguished by the attention it pays to the regional and international context of the crisis. It also contains theoretically sophisticated analyses of organizations such as APEC and the IMF.

Richard Robison is Professor of Asian and International Politics, and Director of the Asia Research Centre, Murdoch University, Australia; he is the author and editor of many books, including, most recently, *The Political Economy of Southeast Asia*. **Mark Beeson** is Lecturer in International Politics at Griffith University, Australia. **Kanishka Jayasuriya** is Senior Research Fellow at the Asia Research Centre, Murdoch University; Routledge recently published his *Law, Capitalism and Power in Asia: The rule of law and legal institutions*. **Hyuk-Rae Kim** is Professor in the Department of Korean Studies, Yonsei University, Korea.

ASIAN CAPITALISMS
Edited by Richard Robison
Director, Asia Research Centre, Murdoch University, Australia

At the end of the twentieth century capitalism stands triumphant. Yet, it has not been the liberal model of free markets, democratic politics, rule of law and citizenship that has enjoyed general ascendancy. Within Asia, a range of dirigiste, predatory and authoritarian systems have emerged under the general rubric of Asian Capitalism. In this series we seek to explain the political, ideological and social bases of this phenomenon and to analyse the collision of these systems with the power of global economic markets and highly mobile capital and their confrontation with emerging social and political interests domestically. In the context of the financial crisis we ask whether we are witnessing the end of Asian Capitalism. Is Asia caught in an inexorable metamorphosis towards liberal capitalism and what factors drive the processes of transformation?

LAW, CAPITALISM AND POWER IN ASIA: THE RULE OF LAW AND LEGAL INSTITUTIONS
Edited by Kanishka Jayasuriya

POLITICS AND MARKETS IN THE WAKE OF THE ASIAN CRISIS
Edited by Richard Robison, Mark Beeson, Kanishka Jayasuriya and Hyuk-Rae Kim

POLITICS AND MARKETS IN THE WAKE OF THE ASIAN CRISIS

Edited by Richard Robison, Mark Beeson, Kanishka Jayasuriya and Hyuk-Rae Kim

London and New York

First published 2000
by Routledge
11 New Fetter Lane, London EC4P 4EE

Simultaneously published in the USA and Canada
by Routledge
29 West 35th Street, New York, NY 10001

Routledge is an imprint of the Taylor & Francis Group

Typeset in Times by Taylor & Francis Books Ltd
Printed and bound in Great Britain by Biddles Ltd, Guildford and King's Lynn

British Library Cataloguing in Publication Data
A catalogue record for this book is available from the British Library.

Library of Congress Cataloging-in-Publication Data
Politics and markets in the wake of the Asian crisis / edited by
Richard Robison ... [et al.].
(Asian capitalisms)
This volume is an outcome of the proceedings of an international
conference in August 1998, organized by the Asia Research Centre,
and Yongsei University.
Includes bibliographical references and index.
1. Financial crises–East Asia. 2. Capitalism–East Asia.
3. East Asia–Economic conditions. I. Robison, Richard, 1943– .
II. Asia Research Centre. III. Yŏnse Taehakkyo. IV. Series.
332'.095–dc21   99-31669

ISBN 0–415–22056–4 (hbk)
ISBN 0–415–22057–2 (pbk)

CONTENTS

v

CONTENTS

CONTENTS

ILLUSTRATIONS

Figures

Tables

CONTRIBUTORS

Mark Beeson is Lecturer in International Relations, Griffith University, Queensland.

Stephen Bell is Associate Professor in the School of Government at the University of Tasmania.

Walden Bello is Professor in the University of the Philippines and Director, 'Focus on the Global South' in Bangkok.

James Cotton is Professor of Politics at the Australian Defence Force Academy, University of New South Wales, Canberra.

Lance L. P. Gore is Research Fellow at the Institute of East Asian Political Economy, the National University of Singapore.

Kevin Hewison is Professor of Asian Studies, Asia Centre, School of Social Science, The University of New England, Armidale, New South Wales.

Richard Higgott is Professor of International Political Economy and Director, the Economic and Social Research Council of Great Britain, Centre for the Study of Globalisation and Regionalisation, Warwick University. He is also Editor of *The Pacific Review*.

John M. Hobson is Senior Lecturer in International Relations in the Department of Government at the University of Sydney.

Kanishka Jayasuriya is Senior Research Fellow at the Asia Research Centre, Murdoch University, Western Australia.

K. S. Jomo is Professor of Economics at the University of Malaya, Kuala Lumpur.

Hyuk-Rae Kim is Assistant Professor and Chair, Department of Korean Studies, and Associate Director, Institute for Modern Korean Studies at the Graduate School of International Studies, Yonsei University, Seoul.

Richard Leaver is a Senior Lecturer in the School of Politics and

International Studies, Flinders University, South Australia.

Yeon-ho Lee is Research Professor at the Institute of East and West Studies, Yonsei University, Seoul.

Chung In Moon is Professor, Department of Political Science and Director, Institute for Korean Unification Studies, Yonsei University, Seoul.

Sang-young Rhyu is Senior Research Fellow, Samsung Economic Research Institute, Seoul.

Richard Robison is Professor of Asian and International Politics and Director of the Asia Research Centre, Murdoch University, Western Australia.

Andrew Rosser is Research Fellow at the Asia Research Centre and Lecturer in Politics and International Studies, Murdoch University, Western Australia.

Khoo Boo Teik is a Senior Lecturer in the School of Social Sciences, University Sains Malaysia, Penang.

Linda Weiss is Associate Professor in the Department of Government, University of Sydney.

Jeffrey A. Winters is Associate Professor in the Department of Political Science at Northwestern University, Illinois.

PREFACE

Asia's economic miracle which dominated the headlines of the popular press and the bylines of academic journals spectacularly collapsed in mid December 1997. The end of the Asian miracle, like the collapse of the Soviet Union, was a scenario that most major social scientists and futurists failed to foresee. Of course it is too late for prediction but as social scientists – and this is a truly interdisciplinary task – we have a remarkable opportunity to examine and understand the dynamics of the crisis, and, yes, even to speculate on possible future scenarios for East Asia. It is in this context that the Asia Research Centre (ARC) at Murdoch University, in association with the Graduate School of International Studies at Yonsei University in South Korea, organized a major international conference in August 1998 to engage in a broad-ranging discussion of issues relating to the political economy of the Asian crisis. This also provided an opportunity to monitor and look ahead at what may be in store for East Asia in the first decade of the new century. This volume is the edited outcome of the proceedings of that Conference.

The Asia Research Centre of Murdoch University, a Special Research Centre of the Australian Research Council, was well placed to hold such a conference. As an internationally recognized institution for the study of economic and political change in East Asia the Centre has a well-established reputation for scholarly research on diverse aspects of social and political change in East Asia. An early study conducted by the Centre on the impact of the new middle class on the changing dynamics of East Asian political economy has helped to shape much of its research agenda in the 1990s.

However, it is clear that the current crisis poses a different set of research questions as we move into the new century. These relate to such issues as the extent to which illiberal markets and the powerful interests entrenched in these structures can resist the shift towards a more efficient economy, the coalitional and institutional politics that underlies the difficult process of policy reform, and the need to explore the role that will be played by international and regional organisations in the post-crisis period. The contributors to this volume are scholars well known for their work on East

Asia, and well equipped to provide an informed and considered analysis of the Asian crisis. The volume deals with the Asian crisis in several East Asian countries, especially the People's Republic of China, South Korea, Taiwan, the Philippines, Indonesia, Thailand and Malaysia and Singapore. All the studies are linked together by a common endeavour to explore the dynamic interaction between global economic forces and domestic structures

The analyses presented here importantly depart from simplistic accounts of the Asian crisis, which swing between an emphasis on convergence imposed by global economic forces and the reassertion of the distinctive patterns of East Asian economic governance that usually goes under the rubric of the developmental state. Indeed this debate on convergence and divergence in post-crisis Asia is merely another instalment in the long-running debate between statist and mainstream neo-classical economic approaches to the Asian miracle. The conventional orthodoxy would suggest that the crisis signals the end of the road for the collusive relationship between business and the state that so dominated East Asian political economies. Of course, what this perspective singularly fails to acknowledge is the role of politics and power in shaping and constraining the process of economic reform in East Asia. Similarly analysts as well as proponents of the East Asian developmental state explain the crisis rather naïvely in terms of a conflict between competing models of capitalism. These theorists conveniently neglect the fact that the reasons for the demise of the developmental state lie in part in the reconfiguration of domestic forces and interests within East Asian political economies. In short, the contributors to this volume argue that politics matters in understanding both the crisis and its aftermath.

An underlying theme of this volume proposes that global forces and domestic structures are engendering new forms of economic and political regulation in East Asia. While the developmental state can be safely consigned to economic historians, this fact in itself does not presuppose a convergence towards a standard model of global capitalism. It is hoped that the critical perspectives presented in this volume will have significant bearing on the construction of a new research agenda for comparative political economy at the dawn of the new century – one that will hopefully go beyond the cul-de-sac of recent debates on East Asia.

This work presents a bold, exciting and invigorating research agenda for the next decade, and we are confident that it will provide a first instalment of a new research agenda for the study of East Asian political and economic change.

Richard Robison
Mark Beeson
Kanishka Jayasuriya
Hyuk-Rae Kim
Perth, May 1999

ACKNOWLEDGEMENTS

This volume is the product of a substantial period of research collaboration that culminated in an international conference entitled 'Miracle to Meltdown: The End of Asian Capitalism?', held in Fremantle in August 1998. It was a conference that involved not only the contributors to this volume, but a range of leading researchers from the region, who acted as discussants. We wish to thank the contributors for their patience as well as prompt attention to editorial requests. This is especially important, given the fact that we were keen to ensure rapid publication of the papers. Our thanks to the discussants who enriched the conference as well as the quality of the final papers in this volume.

That we were able to hold such a long and successful conference is largely due to the financial generosity of several sponsors. These included: The Japan Foundation, The West Australian Department of Commerce and Trade and the Confederation of Asian Chambers of Commerce. We are indeed grateful for their support. The editors also wish to thank Professor Choi, Dean, Graduate School of International Studies, Yonsei University, and Professor Moon, former Director, Centre for International Studies, for their contribution to this project.

Last but not least we owe a debt of gratitude to the administrative staff of the Centre – Del Blakeway, Geoff Paton, Robert Roche and Mandy Miller – who have contributed greatly to the success of the conference. Special mention must again be made of Del Blakeway, the Executive Officer of the ARC, who not only provided efficient management of the conference but also made it a convivial intellectual gathering.

Part I

THE END OF ASIAN CAPITALISM?

1

INTRODUCTION

Interpreting the crisis

Mark Beeson and Richard Robison

In the middle of 1997 East Asia was gripped by a major financial crisis that continues to affect the region. What was initially taken to be a relatively isolated shock has intensified and generated increasingly widespread economic and political effects which threaten to overturn much of the region's established political and economic order. These events have been remarkable enough in themselves. For observers of the region there has been an additional, if rather less traumatic, consequence of the crisis: quite simply, it has forced a major reassessment of our understanding of the way political and economic activity is organised within the region, and about the place of the region in an increasingly integrated international system.

The key question to emerge in the wake of the crisis is whether we are witnessing the end of Asian capitalism in its various dirigiste or predatory manifestations. In short, have East Asian forms of capitalism been undone by inherent structural contradictions that make them simply unsustainable, or have they been undermined by external forces associated with global financial markets and the activities of powerful actors like the International Monetary Fund (IMF) or the United States? Whatever the origins of the crisis, is 'Asian capitalism' in the process of moving towards a more liberal, market-centred order?

Despite differences in emphasis on global and domestic factors, on institutional and social factors, there is a general belief amongst this volume's authors that it is simply not possible to understand the recent events in East Asia without considering the integrated nature of economic *and* political factors. Although one of the central questions with which this entire volume seeks to deal revolves around the form and future of capitalist organisation in East Asia, it is worth emphasising at the outset that *any* form of economic organisation is ultimately an expression of institutional frameworks and the particular sorts of social relations embedded in them. In other words, although there are some fairly basic qualities which define capitalism anywhere, its specific manifestation will reflect the particular constellations of political and economic power within which it is embedded. Hence, the volume is distinguished by its questioning of the neo-classical/rational choice proposition that capitalist markets are mechanisms defined by natural laws of equilibrium, and driven by the rational choices of utility-maximising individuals.

Before introducing the region's more distinctive modes of political and economic organisation, we shall provide a brief sketch of the crisis itself, and indicate the scale of its impact. The broad intention of this chapter is to indicate the main themes that run through the volume and give a preliminary indication of the other contributions that make it up. In addition, we shall identify some of the key questions which have emerged from the crisis. At the outset let us broach the most fundamental of all: is this a crisis of *East Asian* capitalism, or a crisis of capitalism more generally? As the impact of the crisis spreads relentlessly outwards, are the problems being revealed by its progress less to do with the 'crony capitalism' of Asian business–government relations, or even the 'irrational exuberance' of financial markets, than they are with the contradictory and inherently crisis-prone nature of capitalism in general?

What the analyses contained in this volume reveal is the complexity of the factors that have not simply shaped the crisis, but which are determining its continuing evolution. Central in this regard are an array of national and international forces that are increasingly and overtly political. Whether it is the contest to shape domestic policy responses in Korea, or the friction between the IMF and Indonesia, the crisis has never been simply an economic event. Indeed, the IMF's role is indicative of the essentially political impact of nominally economic policy advice. The IMF has provoked both resistance and enthusiasm, influencing the struggle over policy agendas throughout the region, and being instrumental in the downfall of the governments of Korea, Thailand and, most dramatically, Indonesia. Significantly, the results and dynamics of such struggles have been different in each country. Exactly why is a matter of contention, with some stressing the clash between global financial markets and domestic institutions, while others emphasise the importance of constellations of power and interest in shaping outcomes.

It is precisely because the crisis is an inescapably political phenomenon, however, that the essays collected here are able to shed such a penetrating light on what is arguably the most important event in the region, if not the world, since the end of the Second World War. To put the matter somewhat baldly, what is at stake here is the future pattern of economic and political organisation in a region which was until recently routinely taken to be the most dynamic on earth. However – or whenever – the crisis is resolved, the nations of East Asia will continue to be of primary importance, if for no other reason than a substantial proportion of the world's population lives there. What is of equal importance, therefore, is the region's relationship

4

with the rest of the world. The spreading of crisis demonstrates that, for good or ill, East Asia now has the capacity to move the world.

While immediate policy attention focuses on whether existing regimes can emerge intact from the crisis by introducing Keynesian reflationary policies or by attempting to control domestic and global capital markets, the crisis begs other, more fundamental questions. For example, are Asian forms of capitalism simply in transition towards a universal capitalist model shaped by an intrinsic instrumental rationality? Or may various capitalisms exist within a range of institutional frameworks? Most importantly, how do economic systems change?

In the intense debate that has emerged in the time since the crisis took hold there, major questions have emerged. First, is the crisis a phenomenon that has its roots in changes in the structure of global capital markets that make economies more unstable, or in movements in currencies that change international competitive advantages? Or were the crises generated from within, propelled by shifts in the balance of power and interest among political and social coalitions or the collapse of institutions? While there is a general recognition that particular outcomes must be explained in terms of the interaction between a range of political and economic factors at both the domestic and global levels, the authors in this book nevertheless privilege particular forces.

Winters, Higgott, and Leaver, for example, emphasise factors at work in the global political economy, whereas Weiss and Hobson, Moon and Rhyu, Kim and Lee, and Kim all suggest that the disintegration of institutional capacities within particular economies is at the heart of the region's problems. For Robison and Rosser, Khoo, and Hewison shifts in the architecture of power and interest have played an especially critical role. Beeson and Bell, by contrast, suggest that all of these factors have affected Australia's relationship with the region. Clearly, there is a good deal of debate about where the appropriate explanatory emphasis should lie even amongst broadly sympathetic scholars. In order better to appreciate such differences of opinion, it is as well to remind ourselves of both its origins and impact.

Measuring the meltdown

Although the crisis has by now become a staple of popular commentary, it is important to remind ourselves at the outset of quite how profound a transformation there has been in the fortunes of the region. Jeffrey Winters (Chapter 3) provides a detailed analysis of the dynamics that drove the initial currency crisis, which we shall complement here by briefly sketching its impact on the region. Having done that, we locate the countries of East Asia within an overarching global framework. For as Richard Higgott observes in this volume, the East Asian crisis is also the first 'crisis of globalisation'. It is important, therefore, to say something about the increasingly interconnected and internationalised system within which the East Asian meltdown occurred. This will enable us to begin the task of establishing how much of the current crisis is a product of the problems of East Asian capitalism, and how much may be a function of longer term changes in the wider global political economy.

The possibility that a number of East Asian economies might have potentially serious problems first became really apparent as a consequence of the Thai currency crisis. While there were a number of earlier warning signs that might – indeed, *should* – have caused concern in retrospect (see the chapters on South Korea by Moon and Rhyu, and by Kim in this volume, for example), these were overlooked in the euphoria associated with the generalised 'East Asian miracle'. As Kevin Hewison points out in this volume, the Thai developmental experience has been highly distinctive and has little in common with many other countries, yet there was little recognition of these differences or the potential for the Thai economy to collapse. What was perhaps an even greater shock was the possibility that the problems of one economy might by transmitted through the so-called 'contagion effect' to other economies with little obvious connection, other than inescapable geographical contingence.

Not only did a currency like Indonesia's rupiah lose about 80 per cent of its value in the space of a few months, but regional equity markets were equally decimated as 'investors' scrambled to leave what were perceived to have become highly risky investment prospects. This rapid capital exit which has clearly been central to the scale and rapidity of the transformation of the region's position becomes more comprehensible when the *composition* of capital is considered. As Table 1.1 shows, the economies of the region in general, and Southeast Asia in particular, had increasingly utilised and become dependent on highly liquid forms of portfolio or bank-mediated credit. Such inflows of capital were generally denominated in US$ and – compounding the potential risks of this strategy – unhedged.

The consequences of a growing reliance on 'hot' money from the world's increasingly integrated and massive financial markets have by now become all too apparent. As a number of the contributors in this volume make clear, a strategy of currency 'pegging' was always fraught with potential danger: not only was it always vulnerable to speculative attacks from the world's financial markets, but it systematically undermined the competitive position of the overall economy.

Equally rapid was the transmission of these financial sector shocks to the underlying 'real' economies of the region. We shall say more about this important distinction below, but at present we merely want to emphasise the scale of the downturn in the troubled economies. As Tables 1.2 and 1.3 indicate, across a number of key indices like unemployment, interest, inflation and growth rates, the position of the East Asian economies has been profoundly altered. From being synonymous with unparalleled growth rates

Table 1.1   External financing for five Asian economies[a] (US$ billions)

	1994	1995	1996	1997e	1998f
External financing, net	47.4	80.9	92.8	15.2	15.2
Private flows, net	40.5	77.4	93.0	−12.1	−9.4
Equity investment	12.2	15.5	19.1	−4.5	7.9
Direct equity	4.7	4.9	7.0	7.2	9.8
Portfolio equity	7.6	10.6	12.1	−11.6	−1.9
Private creditors	28.2	61.8	74.0	−7.6	−17.3
Commercial banks	24.0	49.5	55.5	−21.3	−14.0
Non-bank private creditors	4.2	12.4	18.4	13.7	−3.2
Official flows, net	7.0	3.6	−0.2	27.2	24.6
International financial institutions	−0.4	−0.6	−1.0	23.0	18.5
Bilateral creditors	7.4	4.2	0.7	4.3	6.1
Resident lending/other, net[b]	−17.5	−25.9	−19.6	−11.9	−5.7
Reserves excluding gold (= increase)	−5.4	−13.7	−18.3	22.7	−27.1

Source: Institute of International Finance
Notes:
a South Korea, Indonesia, Malaysia, Thailand and the Philippines
b Including resident net lending, monetary gold, and errors and omissions
e = estimate, f = IIF forecast

Table 1.2   Unemployment, interest rates

Country	Unemployment (%)		Prime rate (%)	
	June 1997	June 1998	July 1997	July 1998
Hong Kong	2.5	4.2	8.75	10.0
Indonesia	14.2	16.8	18.25	65.0
Malaysia	2.7	5.0	9.45	12.1
Philippines	10.4	13.3	14.5	18.0
Singapore	1.7	2.2	6.0	7.5
South Korea	2.6	6.9	8.5	11.5
Thailand	3.0	8.8	13.25	15.5

Sources: JP Morgan Asian Financial Markets: Third Quarter 1998, Singapore, 24 April 1998
(http://www.stern.nyu.edu/~nroubini/asia/afm2.pdf); 'Charting the Crisis', *Asiaweek* 17 July
1998: 41

Table 1.3 Economic growth and inflation

Country	Economic growth (%)				Inflation (%)			
	1996	1997e	1998f	1999f	1996	1997e	1998f	1999f
China	9.7	8.8	6.5	6.0	8.3	2.8	−2.8	−0.5
Hong Kong	5.0	5.3	−3.0	1.6	6.0	5.7	3.2	−2.4
Indonesia	8.0	4.5	−14.0	−3.5	7.9	6.6	60.0	27.0
Malaysia	8.6	7.2	−5.1	0.1	3.5	2.7	6.1	6.7
Philippines	5.8	5.2	0.4	4.0	8.4	5.1	10.0	7.5
Singapore	7.0	7.8	0.0	0.1	1.4	2.0	1.3	1.7
South Korea	7.1	5.5	−6.0	2.6	5.0	4.4	8.0	3.0
Thailand	7.7	0.5	−6.0	2.5	5.8	5.6	10.0	6.0

Sources: JP Morgan Asian Financial Markets: Third Quarter 1998, Singapore, 24 April 1998 (http://www.stern.nyu.edu/~nroubini/asia/afm2.pdf); 'Charting the Crisis', *Asiaweek* 17 July 1998: 41
e = estimate, f = IIF forecast

and seemingly limitless prospects, the region now finds itself at the centre of an equally dramatic downward spiral of negative growth and rising unemployment.

The long-term position of a number of the most badly affected countries is further constrained by their external debt positions. As Table 1.4 indicates, not only do the troubled economies share significant debt burdens, of which a substantial portion is short term, but this further compounds negative sentiment towards them by potential external investors or creditors. Quite how dramatically the position of the troubled Asian economies has deteriorated is demonstrated in Table 1.5, which indicates the extent of non-performing loans throughout the region.

Although the crisis has assumed an increasingly regional dimension, sweeping up one country after another in an expanding and seemingly

Table 1.4 International claims held by foreign banks (US$ billions)

Country	Total debt (1995)	Short term	Total debt (1996)	Short term	Total debt (mid 1997)	Short term
Indonesia	44.5	27.6	55.5	34.2	58.7	34.7
Malaysia	16.8	7.9	22.2	11.2	28.8	16.3
Philippines	8.3	4.1	13.3	7.7	14.1	8.3
Thailand	62.8	43.6	70.2	45.7	69.4	45.6
Korea	77.5	54.3	100.0	67.5	103.4	70.2
TOTAL	209.9	137.5	261.2	166.3	274.4	175.1

Source: Steven Radelet and Jeffrey Sachs, 'The Onset of the East Asian Financial Crisis', World Wide Web document http://www.stern.nyu.edu/~nroubini/asia/AsiaHomepage.html, citing International Settlements data

Table 1.5 Non-performing loans (percentage of assets)

Country	1997	1998
Korea	16.0	22.5
Indonesia	11.0	20.0
Malaysia	7.5	15.0
Philippines	5.5	7.0
Singapore	2.0	3.5
Thailand	15.0	25.0
Hong Kong	1.5	3.0

Source: Giancarlo Cosetti, Paolo Pesenti and Nouriel Roubini, 'What Caused the Asian Currency and Financial Crisis?', World Wide Web document http://www.stern.nyu.edu/~nroubini/asia/AsiaHomepage.html, citing JP Morgan data
Note:
The figures for 1998 are forecasts

irresistible downward spiral, it is important to recognise that it has gener-ated different effects in different countries. In order to try and untangle those aspects of the crisis that appear to be connected with possibly universal problems of capitalism in general, and those that may be more specifically connected to 'Asian' forms of capitalism, it is important to try and unpack this latter category more carefully and distinguish it from other forms of economic organisation.

The end of Asian capitalisms?

One of the most important issues to emerge during the crisis has centred on the way economic activity has been organised in East Asia. A good deal of attention has been devoted – particularly by the IMF – to developing plans to remedy the perceived shortcomings of Asian capitalism. Before the tech-nical merits of such questions can be considered, however, it is vital to develop a clearer understanding of the much invoked term 'Asian capi-talism'. In particular, we need to consider how East Asian forms of capitalism are organised differently from their counterparts in the Anglo-American economies. To understand how the East Asian variations on the general theme of capitalist development diverge from theoretical abstrac-tions, therefore, we need to place them in specific social and historical contexts.

Capitalism in context

Although the defining qualities of capitalism – market-oriented commodity production; private ownership of the means of production; the necessary sale of labour power by the majority of the population; acquisitive, maximising behaviour on the part of individuals (Hunt 1979: 2) – are well enough known, they merit repetition, as it is important to remember that they are not simply timeless, universal or 'natural' givens, but dependent upon particular constellations of power and interest for their realisation. In other words, although capitalism as an abstraction may have enduring qualities that lend it analytical utility, the way the institutions and social practices that constitute capitalism are actually manifest vary from one historical setting to another. Whether these different forms are stages on the road to a single model or constitute viable alternatives is another question, one that is clearly of central importance in the context of the crisis.

The expansion of capitalism from its original European home to encompass not just Asia but the entire world, made the idea of considering capitalism as one, all-encompassing *global* system increasingly attractive and appropriate. Whether the 'core–periphery' schema (Wallerstein 1974) is the most appropriate way of conceiving of an increasingly internationalised and interconnected system is another question, however. If there is one thing the pre-crisis performance of Japan and the so-called newly industrialising countries (NICs) seemed to demonstrate unequivocally, it was that economic development outside the 'core' was not only possible but could be achieved much more quickly than had been the case in Europe (Amsden 1990).

Yet in an increasingly global and interconnected political economy it is not clear whether any region or country, no matter what form of economic policy or social system it favours, can insulate itself from major systemic disturbances elsewhere. This is an especially significant consideration given that one of capitalism's defining historical qualities has been a chronic proclivity for deep-seated cyclical shifts that manifest themselves as 'booms' and 'busts' (Goldstein 1988). A key question, therefore, is whether the current crisis in East Asia is simply a 'normal' reflection of the internal dynamics of capitalism in general, or whether such inherent instability is compounded by the region's distinctive political and economic structures.

Asian capitalisms

Few would argue with the proposition that there are particular qualities which set capitalism apart in East Asia. Yet within this encompassing conception of 'East Asia' there are a number of distinctive historical patterns of development, very different types of state–business relations, as well as more broadly conceived generic types of capitalist organisation. In trying to understand the way the crisis is likely to impact on the region it is important to acknowledge these contingent factors as they will inevitably help shape the post-crisis political and economic order.

If one idea encapsulates a *Northeast* Asian approach to economic management in particular, or is synonymous with the region's political economy more generally, it is the 'developmental state' (Johnson 1982).

Pioneered by Japan, the developmental state is associated with a range of essentially mercantilist trade and industry policies that are designed to force the pace of industrialisation and promote national economic development. Central to this developmentalist project is the desire to harness the totality of resources available within the politically demarcated space over which the state claims authority in pursuit of some notion of a 'national interest'.

In Japan, the imperatives of post-war reconstruction provided the legitimating rationale for the single-minded pursuit of economic growth. While the desire for rapid economic growth may not have been an exclusively Japanese preoccupation, what distinguished Japan was the way its governing elite set about achieving it. The underpinning dynamic in Japan was still capitalist, but because the pursuit of profit occurred within a contingent Japanese context – with all the historical specificity that implies – it effectively harnessed capitalist dynamism to national purpose (Tabb 1995: 199). In short, what emerged in Japan was a form of *coordinated* capitalism which effectively consolidated and was mediated by existent social relationships and institutionalised patterns of organisation. Of central importance in this regard was the structure of the state–business relationship. Not only was the bureaucracy in Japan technocratically competent and capable of providing a blueprint for national reconstruction, but it had sufficiently close links with, and leverage over, local business to ensure that its plans could be carried to fruition (Calder 1988).

Japan has a wider significance in the context of the current crisis. First, not only is Japan still by far the most important economic power in the region, but it has provided an important developmental exemplar for other East Asian nations. The first generation of NICs to emerge after Japan, especially Taiwan and South Korea, were directly influenced by the Japanese during the latter's period as a colonial power (So and Chiu 1995), reproducing a range of Japanese-inspired industrial structures, policies, and state–business relations. A second generation of NICs in countries like Indonesia, Malaysia and Thailand have subsequently been caught up in a complex web of production structures, loan and aid packages which have tied them to Japanese companies as they have expanded into the region (Hatch and Yamamura 1996). A second, more subtle Japanese influence has been ideational. East Asian economic development has been premised on the idea that domestic governments – unlike their counterparts in the Anglo-American nations – could and should lead rather than follow markets (Wade 1990). In short, thinking about economic development and the appropriate role of government in that process has been shaped by a range of influences and economic models that are significantly different from the nostrums and idealisations that are associated with the neo-classical economic orthodoxy that predominates in countries like Australia and the United States (Fallows 1993). In short, Japan has developed a generic form of capitalism that

11

stands as a distinct alternative to the sort of model that the IMF is currently trying to impose on the region.

Yet the currently parlous state of the Japanese economy raises important questions about the competence and capacity of public servants and governmental agencies in an increasingly complex and interlinked global political economy. The numerous corruption scandals that have plagued the hitherto highly esteemed bureaucracy suggest that there is much that can go wrong when potentially mutually beneficial relationships between state officials and private businesses become entrenched over time. These are issues that are central not only to understanding the origins of the crisis itself, but to trying to judge its impact on the distinctive political and economic structures of East Asia. Key questions revolve around the continuing utility of coordinated forms of capitalism: Are such arrangements only useful in the earlier phases of industrialisation or 'catching up'? Do the enduring, cooperative relations between business and government that facilitate planned economic development inevitably risk descending into self-serving venality? In the longer term, do the processes associated with 'globalisation' make such relationships either unsustainable or irrelevant?

A number of responses to such questions are presented by the authors in this volume. Weiss and Hobson, for example, consider that the 'strong' states of Northeast Asia in particular can 'convert external constraints into domestic opportunities', and emerge comparatively well from the crisis. Similarly, James Cotton argues that the 'enterprise associations' of Singapore and Taiwan provided a rational and structural basis for a specific form of economic and political organisation that has insulated these countries from the worst ravages of the crisis. However, Hyuk Rae Kim argues that the capacity of even the most technocratically competent of East Asian states to respond effectively has been fundamentally undermined by the crisis. Perhaps Kanishka Jayasuriya's paper points the way forward from some of these apparently incommensurate positions: it is not so much a question of an absence or diminution of the state's regulatory effectiveness, but of *new* forms of regulation. In other words, even in the face of an apparently relentless tide of IMF-inspired neo-liberal reform, governments are involved in a process of *re*-regulation rather than *de*-regulation (Vogel 1996; Cerny 1991).

There is another point that merits re-emphasis in any discussion of the role of the state in the region: that is, the importance of distinguishing between the different versions of the 'East Asian model'. A consideration of the *South*east Asian experience suggests that while the Japanese exemplar may have exerted an influence, its realisation in a Southeast Asian context generally owes little to the stylised – not to say idealised – depictions of technocratic elites promoting the collective good. On the contrary, a country like Indonesia, dominated as it has been by a close-knit oligarchy that has been the principal beneficiary of economic development, is closer to a 'predatory' state than the developmentalist ideal (see Evans 1995). True, Indonesia's economic development has generated more widely dispersed benefits than has been the case in comparable African regimes, but the locus of political and economic power has remained with the dominant politico-bureaucratic elite. Indeed, the point to emphasise in the Indonesian case is that state power has been utilised to cement the position of the elite itself, *not* in the pursuit of some more broadly based conception of the national interest (Robison 1997).

Although the Indonesian case is perhaps extreme, it is not unique. A number of countries in the region have demonstrated a potential for predatory statism (Hutchcroft 1994), or for the more entrenched fusion of political and economic power that characterises a country like Malaysia (Gomez and Jomo 1997). The chapters by Robison and Rosser on Indonesia, Hewison on Thailand, and Khoo Boo Teik's analysis of the Malaysian experience suggest that the crisis itself and the reformist ambitions of both external *and* internal actors will profoundly affect domestic political economies across Southeast Asia. If, as seems increasingly likely, the crisis drags on and intensifies, then the possibility that such reforms will either generate nationally based forms of resistance or create further instability by accentuating domestic tensions is all too real. As Beeson and Bell indicate in their consideration of Australia, even a country which has enthusiastically embraced neo-liberal reform is not immune from the discomforting economic *and* political impacts of increased international integration. In short, the preconditions for what Higgott calls the 'politics of resentment' are in place across the entire region.

Nowhere are the social complexities of the crisis more apparent than in the potential for interethnic conflict, particularly involving the so-called 'overseas Chinese'. Although we need to be careful about homogenising a large number of people from increasingly disparate national contexts under this convenient rubric (Brown 1998), there are, nevertheless, sufficient commonalities about Chinese business practices to allow Chinese capitalism to stand as another ideal–typical entity. Chinese capitalism continues to reflect the social, institutional and cultural milieu within which it is embedded (Redding 1990), and represents – along with the Japanese variant described above – an important generic form that could play a potentially important role in the resolution of the crisis, especially in Southeast Asia. As such, it continues to be characterised by relatively small-scale, family-centred business structures, which generally substitute personalism for the supposed rationality of its Anglo-American counterparts. In short, different relationships and connections (*guanxi*) provide the underpinning basis for a complex network-based organisational structure that will not be easily altered by neo-liberal reforms and calls for 'transparency'. Indonesia is perhaps the most obvious illustration of both the economic importance and political influence of Chinese capitalism and of the potential for such relationships to generate widespread social unrest.

The final point to make about this brief sketch of Asian capitalism is that the theoretical and ideological prism through which the East Asian experience is refracted will inevitably colour subsequent conclusions. The theoretical assumptions of much neo-liberal economic thought, particularly the normative and methodological privileging of the *individual* rather than the group (or more specifically in the current regional context, the network), mean that many of the most distinctive qualities of East Asian capitalism are simply not captured (Biggart and Hamilton 1992). The type of theoretical paradigm that is employed, therefore, is likely to determine not only the way we see, or indeed define, problems for analysis, but the sorts of policies that are put in place as a consequence. This possibility is most obvious in the link between the neo-classical tradition of economic thought which has assumed such a paramountcy in the Anglo-American nations, and the normative pursuit (or imposition) of market-centred reforms (Gordon 1994). We shall critically assess a number of the more useful or influential theoretical perspectives in the final part of this chapter. Before that, however, it is important to situate East Asian forms of capitalism in their overarching and increasingly 'global' context.

East Asia and globalisation

In a number of analyses of the crisis writers from a range of backgrounds, from orthodox liberal economists like Jeffrey Sachs (1997), to the more radical perspective of Jeffrey Winters (this volume), have stressed the importance of the global financial system in precipitating the crisis. Such views raise a number of important questions. First, what specific changes in the international political economy may have been implicated in the crisis? Second, what are the implications of such changes for nation-states? In short, is it still possible for a range of national or regional responses to be generated to apparently ubiquitous international pressures, as the analysis of Higgott (this volume) or the recent actions of Malaysian Prime Minister Mahathir seem to suggest? These are critical questions, for if global financial markets in particular and the reconfigured international system in general are responsible for a crisis that shows every sign of affecting non-Asian economies, then dismantling 'crony capitalism' or discouraging dirigiste regimes may do little to address the underlying structural problems of capitalism *per se*.

In order to answer some of these questions, we need to be clear about how capitalism has evolved generally. This section, therefore, sketches the most important structural developments in the interconnected, international economic and political system, changes which are routinely subsumed under the rubric of 'globalisation'.

The industrial and financial sectors

The most visible expression of East Asia's incorporation into what is an increasingly global economy has been, until recently at least, its role in what has been dubbed the 'new international division of labour' (Frobel *et al.* 1978). A number of changes in the way productive processes are organised over recent years have allowed production to be dissaggregated and spatially dispersed over a number of locations that may transcend national borders (Dicken 1992). While the region has clearly enjoyed a number of benefits from its integration into global production processes and networks, the crisis has had the effect of revealing a number of long-term structural problems in the underlying 'real' economies of both the region and the wider international system.

Inward investment flows associated with new, internationally organised structures of production are now generally welcomed, if not actively pursued by host nation governments. Although East Asia has attracted increasingly significant flows of foreign direct investment (FDI), they have recently tended to be overwhelmingly directed towards one country – China. As Lance Gore points out in this volume, China's own political and economic practices in combination with new inflows of capital have contributed to a major build-up in the region's manufacturing capacity. This is exacerbating an historical crisis of excess productive capacity and declining profitability throughout the world, a growing problem that has been manifest in increasingly intense interregional contestation between North America, Europe and East Asia (Brenner 1998). This not only makes any immediate, export-led recovery from the present crisis more difficult, but directs attention to potentially more fundamental problems with capitalism in general. The remarkable increase in the productivity of manufacturing processes in particular has generated the preconditions for a systemic crisis centred on a major imbalance between supply and demand. The crisis, therefore, may be highlighting a global, rather than simply an East Asian problem of structurally entrenched unemployment, saturated markets and chronic overcapacity (Greider 1997).

These problems have been compounded by the prominent role played by financial capital during the crisis. Financial capital is most easily distinguished from FDI by its more attenuated relationship with 'real' economic activity. Simply put, financial capital is not directly involved in or committed to long-term involvement in productive activities, but operates through a range of intermediaries or financial instruments which allow its controllers to maintain a high degree of potential mobility. In other words, financial capital can move rapidly in and out of national economic space in response to changing circumstances. This has become an especially critical issue in an era when by some estimates up to US$2 trillion passes through the world's currency markets every day, of which more than 97 per cent is speculative and unconnected with the production of goods and services (Lietaer 1997: 15). The scale, scope and visibility of the markets is significant enough in itself, but when combined with the apparent inherent historical tendency for disjunctures to emerge in the pace of expansion in the financial and industrial spheres of international economic activity (Arrighi 1994), then the potential for crises is compounded. Certainly, increasing volatility in global equity, bond and currency markets suggests that such systemic crises and imbalances are not confined to the eastern side of the Pacific.

This is an even more important consideration given that one of the more important aspects of the present crisis has been the so-called 'contagion effect', in which what were initially taken to be localised problems rapidly spread to other countries. In the contemporary interlinked world economy, individual nation-states, especially those with smaller economies, appear to be extremely vulnerable to rapid shifts in market sentiment (Beeson 1998). The relative size of the economic forces ranged against individual countries is of critical importance here. The dramatic growth of mutual funds and large-scale institutional investors in countries like the United States means that where the governments of smaller economies have loosened control over domestic economic activity in line with international trends, then national currencies and the course of domestic development may be at the mercy of forces beyond the control of individual governments. While the degree of vulnerability or insulation experienced by individual countries is clearly variable and something that needs to be determined in specific circumstances, it seems plausible that much of the impact of the spreading crisis may be derived from the sheer increased scale and rapidity of financial sector movements.

An inevitable corollary to the resolution of the current crisis will be a re-examination, if not a reformulation, of the regulatory framework within which capitalism operates. Inevitably, however, the construction of a new 'financial architecture' will be shaped by the constellations of political forces within nations, the varying power of individual nations in relation to each other, and the increasing influence of transnational or non-state authorities. Greater capital mobility has had the effect of entrenching new domestic cleavages, not simply between 'capital' and 'labour', but within different elements of nationally or internationally oriented producers (Frieden 1991), and between them and the controllers of more liquid, footloose financial assets. An important impact of the internationalisation of economic activity, therefore, is to reconfigure the interests upon which domestic political coalitions rest (Milner and Keohane 1996: 16).

The potential importance of this realignment of domestic forces in response to international pressures is clearly demonstrated in the case of Japan, the most important economic actor within East Asia. To put the matter briefly, changes in the international financial system have not only reduced the ability of Japanese state officials to manage the domestic economy, but also affected the nature of the relationships between the financial and industrial sectors within Japan. A key change in this regard has been the growth of disintermediated credit in the Japanese system. In other words, the control and more particularly the allocation of credit has steadily moved beyond the purview of governmental control (Leyshon 1994). Not only is this a profound transformation of domestic political relations and the relative influence of key actors within Japan's political economy, but it is emblematic of a fundamental challenge to the very basis of East Asian capitalism. The distinctive East Asian form of a *credit*-based capital provision, (rather than the Anglo-American market-based model of finance), in which the state and the domestic banking sector are the principal sources of credit allocation (Zysman 1983), would seem to be directly threatened by the growing power and ubiquity of international financial markets.

State authority, and the entire interventionist style of economic development in East Asia, appears to be inevitably diminished by the current crisis and the potential imposition of further neo-liberal reforms. While the implications and extent of these changes need to be analysed in specific national contexts, there does seem to be prima-facie evidence, therefore, of a degree of 'convergence' in response to similar imperatives and structural constraints. Importantly in the context of the East Asian crisis, however, there appears to be a desire on the part of key transnational authorities and actors to try and encourage a process of convergence, or even impose structures and practices which conform to 'western' idealisations. In short, there is an increasingly important and overt *political* dimension to the globalisation process.

The politics of globalisation

The idea that the authority of nation-states is seriously compromised by processes associated with globalisation has become one of the staples of popular and academic commentary (Ohmae 1995). Yet as we saw in the case of Japan, while the internationalisation of economic activity does have the effect of reconfiguring the relative power of domestic political forces, this does not necessarily imply that the state itself is a less effective or important actor as a result. Clearly, any form of capitalism is ultimately dependent for its long-term realisation and continuance on the sort of legitimating authority and legal infrastructure that only nation-states can provide (Heilbroner 1985). And yet there clearly *have* been important changes in the state's position, especially as a consequence of the internationalisation of economic activity. Susan Strange (1996: 43) argues that the 'shift [of power] away from states towards markets is probably the biggest change in the international political economy in the last half of the twentieth century'.

States, then, are bound up in a complex web of transnational relationships, interdependencies and commitments which play a fundamental role in defining not only their own position and power, but also the shape of the increasingly multilateral international system of which they are a part. Yet the international political economy which has evolved in the post-war period is a *particular sort* of system, one which reflects the interests, preferences and power of its members. Increasingly, the rules and norms that govern the contemporary international system are associated with the so-called 'Washington consensus', which is predicated upon market-centred policies of privatisation and liberalisation (see Williamson 1994). In short, the consolidation of neo-liberal policies is associated with a range of reforms and initiatives that are designed both to entrench the position of market mechanisms and to advantage those firms and nations that are best able to take advantage of them. In other words, a critical issue highlighted by the crisis is whether market-centred reforms are simply apolitical technical responses to particular economic difficulties, or whether they are part of a wider agenda of reform designed to further particular national interests.

The role played by the IMF in attempting to manage this crisis highlights many of these issues, as Richard Leaver demonstrates in Chapter 15. Given that the IMF not only symbolises the new reality of intergovernmental relations, but has also been the most important and visible agent of neo-liberal reform, it is worth making a couple of brief additional points about this key organisation. The major point to emphasise is the thoroughgoing nature of the reforms being proposed by the IMF. As Robison and Rosser argue in this volume, the IMF reform agenda is designed to 'strike at the heart of politico-business and conglomerate power'. In other words, the IMF is interested not simply in attempting to stabilise immediate economic dislocation in Indonesia, but in making profound long-term changes to the organisation of economic and *political* activity in Indonesia. Given the intimate historical association between the IMF and the United States and its foreign policy goals (Pauly 1997), then it is reasonable to ask whether the key intergovernmental institution charged with resolving the crisis is pursuing a politically neutral agenda of exclusively economic reform, or one which is shot through with national implications and political imperatives. As Higgott argues in this volume, it is a perception that may provide a lightning rod for regional resentment and future conflict.

As the very different perspectives taken in this volume by Winters on the one hand and Weiss and Hobson on the other demonstrate, there is clearly an important debate about the role played by the United States in attempts to reconfigure East Asian political economies. What can be said is that the end of the Cold War has profoundly reduced East Asia's strategic leverage over the United States, and opened up a possibly unique, historic window of opportunity for those forces that wish to restructure political and economic activity in the region along more 'western' lines. This raises a further and critically important question: why do economic systems change? In other words, why do market orders function differently from one country to the next? In order to try and unravel this key question and begin to make theoretical sense of the crisis, we shall critically review a number of the more important and influential perspectives that have tried to make sense of East Asian and capitalist development more generally.

Understanding outcomes: how do markets change?

In the face of overwhelming pressures to reform, it is striking that change in the region has been contested and uneven. As a number of the contributors to this volume demonstrate, entrenched interests across the region continue to resist change. Opposition comes from vested business interests under threat from proposed bankruptcy laws, trade reform and the closure of insolvent banks, as well as from middle classes and workers for whom high interest rates, inflation and fiscal contraction undermine the gains of the past two decades. The varied impacts and effects of the crisis on the region raise broader questions about the way economic structures and social systems change.

How do we understand such contests? Do they represent the final struggles of rent-seekers and predators in the face of the inexorable, timeless and universal rationality of market mechanisms? Or are they conflicts between contending systems of power and interest? Are free markets and political democracy functionally necessary for capitalism? Or are these simply the institutions that emerged from the circumstances in which capitalism arose in nineteenth-century Europe? Can market economies exist within a range of institutional frameworks including political authoritarianism? There are a number of theoretical perspectives that might be utilised in trying to answer such questions, which for the sake of convenience we have divided into a neo-liberal perspective, a paradigm which sees markets as constructions of government and politics, and theorists who see markets as structured by relations of power and interest.

Neo-liberal explanations

In contradiction to their previous optimism that the 'Asian miracle' would continue into the Asian century on the basis of sound economic 'fundamentals' (Radelet and Sachs 1997), neo-liberals have explained the crisis as an inevitable functional breakdown of economies in which governments attempt to resist the rationality of markets (Friedman 1997; Camdessus 1997). As the cost of resisting markets becomes too high, reflected in over-valued assets, poor investment decisions and burgeoning debt, rational individuals seek greater efficiencies in the allocation of economic resources through the natural and neutral mechanism of the market. Likewise, individuals seek to reduce transaction costs caused by lack of information and predictability by constructing rules and regulations to constrain the predatory actions of 'rent-seeking' officials and business interests (World Bank 1983; North 1994).

Despite the elegant and frictionless process of change assumed above, neo-liberals have had to recognise the politically contested nature of economic transition. These contests are seen as resistance by rent-seekers, who prosper from government intervention in the operation of markets, and who capture both rents and the very institutions intended to regulate economic life (Krueger 1974; Olson 1982). Consequently, neo-liberals see the primary task as minimising the influence of the inevitably predatory institutions of state power (Buchanan and Tullock 1962). From this perspective, the crisis is a blessing in disguise. It offers an opportunity to dismantle protective trade and financial regimes, industry policies and the structures of 'crony capitalism'. Consequently, besieged governments seeking investment and debt rescheduling now find it increasingly difficult to resist demands from global funds managers and bankers to liberalise their trade regimes or to reform their banking systems. As IMF Chief Camdessus has argued, to receive the benefits of global financial markets countries had to adhere to its disciplines (cited in Saludo and Shameen 1997). Yet, neo-classical theorists confront a contradiction. They have increasingly recognised that it is only within institutions able to stand above vested interests that collective problems may be resolved. Hence the emphasis placed on institution building and 'good governance' and the recognition that the state has a role to play (World Bank 1997).

Neo-liberal approaches, therefore, embody several major problems. First, if the utility-maximising individual is the engine of change, how are collective interests identified and institutions established to enforce them? Chaudhry's (1997) question is central: who should manage these institutions and on what basis? A second problem lies in the assumption that markets are mechanisms abstracted from state power and social and political interest. The view that changing institutions is a technical matter is contradicted by the continuing inability to impose deregulation and craft 'good governance' in the form of transparent and accountable institutions. In Indonesia, for example, attempts in 1965, 1982 and 1986 to impose liberal market reform failed because economic crises did not break the dominant political and social order. Such cases suggest that market economies may require specific social and political preconditions.

Markets as the creations of governments and politics

Following the traditions of Weber and Polanyi, a range of theorists, including Chalmers Johnson and John Zysman, have argued that markets do not exist in isolation from state power, and are not timeless, universal essences, but the creations of government and politics (Zysman 1994).

Developmental elites within the state apparatus, in this view, can and do *create* specific market structures through a range of coordinated industry policies, strategic trade initiatives and financial regimes. In Wade's (1990) terminology, these are managed or governed markets. What is more, they often survive, as Amsden (1989: 13–14) pointed out, by countering the conventional wisdom of the market and 'getting prices wrong'.

In this view, markets do not exist independently of the institutions that define them. Because change occurs in the context of historically deter-mined institutional pathways, crises are accommodated within a central logic defined by layers of institutions – whether they be British trade union systems of labour or the credit-based industrial economies of Japan or France. Hence, in this view there is not one form of capitalism but many. Such an explanation has the advantage of explaining why it is so difficult to change economic systems and why apparently similar institu-tions when translated from one society to another often produce different outcomes.

But the crisis appears to have seriously damaged the statist position. High-debt strategies balanced on collusive arrangements between govern-ments, banks and business were left vulnerable as the currencies collapsed. It appears that state-managed or governed markets may indeed contain essen-tial functional flaws. Statist theorists have explained the crisis, not as evidence of the irrationality of governed or managed markets but as the consequence of foolish and imprudent reforms that led to the collapse of institutional capacity (Weiss and Hobson, this volume). Hence, the current task is to restore the institutional framework that made previous systems so successful.

There are several difficulties in this approach. Change is explained in terms of incremental rational choices that produce historical layers of insti-tutions which in turn impart a degree of path dependency. There is a tendency to reify institutions to the extent that we are unable to explain great shifts in history and the dramatic collapse of existent institutional frame-works as other than mistakes in design by developmental elites. This is the case in the present crisis (Wade and Veneroso 1998). However, reforms to economic regimes in the 1980s were not simply foolish miscalculations by bureaucratic elites, but the related shifts in political and social power that were reflected in policy and constitutional change, not least in the emergence of democratic politics. Restoring the old institutions is not, therefore, a technical matter but one that implies nothing less than a social counter-revolution. The challenge for institutional theorists that seek to do more than simply describe institutional variety, therefore, is to define the boundary between optimal institutional embeddedness and the development of self-serving distributional coalitions.

Markets as relations of power and interest

In western social theories of markets, originating largely from within the classical Marxist tradition, all economic systems are understood as relations of power and interest. Consequently, the opponents of neo-liberal reform are not dismissed as rent-seekers or vested interests, but as cohesive, entrenched political and social entities. Liberal market economies, no less than any other system, are embedded in particular constellations of state and social power. Change occurs, in this view, when legal, political and economic institutions, which were established to facilitate particular systems of economic production and to impose the architecture of social relations embodied in them, become constraints on the emergence of a new order. Hence, institutions are constructed to maintain and allocate power, not just to impose rational economic regimes (Bardhan 1989). The process of change involves political struggle to shape the rules that govern markets.

Like neo-liberals, although for different reasons, Marxists have also assumed that capitalism would lead inexorably to the development of market economies and political democracy. Embracing the globe, capitalism would contain within it a particular hierarchy of social power and interest, and involve a sweeping away of the existing social order. The fact that capitalism has evolved within a wide range of institutional frameworks – from the highly centralised developmentalist states of Bismarck's Germany and Meiji Japan to the predatory oligarchies of Indonesia and the Philippines – presented problems. While both liberal and Marxist theorists have explained such stages in terms of the absence or weakness of middle classes or business interests, this has not always been the case. Transitional stages are better defined in terms of different historical conjunctures of relationships and alliances between capitalists, the state and its officials, middle classes and workers (Marx 1969). Within the Marxist framework, it is assumed that these stages will be transcended as capitalism matures, markets are entrenched and the bourgeoisie achieve a hegemony that renders their protection under the umbrella of authoritarian states and dirigiste economic systems no longer necessary (Harris 1988).

Within this paradigm, the crisis may be explained in the context of two questions. Will it undermine the structural base of entrenched political and social coalitions, or are they able to accommodate such challenges? Moreover, even if existing regimes decay as they succumb to fiscal crisis and social unrest, is there any guarantee that liberal market economies will spontaneously emerge? As a number of contributions to this volume suggest, a retreat to oligarchy, nationalism or a decline into chaos are possibilities that cannot be ruled out. A second question, therefore, is whether the crisis strengthens reformist coalitions whose interests are served by markets, rule of law and political democracy.

There are, then, a number of theoretical frameworks with which it is possible to try and make sense of the current crisis. While they may all have something to tell us, the key test of their efficacy is their ability to illuminate the contingent dynamics that have shaped recent events. While capitalism may display some universal properties, any plausible account of the crisis must recognise that capitalism in Asia has been realised in distinctive ways that will not easily either be swept aside, or inevitably or painlessly 'converge' in a supposedly technically superior western model. Indeed, as the crisis threatens to spill over into the rest of the world – including North America – the Anglo-American variant of capitalism may come in for an equally searching scrutiny which may remind us of the contradictory and crisis-prone nature of capitalism in general, rather than of East Asian capitalism in particular.

Concluding remarks

This chapter has tried to place Asian capitalism in a specific historical context and identify some of the key issues that will influence its future development in the wake of the crisis. One of the most noteworthy features that has emerged from the crisis has been the extraordinary change in perceptions of the region and its prospects. It is important to remember that until very recently key international institutions like the IMF and the World Bank (1993; 1997) had nothing but praise for the developmental states and the primacy they attached to 'getting the fundamentals right' (Berger and Beeson 1998). Not only do orthodoxies change, it seems, but some views are clearly more salient than others in constructing the conventional wisdom. It is not necessary to be a Marxist to recognise that powerful nations are able to use their positions to make their visions of the way the world works pre-eminent (Ikenberry and Kupchan 1990), and thus the basis for 'cooperative' international actions. As a number of contributors to this volume note (see, for example, Winters), the overarching geostrategic framework within which interregional relations are conducted has been transformed in the wake of the Cold War's end. The United States, often under IMF auspices, has attempted to reshape East Asia and its institutions along neo-liberal lines, unconstrained by formerly dominant strategic imperatives (Beeson 1999). In short, it is inconceivable that the crisis would have unfolded in quite the way it has if the central dynamic of the international system had not shifted from 'high' politics to 'low' commerce (Luttwak 1990).

There are, then, powerful international forces associated with both the creation and the attempted resolution of the East Asian crisis. It is worth reiterating some of the key questions that have emerged from this chapter, and which will need to be addressed – either explicitly or implicitly – if the crisis is to be resolved. First and foremost, is the crisis a crisis of capitalism or of *East Asian* capitalism? Are Asian economic and political structures – even in their most technocratically competent and benign Northeast Asian

manifestations – simply unable to adapt to or cope with the seemingly irresistible array of forces associated with globalisation? Or is the East Asian
crisis a manifestation of some more fundamental and possibly new or
heightened 'contradiction' of capitalism itself? In short, how much of East
Asia's problems are due to domestic incompetence or corruption, and how
much to an international economic system that is fundamentally unstable
and which may ultimately affect the North American and European legs of
the Triad?

Other more immediate questions concern East Asia more directly.
Despite the economic origins of the crisis, the key questions that flow from
it are political. Put simply, how will the crisis affect domestic and international political relations? The dramatic downfall of the Soeharto regime
suggests that if the crisis drags on or becomes worse – as seems all too likely
– there may be further political trauma in the region. Will this encourage
democratisation as optimists hope, or will the pressures exerted by
collapsing economies and concomitant social unrest see a move back
towards authoritarianism? Indeed, will there be a backlash against the entire
project of further neo-liberal reform – and its extra-regional sponsors –
especially if it is unable to deliver any obvious benefits in the short to
medium term? The period between the two world wars provides a sobering
reminder that there is nothing inevitable about the course of economic
development or international relations.

If the current economic dislocation ultimately proves to have more to do
with a crisis of capitalism than it has to do with a crisis of *Asian* capitalism,
then the vectors of influence and admonition that are currently pointing
unwaveringly towards the region may be reversed. In the event of a more
generalised global crisis of capitalism engulfing North America and Europe,
then the sort of state-led economic strategies that East Asia perfected may
well prove valuable again. And yet this may highlight a key paradox if not
contradiction of the crisis: it is possible to argue that there are *still* aspects of
Asian capitalism – particularly its capacity for coordination and its potential
for a more equitable distribution of the benefits of economic development –
that make it functionally superior to its Anglo-American counterpart. But in
an era where power is increasingly shifting from states to markets, and in
which the world's most powerful nation cooperates with increasingly influential intergovernmental authorities to impose a market – rather than a
state-centred economic order – the East Asian model will not survive unless
there is a transformation of the wider system of which it is a part. As the
crisis spreads and more questions are asked about the stability and efficacy
of a predominantly neo-liberal world order, such a possibility cannot be
ruled out.

2

COMMENT

Crisis and the developmental state in East Asia

K. S. Jomo

East Asia's financial turmoil since mid 1997 has focused interest on crony capitalism and rent seeking in the region. In the immediate aftermath of the outbreak of the crises, which began in July 1997, many observers immediately assumed that the crises were due to poor macroeconomic management, as suggested by the second generation of currency crisis theories. The first generation of such theories – which had focused on public sector debt related to fiscal deficits – were quickly seen as irrelevant to Southeast Asia where all the affected governments had consistently maintained budgetary surpluses in recent years. It soon became clear, however, that all the governments affected had been maintaining decent macroeconomic balances except for large balance of payments current account deficits for Malaysia and Thailand, which had been bridged by massive capital inflows. With the debt – including foreign borrowings – mainly involving the private sector, and with continued high savings and growth rates as well as low consumer price inflation, most monetary and financial authorities in the region were being enthusiastically encouraged by the international financial community.

As soon as it was clear that the region's macroeconomic indicators were not seriously awry, and in the wake of the recent debate on Asian values and other differences, commentators began to focus on Asian cronyism and its alleged consequences as the new explanation for the crises. Most condemned rent seeking in the region as the ready-made explanation for the crises, usually ignoring all the subtlety and nuance of extant analyses. One commentator, for example, has claimed that things suddenly went awry from 1996, implying that all was well before that, and, presumably, that crony capitalism and rent seeking were not a problem then. Business organisations, relations, practices and norms that had previously been credited with the East Asian miracle were now condemned as the sources of the débâcle.

There is little serious disagreement that the East Asian economic crises since mid 1997 began as currency and liquidity crises. It is now increasingly clear that the crises have been due to the undermining of previous systems of international and national economic governance due to deregulation and other developments associated with financial liberalisation and globalisation, i.e. the subversion of effective financial governance at both international and national levels created conditions that led to the crises.

This does not mean that all was well from a macroeconomic perspective; as noted earlier, large current account deficits in some countries had been bridged by short-term capital inflows into the stock market and by loans from abroad. Crony capitalism and rent seeking had also been thriving, but, in themselves, did not precipitate and cannot explain the crises. However, cronyism and nepotism have certainly influenced official policy responses to the crises in Malaysia and Indonesia; more importantly, they may be said to have exacerbated the crises and are likely to continue undermining confidence, and thus delay recovery. It is now increasingly acknowledged that the currency and financial crises became crises of the 'real economy' mainly due to poor government and IMF policy responses.

Despite official claims that the regional currencies were pegged to baskets of the currencies of their main trading partners, to all intents and purposes, they had been virtually pegged to the US dollar for many years. Such quasi-pegging offered certain advantages including the semblance of stability – especially low inflation – so much desired by the financial community. The 1994 devaluation of China's currency put greater competitive pressure on Southeast Asian economies, especially Thailand, producing for the same markets. As the US dollar strengthened, especially against the Japanese yen from mid 1995, the pegged ringgit followed suit, adversely affecting Southeast Asia's export competitiveness. This was exacerbated by the region's failure to progress more rapidly to higher value-added production, mainly due to inadequate and inappropriate public investments in education and training as well as limited indigenous, internationally competitive, industrial capabilities. This state of affairs also reflected the political weakness – in influencing economic policy making – of exporting manufacturer interests in the region (where much internationally competitive industrial capability outside resource-based manufacturing is foreign owned), compared with the financial community.

Meanwhile, equity finance, involving financial disintermediation, grew in significance in the 1990s. The establishment of various new facilities in the region to ease access to foreign funds also undermined prudence in related banking practices. These and other reforms, as well as the growth of 'private banking' and 'relationship banking' in the region and increased competition among 'debt-pushing' competitors, also weakened the scope and efficacy of national prudential regulation. Other domestic financial sector reforms had also considerably reduced the powers and jurisdiction of the central banks.

Capital inflows – to the stock market as well as through bank borrowings – helped bridge current account deficits due to the growing proportion of 'non-tradables' being produced in the region, much of which was related to construction activity fed by property price bubbles. These flows were osten-sibly 'sterilised' to minimise consumer price inflation, as desired by the financial community, but instead fuelled asset price inflation, mainly involving real estate and share prices. It has become fashionable to suggest that the resultant property price bubble has its roots in Japanese-type or more generically East Asian culture, norms and relationships which compro-mise relations between the state and the private sector as well as among businesses, invariably involving welfare-reducing, if not downright debili-tating rent-seeking, behaviour. In so far as such relations are believed to exclude outsiders, their elimination is believed to contribute to levelling the playing field and bringing about an inevitable convergence towards suppos-edly Anglo-American-style arm's-length market relations.

The recent currency and financial crises suggest that Southeast Asia's economic boom had been built on some shaky and unsustainable founda-tions (Jomo *et al.* 1997). Much of the retained wealth generated has been captured by the business cronies of those in power, who have nonetheless contributed to growth by reinvesting these captured rents, mainly in the 'protected' domestic economy, e.g. in import-substituting industries, commerce, services and privatised utilities and infrastructure. Despite various weaknesses, this Southeast Asian brand of ersatz capitalism – involving changing forms of crony rentierism – has sustained rapid growth for four decades since independence in 1957.

It has now come unstuck owing to the economic consequences of and policy reactions to the massive deflation due to 'irrational' herd behaviour greatly exaggerating the impact of 'rational' (i.e. rent-seeking) speculative market behaviour to gain advantage from some unintended consequences of the region's currency appreciations. The overvalued regional currencies emerged from a recent conjuncture due to partial financial liberalisation, which also created the conditions for the asset price inflationary bubble that has now burst with devastating consequences for the region, exacerbated by injudicious policy responses. Failure to recognise the nature of the processes of accumulation and growth in the region has generally prevented the design and implementation of an adequate proactive strategy of well-designed and sequenced liberalisation in the face of the apparently inevitable.

It is useful to begin with greater recognition of the different processes of accumulation in Southeast Asia in contrast with Northeast Asia. Whereas the latter successfully employed industrial policy to develop indigenous firms which became internationally competitive, the former has been primarily reliant on foreign direct investment to develop industrial capacities and capabilities. As a consequence, the Southeast Asian bourgeoisie have been much more 'lumpen' in nature, with much more wealth derived from financial and other non-industrial investments as well as political power and influence. Hence, although the US dollar peg undermined Southeast Asian export competitiveness from mid 1995 as the US dollar rose against the yen,

27

it was maintained – with disastrous consequences, as we have seen – until mid 1997 owing to the influence of those holding financial and other assets, who stood to gain most from maintenance of the peg.

There have also been important differences within Southeast Asia. Not unlike Northeast Asia, Thailand and Indonesia have much more bank-based financial systems. However, outside Singapore, there is much less evidence of Southeast Asian banking systems being used as instruments of industrial policy as they were in Northeast Asia in the past. However, with the pressures for international financial liberalisation, even Northeast Asian financial systems have been forced to open up, usually not as part of a systematic programme, but more often than not, as a consequence of compromises in dealing with powerful bilateral partners as well as the changing governance associated with multilateral arrangements. Hence, for example, the liberalisation of the South Korean financial system as it sought and gained membership of the Organisation for Economic Cooperation and Development (OECD) undermined the earlier arrangements involving the government-controlled banks as crucial instruments of industrial policy (Chang in Jomo 1998a).

In Southeast Asia, pressures for financial liberalisation undermined earlier prudential regulatory systems without providing adequate alternatives. Banking reforms in Indonesia from 1988 were extended in the early 1990s with eventually disastrous consequences as the number of banks more than doubled in less than a decade and the reach of foreign banks extended beyond Jakarta into the Indonesian hinterland, effectively undermining monetary authority and constraining the scope for effective macroeconomic policy making and implementation. Similar developments in Thailand saw the establishment of the Bangkok International Banking Facility in 1993 and a provincial equivalent in the following year. The establishment of the Labuan International Offshore Financial Centre (IOFC) in 1993 guaranteed complete secrecy for all types of transactions, with some similar consequences.

The rapid growth of securities markets with the encouragement of the Bretton Woods institutions has also exacerbated the situation, especially in the 1990s. In Malaysia, where the financial system has historically seen a greater role for equity financing and has become decreasingly bank based, massive capital flight was facilitated by the ease of exit guaranteed by the government to attract short-term capital inflows. Not surprisingly then, Malaysia has experienced the greatest collapse of its stock market in the region since mid 1997.

It is now increasingly recognised that the International Monetary Fund (IMF) and the United States have unwittingly exacerbated the East Asian crisis in crucial ways. The IMF failed to recognise the nature of the underlying problems, misdiagnosing the situation and insisting on the wrong policy responses. It also undermined confidence in affected East Asian financial systems by demanding the closure of certain financial institutions, and induced the subsequent recessions in the region by insisting on government spending cuts, higher interest rates and reduced liquidity. Apparently at the behest of the United States, it blocked a Japanese initiative to provide liquidity when it became clear that IMF resources were inadequate and not forthcoming. For quite some time, it seems that the US administration did not recognise the severity of the East Asian crises and their likely consequences elsewhere. Hence, unlike its 'prompt and generous' response to the 1994–5 Mexican crisis on its doorstep, soon after the North American Free Trade Agreement (NAFTA) came into effect, the United States actually delayed more effective multilateral responses to the East Asian crises.

The Malaysian authorities' dramatic introduction of capital controls in September 1998 has highlighted the inadequacy and inappropriateness of extant responses to the crises, but its likely impact has been complicated by the acute power struggle leading to Mahathir's sacking, character assassination and imprisonment of his erstwhile deputy and heir apparent. In the year after the crises first began in mid 1997, there have been regime changes in the other four countries most affected by the crises. In Thailand, a new reform constitution went through with less difficulty than expected and a 'relatively cleaner' coalition came to office in the second half of 1997. In South Korea, Kim Dae-jung, considered a wishy-washy social democrat by some, was elected on a reform manifesto. In the Philippines, the populist Joseph Estrada was elected amidst reform expectations. In Indonesia, General Suharto was forced to resign in May 1998 after massive student and other protests calling for an end to 'corruption, cronyism and nepotism' following the massive collapse of the rupiah in January, the appointment of a new cabinet with an even higher 'crony' component and dramatic price increases of essential consumption items.

The dramatic developments since mid 1997 and the popular characterisation of East Asian regimes as 'cronyistic' raise fundamental questions about the nature of the East Asian states. Were they ever developmental, or was this label a figment of the imagination of analysts? Did they then become 'cronyistic', and, if so, how? Or did cronyism coexist with developmentalism, and, if so, how was this possible? There are, of course, no simple or easy answers to these important questions. However, it seems useful to consider several related propositions.

First, regime survival has been a very important motive for the developmental efforts of many East Asian states (Anderson 1998). Second, the extended incumbency and consequent autonomy of the executive in most of the region and the policy-making capacity of the technocracy in Japan and even Thailand have been conducive to generating investor confidence ('credible commitments') besides limiting short-termism among policy-makers. Third, contrary to the neo-liberal claim of consistently superior outcomes from free market outcomes, the benefits of government intervention may well outweigh its costs. Fourth, in so far as relations other than arm's-length market relations are deemed 'cronyistic', such arrangements and relations – which may emerge from state intervention – may either enhance or undermine development. It therefore becomes necessary to examine the nature and consequences of particular government policies and interventions in order to assess its outcome.

Khan (1996) offers a useful framework for the analysis of rent seeking which allows us to consider whether or not the creation of a rent due to a government intervention is value enhancing. Rent seeking attempts to maintain or reallocate existing rents, or more rarely, to create new ones. Rent seeking imposes avoidable costs; for example, with resource transfers, the resource is transferred, but not lost to the economy. Alternatively, resource use on socially unnecessary and unproductive activities is wasteful as resources are dissipated (see Figure 2.1).

Rent seeking also attempts to influence what might be called the 'regime of claims' (to rents). Rent-seekers may attempt to change the claims regime by establishing new claims. As a new claim is usually more costly and difficult to achieve, rent seeking usually attempts to maintain or to change the distribution of rents in an existing claims regime by trying to secure a reallocation of claims. The outcome of rent seeking would therefore be a claims regime that is net value enhancing, net value decreasing, or neutral. As suggested by Figure 2.1, the net effect depends on both the direct effect of withdrawing inputs from production as well as the efficiency implications of the rights created, both in terms of the inputs as well as the outputs involved.

As Figure 2.2 shows, the outcome of rent seeking in turn affects resource allocation. Resource allocation influences not only rent-seeking activity, but also productive investments, which in turn give rise to particular economic outputs. Thus, the distributional consequences of rent seeking would affect resource allocation, which would in turn affect the deployment of resources, including rents.

	Inputs		Outputs
Rights	1 Transfers		2 Maintenance of existing rights
		→ Rights structure	3 Reallocation of existing rights
Rent-seeking rights	1 Costs (e.g. lobbying)		4 Creation of new rights

Figure 2.1   Khan's rent-seeking input–output function
Source: Adapted from Khan (1996: Figure 3)

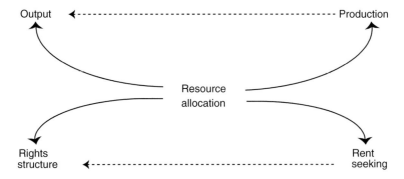

Figure 2.2   Resource allocation at the interface between rent seeking and production
Source: Adapted from Khan (1996: Figure 2)

Khan also lists conditions necessary for the efficient creation of claims. Besides, ensuring low political transaction costs for organising transfers to losers is always important. Since it is usually difficult to ensure transfers to fully compensate all losers with transfer inputs into rent seeking, five other conditions become necessary:

1   State officials are rational and learn from their mistakes, i.e. it is not necessary that officials always get policies right, but they must have the ability to correct themselves.
2   The preferences of state officials should reflect those of society, i.e. not be socially perverse.
3   The state is not fragmented into various competing agencies so that state officials can benefit from value addition.
4   State officials must be potentially able to collect transfers from all agents and sectors so that they will create value-maximising rights – rather than other rights.
5   There should be no political constraints on the creation of value-enhancing rights.

For value-enhancing claims or rights to be efficiently created through rent seeking, Khan identifies several other conditions:

•   Political institutions should facilitate efficient bargaining.
•   Knowledge and cognitive failures should be minimal.
•   The beneficiaries of value-enhancing rights should be able to lobby effectively.
•   Political constraints on the creation of value-enhancing rights should be minimal.

31

Effective governance by a developmental state would ensure that these four conditions are met. State institutions would therefore need to be efficient, but the developmental state should also have the necessary capabilities of facilitating and ensuring the achievement of these conditions, and thus increasing the likelihood that value-enhancing rights will be created as efficiently as possible. A developmental state would thus not only eliminate value-diminishing rents, but also ensure the efficient creation of socially desirable value-enhancing rents. Thus, it would seek to encourage socially desirable investments and discourage socially undesirable resource allocation.

The preceding critique of the rent-seeking literature also implies that non-market institutions (e.g. arrangements, relations and networks based on trust) and other non-government interventions (e.g. collective action based on close business–government relations or interenterprise cooperation) may also have desirable outcomes for capital accumulation and development. It also implies that the simplistic state versus market choice – which dominates so much of the development and other political economy discourses – tends to avoid the much more complex issues involved and thus mis-specifies actual options and their implications. The same may be said of so much else of the literature, e.g. on strong versus weak states. It is increasingly clear that developmental states may well employ market as well as non-market criteria and instruments in the service of industrial policy, which is the essence of what may be considered developmental about so-called developmental states.

At the risk of caricature, it now seems clear that there are important differences between Japan and the first-generation East Asian newly industrialising economies (NIEs) on the one hand and the second-tier Southeast Asian newly industrialising countries (NICs) in terms of the motives, instruments and outcomes of government intervention, on the other. Resource wealth in the latter is often said to have weakened, if not undermined, the imperative, capacity and capability for effective government intervention. Nonetheless, despite the apparent inferiority of industrial policy in Southeast Asia, there is evidence that some government interventions were crucial for the rapid resource accumulation and industrialisation of Malaysia, Thailand and Indonesia in recent decades (Jomo *et al.* 1997).

In so far as the popular caricature of blaming the East Asian crises has become very influential, it is likely that the IMF as well as other like-minded forces will continue to invoke crony capitalism to insist on structural reforms as conditions for providing badly needed credit to the region. Some of these reforms are long overdue and hence desirable owing to failure of financial governance to keep up with the consequences of internationally induced financial liberalisation in the last decade or so, though imposing them as conditions for access to credit has exacerbated panic and other related problems, with onerous consequences. However, other reforms inspired by neo-liberal ideology and related views of desirable economic restructuring will continue to erode and further undermine East Asian states' capacity for industrial policy initiatives. The changing international economic governance of the last decade – inspired by the Washington Consensus' neo-liberal view that 'there is no alternative' (TINA) to free markets – has already promoted global liberalisation in trade, investment, finance and other international economic relations, undermining national governments' capacity for macroeconomic and industrial policy management, and thus the capacity of developmental states. Hence, developmental states in East Asia will be more constrained than ever before, though one should not completely discount existing room for manoeuvre within the still essentially glacial world system.

The protracted nature of the East Asian crises and the failure of international responses have encouraged and will continue to inspire nationalist and populist responses as well as the resurgence of Keynesian and other perspectives which may well coalesce towards a post-Washington consensus (Stiglitz 1998c). However, it still seems more likely that international capital and the most powerful G-7 governments will fail to agree on much needed fundamental reforms to the international financial system, and, instead, only settle on limited stop-gap measures consistent with continuing global liberalisation until the next crisis. After all, the 1944 Bretton Woods conference and the resulting reforms required more than the 1929 crash, but also an intervening world war which radically transformed the international balance of power (Helleiner 1994). Ultimately, however, the policy instability associated with increasingly electoral political systems may have a greater impact in undermining the East Asian developmental states.

3

THE FINANCIAL CRISIS IN SOUTHEAST ASIA

Jeffrey A. Winters

There are many factors that converged to precipitate the crises in Asia starting in 1997. Many of them were intra-national in character, which helps account for the varying degrees and forms of crisis for the countries of the region. But the causes were also rooted in important changes unfolding in the international political economy of the late twentieth century. This chapter emphasizes two of those changes, arguing that international political and economic conditions that once favored the so-called 'Asian model' of development began to work strongly against it, and also introduced a more punishing regime of control over key investment resources.

Before assessing the implications of these developments for the Asian model, it should be noted that there is no consensus on what the Asian model is. For some it is a set of policies – an export-oriented approach to development in which the state aggressively promotes a country's manufacturing base. The developmental state mobilizes national and international resources, builds a domestic private sector (sometimes from within the state), and then proceeds to work hand-in-glove with it. In this view, the 'Asian' part of the model refers only to where this potent pattern of development emerged geographically. For others the Asian model goes beyond mere policy choices and strategies and has a deeper, cultural definition. Confucian traditions, an emphasis on education and hard work, a propensity to save, and a deference to authority and the group (what the region's authoritarian leaders call Asian values) are thought to have produced behaviors and institutions that made the spectacular rise of the Asian Tigers possible. As a set of social characteristics, such a model could not easily be transported to other regions of the world and mimicked. But upon closer inspection, it is not even clear that many parts of Asia qualify socially and culturally for the Asian model.

The most obvious flaw in these definitions is that they are ahistorical in that they fail to incorporate the broader global context that was so crucial to the rise of the Tigers. As Meredith Woo-Cumings makes clear, the stunning development of countries like South Korea and Taiwan was not just a matter of domestic factors, but the result of a complex interaction with quite specific external factors as well.[1] By analytically embedding the emergence of the 'miracle' economies of Asia within the international environment that helped make them possible, and then by focusing on how key elements in that environment changed, we can begin to explain why the Asian model is in trouble and why it is unlikely that countries in Asia or elsewhere will be able to reproduce the developmental paths of Taiwan, South Korea, or even Japan. The first element that changed was the priority of security concerns for the region. As the Cold War has evolved into the Cold Peace, key international actors like the United States have become much less willing to allow trade and investment issues to take a back seat to security concerns. The second is that as private capital flows have replaced bilateral and multilateral official flows as the dominant source of investment capital for developing countries, the motives, interests, and patterns of behavior associated with the flows have changed in ways that conflict with essential elements of the Asian model. The effects of this shift have been magnified by the growing share of highly mobile – and thus potentially volatile – commercial loan and portfolio capital flows to post-colonial states.

During the Cold War, when South Korea and Taiwan were embarking on their rapid rise, the dominant consideration for the United States and the western allies was containing communism. The motives for supplying official capital and for opening up US markets for a mostly one-way flow of Asian exports were heavily weighted toward security calculations. During the several decades of this confrontation, the United States and Western Europe expended tremendous resources not only to build their own armed forces and fight proxy wars, but also to sustain frontline states economically and politically to prevent them from falling into the opponents' camp. This was done by providing bilateral and multilateral credit and aid, and by giving these frontline states access to the US, and to a lesser extent European, markets on terms that were highly favorable to the exporting countries, especially in Asia. It was also done by providing fairly rapid and reliable resources that helped rescue these states when they encountered cycles of crisis. When the economies of the newly emerging Tigers experienced financial problems, steps were taken bilaterally and multilaterally to avoid deep economic disruptions that would make these states more vulnerable to their opponents. The decisive voice in that era came from the Pentagon, not the Commerce Department, the Federal Reserve, or even the State Department. This was especially true for South Korea. From the recipients' perspective, maintaining reliable flows of development capital and continued access to the US market for exports was linked to being a good client state in the Asia–Pacific region and to being staunchly anti-communist. South Korea and Taiwan lived up to their side of the bargain.

By the late 1980s and early 1990s, this geostrategic window of opportunity, used to such advantage by the first group of NICs, had closed. The end of the Cold War altered the balance of influences in US foreign policy, giving greater prominence to long-standing demands of American corporations. Although still concerned with security in the Asia–Pacific region, policy-makers in the United States began to demand that access to markets be a two-way street. In concrete terms this meant yanking the Asian hand from the glove – separating the state from the private sector, lowering protective barriers, and breaking up monopolies in the name of promoting fair competition. Of course, this policy shift was not just limited to Asia. It has become the centerpiece of the entire US foreign policy and is pursued aggressively through the World Trade Organization and various regional trade and investment groupings, such as the Asia–Pacific Economic Cooperation (APEC) forum and the North American Free Trade Agreement (NAFTA).

The surge in private capital flows has had an even bigger impact. In the 1950s and 1960s, government loans provided more than half of all capital flows to developing countries. In 1984 official and private sources were roughly balanced, with total official flows to these states being $33.4 billion, and total private flows being $35.6 billion. But since 1984, private flows have increased at a rate five times faster than official flows. In 1995, private capital accounted for three-fourths of all investment resources delivered to the developing world. Portfolio capital, a particularly volatile form of investment, rose from just 2 percent of total net capital flows to developing countries in 1987 to 50 percent by 1996. And the majority of this staggering sum of money is in the hands of fewer than 100 emerging market fund managers.[2] As a further indicator of the size and significance of private sector flows to developing countries today, consider that in its first fifty years of operation, the World Bank Group supplied about $300 billion in loans for 6,000 projects in 140 countries. By comparison, more than $300 billion was invested in developing countries by private capital controllers in just two years, 1996 and 1997.[3]

The real significance of these changes lies in the motives now associated with these capital flows. Unlike official capital in previous decades, these resources are not being provided institutionally for political goals like rolling back communism or maintaining regional security, but instead move in a more diffused way in search of a combination of market shares and profits in an environment marked by competition. And it is here that we encounter most clearly the increasing contradictions confronting the Asian model. The problem for contemporary Asian economies is that many of the practices South Korea and Taiwan could routinely get away with domestically during the Cold War now clash with the interests and calculations of private capital suppliers now dominating capital flows.

The crisis in Asia was genuinely regional in the sense that no country was spared from damaging effects. But the extent of the damage and whether economic deterioration was sudden or more gradual varied considerably across cases. Thailand, Indonesia, Malaysia, and South Korea were pulled in early and suddenly, and experienced the most devastating effects. Singapore, the Philippines, Vietnam, Taiwan, Burma, and even China were battered, but more gradually and none was knocked to the ground. The key difference separating these groups was not only how deeply they were plugged into international currency and capital flows and transactions, but also whether circuit-breakers and surge-protectors were in place that could dampen the potentially ruinous effects of highly mobile capital controllers who can decide *en masse* to abandon a country or region, or, better still, limit their ability to unleash their economic punishment in the first place. Thus it is not just a matter of degree but also the nature of a country's international exposure.

The dark side of the Asian model has always been its exclusionary politics, nepotism, corruption, and the blurred lines between political and economic power. Umbilically linked to the state are key families, members of the armed forces, and various favored individuals who have built huge conglomerates and become fantastically wealthy. Using rule of law when it suits them, these powerful figures act as if they own their societies – which in a certain economic sense they do. During the Cold War, the United States either overlooked or supported such political–economic arrangements as an efficient means of maintaining solid political control over rapidly changing societies. Since the 1980s, however, these arrangements have become much more problematic because more private capital is involved and decisions about capital flows are much more fragmented and competitive. As long as the game of being above the law is played only domestically and does not involve outside actors and their resources, any conflicts or clashes it generates can be handled strictly internally. But when outsiders are involved, including highly mobile domestic economic actors who are 'outside' the group controlling the state, the clashes spill over into the international arena, but also circle back into the Asian economies with potentially devastating consequences. This is not to say that mobile international investment is necessarily a harbinger of political opening, as some have argued. The key considerations for capital controllers are reliable information, a stable economic climate, and a political system that guarantees property rights and profits by frustrating serious challenges to both. If these fundamentals can be maintained, investors have shown a willingness to go along with wider political participation for the rest of society.

When the stakes are high, information is crucial. Investors operate well with *risk*, where probabilities of different outcomes can be calculated. They do not operate well with *uncertainty*, which means the absence of quality information on which to base investment decisions. Transparency transforms uncertainty into risk. In the world of Asian business, transparency means bringing into public view much more information about who is doing what, who owns what, who is borrowing, from where, how much, for what, and how well everyone is doing (including the government itself), and who is being bailed out, protected, and subsidized, and at whose expense. These questions strike at the heart of the power relations across Asia. Failing to answer them satisfactorily over extended periods, which was the norm during the Cold War decades, is no longer a viable option. Indeed, as hidden information about the economies of Southeast Asia seeped out in July 1997, it triggered an escape psychology among private capital controllers that by November had erased some $400 billion of value in the region's capital markets measured from the beginning of 1997, and shaved double-digit percentage points representing tens of billions in production and scores of millions in jobs off the region's projected growth rates into 1999 (Chowhury and Paul 1997).

The onset of the crisis

'In nearly every economic crisis, the root cause is political, not economic', concluded Singapore's Senior Minister, Lee Kuan Yew, in an address to leading American businessmen at the Fortune 500 Forum in Boston (see Chowhury and Paul 1997). Mr. Lee did not mean political in the same sense as the Malaysian Prime Minister, Dr. Mohamad Mahathir, who blamed the crisis on an international conspiracy of Jews who, he implied, were upset to see Muslims prosper economically (a view that is not only odious but odd, since the crisis began in Thailand). He meant that the behaviors of economic actors are a response to prior decisions and policies of governments. Governments oversee and enforce the context in which economic activity unfolds. Their policies make the opportunities and set the rules. They also create the sort of time bomb that exploded in Southeast Asia at the beginning of July 1997. This is because the interaction does not stop with the context created by governments. Economic actors react in an increasingly connected transnational environment according to their own interests. Speaking from the perspective of policy-makers, one analyst expressed the resulting impact on state sovereignty succinctly: 'We are free to do what we want, but we do not control the consequences' (see Harberger *et al.* 1993).

There are three aspects of the crisis that are particularly surprising. First, that a region everyone believed was so strong could stumble and crumble so rapidly. Second, that so many countries could get swept simultaneously into the crisis. And third, that despite domestic and international efforts to restore stability and confidence, including more than $100 billion in rescue packages sponsored by the International Monetary Fund (IMF), the crisis remained so deep and durable through all of 1998 and into 1999. Indeed, what began as crises in Thailand, Malaysia, and Indonesia soon spread to South Korea, shook Hong Kong, and threatened China and Japan. The

Asian crises caused ripple effects that disrupted the capital markets of Europe and North America, with daily gyrations on the New York Stock Exchange resembling the brain waves of a patient having a nightmare.

Before analyzing the crisis and crises in greater detail, it would be well to bear certain considerations in mind. One is that the crises are not just the result of government policies, but specifically how they interact in an international environment dominated by private controllers of capital who are willing and able to relocate massive resources away from perceived danger in a very short time frame – though not necessarily willing to bring them back as quickly as they withdrew them. Significantly, once this process starts, it does not matter if the danger is real or perceived. This leads to important lessons regarding transparency and information.

Another is that even if analysts or policy-makers can successfully diagnose the superficial and deep causes of crises, it is not obvious what sorts of policies will stabilize the situation. Indeed, even the Mexico crisis in 1994 and 1995 provides few clear parallels and lessons for dealing with the disaster that spread like wildfire across Asia. It appears that many policy-makers in the region, together with powerful international institutions like the IMF, took actions that were tailored more to standard balance of payments difficulties than the specific kind of crisis that hit Asia. As they groped for a policy combination that worked, their actions sometimes helped deepen and prolong the crisis.

And finally, it is crucial that any analysis of the crisis and the responses to it be linked analytically to the struggles over power within the governments of the region. For instance, one consequence of the close arrangement in Southeast Asia between the state and its clients in business and politics is that there is a built-in tendency for economic reformers in government who are marginalized from power in normal times to seize moments of crisis as windows of opportunity to ram through as many fundamental changes in the domestic political economy as possible. Some of these policies may help address the immediate crisis, but just as often they extend it. Far from being a rational, methodical, planned, phased, or integrated set of policies to stabilize the economy and set it on a more prosperous course, the actions of frustrated reformers are sometimes driven by a desire simply to get as many sweeping changes in place as possible before the window closes and power swings back to those who enjoy it during the intervals between crises.[4]

This is of interest for at least three reasons. First, it helps explain why seemingly useful and even crisis-averting policies are delayed so long, as well as why reforms tend to be introduced in wrenching packages that only make sense as acts of desperation. Second, it suggests a twisted relationship between economic crises and the power of economic reformers in clientelist Asian states: crises that sharply increase the influence of reformers must also be solved, often resulting in an equally sharp decrease in influence. And third, it provides an important reminder that despite nationalist public statements and posturing, these economic ministers often leverage the conditions of international agencies like the IMF for maximum advantage in their intragovernmental and intranational struggles. This was especially true in the Indonesian case, where economic ministers insisted on including many policy changes and reforms as conditions for the IMF bailout which the IMF had not demanded, but for which it was later criticized. Thus, those who would cast the conflict as foreign versus domestic forces miss one of the most important political dimensions of the crisis.

Phase 1: the trigger

The general public, and quite a few investors who should have known earlier, had their first indication of problems in Southeast Asia on July 2, 1997 when Thailand announced that the national currency, the baht, would be floated. To the casual observer this was a curious development, but hardly worth much more attention than the thousands of other facts filling the newspapers that day. But to individuals controlling huge pools of investment resources in Southeast Asia, this was a flashing red light signaling danger for the whole region. Within weeks, the Indonesian government also floated the rupiah – yet another stunning announcement for investors, both local and global, whose entire game plan for Southeast Asia was founded on stable exchange rates pegged to the US dollar.[5] It was in this moment that the changes in the nature of control over investment flows into and out of developing countries made their impact felt with a vengeance.

The already thin level of economic analysis prevailing among capital controllers prior to these announcements was soon replaced by a pure psychology of escape. All controllers of liquid capital, including domestic actors, began behaving like spooked wildebeest on the Serengeti. Frustrated policy-makers, economists, and even managers and analysts at major institutional investing firms tried desperately to break the grip of the escape syndrome by pointing out that despite some obvious and even deep problems with the political economies of Southeast Asia, the economic fundamentals in the region simply did not warrant such a mass exodus.

In the weeks and months that followed, several countries in Southeast Asia endured devaluations in their currencies averaging over 50 percent and declines in local stock markets that were even higher. Scores of millions of workers and managers were fired from companies that either went bankrupt or had to scale back their operations because economic growth rates were suddenly much lower, imported components were much more expensive, or major government projects were postponed or canceled. Not only did growth rates slow, but in Malaysia, Thailand, and Indonesia they became negative. At the epicenter of the crisis were the region's ailing banking and property sectors, which only grew more unstable as the crisis deepened.

If it is true that there were serious underlying problems in the political

40

economies of Southeast Asia, then why did the crisis not occur six, twelve, or even eighteen months earlier? In fact, all of the problems mentioned for the economies of the region – weak banks, wasteful and non-productive investment, overbuilding in the property sector, excessive borrowing by private sector firms, and speculation in local stock markets with borrowed funds – have been chronic for years. Part of the answer is that it took time for these pathologies to ripen and to converge in the right combustible mix. But part of the answer also has to do with information, or the lack of it, and a psychology among investors that inflates an economic bubble and a triggering moment that causes the bubble to burst. The moment came when currency traders, suspecting that Thailand's economic situation was much worse than investors thought, were proved to be correct. The day was July 2, when policy-makers in the Thai government, who spent a staggering $23 billion buying baht trying to maintain the dollar peg, gave up their defensive effort because they realized that they would run out of foreign exchange reserves long before there would be any good economic news to report about the country's property and banking sector. Only an immediate, genuine, and reliable upturn in the health of the economy could have stopped the pressure from the currency traders (stopped them by causing them to lose large amounts of money for betting the news would be bad). And given the realities in the Thai economy, there would be no such upturn.

It would be incorrect to draw the simple conclusion that the big problem was the peg to the US dollar. It was a smart thing to do and worked rather well as long as the dollar was weak. This gave Thai and other regional exporters a competitive edge, especially against producers based in Japan. This, in turn, generated high growth, which attracted capital, and helped strengthen the belief, some would say hype, that the economies of Southeast Asia would be able to sustain high growth rates indefinitely. Those who pointed to serious and growing problems in the region's economies were shouted down by others who responded that the countries would grow their way out of the bottlenecks they faced, whether that be national debt, balance of payments problems, insolvent banks, or oversupplies in office space and expensive residential property.[6] No matter how accurately one demonstrated that there were serious problems in the structure and operation of the economy – and the excellent reports from the private think tank, ECONIT, in Jakarta are probably the best example – it was futile to argue with success. Between 1990 and 1995, when the dollar was weak and exports were still booming, Thailand ran current account deficits of 7.7 percent of gross domestic product (GDP), a level that normally signals serious problems to investors, rating agencies like Moody's and Standard and Poor's, and such watchdog institutions as the World Bank and IMF. But no one seemed to care and no alarm bells were rung.

When the dollar appreciated in value, the peg went from being a blessing to a curse as Thailand's exports became relatively more expensive and began to weaken. At the same time there was a global slowdown in key Southeast Asian exports, especially electronics. With a massive devaluation in 1994, China laid the foundation for the competitive export pressures that would undercut exporters in Southeast Asia. By the first quarter of 1997 it was clear that Thai private companies, encouraged by the stable exchange rate, were running up their short-term debts even more aggressively by borrowing tens of billions of dollars from foreign commercial banks. Currency traders were the first to notice the sharp rise in Thailand's current account deficit. And since most currency traders are based in commercial banks, they were also the first to notice the surge in Thai businesses and financial institutions borrowing large amounts of dollars with relatively short maturities. The final blow came in the spring of 1997 when, against the advice of economists who were already worried that Thailand was sitting on a bubble, five new banking licenses were issued to people with strong government connections. It was at this point that currency traders became convinced that Thailand was in trouble, and they began to bet with their resources that they were right.

Phase 2: the chain reaction

This story helps explain how Thailand got into trouble, and even how that trouble quickly pulled the country into a crisis. But why should a crisis in Thailand trigger a chain reaction that not only pulled in other major countries in the region, but spread to distant and diverse areas of the globe? To understand this, the analysis must shift to an entirely different set of actors and forces. The answer lies partly in who controls investment resources for developing countries, how those resources are controlled or channeled (through what institutions and practices), and based on what information, calculations, and motives the resources are invested. It also lies partly in the nature of the political economies in key Southeast Asian states, but, more specifically, in how much weight capital controllers decide to give these political–economic factors in their investment decisions.

The chain reaction was set in motion by currency traders and managers of large pools of portfolio capital who operate under intense competitive pressures that cause them to behave in a manner that is objectively irrational and destructive for the whole system, especially for the countries involved, but subjectively both rational and necessary for any hope of individual investor survival. As an increasing proportion of private capital flowing to developing countries was in the form or commercial loans and portfolio investments, meaning stocks, bonds, and other securities, countries across Southeast Asia have moved rapidly to open up capital markets because selling shares is an important alternative to raising capital from commercial banks. But where does this capital originate and how does it reach the market?

The majority of capital invested in Southeast Asia's capital markets is owned and managed by local actors. But a substantial portion of the capital invested in the region's capital markets comes from many millions of private citizens from around the world. These people usually do not buy shares in individual companies in emerging markets directly, in part because they have no idea where to put their money, and it would be very costly for them to collect the information needed to make such decisions. This money is gathered together in a variety of institutional forms, such as pension funds and mutual funds. These institutions have management teams that decide where to invest the capital and how much to allocate. These allocations are done on the basis of individual companies, but also through much more broad categories such as sectors, geographic regions, and types of market. Various formulas that balance risk, profitability, and other factors are used. The top person in charge of a fund is called a fund manager.

It is from these large institutional investors that, collectively, tens of billions of dollars in portfolio capital get invested in the capital markets of developing countries. But there is still another stage in the system before the money reaches capital markets in areas like Southeast Asia. Often even the largest institutional investors lack the staff and expertise to invest intelligently in emerging markets. To solve this problem, specialized mutual funds arose that were specifically designed to invest in emerging markets. At the head of these funds are 'Emerging Market Fund Managers' (EMFMs). Institutional investors allocate different percentages of their total portfolio at the macro level to different types of investments in different world regions. The portion that gets allocated to emerging markets ends up in the hands of EMFMs. It is the EMFMs who make the more micro-level decisions about which specific countries and companies in emerging markets will receive the investments as purchases of shares in capital markets around the world. This structure for channeling investment capital produces what Mary Ann Haley calls a precarious 'funnel effect'.[7] Hundreds of millions of independent investors and savers entrust their money to a much smaller number of institutional investors, who then entrust a portion of their capital to an even smaller number of EMFMs. The disturbing result is that most of the portfolio capital supplied to developing countries ends up in the hands of just 100 extremely important EMFMs.

Of course, EMFMs are paid very handsomely for serving this specialized role as the eyes, ears, and decision-makers for millions of people and their money. Justified or not, these individual investors (plus a range of institutional investors) expect that EMFMs will act prudently and responsibly with the capital under their control.[8] Even when they are behaving at their analytical best, there are still two major problems for EMFMs: the intense pressure they are under in a highly competitive environment to outperform all the other EMFMs, and the poor quality of information about the world's emerging markets.[9] It is the combination of all three elements – the funnel effect, intense competitive pressures, and bad information – that produced the explosive volatility and the chain reaction that rocked Asia. Having severe problems in one's political economy is a necessary precondition for being vulnerable to the forces of this chain reaction. But it is not sufficient. China and Vietnam shared many of the same political–economic patholo- gies of their Asian neighbors, and should have been swept into the crisis and felt its full disruptive force. But because neither country had a convertible currency and Vietnam lacked a capital market, the behavior of currency traders and EMFMs had a delayed and muted effect. Currency traders lost confidence and unloaded local currencies. EMFMs started selling shares across the region, and then beyond it. Entire banking and corporate sectors that had borrowed heavily abroad sank into immediate insolvency.

With profit-seeking and risk-averse private investors now in charge of most capital flows, displacing bureaucratically and politically motivated actors controlling official flows, the psychology, motivations, and volatility of those commanding investment resources for emerging markets take on great significance. One of the least understood aspects of investments chan- neled through capital markets or, indeed, deposits in banks, is that the decision to invest, to keep the capital where it is, or to pull it out is only partly based on the direct information the individual investor has about the quality, safety, and stability of the investment – whether it is in a country's capital market, a bank, or in an individual company. It is also based on what the investor believes other investors will do.

And so there is a paradox: even if there is no good reason to panic, the more individual controllers of money and capital act to protect themselves in times of uncertainty, the more genuine reason there is to panic. In fact, in this example, the best thing objectively for all the investors to do is avoid panic, since the conditions in Malaysia were relatively healthy before capital controllers hurt themselves and the economy. But subjectively, the escape syndrome is the only course of action that makes sense.[10] And the logic of the syndrome applies equally to foreign and domestic capital controllers. The chain reaction starts because once a major triggering event like the float of the Thai baht occurs, EMFMs realize that the positive (buy/bullish) psychology regarding other similar emerging markets, which is a very deli- cate bubble because it is rarely based on solid data and information, can burst and cause tremendous financial losses. A trigger like that seen in Thailand also causes EMFMs to ask tougher questions, look much more closely at the data on the economies where they are invested, and demand better answers and immediate policy actions to prevent a loss of confidence. If the answers and policies are late or never come, the chain reaction continues and deepens as it widens. Once a crisis starts, it also has the effect of exposing weaknesses in an economy that had previously been well hidden, such as high debt levels, poor sales or export performance, problem loans in the banking sector, or dangerous interlocking relationships between capital markets, banks, and the property sector. As this happens, what begins narrowly as a financial crisis enters a vicious cycle that quickly turns it into a full-scale economic crisis.

Phase 3: the vicious cycle

Although, strictly speaking, it was not the poor condition of the Southeast Asian economies that caused the crisis, the fact is that the political economies of the region were not healthy on the eve of the crisis. For years, corporate and political leaders in the hardest-hit Asian countries had borrowed more money than they could invest productively. And over time the proportion of this commercial borrowing that was short term (maturing in one year or less) increased dramatically. Believing growth rates would remain strong indefinitely, they built hundreds of office towers, thousands of luxury condominiums (where the real shortage is of low-cost housing), scores of resorts, and also used borrowed funds to speculate in the capital markets. According to one estimate, Asian (excluding Japanese) companies had borrowed at least $700 billion from the rest of the world just since 1992. Japanese banks lent Asians $263 billion, European banks lent them $155 billion, and American banks lent Asian firms $55 billion. Conservative estimates were that by the middle of 1997 Indonesia, Malaysia, Thailand, Singapore, and the Philippines had accumulated bad bank loans that totaled $73 billion, or 13 percent of these countries' combined GDPs. That makes Southeast Asia's banking mess larger in relative terms than the Savings and Loans crisis in the United States in the 1980s and the Japanese bubble in the 1990s.[11] Economic ministers in the region had a hard time passing legislation that would regulate all of this reckless activity, and even when they succeeded in getting laws on the books, they found enforcement to be an even greater challenge.

A highly damaging downward spiral was triggered by initial pressures on the region's currencies and capital markets. In Indonesia, as the economic ministers raised interest rates to try to pull rupiah liquidity out of the market and defend the currency, they unwittingly deepened the crisis by increasing investors' alarm about how serious circumstances were in Indonesia and by tempting them to shift their money out of the potentially volatile Jakarta Stock Exchange and into the banking system, especially the large state banks. In Malaysia, Prime Minister Mahathir played to domestic nationalist and religious sentiment by lashing out at currency speculators and others who he felt had turned against the Malaysian economy for no good reason. His accusations overlooked the fact that Malaysian investors, being no less self-interested than any other capital controller trying to protect their assets in the face of tremendous threats, were themselves deeply involved in the selling of Malaysian ringgit and shares on the Kuala Lumpur exchange for the same logical reasons already explained in the previous section. And it is worth recalling that the current governor of the central bank, Datuk Ahmad, was appointed in the aftermath of a scandalous outbreak of currency speculation in 1992 and 1993 undertaken by directors of Bank Negara, the central bank. This speculation resulted in losses of 16 billion ringgit. Mahathir's statements, combined with other signs that his government would not produce any serious policy responses to the spreading crisis, caused the pressure on Malaysia to increase. In Thailand, the crisis provoked infighting among coalition partners in the government, leading to the resignation of the prime minister and the formation of a new government. The initial Thai government response was fragmented, contradictory, and caused investor confidence in the country and economy to drop to unprecedented levels.

The vicious cycle of the crisis was given added momentum in the early months by an attitude of denial, suggesting that leaders in the region did not understand the dimensions of the problems they faced. In August 1997, Indonesia announced that it planned to build the world's longest bridge across the Strait of Malacca, connecting Sumatra to Malaysia. The project belonged to one of President Suharto's daughters. Malaysia refused to cut back on its 'mega projects', which included plans to build the world's biggest dam and longest building (after having already built the tallest). Despite rapidly deteriorating conditions in Thailand, the Thai armed forces insisted on delivery of what they claimed was Southeast Asia's first aircraft carrier, built in Spain and priced at $250 million. By November, the Thais were still bickering among themselves and showing insufficient will to implement IMF conditions for a rescue plan. Meanwhile, Indonesia's President Suharto was sending a dizzying series of mixed signals. First he canceled and postponed a number of big and expensive projects of dubious developmental and productive value, only to reinstate several that were connected to his children and businessmen close to the president. After hammering out a $43 billion IMF-sponsored rescue package, Suharto quietly reneged on most of what he had agreed to in public. When the rupiah fell to 17,000 to the dollar in January 1998, from 2,400 before the crisis started, Suharto revised the national budget and readopted the reforms pushed by the IMF, only to fail again to implement them seriously. In Malaysia, a major and decidedly nontransparent stock deal that effectively bailed out a company closely linked to Mahathir's party apparatus, UMNO, stunned investors on the already weak Kuala Lumpur exchange, causing a sell-off that plunged it to its lowest level in nine years.

One of the most striking examples of self-inflicted harm is evident in the Indonesian case. It also serves as an illustration of how political power and business power weave together to produce an economic fabric in many parts of Asia that is increasingly being worn thin by the vicissitudes of contemporary investor motives and capital movements. Bambang Trihatmodjo, one of President Suharto's entrepreneurial children, opened up a bank, accepted deposits from thousands of Indonesian citizens, and then loaned a big chunk of those deposits to his own company – one that happened to be highly unprofitable despite generous government protections. Strictly speaking, such reckless banking practices are against Indonesian law. But then, no one is strict with the president's children, or, for that matter, with any of the other cronies made rich by their links to state power in Indonesia.

When Mr. Bambang's institution appeared on the list of sixteen troubled banks to be closed as part of the first IMF rescue package, he protested loudly, and then, with a new-found respect for the rule of law and Indonesia's courts, filed suit against the minister of finance and the governor of the central bank. The essence of his claim? That he was being treated unfairly, since '90 percent of the other banks in the country did the same thing'. Observers were not sure whether they should gasp because of what he said or because he had the audacity to say it. Mr. Bambang's tragic story, multiplied countless times across Asia and mixed with foreign financiers that were eager to play along, captures in a nutshell how billions upon billions of dollars in bad debt and unprofitable investments could be accumulated into a massive bubble that has now burst.[12] The Indonesian case is extreme, which helps account for why the crisis was predominantly economic and financial for every other country in the region, but predominantly political for Indonesia.

The blame for the crisis spreads in several directions. The IMF and the World Bank are supposed to be watchdogs that alert governments and capital controllers to serious trouble on the horizon. But these institutions did not perform their jobs. The IMF failed to anticipate the Mexican peso fiasco of 1994–5. After that record bailout, a new 'early warning system' to provide more extensive and timely information to policy-makers and market actors was created. But the IMF provided no warnings in the weeks and months before July 2, 1997. In May the IMF had issued its 'World Economic Outlook' but in it there were no clear signals indicating that Thailand or the other countries in Southeast Asia were in serious trouble. In response to these criticisms, the IMF claimed that it knew there were problems and that it had the internal documents to prove it. But as one observer asked pointedly, 'Is secrecy the hallmark of an early warning system?'[13]

Rating agencies like Standard and Poor's and Moody's Investors Service are given 'privileged access to the books and boardrooms of companies, as well as to finance ministries and central banks'. And yet businesses and banks that they rated highly were crumbling under the weight of the region's financial crisis. Executives from these firms defended themselves by saying that as far back as two years prior to the crisis, they had already sent clear signals of problems, but that these concerns did not appear in their credit ratings. Why? Because according to a top manager at Moody's, such signals are not supposed to appear in the ratings. 'An institution run by a bunch of bureaucrats who couldn't run a corner candy store is not necessarily a bad credit risk', the manager pointed out. What matters is the willingness of governments to intervene and bail out management teams that the man from Moody's admits may in fact be 'dumbos'. A high credit rating does not mean that a company or bank is well managed. It means that despite 'bad management, lax regulations, corrupt lending practices and all other maladies', creditors will be paid because governments can be expected to provide public funds as backing. It happens that these ratings agencies provide another measure, called financial ratings, and it is these that reflect what the agency thinks of a company's or bank's actual management and operation. But investors do not appear to consult these ratings.[14]

The United States has also been criticized for the actions it took, or failed to take, that contributed to the crisis. One example was the almost reflexive response against the idea of setting up a regional monetary authority dominated by the Japanese. Especially when comparing the far more engaged US response to the Mexican crisis, it is important to realize that the mostly counter-productive role of the US government was as much a result of neglect and distraction as design. Because Mexico shares a long and porous border with the United States, and because immigration from Mexico is a political hot potato in Washington, the crisis that broke out late in 1994 received immediate and generous attention. The massive exposure of US investors in Mexico also played an important role in the response from the Clinton administration. There were no parallel economic and political concerns regarding Asia. The crisis that began in Thailand and appeared to be spreading did not immediately set off alarm bells in Washington.

Policy-makers in the United States clearly misread the dimensions of the crisis, and certainly were very late in appreciating the negative impact it could have on the US stock market and economy. Different parts of the government worked at cross-purposes. In the case of Indonesia, which festered politically from December 1997 through May 1998 when Suharto was removed from office, the lead US officials on the case were Treasury Secretary Robert Rubin, who knew virtually nothing about the Indonesian political situation, and Defense Secretary William Cohen, who also was not especially well briefed on Indonesian politics. With Chairman of the Federal Reserve, Alan Greenspan, to round out the team, it was clear the United States was poorly equipped to deal with Indonesia. Meantime, the State Department was in disarray on Southeast Asia – especially Indonesia – and Secretary of State Madeleine Albright was too busy with pressing matters in Russia and the Middle East to weigh in coherently on the deepening political–economic crisis in Asia. By the time the Clinton administration began to engage the crisis more directly, it had a difficult time selling a deeper commitment and intervention in Asia to the people and the Congress. The legislature defeated fast-track authority demanded by the Clinton administration and delayed the approval of funds needed to replenish the IMF.

Lessons from the crisis in Southeast Asia

It is evident that the re-emergence of global finance on a scale last seen at the end of the nineteenth century, in combination with late twentieth-century technology and communications, is a volatile mix that wrenches governments and populations alike. Federal Reserve Chairman Alan Greenspan admitted that 'these virulent episodes' seen in the Mexican and Asian crises may be 'a defining characteristic of the new high-tech financial system'. Greenspan admitted that no one fully understands the workings of that system. 'At one point, the economic system appears stable', he said, while 'the next it behaves as though a dam has reached a breaking point, and water – confidence – evacuates its reservoir'. Hinting at a crack in the dam known as neo-classical economic theory, Greenspan concludes: 'We have observed that global financial markets, as currently organized, do not always achieve an appropriate equilibrium' (Greenspan 1998).[15] The political question is whether people want their fates to be determined so thoroughly, randomly, suddenly, and irrationally by the controllers of mobile capital. Although it would be a difficult struggle, with capital controllers putting up a mighty fight, decisions can be taken to severely limit the power and influence of hot money and those who wield it. Many people around the globe feel immobilized by abstractions like 'globalization'. But the fact remains that it is not technology but rather the policies of states that confer so much power to those controlling and moving investment resources around the globe. In September of 1998, Mahathir decided to pull the plug and impose capital controls in an attempt to use a strong dose of Keynesian stimulation to regain some semblance of control over the domestic economy. Where this bold move will take Malaysia is unclear, but those supporting and opposing free markets are watching closely. That some countries have been much harder hit in this crisis than others – and that this is related to how deeply one is plugged into the global electrical grid of mobile capital flows and whether surge protectors are in place when wild fluctuations occur – is a point leaders across the developing world cannot easily ignore.

On the question of political participation, arguments about the wonders of authoritarianism for rapid economic development have been floating around government, business, and academic circles for several decades. It is striking, however, that Thailand and South Korea handled their crises better than Indonesia, and managed to have peaceful changes in government leadership at the peak of economic disruption in both places. And they did so without violence and bloodshed. In Indonesia, the country faced a political impasse for months as Suharto clung to power despite his age, poor health, and being fully implicated in making the country vulnerable to crisis in the first place. And this impasse played a central role in prolonging the country's economic pain as capital controllers stayed on the sidelines waiting for a resolution to the succession crisis, largely ignoring the huge IMF rescue package. Suharto was finally deposed at the cost of more than 1,000 Indonesian lives. The relatively more participatory political systems in Thailand and South Korea allowed discredited leaders to be eased out and new leaders to take the reins and push through painful reforms with a legitimacy that was utterly lacking in the half-hearted efforts of Suharto's New Order regime, and the Habibie government that followed.[16]

It is not yet clear how this crisis will affect Asian countries and, in particular, the Asian model of development. For the present, controllers of mobile capital are in charge. Either through the direct signals of their capital investments and withdrawals, or through the spins and policy reforms pushed by organizations like the IMF or individuals like Alan Greenspan, these capital controllers are able to punish and reward countries they dislike or favor. Of course, along the way jobs and goods get created. But over time, and with successive crises, especially in finance, it becomes apparent that the motives of these investors have little to do with jobs and production. These are by-products of the profit-making drive, not its central concern or goal. Neo-classical economists consider this to be the genius of market systems. You do not have to want to create employment or develop a society. It happens as if by magic.

In fact, it does not happen automatically or magically. Nor does it happen without a good dose of coercion, conflict, and now the constant threat of tremendous economic upheaval on short notice. Private investors are choosy. Some 80 percent of total private capital flowing to developing countries goes to just a dozen countries. This means that until major changes are made in how capital is controlled, countries are going to face intense pressures to be responsive to the demands of capital controllers. This is going to yield reforms in the short and medium term that could undermine much of what is defining of the Asian model of business–government relations. But just as these crises produce reforms, they could also build and strengthen the resolve of governments and their populations over the medium and long term to gain more control over how capital is controlled.

NOTES

1 In the vast literature on the rise of the NICs, her book stands out as the only work that focuses on the crucial interplay among domestic factors, global financial flows, and security concerns in the Pacific basin. See Jung-en Woo (1991).

2 On these important changes in capital flows see Armijo (1999) and Haley (1999). For an assessment of the impact of these flows on one important case, see Jeffrey A. Winters, 'Indonesia: On the Mostly Negative Role of Transnational Capital in Democratization', in the same volume.

3 Now the World Bank struggles to convince leaders of the advanced industrial countries that it is still useful. In a 1996 speech, the Bank's president, James Wolfensohn, argued that the real significance of the Bank was not in the levels of resources it provides, but in the leading role it plays as chief reformer on behalf of private capital controllers:

Indeed, the post-Cold War world has increased, not reduced the Bank's relevance – not only because of the Bank's ability to reach out to new centres of influence such as civil society, but because the Bank, focusing on systemic change, is perfectly positioned to create the kind of enabling environment so necessary to attract private capital.

(Wolfensohn, speech before the G-7 meeting, 1996)

4 For a fuller development of these relationships, see Winters (1996).
5 One consequence of this bedrock belief in the regional dollar pegs was that most companies in the region who had borrowed billions of dollars abroad did not hedge their debt – meaning they did not buy futures and options to protect them against exchange rate fluctuations.
6 Even Paul Krugman's mild observation that as GDPs in Asia grew ever larger, annual growth rates on a much larger base would have to slow down, was dismissed as overly pessimistic.
7 See Haley (1999), *supra*, note 2.
8 There are indications that many EMFMs in fact did not act prudently and responsibly. 'Before [the crisis], people could just close their eyes and blindly buy Asia as a whole', said Nitin Parekh, regional strategist at Credit Suisse First Boston (HK) Ltd. 'Now you can't do that; you have to pick carefully what you buy and why you're buying it.' Is this not what the high-paid EMFMs were supposed to be doing all along? It would have been a lot cheaper to pay someone to throw darts at a stock market dartboard, if all one wanted to do was close one's eyes and blindly buy Asia. See Pui-Wing Tam (1997). According to one of the world's leading specialists on financial markets:

When the market rises, there may be a rush of 'noise traders' wanting to get in on the action. Noise traders care little about underlying values [of companies' stock] and are simply betting that the rising trend will continue. Their buying can drive prices up, providing them with the capital gains they hoped for. This, in turn, spurs more buying, and so on.

(See Kohn 1994: 727)

9 The case of Richard Hazlewood, who was 'reassigned' from his position as the EMFM based in Hong Kong for Fidelity Investments to the lowly position of 'analyst' back in Boston, is noteworthy. Hazlewood, who was 37 years old, had managed the emerging market fund since July 1993. His fund was deeply invested in Malaysia as the crisis began to unfold. Hazlewood was so overinvested in Malaysia that he found himself trapped because he was 'unable to sell his investments ... because of chaotic market conditions, which would be made worse if a big investor like Fidelity dumped even more stock'. Hazlewood said he found himself 'not selling what you want to sell, when markets go down, they go illiquid'. By any objective standard, Fidelity, one of the world's largest and most reputable mutual funds, should not have been so deeply invested in Malaysia. At the beginning of 1997, the ratio of the country's stock market capitalization to its GDP was 325 percent, the highest ratio of any country in the world. Attractive markets have ratios of less than 50 percent. According to people who knew Hazlewood, he had been courted personally by Malaysian politicians and businessmen, and he 'relished the attention'. Not only did this attention flatter Hazlewood's ego, but it gave him a false sense of security in the Malaysian market that cost investors in his fund to endure huge losses. See 'Fidelity Reassigns Chief of Battered Fund', *Asian Wall Street Journal* 22 October 1997: 8.

10 The situation I just described applies to banks as well, although with one important difference. If depositors think a bank is in serious trouble, they will try to rush to take out their money because banks will honor withdrawals on a 'first come, first served' basis, until their resources are depleted. Even if you happen to know that the bank is not in serious trouble, you will rush to withdraw your deposits because you know all the other depositors who lack your privileged information will withdraw. And when they do, suddenly your savings are threatened because the bank has only a small amount of reserves to cover routine withdrawals (and if other bankers also think the bank is in trouble, it will not be able to borrow on the interbank market to cover the rush of withdrawals). The big difference between a bank and a capital market is that if a bank collapses due to a run, people lose their deposits and the story is over (unless, of course, a 'contagion effect' transforms a run on a single bank into systemic bank panic). But capital market crashes are not so final. Because of the nature of share trading, they tend to be temporary and 'self-correcting', meaning that after shares hit rock bottom, they will rise again as investors start buying eagerly at bargain prices. After the 1987 US market crash, investors regained their losses relatively quickly. The rebound took longer after the 1929 crash, but investors still did very well over the medium and long term. For more on crashes and panics, see Kohn (1994).

11 See Bremner *et al.* (1997).

12 Soon after Bambang dropped his suit, one of his father's close business associates allowed Bambang to buy out his banking license and name and, after a change of costumes and signs, reopen for business.

13 The IMF was asleep and silent during other crashes as well, including the European Exchange Rate Mechanism (1992 and 1993) and the Czech Republic (1997). See Hanke (1997).

14 But then, why should they? As long as the IMF and bilateral rescuers can be relied upon to jump in and bail out the companies and their incompetent and even criminal managers, why bother to look at the financial ratings? The point is that creditors will get paid, and if that is all they care about, then looking at the financial ratings will only spoil an otherwise pleasant day. See Ipsen (1997: 1).

15 See Greenspan (1998) for the complete text of testimony by Federal Reserve Chairman Alan Greenspan on Friday, January 30, before the House Banking Committee.

16 It also appears that this political impasse in Indonesia undermined progress on rescheduling the private debt of Indonesian companies. According to one report:

> U.S. commercial banks, which were pressured by the Treasury Department and the Federal Reserve to roll over their loans to South Korean banks, are not getting similar pressure with regard to loans to Indonesian corporations for a number of reasons. In South Korea, which has just elected a prominent advocate of democracy to be its new president, U.S. and International Monetary Fund officials could argue to bankers that the fundamentals in the country, which happens to be a key U.S. military ally, were positive – if only it could get through a short-term credit crunch. Indonesia, in contrast, is plagued by the political instability of President Suharto's 32-year regime – and his certain victory when he stands for a seventh five-year term next month.
>
> (Wessel 1998: 6)

4

STATE POWER AND ECONOMIC STRENGTH REVISITED

What's so special about the Asian crisis?

Linda Weiss and John M. Hobson

Introduction

This chapter addresses one of the most influential views that inform contemporary debate about the Asian crisis in particular and global economic change in general. This is the view *that state power is inimical or at best irrelevant to economic strength in an increasingly integrated world economy (so-called globalisation)*. Such a perspective is directly at odds with the thesis of our earlier study, *States and Economic Development* (SED) (Weiss and Hobson 1995). SED's central thesis is that 'state power enables economic strength' . In the light of the Asian events of 1997, we revisit that thesis, asking to what extent it has been blown apart by the winds of global finance, as manifested most recently in the Asian meltdown.

We therefore set out in this chapter a response to the following question: has the relevance of the SED thesis on state power and economic strength been undermined by the advent of global finance and the Asian crisis? Our response is in two parts. Part 1 briefly compares responses to external shocks from an historical perspective. It argues that state power is an important variable in explaining historically how states have typically responded to external crises closer to home. Part 2 proposes that state power is also of central importance in explaining both the sources of the Asian crisis and its ensuing severity.

Our larger argument is that the so-called 'global' economy is mediated by domestic institutions generally and in particular by state power (read 'transformative capacity'). The more stable the institutional capacity of the state to coordinate economic change, the stronger the ability to minimise the economic vulnerabilities that may expose a country to external shocks.

Conversely, the weaker the transformative capacity, the greater the potential vulnerability.

The argument in brief

First, we propose that state capacity (to be defined below) is vital to sustained economic strength. This is linked to a second proposition: that states imbued with capacity are not only able to survive external crises but, more importantly, able to convert external constraints into domestic opportunities. In general states imbued with capacity have emerged stronger and fitter at the end of a crisis. Conversely, states with low levels of capacity have been weakened by external crisis. Part 1 illustrates this proposition in the historical period 1650–1900. Part 2 analyses the sources and deepening of the Asian crisis. The central explanatory task is to account for why unexceptional vulnerabilities could lead to overwhelming financial havoc. It proposes that this outcome can only be explained by analysing the interplay of relatively weak domestic capacities (of the Asian states embroiled in the crisis) on the one hand, and the relatively strong external powers of a leading state (like the United States) acting directly and through its agencies, on the other hand. In short, weak (or, in the case of Korea, weakened) transformative capacity has rendered certain Asian states vulnerable to financial upheaval and in that sense has been a condition, not a cause, of crisis. US interventions together with calculated non-interventions have converted what might have been a 'normal' crisis (that could have been overcome relatively quickly) into a full-scale financial meltdown with prolonged after-effects.

Defining state strength

What constitutes strong state capacity? We contrast our position with that of traditional statists such as Theda Skocpol (1979) and Stephen Krasner (1978). First of all, state capacity is founded not on the ability of a state to go against the interests of powerful social actors; rather, it rests with the embedding of relatively insulated state institutions within key social structures. Of central importance is the ability of the state to negotiate and collaborate with strong social actors, notably the dominant economic class. Through a collaborative rather than arm's-length or antagonistic relationship, the capacity of the state to pursue a transformative project and the developmental prospects for the economy are mutually enhanced (Weiss and Hobson 1995; Hobson 1997; Weiss 1998). Conversely, states that fail to enjoin collaboration not only undermine their capacity, but also weaken the developmental prospects for the economy. The other equally important ingredient of state capacity is institutional autonomy, which is derived from the differentiation of state institutions from the private interests of individuals within society. Moreover, states must have what Mann (1988: ch. 1) calls 'infrastructural power' – that is, the ability to reach into society so as to govern the economy. But in the context of the modern industrial economy, the mere fact of institutional differentiation will not secure the autonomy necessary for the state to project independent goals. What is also required for a transformative project is an insulated pilot agency able to stand at some remove from the push and pull of sectional interest politics. In short, institutional autonomy must go hand-in-hand with social embeddedness if state involvement in economic processes is to be effective. The term 'governed interdependence' is a way of capturing the *reciprocal* relationship that underpins this institutional arrangement. But at the same time, governed interdependence goes beyond the notion of reciprocity to convey the idea that government–business interaction is regularised and subject to – that is, *governed by* – larger goals and rules laid down at the centre rather than being determined primarily by sectional interests. Governed interdependence is the institutional equipment of a transformative state; the evolution it undergoes over time and the various forms it may take are analysed elsewhere (Weiss 1998). Without the institutional insulation, the state lacks a coordinating intelligence and is vulnerable to capture by special interests (as in Thailand, Malaysia and Indonesia). By the same token, without the institutionalised cooperation between government and business, the state lacks the embedded (quasi-corporatist) quality of effective policy design and implementation and is vulnerable to information blockage and policy failure. In either case, governed interdependence can have little institutional basis and the capacity for domestic response and adaptation to change will be accordingly restricted and diminished.

Finally, we argue that states are embedded not only in domestic social relations, but also in international relations, and, conversely, global structures are embedded in national ones. International crises are often portrayed, especially in Marxism and liberalism, as forces which constrain the 'autonomy' of states. At the extreme, such theorists propose that globalisation is 'bringing the state to heel'. This popular view is one that is applied by many commentators to the current Asian crisis, such that globalisation is perceived as wreaking its revenge on the Asian developmental state and forcing it to reconfigure itself along the lines of the western liberal–regulatory state. We are sceptical of this convergence presumption not only for path-dependent reasons but because it falsely polarises 'national' and 'global' as being mutually exclusive rather than interdependent structures. History of course furnishes many examples of states which have managed to use external shocks as opportunities to enhance their domestic power along with the developmental prospects of their particular economy. But much closer to home, the evolution of and responses to the Asian crisis have perhaps more than any other recent event offered a timely reminder of the limits to, rather than irreversibility of, financial liberalisation, and thus the dependence of the global on domestic structures.

Part 1: domestic responses to external shocks

State power and economic strength (1650–1800)

Historical examples of strong external crises are useful not only for teasing out the relationship between states and economic crisis, but also for reflecting on the current Asian crisis. Here we begin with the profound seventeenth-century crisis that was a European-wide phenomenon. By 1650 Europe reached a critical threshold in which states faced a dramatic international crisis that was fiscal, economic, social, ideological and political in nature. States responded differently to this crisis, and accordingly promoted different forms of production relations. It was ultimately a fiscal crisis (rather than a financial crisis), although it had strong economic origins (as well as military origins).

The key question is: how did the different states respond to this crisis? Where state capacity was moderately developed, as in Britain, the state could use the international crisis to restructure domestic social relations in order to enhance its power further, in the process enabling the rise of capitalism. Where state capacity was relatively underdeveloped, rulers had to pursue 'sub-optimal' strategies in order to enhance their power. Thus Russia and Prussia promoted the second serfdom, and France, with moderate state power, took an alternative path and promoted communal agrarianism.

In France, as in all other European states, rulers had been competing with the nobility over control of the means of taxation. Nobles had acted as fetters to the development of state power because they had kept much of the tax revenues for themselves. Thus in order to enhance state fiscal power, the state looked to undermine the power of the nobility and to free the peasants from the grip of the feudal dominant class. This would enable the state to tax the population directly without noble interference and thereby enhance revenue accumulation. The French state had sufficient infrastructural reach to be able to expropriate the peasants from the clutches of the nobility and relocate them into agrarian communes (what we call the 'militarised-agrarian' path of economy and state formation). This enabled the state to extract taxes directly from the peasantry free of noble interference. Nevertheless, despite using the 1650 crisis as an opportunity to assault the power of the nobility, the state had insufficient power to be able to free the peasants from agrarian forms of production and move them into capitalist production relations. Capitalism would have been the optimal solution since it generated indirect taxes which were far more lucrative than peasant land taxes. But communal land taxes were much easier to extract by the French state that had only a moderate level of institutional autonomy.

This contrasted strikingly with the British strategy of 'militarised-capitalism'. The British state had a relatively high domestic institutional power. It had by far and away the strongest fiscal bureaucracy in Europe. Accordingly the state was able to rely substantially on excise and customs taxation, unlike its continental counterparts (such that indirect taxes comprised some 66 per cent of total tax revenues from 1700 to 1850). The state thus set about to expropriate the peasants from the land and enabled the development of noble enclosures. Having been cast from the land, the landless labourers moved to the towns and rising industrial centres to be absorbed in emergent industrial production. Rising market production and growing international commerce were then taxed by the central state. Indirect taxes proved to be far more fiscally lucrative than the alternative land taxes that were imposed by continental absolutist states. This capitalist–fiscal strategy was unavailable to the weaker French and Russian and Prussian states. The key point here is that the British state responded by embedding itself in the capitalist class, through which it maximised its tax accumulation and emerged stronger than any other European state (Weiss and Hobson 1995: chs 2–4).

In the weak states of Prussia and Russia, the 'militarised-feudal' path was chosen. Unable to frontally assault the power of the nobility as in France owing to infrastructural weakness, these states had to continue to rule through their nobilities. The Black Death of 1347 had led to a massive rural depopulation in Eastern Europe. This led to fiscal crisis for the state and economic crisis for the nobilities, since there was no way for tax revenues to be collected (the peasants having fled the feudal locale from which taxes and 'surplus value' had previously been extracted). Thus the Russian state reimposed serfdom, and forced the peasants back into the feudal locale where taxation was extracted by the nobility and passed onto the state. This was not a sufficient long-term solution since it reimposed the power of the nobility over the state. Nevertheless, it was the only available option open to the weak institutional power of the states in the face of fiscal–military crisis.

Thus the key point here is that differentials in state institutional power and embeddedness led to new forms of economic production, as states responded to the profound economic and fiscal–military crisis of the seventeenth century. The states with low capacity implemented sub-optimal economic strategies and fared poorly from the crisis. But the crisis was converted into an opportunity for the British state as it moved towards capitalism. Defining the nature of the shock cannot be done simply by examining the crisis itself, but the way in which it was mediated by the state must also be investigated.

Part 2: sources and severity of the Asian crisis; domestic and international

State power

The argument to this point is that crisis (financial and otherwise) is nothing new in the history of modern states and that infrastructurally strong states managed crises relatively effectively, while weak states responded poorly. In this way, crisis became a kind of crucible for enhancing the capacities of strong states. But this is an argument about the differential response to generalised crisis. It does not address the problem of differential vulnerability to external shock.

We must therefore extend the argument in a new direction in order to make sense of a different set of issues. There are two such issues. The first is a question of the *sources* (rather than the impact) of crisis: that is, why Asia became embroiled in financial upheaval in the first place. The second is a question of its evolution: that is, why the crisis became so severe, unrelenting and damaging, relative to other such episodes and to the pre-crisis state of the economies in question.

Finally, we appraise the impact of the crisis in allegedly terminating a distinctively East Asian (i.e. 'Japanese') form of capitalism. In the language of the new globalism, is convergence on the American model (or something close to it) a plausible outcome?

The two faces of the crisis in Asia

The main question considered here is why a region once considered so economically vibrant is now in the throes of financial depression. Does this invalidate SED's central thesis (about the relationship between economic strength and political capacity)? Or does it raise further important questions about the differential presence of political capacity in East Asia? In short, how is state power relevant to an understanding of the crisis?

Though commentators disagree about the fundamental causes of the crisis, explanatory efforts by and large have taken one of two different tacks. One gives primacy to domestic weaknesses (e.g. flawed policies or institutions or some combination of the two), the other to international and global financial markets (e.g. investor panic).[1]

Rather than appraising the respective merits of an 'outside' or an 'inside' approach, it seems more fruitful to move to a different starting point. Where the crisis is usually discussed as a totality, we begin with the observation that this particular crisis has *two* facets, not one: a 'normal' aspect and an 'abnormal' one.

To say that there is a normal aspect to the crisis is to make the simple but important point that there is *little novelty* to financial crises. Though they occur suddenly and unexpectedly, and at times perhaps even arbitrarily, they do so with great regularity. Though the latest crisis is always viewed as the most compelling, such events as we have witnessed in Asia at least before the crisis deepened – including falling asset prices, declining currency values, and weakened banks – have a long history. Whether one's perspective is that of fifteen years or 150 years, it appears that the history of capitalism is strewn with financial crises of one form or another. Their recurrence over a very long period suggests that crashes, panics and manias are endemic in modern capitalism (see e.g. Kindleberger 1996).

The implication is that no country can be considered immune. This does not mean of course that all countries are equally susceptible to financial crises. Rather, in a world of volatile capital flows, some countries may become more vulnerable to crisis than others. What makes them so? Students of financial crises suggest that vulnerability is a function of some domestic weakness or weaknesses which before the crisis were generally regarded as benign. Generally speaking, then, the *normal* face of the Asian crisis directs analytic attention to *national-level* variables.

But we cannot leave the analysis at this point. No matter which domestic 'weaknesses' are singled out, the very act of doing so runs the risk of over-statement and distortion. The afflicted economies were not basket cases, but reasonably sound, generally with moderate if not striking prospects for improvement. Most of them enjoyed high savings, balanced budgets, strong private sector investment, low inflation, a relatively egalitarian income distri-bution, and a strong export drive. 'Vulnerability' therefore needs to be placed in perspective: it is, after all, merely a condition, not a cause, of the upheaval that ensued. It cannot be emphasised too often that, regardless of one's theoretical perspective, *there is a real danger in the temptation to make overly coherent – and thus apparently inevitable – an outcome which remains, in several important respects, genuinely confounding.*

Separating out for special explanatory treatment the *abnormal* aspect of the crisis is one way of guarding against this tendency. In so doing, we propose to explain why a problem that should have been transient and quite quickly rectified like so many others before it (cf. Kindleberger 1996), turned into a full-blown disaster.

To emphasise the 'abnormal' face of the crisis is to draw attention to its *severity*, and thus to highlight what was special about the Asian experience. Abnormality in this context refers to outcomes far in excess of what one could reasonably anticipate or justify in the light of what is known about pre-crisis conditions of the affected economies. Domestic weaknesses may explain country vulnerability, but such weaknesses are unlikely to be lethal. That is, they are unlikely to explain the way the bursting of the property bubble in Thailand, for example, turned into full-blown capital flight. For there is much about the Asian crisis – its timing, its pattern of contagion and, above all, its magnitude – that has only a tenuous connection with the fundamental state of the economies in question. Many have remarked on the peculiar depth and severity of the phenomenon. Few have attempted to theorise it. We do so here turning to political power variables, but this time originating *outside* the nation-states in question.

International markets vs. national institutions?

We propose, then, a two-pronged approach to the issue. If we take this duality seriously, it stands to reason that monocausal approaches will not take us very far. Rather than adding to the steadily growing collection of monocausal explanations presently competing for attention, we therefore take a different tack. A state power framework enables one to address the question of the sources and evolution of the crisis in a theoretically rigorous way which, at the same time, gives due weight to national and international factors. We argue that far from being at the mercy of 'global' financial markets, the impact of the latter depends, in the first instance, on the strength of domestic political institutions, and ultimately on the strength and cooperation of other leading (international) power actors This is a state capacity (though non-statist) explanation (the distinction is discussed in Weiss 1998: ch. 2). It is able to encompass both *domestic* and *international* variables while at the same time making power relations – particularly those connected with *state* power – the focal point of analysis.

The general argument is that while global financial markets somewhat obviously and directly produced the outcomes commonly labelled as the Asian crisis (i.e. by speculative runs and sudden withdrawal of funds – so-called investor panic or 'herding'), they were not the primary determining factor. For financial markets to have wrought their effects in the first place (and in differential measure), two less obvious variables had to be present. The first – a 'normal' pull factor – is some sort of domestic vulnerability in the real economy, in this case, we shall argue, one whose common denominator is weak or decomposing institutional capacities. The latter, in turn, depending on the context, considerably exacerbated real economy vulnerabilities such as falling exports, rising current account deficits, and surplus capacity.

The second variable – an 'abnormal' push factor – consists in vulnerability which is externally induced or intensified. The common denominator of this second-order vulnerability is the strong external power of a leading state (the United States) pursuing its own national economic agenda (with a strong input from its domestic interests), partly on its own and partly in concert with the IMF.

Thus two theses are advanced. Both implicate state power. The more general thesis is that *the relative weakness of state capacity (in Southeast Asia) and its marked, if incomplete, decomposition (in Korea)* made these economies more prone to speculative investment (in the Korean case, overinvestment), to asset bubbles and current account deficits, and consequently more vulnerable to financial upheaval. In the Korean case, it was not institutionalised weakness *per se* but the gradual decomposition of governed interdependence that paved the way for the high-risk borrowing strategies and overinvestment of the *chaebol* which exposed Korea to sudden downturns and capital flight. In the Asian episode at least, one can generalise that by virtue of both weak and decomposing state capacities, certain economies became significantly more vulnerable than others to capital flight (triggered in the first instance by the bursting of the property bubble in Thailand). But in saying this, one is merely drawing attention to the ordinary, *normal* (read endemic) face of financial crisis.

The second more specific thesis is that it was an outside force, namely *the relative strength of US international state power*, which – as will be shown below – partly through its own independent actions and partly through the auspices of the IMF helped turn an otherwise ordinary event (that is to say, transient and quickly repaired) into an unusually severe and protracted phenomenon.[2]

In sum, global markets were a key (if somewhat obvious) factor in the Asian financial crisis, but not in a primary determining sense. For financial markets to have impacted so dramatically on the economies in question, two critical if less obvious variables had to be present: a pull factor in the form of domestic vulnerability, in this case afforded by weak or decomposing state capacities; and a push factor in the form of a strong external impulse which served to deepen that vulnerability, in this case the organised expression of US economic power, otherwise known as the Treasury–Wall Street–IMF complex.[3]

State power and the Asian crisis

In what way, then, is state power at issue in the crisis? There is no shortage of commentary on the alleged role of the state in the Asian crisis, much of it couched in terms of 'crony capitalism', which concludes that the crisis is readily understandable as the result of too much state involvement in the economy (e.g. Emmerson 1998: 48). This is the dominant view on the state power issue. It is favoured by the IMF and by those antagonistic to deviations from the free market (American?) model of capitalism. If state involvement is seen as a recipe for unstable economic foundations, this is because in most such reasoning it is virtually inseparable from rent-seeking, political favouritism and straightforward corruption. It must be emphasised, however, that to the extent that such practices are the norm rather than the exception, they are manifestations of *weak* – not robust – state capacity; to this extent, evidence of their existence in the troubled economies is more likely to support the SED thesis than to refute it.

For others, however, the problem of state power is one of inadequate or too little state control rather than too much. As Joseph Stiglitz, Chief Economist and Vice President of the World Bank puts it, 'The crisis was caused in part by too little government regulation (or perverse or ineffective government regulation)' (Stiglitz 1998: 2). The 'too little' proponents are chiefly concerned with the laxity of regulatory control over capital inflows consequent upon financial liberalisation (hence overexposure to unhedged, short-term debt). This is undoubtedly important since it turns directly on the weak regulatory capabilities of the state in the financial arena. While the Stiglitz thesis has much to recommend it, *there is, however, much more at issue than regulatory capacity*, as we shall argue in the next section.

Economic vulnerability and weak transformative capacity

Our account therefore takes a different tack to the Stiglitz approach ('too little regulatory control'). For in all the troubled economies, we are confronted with another kind of institutional debility: that is to say, weak or weakened 'transformative capacity'. This is a term deployed elsewhere to indicate an institutionalised capability for guiding industrial change: coordinating investment, diffusing innovation, and generally ensuring permanent upgrading of the industrial portfolio, especially in the tradables sector (Weiss 1998).

Transformative capacity is important in this context for at least two reasons. First, transformative weakness in the Asian industrial arena has almost always underpinned, preceded or paved the way for regulatory weakness in the financial sector. In Korea, where the ideological and institutional underpinnings of transformative capacity have gradually unravelled, slowly in the 1980s, much more quickly in the first half of the 1990s, financial liberalisation took a neo-liberal direction. It was the gradual erosion of the ideological and institutional basis for strategic coordination in the Korean setting that helped shape a particular approach to financial reform. That approach was to view the process of liberalisation as a means of minimising rather than affirming or strengthening the state's involvement in economic management. This was in striking contrast to the Taiwanese experience where, because of different domestic and international pressures, both transformative ideology and institutions remained intact (Weiss 1999). That legacy ensured a different approach to financial reform, which accordingly became a means of securing rather than minimising state involvement.[4] In the Korean context, by contrast, the first great step towards state disengagement and neo-liberal reform occurred in the early 1980s under the impetus of domestic political pressures. Domestic politics and intra-state conflict rather than international pressures provided the primary driving force for the first great step in this direction in the 1980s. Push turned to pull in the mid 1990s with the promise of OECD membership held out to Korea in return for greater opening of its capital account. In this context, insistent prodding from the United States gave leverage to economic liberals within the financial bureaucracy and the government-sponsored think tanks like KDI which pressed for complete dismantling of the Economic Planning Board, the central coordinating intelligence or pilot agency which had presided over Korea's rapid transformation.

There is, however, a larger point to be made, which dovetails with the argument being advanced here. By the early 1990s, having already ceded a large chunk of its investment coordination and upgrading role to a private sector enthusiastic for independence, it was for the Korean government merely a short step to relinquishing control over the financial system. To say – as many have indeed pointed out – that liberalisation took place in a 'flawed' manner, i.e. without accompanying regulatory controls, may be somewhat beside the point. For the Korean authorities appear to have undertaken liberalisation with a view to further dismantling, not securing, the state's core transformative capacities (see Weiss 1999a). In the process, of course, they relinquished much more than they bargained for.

The implication of the present argument is not that transformative capacity inhibits full capital opening, but rather that it offers a form of in-built protection against volatile inflows in so far as it calls for coordination of investment and upgrading, and thus greater oversight of capital flows. This at least is the story for Taiwan (see Weiss 1999).

The second major consequence of transformative weakness is that of vulnerabilities in the real economy, in particular the phenomenon of worsening current account deficits, which for investors are among the most important indicators of a nation's economic prospects. In the Asian setting on the eve of the crisis, current account deficits (most marked in Thailand) grew as exports slowed and as borrowed capital was invested in non-tradables (especially real estate). As the current account deficits ballooned, the demand grew for foreign capital to sustain them. Attracting such capital meant raising domestic interest rates, which in turn resulted in a dramatic fall in real estate prices, thus bursting the bubble economy. Thailand manifested in exaggerated form the problem common to the Southeast Asian economies: a consumption boom, stock and property bubbles, and asset price inflation. These were the immediate source of its increasing current account deficits. At a more fundamental level, however, these outcomes were ensured by the fact that Thailand had ceased to be a low-cost producer, yet it remains poorly equipped to supply more sophisticated, less price-sensitive goods. Weak transformative capacity is reflected in low high-school completion rates, in the underdevelopment of domestic production of capital goods, and in the increasing gap between productivity growth and rising wage levels. In short, the move to upgrade the industrial portfolio, and thus the shift upmarket of cheaper producers in China and Vietnam, has been delayed. The end result for Thailand has been massive capital inflows whose composition and destination a relatively weak state was neither able nor willing to determine or coordinate. Below we indicate the ways in which Southeast Asian states failed to institutionalise such powers for sustainable development; and how the slow unravelling of Korea's powers quickened in the 1990s.

Ironically, as we shall see, only in one area has 'too much' state power been of relevance. This concerns the international arena and the role of the United States as 'opportunistic hegemon', whose interests and actions have deepened, and in turn been served by, the Asian crisis.

Southeast Asia: in search of the effective state

The fast growth of the Southeast Asian economies has tempted many to assume a fundamental similarity in the political economies of Southeast and Northeast Asia (hence the widely touted notion of an 'Asian model'). One consequence of this geographical elision is the tendency to see state involvement in the economy as all of a piece, the state's role in the Indonesian (or Thai) economy being considered much the same as for Korea or Taiwan. The result, say the same sources, is 'crony capitalism', a normative rather than analytical term to suggest that close ties between government and business are harmful to economic performance, in so far as they produce decisions based on non-economic criteria and are therefore market subverting. But whatever the extent of such practices in Southeast Asia in particular or the region more generally (leaving aside the issue of explanatory relevance), they are not the building blocks of developmental states.

Indeed Malaysia, Thailand and Indonesia, in spite of the frequent rhetoric of growth *über alles*, have never institutionalised 'developmental market economies' of the kind found in Japan, Korea and Taiwan. If one takes the high-growth period of each country, the differences in fundamental national goals, in state architecture and in coordinating capabilities remain striking, at times profound. While government–business ties have often been close, they have rarely approached the 'governed interdependence' model of Northeast Asia, whereby a skilled and relatively insulated economic bureaucracy institutionalises a negotiating relationship with well-organised industrial groups in order to pursue transformative projects (see Weiss 1998: x–xv, ch. 3).

In Malaysia, where the bureaucracy for the past two decades has been preoccupied with ethnic redistribution, industrial policy has been much more a tool for resource redistribution than an instrument of industrial transformation (Jomo *et al.* 1997: 105–7). The story for Indonesia again is one at odds with the transformative capacity of developmental states.[5] While ethnic distance gives the state some autonomy from the dominant (Chinese) entrepreneurial group, and while the state in the Suharto era has been surprisingly insulated from organised societal pressures, the overall picture is one of a weak bureaucracy unable to monitor and enforce policy preferences

(MacIntyre 1992: 161). In his study of the politics of credit activism in the Suharto period, MacIntyre concluded that notwithstanding the development of an elaborate system of preferential credit, official policy preferences were routinely subverted by a 'patrimonially based allocation of rent-taking opportunities within the state elite' (1992: 151). Thus for all its interventionism and autonomy from societal pressures, a developmentally configured state – that is, one oriented to the pursuit of transformative projects that are not reducible to particularistic interests – Indonesia is not. A similar conclusion applies to Thailand. In contrast with Indonesia where oil played the major role, Thailand's rapid growth since the 1980s has a stronger base in manufacturing exports. But Thailand's growth owes little to an interventionist industrial strategy (Doner and Unger 1993). Indeed in spite of expanding manufacturing exports since the mid 1980s, Thailand appears to be trapped at the low end of technology, pursuing what neo-classical economists consider a key plank of economic success: static comparative advantage. Again, the contrast with first-generation industrialisers to the north remains striking. Lacking the transformative priorities and the coordinating institutions of its northern counterparts, Thailand has been relatively slow to upgrade skills and technology. According to a recent study, for example, there has been no significant structural shift away from the lower skilled, lower valued-added end of production. Even by the year 2000, it is estimated that over 70 per cent of the labour force will still have reached only an elementary level of education (Jomo *et al.* 1997). Sustaining development in these circumstances is likely to be a daunting task, not least because it is constantly vulnerable to the diversion of resources to non-productive ends, as witnessed in the recent speculative bubble that preceded the crisis.

More generally, while there may be considerable 'embeddedness' of Southeast Asian states in their surrounding societies (more precisely, in leading economic groups), these states have long lacked the pilot agencies of their northern counterparts, where transformative projects can be pursued at some remove from sectional interest politics. In contrast to the Northeast Asian experience, the interdependence of government and business has not been governed primarily by transformative goals and, in consequence, public policy has much more often been driven by the push and pull of short-term sectional interests.

Korea: revenge of the international market against transformative state – interdependence ungoverned?

In Korea, what began as a banking crisis was precipitated by a series of corporate collapses throughout 1997, beginning with the Hanbo group in January. Indeed the *chaebol* loom large as the villains of the Korean débâcle. If one is seeking a common denominator in these events, it was not that of weak-state cronyism, or even of a strong state overriding efficient market logic. Rather it was one of uncoordinated overinvestment (read 'non-directed lending'): that is, massive private borrowing for investments in sectors not only already well supplied by other *chaebol* (e.g. petrochemicals, steel, semiconductors) but also subject to cyclical downturn.

This was a pattern that would become increasingly marked in the decade just prior to the financial meltdown, as government abandoned its long-standing role of coordinating industrial investment. First under Roh Tae Woo's presidency, then under Kim Young Sam's, policy loans were phased out and financial liberalisation speeded up. Ironically, it was a pattern that marked the loosening of the business–government relationship and gradual decline of transformative capacity in Korea. There can be no clearer symbol of this change than that offered by the definitive dismantling of the Economic Planning Board (merged with the MOF) in 1993, for some years already marginalised. As SED pointed out, the state's declining ability to coordinate *chaebol* investments and thereby promote industrial upgrading added to industry's own incapacity for self-governance. As government became less involved in managing credit, in allocating subsidised loans, and in industrial policy more generally, so its efforts to curb excess output by promoting producer cartels had little effect. Decomposing political capacity in turn unleashed a frenzied scramble for market share among the *chaebol* (especially among middle-level conglomerates seeking expansion), resulting in overinvestment and high-risk borrowing strategies. Thus, as 'interdependence' became steadily 'ungoverned', the *chaebol* took the easier course of expansion rather than upgrading. This pattern became a hallmark of the Korean industrial landscape in the democratisation decade.

But the Korean pattern of overinvestment and massive foreign borrowing was far from being fatal. It was certainly not Korea's first encounter with economic downturn, difficulties of foreign debt repayment, or even IMF intervention. Because of its massively leveraged conglomerates, Korea has always been vulnerable to external shocks (leading in 1980 to a 6 per cent loss in GNP). Such shocks, however, had proved more containable in the past. So why was it so uncontainable now? What was new? Was it the composition of external debt, or perhaps its level or provenance? Surely not, for even in a more protected financial system, Korea managed to scale the heights of foreign indebtedness and was no stranger to repayment difficulties. (High short-term debts prompted Korea's first big crisis of 1971–2; and the debt crisis of 1979–83 involved difficulties servicing a huge foreign debt.) Yet these were quickly resolved in the past (cf. Woo 1991).

Thus, to understand what was new about the 1997 experience, we need to consider the role of external factors in turning a run-of-the-mill debt crisis into an over-the-top financial crash. One thing had altered fundamentally – the geopolitical landscape. Since the end of the Cold War, the US–Korea security relationship had gradually weakened. Consequently, Korea in the

1990s was no longer a special case whose deviation from the free market norm could be tolerated for larger political goals.[6] Thus, far from seeking to buttress the Korean state as it had done in other times of difficulty, the United States was now prepared to stand back and let the crisis rip through the institutional fabric it so wished to tear apart.

When crisis turned to tragedy: international power actors

We have argued that weak or weakened transformative capacity rendered some economies more vulnerable to economic turmoil. But the fact remains that vulnerabilities of various kinds do not necessarily produce a banking or currency crisis. Moreover, the kind of weakness identified here is far from lethal. It is certainly no candidate for explaining the scope or depth of the crisis – in short, why it turned abnormal.

To the question 'Why is the crisis so much worse than it is supposed to be?', several authorities have suggested it is because of investor panic, self-fulfilling expectations and sheer 'herd' behaviour whereby everyone withdraws from the market simply because that is what everyone else is doing. But what nurtured and sustained the panic? It may well be that the herding phenomenon is more prevalent in a global environment where the world's money is controlled by fund managers who feel most secure when they follow everyone else. However, to invoke panic, herding and similar behavioural metaphors is to provide not an explanation but a restatement of the problem. Why was capital flight so massive, so relentless, and thus so damaging? To answer this we must look outside the nation-states in question, to the role of external power actors which coalesce around and within the US federal administration.

The explanation thus requires that we turn our attention to the exercise of state power (and the constellation of interests therein embedded) – but this time state power which is being applied externally by the world's most powerful nation-state. SED advanced two propositions. The first is that economic strength and (domestic) state power are highly correlated rather than antithetical. The second proposition is that (externally oriented) state power could in certain though limited cases – the United States being the exemplary case – provide a (temporary) substitute for domestic capacity by forcing other nation-states to relinquish their internal transformative powers.

Today, the most vivid illustration of that proposition can be seen in the extraordinary behaviour of the United States in the Asian region in seeking to force systemic change in the troubled economies. This has been a persistent pattern in the post-war American experience, whereby the leading power, relatively weak in domestic transformative capacity, but strong externally, compensates for that weakness by attempting to force change upon others and, if possible, conformity with its own system. Such power inversion invokes the idea of the United States as an 'opportunistic' hegemon with a free-riding strategy: shifting the costs of change onto others rather than adapting its own institutions.

The role of the US Treasury–Wall Street–IMF complex

Of the three power actors involved in deepening the crisis, it has been the US Treasury–finance nexus that has been the least visible yet the most damaging. While the IMF is also implicated in the unfolding drama, its role has differed on two counts: its interventions have neither enjoyed the level of autonomy disposed of by the other actors (though strongly desired by the Fund), nor been deployed by their more calculated self-interest. The key proposition is that the US administration has not merely used the crisis as a leveraging opportunity to prise open markets once closed to foreign financial institutions; it has played a critical role in deepening the crisis in the first place.

By way of summarising the argument, the impact of external power sources coalescing around the US administration can be seen in the following three main ways.

Securing the door after the horse has bolted

The key point here has to do with actions of the US administration that entailed both calculated non-intervention as well as prevention of intervention, which would in all probability have circumvented investor panic. Even a slight familiarity with earlier financial crises indicates that when the foreign exchange turmoil struck Korea, the primary need was clear and straightforward. It was to maintain liquidity and thus to persuade foreign creditors to maintain lending by rolling over existing loans as they came due. That could be done without IMF guarantees, simply by ensuring that lenders understood that Korea's problem of inadequate reserves was a temporary problem of liquidity, not insolvency. Above all, Korea needed 'coordinated action by creditor banks to restructure its short-term debts, lengthening their maturity and providing additional temporary credits to help meet the interest obligations' (Feldstein 1998: 25–6, 31). But it was not until Korea's reserves were almost depleted and after the damage had already been done that the US Federal Reserve took the steps (in January 1998) that would earlier have averted the 'deep' crisis: bringing together the major players to coordinate a program of debt restructuring and short-term loan rollovers.

The unwillingness to intervene in a timely manner to stem the degradation of the currency poses a striking contrast with US action in earlier such episodes in Europe and Latin America (where recovery was relatively quick). For instance, when sovereign debt led Mexico to the brink of bankruptcy in

1982, and twice more in 1994 and 1995 in response to massive capital flight and the peso crisis, the US moved quickly to coordinate a rescue plan. In the recent peso crisis, the US government and the IMF took early action to rescue the currency, first with a credit line of $6 billion, finally orchestrating a rescue fund of $50 billion, engineering a massive international loan which restored investor confidence. This is not to suggest that the Mexican and Korean crises were similar, merely that the international responses were very different. Timely intervention was at hand in the Mexican case – and it worked. As Kindleberger has remarked, the strategy 'proved persuasive'. 'The hemorrhaging stopped, capital returned' (1996: 187). As Kindleberger's study of financial crises indicates, whenever international cooperation or even a lender of last resort has come to the rescue – and such instances appear to be the rule, not the exception – the business depression that follows financial crisis is momentary, slowing the economy only briefly; recovery after the panic is swift, without deeper significance.

By not intervening (in spite of the Korean government's urgent pleas in November 1997 for US assistance in its efforts to support the currency), it could be argued that the United States was merely bringing policy into alignment with the new geopolitical reality. In a post-Cold-War environ-ment, there was no longer the significant national (security) interest in protecting Asia that in the past would so often override the economic interest of opening Korean markets to US goods and finance.

Should one therefore leave it at that: calculated inaction occurred because it was not in US interests to intervene? Such considerations surely played a part. But more positively, one might also argue that it was now very much in US interests not to intervene. Greater leverage over the stricken countries – and thus over market access – was the ultimate payoff. A number of top-level officials conceded as much in public statements as the IMF was reluctantly called in by the Koreans. In a now widely publicised statement, Deputy Treasury Secretary Lawrence Summers proclaimed in February 1998 that 'The IMF has done more to promote America's trade and investment agenda in Korea than 30 years of bilateral trade talks'. Certainly no one anticipated quite how stricken the Asian economies would become, but that does not weaken the proposition that there was an element of calculation involved in the 'failure' to intervene. While it is highly plausible that the US administra-tion could not have anticipated just how devastating the impact of the crisis would become in the absence of coordinated intervention, it is implausible to suggest complete ignorance of the seriousness of the situation. The fact that the Japanese authorities had declared themselves prepared to intervene rela-tively early in the crisis (i.e. in July–August 1997) with the offer of a massive bailout – subsequently scuttled by the US administration – would surely have conveyed some sense of the gravity of the situation unfolding.

Indeed, we can add one further piece of evidence to this proposition. The US government also actively prevented intervention by another nation-state.

When the Japanese stepped forward in August of 1997 with an offer to redeem some of their neighbours' debts, and a proposal to create an Asian monetary fund with $100 billion to bolster resources available to ailing economies in the region, the Americans quickly scuttled the plan (Johnson 1998). Perhaps, as Johnson suggests, the worry was that the Japanese would begin to deploy their surplus capital for the benefit of Asian countries, thus withdrawing it from the world's largest debtor nation (namely, close to US$350 billion of Japanese money invested in US Treasury bonds). Perhaps, more simply, Japan's proposal was rejected because of the fear that a contender to the IMF would not be quite so US-friendly in the conditions it imposed on those seeking assistance.

How then is one to interpret calculated non-intervention – as a matter of indifference or of national interest, or perhaps some combination of the two? The geopolitical argument leans towards indifference: 'If we don't help the Koreans it won't impact negatively on our security interests'. The interest argument leans towards positive benefits: 'If we don't help the Koreans this time it may just help to advance our economic interests that little bit further'. Attributing motives, even in the best of circumstances, is an exercise fraught with imprecision. It is especially difficult when consensus among the key decision-makers is often hard to discern. The real issue is: 'Could the US Treasury and the Federal Reserve have intervened earlier to prevent the crisis deepening, as they had on other occasions?' The Koreans certainly thought so, making urgent approaches in November of 1997 (in an effort to prevent calling in the IMF) to both the US government and a consortium of banks in the United States. They were turned down. It is now on public record that the Koreans believe their efforts at crisis management were given less than wholehearted support because the US authorities wanted the IMF to have a free hand in Korea. The Koreans tend to see conspiracy; but calculation is probably more accurate, in the sense that in holding back until the last minute, the US authorities were more cognisant of the benefits to the United States than of the costs to the Asians. But whatever the true political motives driving these events, there can be no denying their devastating consequences.

'Screaming "fire" in the theatre'

The second way in which external power deepened the crisis has to do with the imposition of a US trade and investment agenda in the IMF agreements. The latter have already received wide discussion, so let us simply note two points. First, the documents leave little doubt as to the embeddedness of the US Treasury in the financial interests which dominate Wall Street. (While the IMF is no mere instrument of US interests, seeking to maintain an independent role, it nevertheless depends on US support and is inescapably drawn into a close relationship with the world's leading nation-state and 'its' finance capital.) The IMF plan for Korea, for example, imposes as a condition of funding a series of institutional makeovers which have nought to do with dousing the fire or even making the structure fireproof. These include the opening of capital markets to enable hostile takeovers and foreign (majority) ownership of Korean firms, as well as greater access for foreign banks and insurance companies. It should be noted, however, that in Korea's case some aspects of structural reform, mainly those concerning the troublesome *chaebol*, have long been sought by Korean governments. To this extent, it has been suggested that the crisis may be a 'blessing in disguise' – allowing more foreign ownership of Korean assets, at least in the short term, but also restoring balance to the government–business relationship by granting state authorities the power to discipline the conglomerates (see e.g. Mathews 1998).

In some cases, the reform measures were sound but poorly sequenced. Thus, for example, the IMF's insistence that the Indonesian government take tough action to clean up its banking system led to the sudden closure of fifteen banks with links to the Suharto family, which in turn precipitated a run on deposits that became a haemorrhage. This is because the closure was undertaken before Indonesia had established a system of deposit insurance. A stunned populace, faced with the prospect of a massive bank collapse, rushed to withdraw its savings. Similarly abrupt closures of financial institutions in Thailand and Korea precipitated among investors a rush for the exit, thus giving rise to the image of an IMF whose actions – to use Jeffrey Sachs' vivid imagery – amounted to 'screaming "fire" in the theatre'.

But the main outcome of the IMF agreements was the unintended one of inviting panic by undermining investor confidence.

> Lenders who listened to the IMF could not be blamed for concluding that Korea would be unable to service its debts unless its economy had a total overhaul. ... Unsurprisingly, after the program was announced, the bond rating agencies downgraded Korean debt to junk bond status.
>
> (Feldstein 1998: 31)

By emphasising the need for major structural overhaul, the IMF prescriptions suggested to investors a systemic weakness that did not exist, thus fuelling further investor panic resulting in currency plunges and capital outflows. In this way, by shouting 'fire' in the theatre, the IMF helped engineer the very outcome that it was supposed to have prevented (Feldstein 1998; Radelet and Sachs 1998; Stiglitz 1998; Wade and Veneroso 1998).

Striking the fallen

There is a third aspect to the 'external power' story, which has attracted the widest commentary and discussion. This concerns the uncalculated but significant harm wrought by standard IMF austerity measures, such as the imposition of high interest rates in highly inappropriate circumstances. These measures exacerbated the liquidity problem, thereby helping to kill off sick and healthy companies alike. In the Indonesian setting, in particular, IMF measures often had the most perverse results, threatening to kill off the patient whose health they were designed to restore. (The case of the sudden bank closures mentioned earlier provides a powerful illustration.)

As for the standard IMF austerity measures of high interest rates and reduced public spending, these too added significantly to the economic and social hardship (and indeed were scaled back considerably in the second half of 1998). But the IMF measures have had less causal impact than the other two areas of US intervention. This is because they were introduced after the main damage had been done. In short, capital had already left – and this is, after all, our main explanatory target in this context.

Now in making these points about the role of the world's major power in deepening the crisis, it is important to be clear about what is not being claimed. We are not suggesting that the US government or American financial institutions or even the IMF set out deliberately to deepen the crisis. Rather, we are proposing that some of their actions and inactions were critical in deepening the crisis; that some of these actions were calculated to further US interests; and that in so doing they were more cognisant of the benefits to the United States than of the costs to the Asians; and that they had the unintended consequence of exacerbating a situation that should have been quite quickly repaired.

Conclusion

So we have then a two-pronged approach to the Asian meltdown: why Asia became embroiled in financial turmoil in the first place, and why it turned so savage. Institutional weaknesses (weak-state capacities) gave rise to real economy vulnerabilities, which then acted as flashpoints to investors as other events, above all the actions of external power actors, helped to precipitate full-scale panic (i.e. the deep crisis).

Thus the Asian crisis appears to reinforce our 1995 thesis in two ways. First, it suggests how weak domestic power can increase vulnerability to external shocks like financial crises. With regard to domestic weakness, the Asian crisis and the problems suffered by Thailand and Indonesia are widely perceived as events which demonstrate the futility of 'state-guided' capitalism with its Japanese-style developmental state. But this conclusion is based on flawed premises. As institutionalists, including ourselves, have always sought to make clear, the Southeast Asian countries have never been guided by transformative states pursuing structural change as a national priority. Both ideologically and organisationally, they have had comparatively low transformative capacity, making them more dependent on capital inflows, less guarded about capital account opening, and more vulnerable to financial volatility. By contrast, South Korea – once a powerful example of state-guided capitalism – has seen its coordinating powers unravel, beginning with a process of ideological osmosis in the 1980s with the rise of neo-liberalism in the upper ranks of the economic bureaucracy, and ending with the dismantling of its pilot agency by 1993. The result – in striking contrast to the Taiwanese experience, where transformative goals and institutions remain largely intact – has been a virtual abandonment of investment coordination and of control over the composition of capital flows.

Second, the Asian crisis illustrates how the 'transformative' role of state power applied externally can exploit vulnerability and deepen the effect of international shocks. Here we have in mind the 'opportunistic' behaviour of the United States, which directly and indirectly helped to deepen and extend the crisis, turning the historically 'normal' face of financial crisis into something 'abnormal' and extraordinary.

As to what all this means for the so-called replacement of capitalist diversity in Asia with free market liberalism or with some variant of the American model of capitalism, one thing can be said with some confidence. While 'global' and 'national' are commonly portrayed as antithetical, mutually exclusive principles of organisation and interaction, 'Asia in crisis' has shown that they are in fact in critical respects interdependent, mutually reinforcing. The extent and sustainability of financial liberalisation will continue to depend on the solidity of domestic structures. Where these are weak, global networks merely end up undermining their own conditions of existence. The extreme case is that of Indonesia where domestic collapse has gone hand in hand with the country's involuntary detachment from the global financial system. At the other extreme lies the Malaysian response of voluntary semi-detachment from global finance, ostensibly in an effort to build and strengthen the institutional capabilities of Malaysia. Somewhere between these two extremes, others are drawing lessons from the crisis by tightening and improving capital controls. Above all, 'Asia in crisis' vividly illustrates the implausibility of a world economy sustained by unlimited global flows, and draws attention instead to the underlying (institutional) limits to liberalisation. Based on the variety of national-level responses, as well as the growing international demands at the highest levels for re-regulation of global finance, is it plausible to anticipate that post-crisis Asia will edge more closely towards neo-liberal American ways than those of state-guided Japan?

NOTES

1   For a fruitful classification of the different approaches to the crisis, see Jayasuriya (1999).
2   On the notion of 'episodic events', such as depressions and wars, which act as historical watersheds, see Skocpol (1985).
3   The expression is that of Wade and Veneroso (1998).
4   For an account of how and why Korea and Taiwan diverged in their approaches to financial liberalisation, see Weiss (1999a).
5   For the pioneering study of Indonesia from a political economy perspective, see Robison (1986).
6   For a similar, though more elaborate, argument along these lines, see Woo-Cumings (1998).

Part II

CRISIS OF THE DEVELOPMENTAL STATE

5

THE STATE, STRUCTURAL RIGIDITY, AND THE END OF ASIAN CAPITALISM

A comparative study of Japan and South Korea

Chung In Moon and Sang-young Rhyu

Introduction

Japan and South Korea have long been touted as the stellar examples of successful economic transformation since the end of World War II. Despite poor factor endowment and devastating legacies of the Pacific war, Japan has emerged as an economic superpower in a relatively short time. South Korea has also shown a remarkable pathway from the periphery by becoming the eleventh largest economy in the world as well as joining the Organization for Economic Cooperation and Development (OECD) in 1996. Their economic success has offered a rich empirical research site for refuting the Anglo-American model, while supporting the thesis of the 'late-industrialization' model (Amsden 1989). By neo-classical economic standards, indeed, the economic performance of Japan and South Korea in the past four decades, along with Singapore and Taiwan, is rather anomalous. Such anomaly has stirred new debates on Asian capitalism (Krugman 1994; Lucas 1993).

Asian capitalism is differentiated from other forms of capitalism on three major accounts: culture, state, and networks. The Confucian cultural tradition and authority structure associated with it have endowed East Asian nations with strong state machinery and organic social networks. While strong state, devoid of social capture, has been able to formulate efficient, coherent, consistent, and flexible economic policies and to implement them effectively (Johnson 1982; Cumings 1987; Haggard and Moon 1983; Weiss and Hobson 1995; Weiss 1998), organic social networks formed through close blood, school, and social ties have bred shared norms and values, reduced transaction costs, and enhanced information flows (Evans 1995; Fukuyama 1995; Sakakibara 1995; Aoki 1995). The combination of state capacity and social networks embedded in the East Asian social and cultural fabrics has not only distinguished the East Asian form of capitalism, but also served as the locomotive of economic dynamism in East Asia. But after four decades of uninterrupted economic growth and expansion, both Japan and South Korea are undergoing hard times. While the Japanese economy is faltering under the protracted economic recession, the South Korean economy has been placed under IMF economic trusteeship after requesting rescue financing in the wake of major foreign exchange and financial crises in December 1997. Negative growth rates, corporate bankruptcies, paralysis of the banking and financial sector, unstable foreign exchange regimes, steep asset deflation, and pervasive unemployment, all of which are quite foreign to the populace of these nations, underscore the dark side of today's economic reality in Japan and South Korea. What went wrong? Does it imply the end of East Asian economic dynamism? What is the future of Asian capitalism? This chapter is designed to explore these questions by looking into the nature of economic crisis in Japan and South Korea, eluci-dating its behavioral and structural causes, and drawing theoretical and empirical implications. We argue that the current economic crisis in Japan and South Korea is a product of government and policy failures, which can be attributed to a structural rigidity deeply embedded in a social and polit-ical terrain. The age of the developmental state is now gone, and East Asian capitalism can neither be engineered nor saved. Convergence toward Anglo-American capitalism is likely to be accelerated in the name of globalization and global standard.

Economic crisis in Japan and South Korea: a comparative overview

The historical trajectory of economic performance in Japan and South Korea has not been unilinear. Constant cycles of boom and bust have char-acterized their economic profiles. Since the early 1990s, however, the Japanese and Korean economies have shown a persistent pattern of economic downturn without signs of immediate recovery. A relatively long recession flared up into an acute crisis in South Korea. Crisis has not yet been manifest in Japan, but its countdown appears to have started.

Japan: from bubble to protracted recession

Japan recorded the highest economic growth rate among OECD members during 1987–90. While the United States, the United Kingdom, and other advanced industrialized countries were suffering from slow growth and extensive structural adjustment, Japan enjoyed an average annual growth rate of 5 percent. Fiscal stimulus, export expansion, booming real estate, and capital markets have all enabled and sustained its economic boom. Land prices appreciated by more than three times during 1987–90, and the stock price index rose by twenty-five times from 100 in 1968 to 2,569 in 1989. Japan enjoyed unprecedented economic expansion in the second half of the 1980s. As Table 5.1 illustrates, however, the Japanese economy began to show a sharp downturn since 1992. Growth rates faltered from 4.3 percent in 1991 to 0.8 percent in 1997. As of June 1998, Japan's growth rate recorded −5.3 percent. It is the first major negative growth rate. An acute depreciation of stock prices has also haunted Japan. Compared to that in 1989, the value of stock prices dwindled to 53.8 percent in 1996 and 42.7 percent in 1997. Along with stock prices, real estate value has been sharply depreciated, aggravating asset deflation. Compared to 1990, real estate value was deflated by more than 20 percent in 1996 and 42 percent in 1997.

More troublesome is a gradual paralysis of the Japanese financial and banking system. Sharp depreciation of stock prices and real estate values has proliferated non-performing loans. Table 5.2 presents summary figures on non-performing loans or 'bad' loans held by Japanese banking and financial institutions. As of September 1997, the Ministry of Finance (MOF) estimated non-performing loans to be 21 trillion yen, accounting for 3.48 percent of outstanding gross bank loans (*Nihon Keizai Shimbun*, June 21, 1998). But as indicated in Table 5.2, the official figure seems quite deceptive. In July 1998, the Japanese Financial Supervisory Agency gave a revised figure of total non-performing loans which amount to 87.5 trillion yen, accounting for more than 13 percent of gross outstanding loans. Despite government efforts to deal with the problem of non-performing loans in an incremental manner, seventeen banking and financial institutions have become bankrupt since December 1994. Two leading banking and financial

Table 5.1   Main economic indicators in Japan (1989–98)

	Real economic growth rate (%)	Stock price index (TOPIX: 1968.1 = 100)	Land price index (1990 = 100)	Exchange rates (yen/dollar)
1989	4.7	2,569.27	86.3	138.12
1990	4.8	2,177.96	100	144.88
1991	4.3	1,843.18	111.5	134.59
1992	1.1	1,364.19	109.2	126.62
1993	0.1	1,525.09	101.0	111.06
1994	0.5	1,600.32	93.5	102.18
1995	1.5	1,378.93	87.1	93.97
1996	3.9	1,606.37	79.9	108.81
1997	0.8	1,394.88	–	120.92
1998*	−5.3	1,191.15	–	140.57

Sources: Bank of Japan, *Economic Statistics Annual*; *The Monthly Toyo Keizai Economic Statistics*; Kwon (1998). * = to June

Table 5.2   The size of 'bad' (non-performing) loans in Japan[a] (units: yen billions)

	The gross amount of loans (G)		624,864	
	Normal loans		548,156	
Non-performing loans	Classified by debtor	Classified by loan (repayability)		
	Secondary loss	Precautionary (A)	65,289	
	2nd, 3rd, 4th losses	Doubtful (B)	8,724	
	2nd, 3rd, 4th losses	Estimated loss (C)	2,695	
Non-performing loan (A+B+C) announced by MOF (September 1997)			21,730	(3.48%)
Non-performing loan (A+B+C) announced by MOF (January 1998)			76,708	(12.28%)
Non-performing loans announced by Banks Federation (July 1998)			35,207	
Non-performing loans announced by Financial Supervisory Agency (July 1998)			5,217	(14.0%)

Sources: Kwon (1998); *The Weekly Toyo Keizai* (August 1, 1998); *Nihonkeizai Shimbun* (June 21, 1998); *The Yomiuri Shimbun* (July 18, 1998)

Notes:
a Includes commercial banks, long-term credit banks and trust banks; parentheses mean the ratio of non-performing loan (A + B + C/G)

institutions, the Hokkaido Takushoku Bank and Yamaichi Securities, collapsed ahead of the government schedule in 1997, and their bankruptcy sent shock waves through the Japanese economy by creating panic behavior and a severe credit crunch. Faltering performance of the Japanese banking and financial institutions has not only activated the collapse of small- and medium-sized firms, but also lowered its international credit rating and foreign exchange rates. In the first half of 1998, 10,100 firms went bankrupt. It is also ironic to note that Japan, as the number one creditor nation in the world, suffers from the threat of sharp depreciation of its own currency.

The Japanese economic recession has other dimensions too. By the end of 1997, the Japanese government's accumulated long-term debts had reached a record high of 544 trillion yen, which is larger than its GDP. The fiscal deficit in 1997 alone was equivalent to 6.7 percent of GDP. In addition, the myth of lifetime employment has also disappeared. Unemployment reached 4.3 percent (2.84 million) in June 1997. Widespread unemployment is causing a new social trauma such as a rise in the suicide rate. In 1997 alone, 3,500 persons committed suicide for reasons of economic hardship, a rise of 2.8 times rise compared to 1990.

South Korea: globalization and economic crisis

While the Japanese case reveals a pattern of protracted recession and crisis of management, the South Korean crisis was much more abrupt and traumatic. In 1994, the Kim Young Sam government adopted the *segyehwa* (globalization) strategy as 'the shortcut which will lead us to building a first-class country in the 21st century' (*Korea Herald* January 7, 1995). As part of the globalization strategy, the Kim Young Sam government ratified the Uruguay Round and maneuvered to join the OECD. Along with this, South Korea liberalized its foreign trade, banking and financial systems, and foreign investment regimes. However, even before reaching the twenty-first century, globalization brought about a major setback during his tenure, the sudden collapse of the Korean economy in November 1997, which alarmed the entire world. After a series of financial and foreign exchange crises, the Kim Young Sam government filed for national economic bankruptcy by asking the IMF (International Monetary Fund) for $57 billion in bailout funds on December 3, 1997. The myth of the Korean economic miracle was shattered, and national shame prevailed.

Table 5.3 presents data on the dark side of the Korean economy under the Kim Young Sam government. During his term in office, South Korea's foreign debts increased from $43.9 billion to $160.7 billion in 1996 and $153 billion in 1997, while foreign reserve assets dwindled from $20.2 billion in 1993 to $12.4 billion in 1997. At the peak of the currency crisis, foreign reserves held by the central bank were less than $8 billion, spreading the fear of default. With foreign reserves being depleted, the Korean currency rapidly depreciated. In 1993, the won/dollar exchange rate was KW808.1, but the Korean won devalued by almost two times by the end of 1997, posting an exchange rate at 1,415 won/dollar. At one point, the exchange rate reached 2,000 won/dollar.

More troublesome was the private sector. As Table 5.3 illustrates, the banking and financial sector as well as the corporate sector have shown the worst performance in recent history. The stock price index is generally considered the most reliable barometer of economic vitality. The average annual stock price index was 866.2 in 1993 and 1,027.4 in 1994. But it continued to slide down throughout 1995 and 1996, falling to 376 by the end of 1997, the lowest since the opening of securities markets. Falling stock prices amidst rapid currency devaluation have drastically reduced the value of Korean firms' assets. According to an analysis by the *Financial Times*, total assets of all 653 Korean firms listed on the Korean Securities Exchange Market were estimated to be only 66.3 trillion Korean won, which is the

Table 5.3 Main economic indicators in Korea (1992–8)

	1992	1993	1994	1995	1996	1997	1998
Economic growth rates (%)	4.7	5.8	8.6	9.0	7.1	5.5	−3.8 (Feb.)
Stock price index (KOSPI: 1980.1=100)	678.4	866.2	1,027.4	882.9	651.2	376.3	297.9 (June)
Current balance ($ million)	−4,529	385	−4,531	−8,948	−23,005	−8,168	22,383 (June)
Foreign exchange holdings ($ million)	17,154	20,262	25,673	32,712	33,237	20,410	43,020 (July)
Exchange Rates — Won/$	788.4	808.1	788.7	774.7	844.2	1,415.2	1,236.0 (July)
Won/100 yen	631.98	772.49	790.68	749.23	726.51	1,087.82	873.77 (July)
Ratio of dishonored bills (%)	0.12	0.13	0.17	0.20	0.17	0.40	0.42 (June)
Total debt per GDP (%)	19.17	17.07	20.91	25.82	32.79	34.02	–
Financial capital market openness[a] (%)	4.65	4.88	9.11	12.58	15.03	6.97	–

Sources: Bank of Korea, *Economic Statistics Yearbook*; IMF, *International Financial Statistics*; Samsung Economic Research Institute, *Principal Economic Indicators*

Note:
a Ratio of financial capital transactions to the value of GDP. Financial capital transactions are the sum of financial capital inflows and outflows

equivalent of assets held by one European company, ING Group, a Dutch banking and financial firm ranked as the seventieth largest firm in the world (*Financial Times*, December 29, 1997).

Another important indicator of microeconomic health is the size of non-performing loans since it tells us about the magnitude of corporate bankruptcies. Total non-performing loans were KW2.4 trillion in 1993 and KW1.9 trillion in 1994. By the end of September 1997, they rose to KW4.8 trillion (Samsung Economic Research Institute 1995; OECD 1998). Given the avalanche of corporate bankruptcies including major chaebol such as Hanbo, Kia, Jinro, Daenong, Newcore, and Halla,[1] the size of non-performing loans must be much higher than 4.8 trillion won. In fact, the IMF estimated that non-performing loans amounted to KW32 trillion, about 7 percent of GDP, in 1997 (International Monetary Fund 1997). A sharp increase in non-performing loans literally paralyzed the banking and financial sector, precipitating the financial crisis. Non-performing loans accounted for 6.8 percent of total bank loans as of the end of September 1997. In addition, most firms in South Korea, especially small- and medium-sized ones, have traditionally relied on discounts of corporate bills such as promissory notes in raising corporate funds. Thus, a high ratio of dishonored corporate bills implies a severe liquidity shortage and greater corporate delinquency. In the first three quarters of 1996, the ratio of dishonored corporate bills was 0.24 percent, a dramatic increase from 0.13 percent in 1993.

Japan and South Korea share a common denominator of steep economic downturn and prolongation of economic recession. Ironically, the recession and subsequent crisis (in South Korea) and quasi-crisis (in Japan) were followed by banking and financial liberalization. But they differ in behavioral and structural configurations. While the Korean economic crisis was acute and manifest, the Japanese one was gradual and latent. Strictly speaking, the Japanese case might not be labeled as a crisis, but as a gradual and structural deterioration (Krugman 1998b). Another contrasting point is that while the South Korean crisis was initially triggered by exogenous variables such as high foreign debts and liquidity shortage, the Japanese problem was more endogenous in origin involving depressed domestic demand and asset deflation.

What went wrong? Government failures and economic crisis

What went wrong? There has been an extensive literature focusing on internal and external variables.[2] While some attribute the economic crisis of Japan and South Korea to domestic factors such as crony capitalism, moral hazard, and government failures (Bello 1998; Hollerman 1998; Roubini *et al.* 1998; Mauro 1997; Fischer 1998; Fitch IBCA 1998), others argue that macroeconomic fundamentals in Japan and South Korea were good, and such exogenous variables as panic behavior, contagion effects, and hot money and international conspiracy are to be blamed (Radelet and Sachs 1998; Moon 1998; Krause 1998). But we argue that the genesis of the Japanese and Korean economic crisis can be found in domestic mismanagement. It is more of a home-grown crisis (*The Economist* 29 November 1997). Inasmuch as the East Asian economic miracle was a product of a rational, interventionist state, its collapse was an outcome of rigid, incompetent, inertia-driven state behavior.

Trapping structure of incrementalism: policy failures in Japan

The Japanese economic crisis can be seen as a state-made disaster. When the bubble was lifted from the real Japanese economy, causes of its economic malaise became apparent. Fiscal and monetary reforms, banking and financial reforms through big bang, and overall deregulation and liberalization emerged as self-evident policy prescriptions of the malaise. The Japanese government knew about them, but was painfully slow in formulating and implementing reform packages. As Wolferen (1990) argues, the Japanese state was nothing but an elusive state without any significant power core where incremental tinkering of macroeconomic and microeconomic policies had become a shared norm. Consultation and consensus are virtues in good times, but in hard times they can turn into ferocious vices (Nakatani 1996; Sheard 1997; Tanaka 1998; Noguchi 1995; Aoki 1995). That is what happened to Japan.

A major policy failure came in June 1996. Facing a sharp economic downturn since 1992, the Japanese government undertook various fiscal and monetary measures to stimulate the ailing economy. Fiscal expansion, progressive tax cuts, and other measures to boost private consumption revived the Japanese economy in 1996. Growth rate rose from 0.5 percent in 1994 and 1.5 percent in 1995 to 3.9 percent in 1996. As the Japanese economy strengthened, its currency also appreciated, recording 102 yen/dollar in 1994 and 93.97 yen/dollar in 1995. Assuming a complete economic recovery, the Hashimoto cabinet undertook the long-delayed fiscal reforms (Sakakibara 1997; Otake 1997; Kwon 1998). In order to arrest snowballing fiscal deficits, the government set a goal to downsize fiscal spending by 13 trillion yen in 1997 alone. At the same time, the government adopted a measure to increase its revenue by raising consumption tax from 3 percent to 5 percent as well as levying an additional income tax of 2 trillion yen. Along with this, the Hashimoto cabinet cut medical insurance expenditure by 2 trillion yen by transferring its costs to beneficiaries. Expenditures for public works were also cut by 4 trillion yen.

The announcement of the fiscal reform package immediately dampened the private sector, however. Private consumption was literally frozen, and the stock market lost its vitality (*Nihon Keizai Shimbun* June 21, 1996). Realizing the negative boomerang effects of the fiscal reform measures, the Hashimoto cabinet reversed the fiscal initiative and introduced four major fiscal stimulus packages until Hashimoto resigned in July 1998. But the measures came too late. Although Hashimoto was aware of the negative impacts of the Financial Structural Reform Act, he was hesitant to revise it simply because the revision could imply the end of his reign (*Japan Times* March 20, 1998). Keizo Obuchi, the new premier replacing Hashimoto, also introduced new fiscal and financial stimulus packages. Obuchi pledged to pump in 16 trillion yen to boost the national economy and another 30 trillion yen to resolve the financial crisis by establishing a series of bridge banks. However, the markets have not responded to such incentive packages. Although the Bank of Japan increased money supply by 9 percent, bank loans have declined, while private savings are on the rise. A liquidity trap was in motion (Krugman 1998c). Moreover, tax reduction measures have not been able to reactivate private consumption. The errors of timing in macroeconomic management proved to be a major source of the current economic difficulties in Japan (*Nihon Keizai Shimbun* July 19, 1998).

Equally critical are the policy failures in the banking and financial sector. As Table 5.2 illustrates, the most serious issue confronting the Japanese economy is the ever-expanding size of non-performing loans. The Japanese government also failed to deal with delinquent loans. As the United States did during the Savings and Loan crisis in the 1980s, the Japanese government should have taken sweeping big bank measures. Yet the Japanese government decided to adhere to its traditional policy posture of an incremental, medium-to-long-term solution. In 1995, four years after the collapse of the bubble economy, the Ministry of Finance announced that it would resolve the question of non-performing loans in the next five years. It implied that troubled banks and financial institutions would be allowed to stay until 2001, and they would go bankrupt if they could not recover within the period. Such incremental measures did not work. Leading banks and financial institutions such as the Hokkaido Takushoku and Yamaichi Securities went bankrupt despite government pledges. Their collapse triggered panic in the financial markets, giving birth to a severe credit crunch.

Lukewarm measures in dealing with the case of Jusen (Japan Housing Loan Firm) also precipitated the loss of public and foreign confidence in the Japanese government. A sharp and protracted asset deflation dealt a critical blow to Jusen, the primary source of financing for the housing and real estate markets. Non-performing loans held by seven major Jusens reached a record high 6.4 trillion yen in 1996. The Murayama cabinet attempted to save Jusen firms through fiscal intervention. It not only appropriated 685 billion yen from the general budget account to assist the ailing Jusens, but also rescued investments by subsidiaries of the Agricultural Cooperatives. Out of 5.5 trillion yen which the Agricultural Cooperatives invested in Jusens, they were guaranteed a recovery of 90 percent of their total investments (Mabuchi 1997; *Weekly Toyo Keizai* May 11, 1996). Such inconsistent and discretionary banking and financial policy critically undermined the general reform efforts.

Policy failures involving fiscal as well as banking and financial reforms can be seen as the primary factor of the current economic crisis. In addition, persistent economic regulation, the old inertia of industrial policy, and the politics of crisis and compensation (Calder 1988) and fiscal weakness have all contributed to the economic downturn in Japan.

South Korea: incompetent state and policy failures

Government failures have been much more pervasive in South Korea than in Japan. The current economic crisis can be dated back to the early part of the Kim Young Sam government in 1994. The problem was inconsistent macroeconomic policy management: the fluctuation between contractionary and expansionary, anti-business and pro-business, and intervention and non-intervention policies. Disregarding inflationary consequences, the Kim government undertook an expansionary policy to stimulate the economy in the first year of its tenure (Kim Dae Jung 1997). Then it swung into contractionary policies. This erratic macroeconomic management sent confusing signals to the private sector.

Failure to discipline the corporate sector, especially big business, also served as an important impetus for the economic crisis in 1997. Facing eroding international competitiveness, big business in South Korea attempted to ensure its corporate survival through expansion and excessive investment with borrowed money. Such behavior became the primary source of the economic crisis as its borrowings became delinquent with declining levels of profits. If the Korean government had been tough on big business through tight enforcement of prudent competition policy, such developments could have been prevented. The banking and financial sector cannot avoid blame either. As the IMF aptly points out in its memorandum to the Korean government, financial institutions have priced risks poorly and have been willing to finance an excessively large portion of the investment plans of the corporate sector, resulting in high leverage. Financial institutions' persistent moral hazard and lack of market orientation have contributed to a worsening of the financial crisis. Here also there arises the issue of government failure. Government's prudent monitoring and supervision could have deterred banking and financial institutions from engaging in such practices.

In reality, despite repeated pledges for democratic reforms to corporate governance structure and *jungkyung yuchak* (the political–business connection), the old practices were not wiped out. While credit allocations were still heavily influenced by political connections, cross-investment and cross-payment guarantees among subsidiaries of chaebols were allowed as leverages for excessive borrowing and corporate expansion. The Hanbo scandal presents a classic example in this regard. Despite bleak business prospects and a low ratio of self-owned capital (about KW300 billion), Hanbo Steel was able to borrow KW5 trillion for investment in a steel plant. It was later revealed that political influence played an important role in securing loans for Hanbo. Kim Hyun-chul, son of President Kim Young Sam, and an array of politicians from both the ruling and opposition parties were implicated in exercising influence over the banks' loan decisions. The Hanbo case represents just the tip of the iceberg. A large proportion of bank loans have been arranged through political connections. The slush fund scandal involving two former presidents, Chun and Roh, offers persuasive evidence of this.

Apart from structural failures emanating from the instrumentalization of banks for state industrial policy, the Korean government made several critical mistakes in dealing with the economic crisis (Moon 1998). First, a rigid management of foreign exchange rate policy backfired. As early as June 1996, pressures for the devaluation of the Korean currency were mounting, but the government did not take any measures. Fear of inflation, disciplining the corporate sector, and lobbying by banks, firms, and state enterprises which benefited from heavy foreign borrowing prevented the government from making a timely devaluation of the Korean currency.[3] The overvaluation of the Korean currency depressed exports, while encouraging imports, eventually contributing to a worsening balance of payments.

Second, grave decisional mistakes were made during the crisis (*Donga Ilbo* April 11, 1998). At the end of 1996, the current account deficit reached 5 percent of GDP, and foreign reserves held by the Bank of Korea were $30 billion, which could pay for only three months' worth of imports. Despite such indicators, the government was optimistic about the future by citing the health of macroeconomic fundamentals. More importantly, during the height of the crisis (November 11–21), the Bank of Korea's disposable foreign reserves were downsized to $19.5 billion. Yet, the Bank wasted $6.7 billion defending the Korean currency. Consequently, foreign reserves dwindled to $12.7 billion by the end of November, aggravating the crisis. The worst mistake was the poor timing in calling for IMF rescue financing. Since mid October, IMF officials had been urging the South Korean government to ask for rescue financing. But the Korean government wasted almost a month before doing so. This was partly due to bureaucratic politics, and partly because of political factors. Those surrounding president Kim Young Sam did not want him to be a disgraceful president who filed for state bankruptcy.

Finally, the government's failure to monitor and supervise the situation played an important role in causing the crisis. Financial and capital liberalization in 1994 triggered an overseas rush by Korean city banks and merchant banks (Chung 1998). They were inexperienced in international banking and finance, but they aggressively ventured into high-risk, high-yield capital games. In addition, they were investing with borrowed short-term loans in the high-risk bonds of Southeast Asian countries, Russia, and Latin America (Brady Bond) (Chung 1998; *Chosun Ilbo* January 8, 1998). When these countries got into trouble, Korean banks and financial institutions lost their money. Deep and mobile international capital also made it difficult for the Korean government to track capital movements. Apart from short-term loans, overseas financing by Korean firms could not be accountable either. In a sense, the Korean economic crisis was a crisis of monitoring, supervision, and accountability. The fact that official government figures on foreign debts emerged in March, 1998, more than three months after the peak of the crisis, underscores the gravity of government failures.

An overview of government failures in Japan and South Korea illustrates three convergent and divergent points. First, Japan was too slow in making macroeconomic policy adjustment, while South Korea was too quick. Incremental tinkering has prevented Japan from dealing with the dynamic changes of market forces. Consensual policy formation through extensive consultation has undercut its effective momentum. On the other hand, South Korea has made too frequent and often erratic macroeconomic policy adjustments, eventually undermining policy consistency and coherence. Second, both Japan and South Korea have shown difficulties in steering their structural adjustment policies. Inertia-driven policy behavior has prevailed in both countries, blocking effective reform efforts. Failure to deal with non-performing loans is testament to this. Finally, governments in Japan and South Korea have revealed fundamental limits to their operational capability. Despite an array of competent economic bureaucrats, neither of them could effectively monitor and supervise the banking and financial sector.

State structure, rigidity, and economic crisis in Japan and South Korea

Where do these failures come from? They have originated from a structural rigidity of governance. As proponents of the developmental state have long argued, the state in Japan and South Korea has been characterized as a rigidity-free entity. Executive dominance, bureaucratic unity and competence, and insulation of economic policy making from social interests have made the East Asian state strong, autonomous, and wilfully maneuvering. Efficient and flexible policy formulation and effective implementation have resulted from this unique configuration of state structure in Japan and South Korea. However, a closer look at recent developments in Japan and South Korea reveals that the old template of the developmental state has been on the wane. The state is no longer rational, competent, unified, and insulated. It is entangled by its own internal actors, and is increasingly being captured by social and political interests (Moon and Prasad 1994). Profound changes in the internal configuration of state structure have not only constrained the formulation of efficient, coherent, consistent, and flexible economic policies, but also impaired their effective implementation.

Waning executive dominance appears to be one of the major factors underlying policy failures in Japan. The power, autonomy, and influence of the chief executive (namely, the prime minister) in Japan are often considered a function of leadership style, which varies from one prime minister to another. For example, Yoshida, Ikeda, Sato, and Nakasone have usually been characterized as strong prime ministers, but Hatoyama, Kishi, Miki, Ohira, and Kaifu have been considered relatively weak. Hashimoto was considered to have strong leadership style, but failed to achieve his policy goals. His fiscal reform efforts met an ill-fated end, while the banking and financial fiasco has remained virtually intact.

Policy failures under the Hashimoto cabinet can be ascribed to his political limits. Hashimoto came into power by forming a coalition with the Social Democratic Party and the New Party *Sakigake* (see Table 5.4). The multiparty coalition entailed a fundamental dilemma of policy coordination due to inherent ideological and policy differences. Precarious factional politics within the Liberal Democratic Party (LDP) also constrained his executive power (*Yomiuri Shimbun* July 22, 1998). No single faction dominates the coalition in LDP politics, and the selection of the prime minister is undertaken through dynamic coalition building. Therefore, those who are elected as prime minister should respond to, and accommodate, various demands from supporting factions. For example, the LDP was divided into two camps regarding fiscal reforms. While Kato, secretary-general of the LDP, and Yamazaki, chairman of the powerful LDP Policy Affairs Research Council, strongly favored fiscal reforms and contractionary macroeconomic policy, Kamei Sizuka and LDP's non-executive members advocated expansionary policy by opposing the fiscal reform efforts. Prime Minister Hashimoto had to muddle through these two conflicting policy camps, resulting in an ill-timed policy intervention.

In contrast, chief executives in South Korea have consistently enjoyed a high degree of power and autonomy. Ruling parties have been virtually subjugated to the arbitrary rule of chief executives. The Liberal Party under Rhee, the Democratic Republican Party under Park Chung Hee, the Democratic Justice Party under Chun Doo Hwan, and even the Democratic Liberal Party under Roh Tae Woo have all had limited or no influence on their president. These ruling parties were merely props for their presidents. Factional politics has existed within ruling parties, but presidents have always remained above such intramural politics. The only exception was the Second Republic under Chang Myon. Even after the democratic transition in 1987, the ruling party did not appear to exercise any autonomy or power over the president. Thus, it can be safely concluded that Korean chief executives have enjoyed a much higher degree of executive dominance than their Japanese counterparts.

Until very recently, legislative supervision and checks and balances did not exist. The legislative branch was nothing but a rubber stamp. The president and his secretariat (the Blue House) played the role of an inner cabinet standing above the regular cabinet. The chronic paralysis of the electoral system, symptomatic of an authoritarian regime, also deepened executive dominance by making the chief executive less responsive to grassroots pressure. Of course, this does not mean that chief executives

Table 5.4   Party segmentation in Korea and Japan (July 1998)

Korea		Japan			
		Sangiin *(Upper House)*		*Shyugiin* *(Lower House)*	
The Grand National Party (Hanaradang)	151	Liberal Democratic Party (Jiminto)	102	Liberal Democratic Party (Jiminto)	263
The National Congress for New Politics (Kukmimhoeui)	88	Democratic Party of Japan (Minshuto)	47	Democratic Party of Japan (Minshuto)	92
The United Liberal Democrats (Jaminryon)	49	Japanese Communist Party (Kyousanto)	23	Club for Reform (Kaikaku Club) – Peace (Heiwa)	47
The New Party by The People (Kukminsindang)	8	Komei Party (Komeito)	22	Liberal Party (Jiyuto)	40
Independents	3	Social Democratic Party (Shaminto)	13	Japanese Communist Party (Kyosanto)	26
		Liberal Party (Jiyuto)	12	Social Democratic Party (Shaminto) – Citizen Coalition (Shimin Rengo)	15
		New Party Sakigake (Shinto Sakigake)	3	Independents Club	5
		Others	4	New Party Sakigake (Shinto Sakigake)	2
		Independents	26	Independents	9
TOTAL	299	TOTAL	252	TOTAL	500 minus 1

Sources: *The Hankook Ilbo* (July 27, 1998); *Nihon Keizai Shimbun* (July 14, 1998)

never responded to pressures from the grassroots. Even in an authoritarian setting, chief executives were sensitive to electoral cycles. Evidence for this can be found in chronic fiscal expansion before and during the election years. Nevertheless, electoral cycles never imposed any significant constraint on chief executives in the past.

Despite the executive dominance inherent in South Korea's authority structure and presidential system, Kim Young Sam became a failed leader. This was due partly to a lack of competence and knowledge on the part of leadership. In fact, the most critical element for the escalation of the financial and foreign exchange crisis in November 1997 was a result of his leadership failure. President Kim was totally ignorant of economic policy and left its management to his aides. But his aides were divided on the diagnosis of, and prescriptions for, the impending crisis. The Bank of Korea (BOK) alerted President Kim of the danger of a foreign exchange crisis as early as July 1997. But the Ministry of Finance and Economy (MOFE) and the presidential economic secretary downplayed it by emphasizing 'healthy fundamentals' of the macroeconomy. Kim's aides thought they could put off the IMF bailout until Kim's tenure was over. His poor monitoring and mismanagement aggravated the crisis by mistiming effective intervention. The principal–agent dilemma haunted President Kim.

The deformed executive–bureaucrat nexus also deepened structural rigidity, aggravating economic difficulties. Japan is characterized by a bottom-up pattern, in which bureaucracy plays a major role in formulating and implementing policies (Yamaguchi 1995; Io 1995). Although prime ministers lay down a macro framework within which detailed policies are mapped out, they cannot directly intervene or interfere with ministry-level policy making. This horizontal executive–bureaucratic nexus turned out to be a major source of structural rigidity in Japanese economic policy making.

One of Hashimoto's major fiscal reforms was the separation of fiscal and financial functions. This measure was designed to prevent the subjugation of finance to fiscal needs (Mabuchi 1994). The issue became controversial since it was predicated on a fundamental curtailment of the powerful Ministry of Finance (Okurasho). However, Okurasho blocked such a move by forming an effective coalition with the Ministry of International Trade and Industry (MITI). An interministerial coalition was able to defy the executive mandate (*Asahi Shimbun* August 17, 1997). A similar case can be found in the Jusen scandal. As noted above, Agricultural Cooperatives invested 5.3 trillion yen in seven Jusen firms. When these firms were on the verge of collapse with mounting bad debts, other investors lost their investments, but 90 percent of investments made by Agricultural Cooperatives was bailed out. This was made possible through a secret agreement between Okurasho and the Ministry of Agriculture, Fishery, and Forestry (Mabuchi 1997: 8–24). Such an interministerial coalition severely undercut Hashimoto's efforts to push for a big bang in the banking and financial sector. Likewise, the loose executive–bureaucratic nexus and relative autonomy of bureaucracy have not only weakened executive power, but also prevented an effective and flexible policy adjustment.

South Korea is quite different. The executive–bureaucratic nexus has traditionally been rigidly vertical. It can be depicted as a 'sunflower (*haebaragi*)' model, in which both junior and senior bureaucrats radiate around the chief executive, or the Blue House. The president exercised virtually unrestricted command and control over the bureaucracy, and, therefore, bureaucrats played a lesser role in formulating and implementing public policies. Chief executives can and do interfere with minor details of policy contents, such as the landscape design of highways (Park Chung-Hee) and the method of highway paving (cement paving under Chun). Korean bureaucrats, whether low or high, did not exercise any significant autonomy or power. The lack of bureaucratic autonomy *vis-à-vis* the chief executive and the vertical nexus can be attributed to several factors: the concentration of administrative and personnel power in the hands of the president, the limited role of ministers and vice-ministers, and the lack of bureaucratic neutrality and professionalism.

But Kim Young Sam was not able to exploit the vertical nexus effectively, leading to policy failures and economic crisis. First, the Blue House and its staff failed to monitor and supervise economic trends and policy movements adequately. Second, presidential staff also failed to coordinate economic policies. As will be discussed below, there were ongoing policy debates among economic agencies on how to deal with the emerging foreign exchange and financial crises. But they did not pay due attention, and accordingly they were not able to formulate timely and appropriate policy measures. Finally, Kim Young Sam failed to ensure bureaucratic and policy stability. Macroeconomic policy instability and the subsequent economic crisis was in fact aggravated by frequent reshuffles of the economic cabinet. During the Kim Young Sam government, deputy prime ministers in charge of finance and economy were reshuffled seven times for reasons of policy failures such as price instability, current account deficits, and the Hanbo scandal, and their average tenure was less than eight months. It is virtually impossible for the Ministry of Finance and Economy to formulate and implement consistent and coherent economic policy with such a short tenure. And as the Hanbo scandal illustrates, the imperial power of the presidency and the blind obedience of economic bureaucrats and bankers resulted in extensive moral hazard and rent seeking, eventually undermining banking and financial reforms.

Bureaucratic politics also contributed to the deepening economic crisis in Japan and South Korea. Despite similar cultural traits, close school ties, unity of purpose, and a high degree of sectionalism, the Japanese bureaucracy can be characterized by compartmentalization and intense interagency rivalry. Thus, forming a consensus and reaching a compromise among bureaucratic agencies requires prudent, time-consuming, negotiating processes. Minimum commitment and muddling through become the basic rules for resolving bureaucratic politics. The prime minister plays an important role in mediating between contending agencies, but the LPD (especially the Policy Affairs Research Council or *Seimu Choshakai*) serves as the critical mediator in resolving bureaucratic infighting.

Viewed from the recent economic crisis in Japan, however, bureaucratic politics (Kato 1994) can be seen as a major catalyst of the economic downturn. A good example can be found in the case of the non-performing loan problem. As bad loans have been a salient public issue since 1991, Okurasho and the Bank of Japan (BOJ) have long deliberated on their effective management. The two agencies have differed on both the definition of non-performing loans and on their management. The BOJ attempted to apply a broad concept of non-performing loans and favored an immediate and sweeping resolution by letting delinquent banks go bankrupt. But Okurasho opposed the BOJ's position. It favored the minimal figures of non-performing loans and advocated a medium- and long-term solution. The agencies only reached a consensus on the definition of non-performing loans after four years of fierce policy debates. While they were engaged in these bureaucratic debates, the size of non-performing loans grew exponentially and went beyond government control. Bureaucratic infighting between Okurasho and MITI has also delayed fiscal reforms. While Okurasho strongly opposed permanent tax cuts, MITI insisted on tax cuts as a way of pump priming the recessionary economy. Likewise, bureaucratic rivalry and failure to coordinate their policy differences by the coalition government have undercut reform measures, heightening the sense of economic crisis in Japan.

Bureaucratic sectionalism and compartmentalization also exist in South Korea, and interagency rivalry has traditionally been fierce. However, the intensity of bureaucratic divisiveness is not as strong as in Japan. Executive dominance, clearly defined hierarchical ordering of ministries, and frequent circulation of economic bureaucrats have minimized such deep cleavages. There are several interministerial consultative mechanisms such as the Economic Ministers' Consultative Meeting designed to resolve any inter-bureaucratic conflicts and to enhance interagency cooperation. Those issues which cannot be resolved in these various interministerial meetings are ultimately determined by the chief executive. The ruling party has limited power in resolving interagency conflicts.

Nevertheless, bureaucratic fragmentation, indecisiveness, and incompetence played an essential role in triggering the entire financial and foreign exchange fiasco. Analysts trace the origin of the current economic crisis to the mismanagement of the case of Kia Motors. Kia Motors, the seventh largest business conglomerate, was on the verge of bankruptcy in the summer of 1997. The government's original plan was to let Kia go bankrupt. But two factors delayed the government's final decision. One was public critiques, and the other conflict of interests involving Kang Kyung-Shik, then deputy prime minister. It was known to the public that the plight of Kia Motors was engineered by the Samsung Group, which has long attempted to take it over. Kia had a better public image because of its ownership structure, while Samsung used to be blamed for its cold business ethics. In the Kia–Samsung bout, the public sided with Kia, making the latter's bankruptcy difficult. Meanwhile, Kang, while serving as a national assemblyman in Pusan before his appointment to the position, played a key role in bringing Samsung's new auto plant to the Pusan area. Thus, Kang's initial efforts to let market logic prevail over Kia were interpreted as a joint conspiracy with Samsung to kill off Kia. Kang was hesitant, and after a three-month delay, the government announced that it would turn Kia into a public enterprise. The government's indecisive actions as well as its ultimate decision to bail Kia out betrayed the expectation of foreign investors, and significantly damaged the government's credibility.

Equally critical was intra-bureaucratic fragmentation. As part of the administrative reforms, the Kim Young Sam government merged the Economic Planning Board (EPB) and the Ministry of Finance (MOF) into a superministry, the Ministry of Finance and Economy (MOFE). The merger did not bring about the positive effects which Oliver Williamson's theory of internal organization predicted. The MOF segment within MOFE has consistently warned of the danger of foreign exchange and financial crises and urged immediate counter-measures including IMF rescue financing. But the EPB segment, which dominated the MOFE decision-making machinery, ignored MOF warnings by pointing out the 'fundamental health' of macro-economic indicators. If the MOF had remained as a separate bureaucratic agency, the liquidity crisis could have been avoided. Worse still was inter-agency feuding. The South Korean economy began to show apparent signs of economic crisis by early November 1997. But two principal agencies in charge of economic policy, namely MOFE and the BOK, were entangled in fierce bureaucratic battles over the newly proposed BOK law which could considerably limit the power and autonomy of the BOK as the central bank. Kang Kyung-shik, then deputy prime minister in charge of MOFE, spent most of his time at the National Assembly in the first three weeks of November in order to lobby the passage of the bill, while employees of the BOK staged street demonstrations. The South Korean state was held at bay by bureaucratic infighting at the critical moment of the economic crisis.

Finally, social capture of economic policy making fundamentally constrained flexible policy choice and its effective implementation. Japan and South Korea have traditionally maintained a corporatist structure of political organization and coordination and the executive branch's pre-emptive power. Such institutional arrangements have prevented a western type of interest aggregation and articulation through political parties and parliament, while fostering interest groups' direct interaction with bureau-cratic agencies. Thus, bureaucratic agencies in Japan and Korea maintain close connections with their social constituents, and depending on issues and the macro political setting, they protect, reward, discipline, and sometimes punish interest groups in their jurisdictions. Likewise, the primacy of the bureaucratic system over civil society has facilitated the insulation of economic policy making in both countries. But viewed from the recent economic crisis, there has been a gradual erosion of the corporatist control, and social capture has been on the rise, cracking the insulating shield of state machinery.

Bureaucrats in Japan maintain close ties with their social constituents through administrative guidance and consultation. As the cliché Japan Inc. implies, business associations, and sometimes labor unions, are very much incorporated into the bureaucratic decision-making and implementation process, and even considered 'co-responsible parties in governance and societal guidance' (Okimoto 1989). The effective operation of 'advisory commissions' (*shingikai*) is a primary mode of interest group participation in bureaucratic politics. Collaboration with and consent from constituents are essential elements for policy adoption and implementation. Private interests are actively consulted, and their concerns weigh in final decisions. When needed, social constituents extend formidable and credible political support to corresponding bureaucratic agencies. Accordingly, the overall links between bureaucrats and their constituents can be characterized as a kind of organic symbiosis. 'Trust' emanating from long-term interactions, school ties, local connections, and a Japanese version of the revolving door (*amakudari*) facilitate the formation of organic networks between bureaucratic agencies and their constituents.

But this organic network between the state and the private sector turned out to be a major liability. The current economic difficulty in Japan is by and large a product of expansionary fiscal policy in the 1980s and the subsequent rise of the bubble economy. The fiscal expansion was in turn facilitated by extensive lobbying of business organizations, interest groups, and policy tribes (*Zoku*). In view of this, economic bureaucrats in Japan were not free from social and political pressures. The Japanese financial crisis offers us a more telling example. A major actor of Japan's current financial crisis is Jusen. But executives of Jusen firms have been staffed by retired Okurasho officials through *amakudari*. Out of twenty-six heads of seven Jusen firms since its inauguration, ten originated from Okurasho (*Nihon Keizai Shimbun* January 27, 1996). It was in this context that Jusen firms were allowed to remain in markets despite their falling profits and mounting delinquent loans. Moral hazard and monitoring failures, the primary causes of banking and financial crises in Japan, were an inevitable outcome of organic social networks.

As in Japan, such cultural variables as school and regional ties enable bureaucrats in South Korea to forge and maintain close working relationships with their social constituents, but the pattern of interactions is somewhat different from that of Japan. Social constituents, mostly business organizations, are officially recognized as interest intermediaries, but only selectively incorporated in bureaucratic decision making and implementation. Their collaboration is essential for policies to be implemented, but their consent is not necessary for policies to be adopted. They are sporadically consulted, but their pressures do not weigh all the time. Especially in the case of social constituents who do not share any common interests and ideology with their respective agencies, such as labor and farmers, inputs from below are often not heard and have even been systematically repressed. Bureaucrat–constituent ties change over time and across sectors, but they have basically remained vertical and exclusionary, in that bureaucrats have occupied the strategic position of command and control over the private sector. Functional interdependence exists between the two sectors, but its nature is instrumental rather than consummate.

Nevertheless, the South Korean state was also heavily penetrated by the private sector. The immediate origin of the foreign exchange crisis in November 1997 can be attributed to the failure to make a timely devaluation of the Korean currency. Despite the government's official position, such a posture was not dictated solely by policy considerations such as enhancement of international competitiveness and avoidance of inflationary consequences. Intensive lobbying by banks, big business, and state enterprises, who enjoyed windfall profits from external borrowings, played a more critical role. As the Kia episode illustrates, the government could not take aggressive measures in phasing out delinquent firms and resolving non-performing loans precisely because politicians and bureaucrats were captives of the private sector through either corruptive ties or social networks.

In view of the above discussion, the state structures in Japan and Korea are not similar, but divergent in many aspects. South Korea's state structure shows a high degree of executive dominance and centralism, a vertical and sunflower shape of the executive–bureaucratic nexus, dysfunctional bureaucratic dynamics, and mechanistic ties with social constituents. On the other hand, Japan's state structure can be characterized by only a moderate degree of executive dominance, a horizontal or parallel executive–bureaucratic nexus, compartmentalized but symbiotic bureaucratic dynamics, and organic networks with bureaucratic constituents. Of course, the state structures outlined above are neither fixed nor static. They vary over time and across policy issue areas.

Despite this divergence, Japan and South Korea share several similarities. First, the states in Japan and South Korea are no longer autonomous. They are being increasingly captured by social and political interests, delimiting their policy maneuverability. Second, the internal cohesion of state structure in both countries appears to be fictional. The states in Japan and Korea are profoundly divided and fragmented, lacking the unity of bureaucratic purpose previously contained in the ideology of developmentalism. Third, the competence and meritocracy of Japanese and Korean bureaucrats also seem misleading. Quite simply, they cannot cope effectively with the deep and mobile movements of international and domestic capital. They are not equipped to monitor and supervise the private sector in the age of globalization. Finally, politics matter. Democratization in Korea and the dissolution of the conservative ruling coalition in Japan have opened up a new space for social penetration in economic policy making, deterring decisive, flexible, and effective policy responses. The political and social terrain in Japan and South Korea is rapidly changing in the direction of deeper structural rigidity, signaling a greater probability of government failures.

Conclusion: some thoughts on the future of Asian capitalism

In view of the above discussion, we can draw several interesting theoretical and empirical implications for the future of state and Asian capitalism. The first implication concerns the role of state stewardship in economic engineering. Episodes of economic crisis indicate that the era of the developmental state is over. The state is not only incompetent, but also immobile. The relative longevity of economic booms has turned both countries into normal states where new patterns of distributional coalition can cripple the effective functioning of the developmental state (Olson 1982: 75–76; North 1990: 52). It is an irony of historical evolution. Japan and South Korea enjoyed the advantages of latecomers, but now it is time to feel the pain of forerunners. As Peter Evans (1997) aptly noted, current economic crisis, neo-conservative remedies, and waves of globalization might not entail the complete eclipse of the state. But the reciprocal consent (Samuels 1987), the misunderstood miracle (Friedman 1988), the disciplined state (Amsden 1989), the governed market (Wade 1990), strategic capitalism (Calder 1993), embedded autonomy (Evans 1995), and governed interdependence (Weiss 1998) are no longer likely to reflect today's reality of Japan and South Korea.

Second, can East Asian capitalism be viable in the absence of the guiding and husbandry roles of the state? A cultural template, dynamics of organic networks, and even crony capitalism can exist and function without their relations to the state, for capitalism is all about how to organize property rights and market transactions. But central to East Asian capitalism has always been state authority. In the Hegelian analogy of master and servant, the state has served as the master without which civil society and even market transactions would not function as they did in the past. Thus, with the passage of state power, East Asian capitalism is likely to lose its power and momentum

Finally, the coming end of East Asian capitalism signals the triumph of Anglo-American capitalism. Crisis is pushing Japan and South Korea closer to the American-style free market. Global standards, transparency, removal of moral hazard, and the phasing out of the state all indicate the profound limits to Asian capitalism and values. Convergence to western capitalism is likely to be the fate of the Asian economy. In a sense, Asian capitalism could have been a temporal detour in the longer historical evolution.

NOTES

1 The number of corporate bankruptcies rose from 9,502 cases in 1993 to 12,000 cases as of October 1997. See *Weekly Chosun* January 1, 1998, p. 98.
2 For a comprehensive and comparative overview, see Corsetti *et al.* (1998), and Radelet and Sachs (1998). Roubini's website is particularly useful.
3 Devaluation also had political and symbolic implications. Devaluation could compromise the government goal of maintaining and upgrading per capita income of $10,000. Thus, devaluation was opposed for political reasons too.

6

FRAGILITY OR CONTINUITY?

Economic governance of East Asian capitalism*

Hyuk-Rae Kim

Introduction

For the past several decades up to the early 1990s, three East Asian countries – South Korea (hereafter Korea), Taiwan, and Japan – have achieved and sustained remarkably high economic growth rates. The 'miraculous' record of economic growth in East Asia has been referred to as the driving force of growth in the global economy and further regarded as one of the most noteworthy economic success stories in the history of capitalist development. Although similarities among the three countries, such as heavy involvement of the state in industrial and financial systems, an export-oriented growth strategy, and a common Confucianist cultural heritage with a hard work ethic, might suggest a convergence toward a uniform East Asian capitalism, the three East Asian countries have shown different trajectories of capitalist development.

There has been considerable variation in the form of economic governance of the national economy: namely, chaebol capitalism in Korea, family capitalism in Taiwan, and alliance capitalism in Japan (Hamilton and Biggart 1988; Kim 1993; 1994). Industrial development in Korea has followed the pattern of dominance of large-scale production in a wide range of industries and the bias toward growth has resulted in a concentrated and vertically integrated market structure dominated mostly by business groups – chaebols (Amsden 1989; Jones and Sakong 1980; Kim 1998a; 1988b). In contrast, the Taiwanese economy has been characterized by the predominance of small- and medium-scale family businesses with informal patrilineal networks in both domestic and export sectors (Greenhalgh 1988; Redding 1990; Wong 1985). Unlike Korea and Taiwan, Japan relies upon extensive alliance networks between small-scale enterprises, large-scale business groups, and the institutional linkage of subcontracting (Fruin 1994; Gerlach 1992).

The economic governance of the three East Asian countries clearly shows variation that indicates there is not a single optimal institutional arrangement for organizing national economies. The large array of institutional arrangements for effectively organizing modern economies arises from the broader political–institutional environment in which economic activity is embedded (Chandler 1990; Granovetter 1985; Maurice *et al.* 1980; Rose 1985). Therefore, considerable divergence rather than convergence suggests that there is no particular set of general contingencies that inexorably leads to a single way of structuring economic units and coordinating their activities (Hollingsworth and Boyer 1997; Whitley 1992).

But by the mid 1990s, symptoms of both inherent and structural failure to adapt to rapidly changing environments of globalization and financial liberalization appeared in East Asia. A major reversal in the fortune of East Asian economies began in July 1997 when Thailand was struck by a currency crisis and widespread economic troubles. In a very short period of time, the crisis spawned in Thailand and spread to the neighboring countries of Southeast Asia and eventually triggered serious turmoil in the currency and financial markets of Japan and South Korea. While the extent of crisis differed from country to country, the Asian economies were brought face to face with serious difficulties that came from overreliance on short-term foreign capital, speculative investments, and poor supervision by financial authorities. Even the resilient economies of Singapore, Taiwan, and Hong Kong have shown related problems, slowly being eroded by the persistent weaknesses of their neighboring economies.

After several decades of miraculous growth, the East Asian economies have faced unprecedented challenges and a full-blown crisis. Economic turmoil in East Asia is threatening not only to undermine the viability of the regional economy but also to adversely affect the overall global economy. The various systems and institutions such as state intervention and export-oriented strategy, which previously were seen as contributing factors for rapid economic growth, began to be viewed as the main culprits of economic turmoil. Furthermore, doubts emerged about the capacity of the nation-state to maintain its role as the main governing mechanism in the East Asian development model.

Several questions will be addressed in this chapter: Does the economic crisis signal the end of the East Asian economic growth miracle or the demise of the East Asian developmental model? Does it truly indicate the possible collapse of divergent forms of East Asian capitalism and hence the East Asian economies? How much fragility exists in economic governance as a system in face of economic turmoil? How resilient are systems of economic governance in East Asia? Will the nation-state continue to be salient as a locus of economic governance after economic reforms are completed?

This chapter will attempt to answer these questions by suggesting that the economic crisis is a crisis of governance. In other words, the economic crisis is due to the accumulation of the state's inability to fulfill its capacity as the center of economic governance in the transformation toward a market-enhancing economy. It further suggests that the nation-state will continue to have salience and remain an important actor and level for the coordination of economic activity if the nation-state successfully implements major economic reforms against built-up structural impediments and moves toward a market-enhancing economy.

Globalization and uneven crisis in East Asia

During the 1980s, there was a dramatic shift toward emphasizing the efficacy of self-adjusting market mechanisms. Indeed, the apparent failure of Keynesian economic policies and the collapse of Eastern Bloc economies led many to believe that capitalism and the free market system had finally triumphed. In an era of globalization, the development and proliferation of information technology has reinforced international networks for all economic activity including trade, finance, and production. As a result, national economies are breaking down territorial boundaries as they become more globalized. It is widely asserted that a truly global economy has emerged or is emerging in which distinct 'national' economies and, therefore, domestic industrial strategies are increasingly irrelevant. Moreover, the nation-state is believed to have lost its capacity as a locus of economic governance.

Since the onset of the currency crises in Asia, the neo-liberal view has highlighted the fundamental weaknesses of the East Asian model of developmental state. In the nations currently suffering from the economic crisis, state intervention has impeded the full development of financial and corporate sectors, which led to the formation of 'crony capitalism' in Asia. As global capital markets have played a more prominent role in East Asia, significant amounts of non-performing loans, excessive and poor lending practices, and increasing levels of risky assets have left the financial sector vulnerable to fluctuations in the availability of credit. In addition, the corporate sector has been characterized by potentially unsustainable investments in a few industrial sectors and related excessive short-term corporate borrowing that have left this sector highly leveraged. According to the neo-liberal view, the crisis can only be overcome through a fundamental shift to a new paradigm toward a truly democratic and market-driven economic system.

Unlike the dominant western neo-liberal view, other views emphasize international factors and trace the source of the crisis to the rapid deregulation of Asian financial markets. This deregulation exposed immature financial markets and developmental levels of corporate debt to the financial vicissitudes and flows of 'hot' money from international capital markets.

These views suggest that the devastating force of borderless capital has led to a series of foreign exchange crises in many parts of the world.

Even though the currency crisis in Korea was in part instigated by the growing market instabilities engendered by the broader Asian crises, it should be noted that various fundamental problems of the national economy had surfaced well in advance of the currency crisis. By mid 1997, overinvestment by the major conglomerates, the accumulation of non-performing loans by financial institutions,[1] and an unprecedented number of bankruptcies of highly leveraged business groups and financial institutions[2] were becoming major immediate problems which resulted in successive downgrading by international credit rating agencies and a sharp tightening in the availability of external finance. More importantly, market liberalization and the massive movement of capital across national borders have shifted the Korean government out of its dominant position as the center point of economic governance. As a result, Korea now relies on a $57 billion rescue package from the International Monetary Fund (IMF).[3]

The crisis brought an end to the prosperous era of $10,000 per capita income as the nation's per capita GNP declined by 9.78 percent in 1997. More significantly, the nation's economic growth rate, as measured by GDP, shrank to 5.5 percent in 1997 and to −3.8 percent during the first three months of 1998 (Bank of Korea 1998). Thus, the Korean government can no longer avoid a comprehensive restructuring program that will revitalize the financial sector, restructure the corporate sector under market principles, reform the labor market, and move toward a lean and efficient public sector.

Japan has not been able to recover fully from the effects of the collapse of the 'bubble' in the early 1990s and is now in the midst of its worst post-war recession. With both unemployment and bankruptcies mounting, Japan's gross domestic product for the fiscal year ending March 1998 shrank by 0.7 percent, the first year of negative growth in two decades since 1974. Japan's mountain of bad loans and fiscal deficits lies at the heart of the economic troubles in the world's second largest economy, stifling new loans and threatening the collapse of top banks.[4] Writing off bad loans and downsizing fiscal spending have absorbed most of the excess cash in the Japanese financial system, instead of allowing for more productive use in new loans to business. This has in turn driven the yen to an eight-year low against the US dollar. Thus, Japan must revive the financial system and develop credible policies for structural reforms, including tax reform and public spending.

Taiwan has been relatively unaffected by the crises because of adequate foreign reserves and relatively small amounts of foreign debt. The Taiwanese economy has adjusted itself to the production of higher value-added products, while the industrial structure is sound and supported by a large population of small- and medium-sized enterprises. Despite Taiwan's 'sound economic fundamentals', however, the Taiwan dollar has lost about 20 percent of its value against the US dollar since the Asian financial crisis began and its GDP is forecast to move below 5 percent for 1998. With the yen having reached its lowest level in eight years, Taiwan is also likely to see its exports fall and post the first negative growth in 13 years.

What then accounts for the uneven economic crises observed across the three East Asian states? This study presumes that the political–institutional environments of the state, and the industrial strategies pursued by the state as the main governing mechanism, significantly influence the design of economic governance as well as the course of economic crisis. The current economic turmoil in East Asia seems to have emerged out of the manifestation of the flaws of the governance system of individual national economies. Because of the divergent forms of economic governance across the three East Asian countries, variations exist in the intensity as well as the extent of crisis. This study claims that the different modes of economic governance that emerged from the three East Asian states appear because economic organizations are embedded in political institutions and that these institutions, which are different in each society, have an effect on the design of the economy's governance system and its current period of economic turmoil. The analysis of economic governance should illuminate the unique nature of East Asian capitalism and assist us in understanding the origins of the economic crisis in this region.

Economic governance: definition, mechanisms, and modes

Definition and mechanisms

In recent years, governance issues have come to occupy center stage in economic development literature. The term 'governance' originally derives from the Greek *kybernetes*, which means navigation or helmsmanship. In general, governance has been loosely employed as a user-friendly 'umbrella' concept (Frischtak 1994). If governance means the same as government, governability, or democratic political system, there will be a lack of conceptual clarity. Thus, it is imperative to delineate the constituent components of the concept as well as to establish the boundaries of the usage of the concept.

According to the World Bank (1992: 1), governance refers to the 'manner in which power is exercised in the management of a country's economic and social resources for development'. In this definition, the term governance entails the notion of efficiency in the state machinery and bureaucracy (Frischtak 1994; Frischtak and Atiyas 1996). It refers precisely to the capacity to deploy power from society and to organize social and economic activities for development. Thus governance becomes both an independent, dynamic feature of government and the underpinning rationale 'steering' the state's development policies.

In this way, economic governance refers to the capacity of governments to credibly ensure a secure economic environment (Dhonte and Kapur 1996; Weiss 1998; World Bank 1992). The creation of a secure economic environment is crucial to sustained growth in a market economy. Such security results from the assurance that the return on enterprise and investment will accrue to the entrepreneur and investor. In this regard, the credibility of government policies is critical to reducing uncertainty and thus establishing a secure environment. Thus, it is not enough for a government to propose a set of policies; it is essential that the process of proposing and implementing these policies be such as to give them credibility.

The state in East Asia is believed to be the key player whose goal is to maintain an economic and regulatory environment conducive to efficient private activities. The nation-state should be regarded as a locus of management of economic policies, coordination among economic actors, and control over the allocation of scarce resources through the interplay with diverse social interest groups. Even though governing mechanisms other than the state exist in East Asia, the alternative mechanisms such as markets, hierarchies, associations, and networks have not played important roles (Hollingsworth and Boyer 1997; Williamson 1996). In East Asia, the nation-state has been a coordinating mechanism that sanctions and regulates economic transactions by economic actors through various mechanisms, including the definition and enforcement of property rights, fiscal and monetary policies, and other industrial policies. At the same time, the state has been a key economic actor by engaging directly in production and exchange relations. East Asian nation-states continue to have salience as a locus of economic governance in the face of economic turmoil.

Governance modes

The governance mode of the national economy is constituted and shaped through the embodiment of the three different aspects of state capacity – management capacity, coordination capacity, and control capacity. Even though each aspect is interdependent, each represents a different aspect of the governing role of the state.

First, the management capacity basically refers to the capacity of the state and its bureaucracy to formulate and implement economic policies and discharge its functions. Asserting a dirigiste form of control over the process of industrialization requires a cohesive and concentrated state bureaucracy that not only commands a wide range of policy incentives and has extensive control over production resources, but also possesses substantial information resources. The management capacity through a centralized chain of command allows state officials not only to choose the policy priorities among various macroeconomic objectives and industrial strategies, but also to enforce monitory and disciplinary actions on economic actors and activities. But, if the economic bureaucracy is fragmented and political power diffused, the state lacks the management capacity to ensure a secure economic environment. However, in order to enhance this capacity, a state should address the issues of transparency in government management of decision-making and budgetary processes, effectiveness of public resources management, and in developing a stable regulatory environment conducive to efficient private sector activities.

Second, the coordination capacity of the state is derived from the institutional link between the state and the private sector to govern the activities of the private sector and to derive collective decisions in an economy. Peter Katzenstein (1978) introduced the concept of 'policy network' to delineate the variety of relations that prevail between the state and the private sector. These relations refer not only to formal policy consultation bodies, deliberation councils, state-sponsored industrial associations, and export cartels, but also to informal discussion groups, *ad hoc* meetings and communications, and other interpersonal connections. The relational aspect of policy networks is based on long-term exchange relationships and is thus viewed as having a loose organizational structure (Katzenstein 1978). This institutionalized collaboration between the state and business can be understood as a form of economic governance through which both sides interact to address market failures in various forms (Hollingsworth and Lindberg 1994).

In the East Asian countries, the linkage between the government and the private sector is specially viewed as a relation of 'reciprocity' (Amsden 1989; Wade 1990) or as a type of 'quasi-internal organization' (Lee and Naya 1988). In the context of this policy network, policy implementation is viewed as the internal organizational mode of policy implementation in contrast to the market mode. The point of their argument is that the quasi-internal or reciprocal network functions more like an arm of the state bureaucracy in state-dominated East Asian societies.

Third, the control capacity is based on the nature of state–society relations. Although this study primarily revolves around the permeability of state institutions and their roles, emphasis on the management or administrative capacity of the state bureaucracy and its coordinating linkage with the private sector is not enough. A study of state structures and their effects must go beyond an examination of administrative institutions and their relations with other sectors: that is to say, the capacity of the state should not be simply assumed to derive from administrative capacities and institutional linkages. This study assumes that state autonomy is a necessary and a primary condition for governance and the more autonomous a state is from society, the more effective it will be in aggregating diverse social interests into policy.

This study posits that the broader relationship between the state and society sets the limits on the state's authority. If social groups are allowed to organize for the purpose of influencing policy, distributional coalitions could possibly constrain the range of state development strategies (Olson 1982). A certain set of development strategies is more likely to be adopted and succeed when the state has independence from the demands of social groups. The degree of insulation from societal pressures, which is the function of the institutional arrangements linking state and society, imposes constraints and incentives on the state officials in formulating and implementing state development strategies. Such a distributional coalition is only possible if the state performs another function – that is, the orchestration of social consensus.

This requirement is of particular importance in the study of the East Asian states. Although much of the literature focuses on the directive role of these three states with the assumption of a weak society, there exist substantial variations in the type of political regimes and coalitional bases. Each country has articulated the connections between state agencies and private interests of big business, labor, and landowners within a distinctive political regime. Even though there are many ways of classifying the types of political regimes among the East Asian societies, this study utilizes two broad types of corporatism: societal corporatism and state corporatism.

This distinction would provide an appropriate scheme for explaining differences in the historically shaped coalitional relationships between the state and society, and their implications for formulating and implementing state development strategies. Societal corporatism is one in which private interests have gradually become more singular and hierarchically organized to represent the interests of their coalitions. Japan's policy-making and development model is broadly based on the societal corporatist system (Okimoto 1989; Pempel and Tsunekawa 1979). On the other hand, state corporatism involves a much more active role on the part of the state and is less likely penetrated by social forces. The policy-making and development model in Korea and Taiwan is based on state corporatism (Cheng 1990; Wade 1990).

Economic governance of East Asian capitalism

Korean economic governance

For the past several decades, the Korean economy has grown rapidly. Korea has tripled the size of its economy every decade since 1960. Korea has successfully developed distinctive forces of economic governance as the process of economic growth took place (Kim 1998b). However, by mid 1997, various fundamental problems of the national economy such as overinvestment by the major business groups and the accumulation of non-performing loans by financial institutions have surfaced. Under the austerity measures prescribed by the IMF program, the sustainability of rapid economic growth in Korea is now widely questioned with rising inflation, bankruptcies, unemployment, and an unstable currency.

Among the three East Asian states, Korea showed the most elaborate and centralized economic bureaucracy. The management capacity of the state was strengthened through a centralization of economic policy made after the seizure of power by the military in 1961. In particular, the creation of the Economic and Planning Board (EPB) in June 1961 combined and concentrated various enclaves of developmentalist thinking that previously had been scattered and separated. Its centrality in hierarchical interministerial coordination as well as in control over the budget and monetary policy has allowed EPB and now the Ministry of Finance and Economy (MOFE) to exert tremendous power over economic decision making.

Acting through positional commanding hierarchies, top state officials were assured of the private sector's compliance with their plans. The management capacity of the state was considerably more direct than influencing the economy through market forces. The state was then viewed as a Myrdalian 'hard' state in the context of its monitoring and disciplinary capacity to implement its development strategies through the enforcement of obligations via compulsion. Effective implementation via hardness was regarded as a major causal factor in achieving economic growth in Korea (Jones and Sakong 1980). Overall the centralized state bureaucracy with a hierarchical channel of command definitely had the upper hand and asserted substantial authority over the national economy.

Direct state intervention was further facilitated on the basis of a unique relationship between the state and large business. The relationship was established through a historically shaped growth-oriented alliance among the military elite, state bureaucrats, and big business. It operated on the principle of hierarchical state dominance that functioned more like an arm of the state bureaucracy. A direct hierarchical relationship permitted information sharing that would otherwise have to be done indirectly through market mechanisms. Through this long-term hierarchical exchange relationship between government and large private enterprises, the state formed growth-oriented policy networks

In addition, Korea retained substantial autonomy from powerful social coalitions, be they agricultural interest groups, industrial working classes, or business interest groups. State intervention and economic policy making were effectively insulated from domestic distributional coalitions. Thus, the state corporatist system in Korea, which involved a much more directive role on the part of the state and was less likely to be penetrated by social forces, contributed to the government's dirigiste approach to industrial transformation and economic growth rather than to economic stability and redistribution.

Consequently, the concentration of state bureaucratic power through its responsibility for the budget and monetary policy, the hierarchical dominance of state in policy networks, and its relative autonomy from societal pressures helped explain the dirigiste approach to industrial transformation. Particularly in the 1970s and 1980s, the state aggressively orchestrated large private firms toward heavy and chemical industrialization, involving steel, non-ferrous metals, petrochemicals, machinery, automobiles, shipbuilding, and electronics. In the process, the Korean government made extensive and forceful use of a wide range of instruments designed to assure private industry's compliance with its plans. Among them, the most widely used has been allocation of credit through the control of commercial and special banks. In addition, foreign loans, an attractive source of borrowing, and their allocation required government authorization. Under these circumstances, access to a stable and low-cost source of credit has been considered to be crucial for the private sector. In addition, the implementation of economic policies relied heavily on discretionary command and control to foster industrial growth with penalties for non-compliance ranging from the removal of an existing privilege to a complete cutoff from credit. This implementation system in Korea was a main source for state capacity to govern the national economy.

The economic governance constructed throughout the past several decades has now begun to display weaknesses. The current crisis in Korea has its roots in weaknesses of all three areas of state capacity. Korea's management capacity problems began as the state bureaucracy lost its centrality in maintaining a secure and consistent macroeconomic environment. While making efforts to overcome difficulties that arose following its admission to the OECD, namely competing with developing countries for export market share and surmounting the protectionist barriers of advanced capitalist countries, the state failed to maintain its function as a locus of economic management in an era of globalization. Structural rigidity of state bureaucracy and the waning of executive dominance weakened the monitoring and disciplinary capacity of the state (Moon and Rhyu, in this volume). In addition, the merged MOFE intensified intra-bureaucratic segmentation that led to the formulation of inconsistent macroeconomic policy management; in particular, the mismanagement of the cases of Hanbo Steel and Kia Motors in 1997 led the Korean government to lose credibility in maintaining a secure economic environment.

The deterioration of the state's management capacity led to the development of weaknesses in its coordination capacity as its ability to influence economic decision in the private sector decreased. The expansion of the private sector, in particular the size and power of the chaebols, eroded the ability of the state to function with its former autonomy and strength. As a result, the growth-oriented policy network was transformed into a rent-oriented policy network in which the private sector heavily penetrated the formulation and implementation of economic policies by the state. The frequent changes of economic policies during the Kim Young Sam government, for example, from contractionary to expansionary or from anti-business to pro-business were the reflection of a rent-oriented policy network by the private sector.

It was during this period too that the control capacity of the state became another issue of concern. As Korea began to move away from its traditional state corporatism into societal corporatism, societal interests began pushing into the economic policy-making process. The elections of 1987 and 1992 signaled a significant change in Korea's post-war political history as democratic influences began to permanently alter the nature of state–society relations and the autonomy of the Korean state was curtailed. Simply put, the state became a captive of societal interests, reflecting extensive private penetration and its corresponding loss of credibility. Therefore, the economic turmoil in Korea has its roots in the peculiar system of economic governance that had been shaped throughout the past several decades.

Japanese economic governance

Japan has shown its economic growth on the basis of a dirigiste model of government-regulated capitalism. But now it is clear that the system that provided such strong growth in the post-war period is not working. Historically, the Japanese government, and especially the centralized bureaucracies such as the Ministry of International Trade and Industry (MITI) and the Ministry of Finance (MOF), were important to the success of post-war Japanese economic growth. MITI and other economic ministries had management capacity over a wide range of policy tools in their efforts to guide the Japanese economy. From the 1950s, MITI and MOF controlled all aspects of foreign economic relations, including imports of foreign goods and technology, access to foreign exchange, and direct and indirect investment. Thus, the predominance of administrative guidance as a regulatory form of government intervention in the economy helped to achieve post-war economic growth.

In the process of encouraging economic growth, much emphasis was placed on the governing triad of interlocked private, political, and public institutions – large industrial and financial enterprises, the Liberal Democratic Party (LDP), and the MOF and MITI which shared a common regard for the importance of aggregate economic performance (Stockwin 1988). This exclusive coalition of the governing triad with the ability to arrive at a shared consensus about basic macroeconomic goals was a hallmark of Japan's political economy. Throughout the last decade, however, the coherence and concentration of the state bureaucracy in initiating and implementing a state development strategy became increasingly diffuse. With increased economic power, the corporate world became less dependent on the bureaucracy for such handouts as foreign exchange, import protection, and technology, and thus more independent in charging its own investment decisions. In addition, other ministries began chipping away at the dominance of MITI and MOF over economic policy making itself. Even though the management capacity of the bureaucracy is clearly declining, it should be emphasized that the power of state bureaucracy is not yet open to capture by the private sector. The ministry–LDP partnership can still enforce compliance through various forms of administrative guidance on the basis of consensus.

A qualitative difference peculiar to Japan in the institutional linkage between the state and the private sector was its structural interdependence through a stable long-term relationship. This interdependence is sometimes called 'reciprocal consent' (Samuels 1987), 'network state' (Okimoto 1989), or 'obligated reciprocity' (Dore 1986). The characteristic of this interdependence is mainly from the mutual penetration of the state's organizational element and the private sector's market element (Imai and Itami 1984). In other words, the state and business were informally bound together over a long period of time through a more interactive and consensual form.

In the Japanese policy network, business interests were generally aggregated and formally and informally integrated into bureaucratically sponsored negotiation through a consultation and consensus-building process. In formulating and implementing a development strategy, the state explicitly invited business to share in the policy-making process in exchange for cooperation in the matter of long-term investment decisions. This institutionally legitimate mechanism of exchange formed the symbiotic interdependence that is the heart of the Japanese policy network.

The bureaucracy was politically insulated from the legislature and other social forces like Korea and Taiwan. However, Japan differs from both Korea and Taiwan in that it is a democracy, and its style of corporatism is closer to the European style of societal corporatism by virtue of the greater equality in relations between the bureaucracy and societal interest groups (Johnson 1982; Wade 1990). Under democratic rules one party has enjoyed a virtual monopoly of legislative power since the party's formation in 1955. The legislature from the beginning until the present has had less influence in the major decisions than in any other industrial democracy and its societal corporatism largely excludes labor, like Taiwan's and Korea's (Pempel and Tsunekawa 1979). But only in Japan is there the institutional legitimacy for the creation of formal mechanisms of exchange between government and social interest groups.

Formal inclusion of interest groups in policy implementation was the essential pattern of Japanese corporatist government. Influence over policy making became increasingly diffused among the different segments of the governing triad of the LDP, bureaucracy, and big business. However, the greater emphasis on consensus made it difficult to establish government leadership. The government usually did not act until there was enough agreement between the government and the concerned firms for a consensus to be declared. Thus the ability to arrive at a consensus about basic goals became a hallmark of Japan's political economy.

The Japanese government has utilized a variety of instruments for administrative guidance: redistributive land reform, exchange rate controls, protection, direct foreign investment controls, export promotion, long-term technology policies, etc. (Johnson 1982). It also utilized various stabilization programs, and capacity reduction plans like depression cartels and rationalization cartels. However, administrative guidance has no statutory or legal basis (Hamilton and Biggart 1988) and most of its instruments tend to be an agglomeration of *ad hoc* responses to special circumstances (Okimoto 1989). Generally, the visible hand of the state worked in conjunction with the invisible hand of the market to create Japan's distinctive policy instruments.

Although the Japanese government has successfully kept its economy from complete collapse, its policy tools appear increasingly ineffective. Moreover, the bureaucracy, which has effectively run the country for five decades, is in growing disarray due to recent policy failures of expansionary macroeconomic management in the 1980s and corruption scandals. The Hashimoto cabinet undertook the long-delayed fiscal and financial reforms basically for non-performing loans to reduce fiscal deficits through the means of tax increases and welfare spending cuts. Domestic mismanagement led many to believe that the state bureaucracy was incapable of responding quickly to the rapidly changing economic environments of globalization and financial liberalization. Although there remains strong faith in the Japanese style of capitalism among the bureaucrats and politicians, many long-delayed economic reform packages have been disastrous policy failures in recent years.

Japan's state capacity problems or its coordination problems with the private sector arise from the nature of the relationship. Although the relationship between the state and the private sector is more cooperative and reciprocal in Japan than in Korea or Taiwan, the process of policy making on the basis of consultation and consensus became too complex as opposing factions in both the state and private sector emerged. A great deal of time was lost in the process of building up consensus, which in turn resulted in policy failures. Japan now needs the courage to move to a more flexible and market-driven economy by developing credible policies as well as by developing a speedy implementation mode for the reform and liberalization of the financial sector.

Taiwanese economic governance

Historically, the Taiwanese government was less centralized, with power over industrial policy issues dispersed among more ministries and agencies, than in the case of Korea or Japan. The state agency, the Council for Economic Planning and Development, plays mostly an advisory role in the policy process, and the Ministry of Economic Affairs has a limited management capacity over fiscal and credit policy instruments. Unlike Korea, the central bank (Central Bank of China) is independent of the cabinet and asserts absolute control over the domestic banking system. The Central Bank of China supports the Kuomintang's conservative economic policy and has great influence over the formulation and implementation of stability-oriented fiscal and monetary policies via the Ministry of Finance.

While relying less on selective credit, the Taiwan government has relied more on arm's-length fiscal and trade instruments and infrastructural investment to steer private firms. The government has also used to a greater extent state-owned enterprises to develop selected industries rather than create 'national champions' of large private firms. But state planning is usually done in a loose, non-command style and since there is no rigorous enforcement of obligations via compulsion in state planning in Taiwan, it is even claimed that there are no real implementation procedures (Hamilton and Biggart 1988). The state economic bureaucracy in Taiwan asserts substantial influence over the national economy, but less authoritatively and forcibly.

Driven by an anti-big capitalist conviction reinforced by fear of the political potential of native Taiwanese economic power, the government has only weakly developed a policy network and discouraged large-scale organization and the accumulation of economic power in private hands (Cheng 1990; Wade 1990). Thus, the state and the private sector have remained apart. This lack of an extensive web of channels to the private sector constrains the organizational capability of economic officials in initiating and implementing a state development strategy. There exists, however, a vigorous policy network linking the central economic bureaus with public enterprises, public banks, and public research and service organizations. In Taiwan, the state and the state enterprise sector constitute a quasi-internal organization (Lee and Naya 1988).

Within this thin policy network with the private sector, the government gets some information about the production capability of individual firms only through such means as the export quality control scheme, the loan guarantee scheme, and the external marketing agency (Wade 1990), and undertakes administrative guidance to steer private investment decisions. But the guidance mostly takes place in bilateral negotiations between state officials and private firms. State–private sector negotiations are event based and take place with individual firms rather than with aggregations of firms. The informal, short-term negotiation as well as the sub-ethnic tension allowed Taiwanese society to form patterns of interdependence between the state and private firms without being vertically integrated and tightly controlled by either one of them.

Following a ruthless liquidation of oppositional groups during the years 1947–9, virtually all the remaining social groups were subsidized by the ruling party and this led to the development of a quasi-corporatist structure in Taiwanese society. There are no peak associations, but there exist informal collaborative relationships as structured in Japan. An additional factor peculiar to Taiwan society is that the separation between political power and wealth roughly parallels the ethnic cleavage between the Mainlanders and the Taiwanese. Hence policy choices inevitably favor those measures that would fragment business, disperse economic power, and expand the latitude for economic distribution. But the fact that the government is not vulnerable to interest group pressure or 'the absence of special interest organization' that Olson pointed out (1982: 218), does not guarantee the monopolization of policy initiation. The government monopolizes policy initiation to a greater degree than in Japan, but to a lesser degree than in Korea (Haggard 1990; Wade 1990).

In face of the current financial and economic crises of the Asian region, Taiwan has not yet developed serious symptoms of the crisis due to its horizontally integrated networks and a flexible private sector based on small- and medium-scale businesses that can adapt to the rapidly changing economic environment. In Taiwan's case, small- and medium-scale firms have historically played the most important roles. These firms form very flexible production networks relying heavily on extensive subcontracting. Unlike the rigidly controlled, vertically integrated chaebol in Korea, the Taiwanese economy is characterized as being loosely coupled networks of arm's-length transactions among family businesses (Greenhalgh 1988; Wong 1985). This form of family capitalism becomes evident in the capital and ownership networks. Ownership and control of businesses are in the hands of individuals or in their personal network of acquaintances, which in Chinese is called a *quanxi* network.

But this form of family capitalism in Taiwan would be fragile in an era of globalization in which economies of scale work in some strategic industries. In Taiwan, these industries have been governed by the public sector, composed of mostly upstream industries like energy, heavy machinery, shipbuilding, and steel, and have proven to be the most inefficient sectors in the economy. The use of state-owned enterprises as an instrument to develop selected industries became an impediment for further development of the Taiwanese economy. Once producing more than half of the GNP, the state-owned enterprises account for just over 10 percent in recent years. Unless this sector is decentralized and state involvement in these potentially private sector industries reduced, there is the threat of a future crisis developing.

In addition, the Taiwanese family capitalism becomes sensitive to the changing pattern of demand generated by manufacturing networks of the small- and medium-scale firms. Heavy reliance on export markets is easily affected by the ups and downs of the regional economy that is now facing unprecedented challenges and an economic crisis. The Taiwanese government together with the private sector immediately deals with declines in exports and the first negative growth through enhancement of a limited management capacity of the state and the public sector. In short, sources of flexibility and dynamism of the Taiwanese economic governance need to be checked in face of an East Asian economic crisis.

Conclusion

After several decades of miraculous growth, the East Asian economies are now facing unprecedented challenges. Since the onset of the currency crises in Asia, the same industrial structures and institutions, which until a short time ago were being lauded as the key to the region's success, have now come under scrutiny as the alleged source of these crises. Furthermore, the Asian values that have been praised for so long are now being identified as a contributing cause of the economic turmoil. More importantly, the current economic crisis in the region has led to the belief that the nation-state, in the role of the main governing mechanism in the East Asian development model, is losing its capacity as a locus of economic governance. Thus, this chapter posits that the economic turmoil in East Asia is a manifestation of a crisis of economic governance.

Rather than proposing a single overarching model, this chapter begins with the comparative problems of divergent economic governance of East Asian capitalism. It assumes that the organizing mode of economic governance does not result simply from instrumental behavior by state officials, social groups, or economic actors, nor are they explicable in terms of the functional logic of efficiency and bureaucracy. Rather, the mode of economic governance is posited to be specific to the institutional environment which emerges from distinctive national experiences.

This chapter examined the governance modes of the three national economies that have been constituted through the embodiment of the three different aspects of state capacity. These capacities are, in turn, proposed to constrain the interests and power of the state as an actor and to enable the possibilities for strategic action. This cross-national comparison and in-depth historical investigation contributes to generalizing the contingent principles proposed in linking the institutional structures of the state with strategic choices and the organizing mode of economic governance.

In the analysis of the economic turmoil in East Asia, this study argues that the economic crisis is a manifestation of the problems of state capacity in the East Asian nations and these economies have experienced fundamental and severe setbacks because of a weakening capacity of their states to credibly ensure a secure economic environment. The fragility of the economies, therefore, reflects the weaknesses in economic governance. Governance crises generally take place when the state's monitoring and disciplinary capacities become weak and fail to adjust to the rapidly changing environment. Specifically, they occur when the state's economic policies become unpredictable and inconsistent; when the state's coordination with the private sector is shaped in the form of a rent-oriented network; and when the nation-state becomes a captive of societal interests, reflecting extensive private penetration of the state and its corresponding loss of credibility.

Now we must look past the economic crisis to the present state of the economies, their modes of governance, and their state capacities to answer questions of whether or not the East Asian model of capitalism has become redundant. Although major reforms are being implemented in Korea and Japan, the basic institutional structure of the East Asian states remains largely intact. In the process of reformation, however, the states as a governing mechanism have begun to address their capacity problems and perhaps have found a new path toward economic stability and success.

NOTES

* This research was supported by the Center for International Studies at the Yonsei University in 1998. Direct all correspondence and comments to Prof. Hyuk-Rae Kim, Department of Korean Studies, Graduate School of International Studies, Yonsei University, Seoul 120–749, Korea.
1 As of the end of March 1998, the estimated total of bad loans of all financial institutions amounted to 118 trillion won (or about US$84 billion). This figure includes non-performing loans totaling 68 trillion won, and 50 trillion won of loans classified as 'recutionary' (Ministry of Finance and Economy 1998).
2 The average debt-to-equity ratio of the thirty newly designated largest conglomerates was up to 518.9 percent in 1997 from 386.5 percent in 1996 (Fair Trade Commission 1998). The Ministry of Finance and Economy (1998) reported that the total foreign debt in the private sector was US$95.5 billion, almost half of the national total foreign debt (US$170 billion). Among these private foreign debts, US$42.3 billion came from domestic financial institutions and US$53.2 billion from short-term overseas borrowing. In Korea, rolling over the short-term foreign liabilities of the private sector became a central issue.
3 The IMF prescribes budget deficit reduction through raising taxes and cutting government spending as well as a tighter monetary policy through higher interest rates and less credit availability. The IMF proposes a set of reforms that comprise three broad elements: a clear and firm exit policy; strong market and supervisory discipline; and increased competition. The IMF believes that an effective system of corporate governance and deregulated capital market are essential ingredients to ensure an efficient allocation of resources in the future. However, these short-term macroeconomic policies in the face of temporary illiquidity rather than fundamental insolvency become controversial (Feldstein 1998). Regardless of the appropriateness of the IMF's role, the IMF regime is apparently providing the chance for Korea to restructure the national economy.
4 November 1997 witnessed the high-profile collapse of three financial institutions – Sanyo Securities, Yamaichi Securities, and Hokkaido Takoshoku Bank. More importantly than these bank bankruptcies, major banks in Japan wrote off a staggering 11 trillion yen ($76 billion) in bad loans in the year to March 1998. The nation's top nineteen banks admitted in March that they hold a total of 22 trillion yen in bad debts. As a result, thirteen of the banks suffered pre-tax losses and their total assets shrank by 34 trillion yen. Many analysts fear the total size of Japan's problem bank loans could be as large as 100 trillion yen.

7

THE DILEMMA OF MARKET LIBERALIZATION

The financial crisis and the transformation of capitalism

Yeon-ho Lee and Hyuk-Rae Kim

The problem and the argument

North American liberalism in general and market-centred economic ideas in particular have come to dominate debates about economic liberalization. The assumption is that state intervention has to be minimized if the market is to be liberalized; that is to say, the state's non-economic intervention in the market is not justified. But its application to East Asian economies is highly problematic and even dangerous, where the state has played the role of 'market planner or governor' for compressed economic growth. The economic logic, of course, addresses a crucial point of liberalization; that is, excessive and unnecessary regulations must be minimized.

The assumption, however, might be based on a myopic analysis. The state–market relationship involves political and social aspects as well as economic and material dimensions. Liberal economists have criticized East Asian states for intervening in and regulating market processes. However, these states, in fact, could not significantly advance deregulation, since regulation was also a means of controlling monopolistic capital which had accumulated under patronage of the state. Ironically, in order for them to create a freer market in which fair competition operates, a more effectively reinforced regulatory system needs to be instituted. The state has to be powerful enough to supervise market actors and punish those violating rules. To advance economic liberalization, the developmental state which strategically supports or protects the market to promote industrialization needs to be restructured. This, however, does not imply that the state must become a weak state, surrendering means of regulation in order to liberalize the market. The state has to become stronger to manage the market liberalization process successfully.

The South Korean case illustrates this point. It shows that if economic liberalization is not institutionally supported by an effectively reinforced regulatory system, the political and economic foundations of stability and growth can be eroded. In South Korea financial crisis resulted from a weak state's failure in managing the liberalization process. Emulating neo-liberal or neo-conservative reforms that had been undertaken by the United Kingdom and the United States since the 1980s, the Kim Young-sam government (1993–8) announced the *Segyehwa* (globalization) policy in 1994, in an attempt to facilitate economic liberalization. The policy was predicated on a criticism of the mercantile industrialization strategy that had been taken by previous authoritarian governments.

In an attempt to liberalize its economic system, the South Korean government mimicked neo-liberal reforms. The axiom of the reforms was to liberate the market from the state. In the United Kingdom, the Thatcher and Major governments attempted the following: (1) to enhance the efficiency of labor utilization by rendering the labor market more flexible and by weakening the political power of workers, (2) to relieve the state's welfare burden, (3) to introduce competition to the market by getting rid of protection and support of industries, and (4) to encourage capital accumulation by removing regulations on the financial industry (Hutton 1997: ch. 1; Eric Evans 1997). The state effectively abandoned trying to provide certain public goods. Instead, it encouraged privatization policies, the expansion of the private sector, and the influence of market principles. As a result of the reforms, the welfare state was transformed into a 'competition state' (Cerny 1990: ch. 8). The market that used to be regulated by the state became increasingly autonomous and outside government control, with the state playing a minimal role as a supervisor or umpire (Ling 1998: ch. 6). In short, 'the retreat of the state' took place in consequence of liberalization (Strange 1996; Ohmae 1995).

But, in Korea, the emulation of neo-liberal reform induced numerous problems. Most of all, the confusion of the state's role required in the process of economic liberalization as well as the concept of regulation caused critical problems. Liberalization refers to the introduction of more competition through the introduction of market principles, and the reduction or elimination of government regulations (Vogel 1996: 3). While most East Asian countries, including South Korea, understood that the neo-liberal reform implied removing government regulations on capital, they overlooked the possibility that withdrawing state regulation may undermine political and economic stability (Hawthorn 1993). In developing countries where no institutional apparatus existed to ensure fair market competition, deregulation weakened the state's capacity to supervise and control the activities of monopolistic market forces. In theory, regulation can be distinguished from supervision; while the former is the government's tool for intervening in industries, the latter is a means of maintaining the stability of the market. In practice, however, it was impossible to separate the two. In effect, the relaxation of regulations destabilized the market order as large capital abused its monopolistic status in the market.

East Asian developing countries employed the mercantile industrialization policy that was based on the state's strong support in their early stages of industrialization. In consequence, state-managed politico-economic systems emerged in those countries (Kim 1998). The state selectively supplied industries with financial resources that were virtually nationalized for an effective accumulation of national wealth. With no autonomous market institution supporting fair competition, industrial capital, which had grown under the patronage of the state, could be controlled only by the state's strategic intervention. Market liberalization in East Asian developmental states advanced only to a limited extent, since the state was reluctant to abandon the means of regulating capital that abused its monopolistic status in the market and challenged the state's authority (Lee 1998; 1997a). Ironically, strong regulatory and monitoring systems were necessary to allow the market to operate autonomously from the state.

This chapter analyzes the cause of failure of the economic liberalization scheme of the Kim Young-sam government. The central argument developed here is that the state's capacity to monitor the market was diminished by deregulation, which further undermined market stability. If market liberalization is to be achieved successfully, the effectiveness of regulations must be enhanced and the state's capacity to oversee the market reinforced. For economic liberalization, the state has to be capable of coordinating the interests of capital and labor and compromising inner conflicts of the state.[1]

Liberalization and the role of the state

The political economic atmosphere in which East Asian countries attempted economic liberalization was in many ways similar to what European states underwent in the nineteenth and the early twentieth centuries. During the so-called 'golden age of liberalism', mercantile economic elements – that is, those enjoying state support, protection, and political supervision – were replaced by market-centered competition (Polanyi 1944; Hill 1985). During the period of mercantilism, alliances were formed between the state and the capitalist group consisting of the landed class, merchants, and manufacturers. The core idea of mercantilism was to build physical and commercial infrastructures, a strong army, and a wealthy nation, and for the state to secure an advantage in competition with other states. In order to protect domestic industries, the state installed trade barriers and granted industrial subsidies (Cameron 1993: ch. 6). Denouncing the mercantile industrial policies that hampered the effective distribution of resources and oppressed the liberty of individuals, Adam Smith deplored the economic situation of the time in which economic policies were made not by professionals with economic knowledge, but by corrupt politicians allied with the capitalist class (Smith 1993: 289–301).

And yet the relationship between the state and the market is in fact inseparable. The neo-classical economic position tends to posit that the market is independent of the state, neutral and self-regulating, without taking the political economic origin of the market into consideration. However, the market has been created by the state, adjusted by institutions, and sustained by regulations (Wilks 1996: 538). The process of market creation is a struggle between economic actors. For fair competition, therefore, rules must be observed. Regulation is a kind of rule that market actors are forced to abide by since it cannot be otherwise observed. The market is a social institution ruled by regulations, set up by government authority. As Polanyi observed, in the nineteenth and the early twentieth centuries when free trade blossomed in the United Kingdom, centralized regulations to operate a liberal market system evolved rather systematically.[2] Even liberals, who attempted to remove many of the functions of the state, had no choice but to entrust the state with a new institutional power to build a liberal economic system. In short, the *laissez-faire* economy was a consequence of the state's planned activities (Polanyi 1944: ch. 12).

In the era of classical liberalism in the United Kingdom, the systemization of regulations for building up market autonomy was equally as important as the curtailment of state intervention, e.g., support and protection, in the market. The type of state that South Korea needed to become to attempt structural adjustment – that is, converting a mercantile economy into a liberal economy – was one able to enforce the principle of market competition upon capital and labor. The institutional apparatus to curb the ill-effects of deregulation should have been installed before the state relaxed regulations on capital. Regulation was the price to be paid by selected capitalists who enjoyed special benefits in the process of compressed economic growth orchestrated by the government. It is no wonder that three chaebol-regulatory policies, namely, the fair trade system, the loan and payment guarantee management system, and the main line business system, were established and strongly implemented by the Chun government, which suggested economic stabilization and liberalization as economic principles of the regime. The state adopted these regulatory measures in order to establish a liberalized and stabilized economic foundation by weakening the economic power concentrated in the hands of big businesses in the course of the state-led economic development (Lee 1996). The reason the Roh government's economic deregulation attempts failed was that economic concentration remained undiluted. If regulations had been drastically withdrawn, the market order sustained by state intervention could have become unstable due to the market actors abusing their monopolistic powers (Lee 1997a).

The public interest theory of regulation argues that regulations take place to cure market failure. It assumes that the goal of the government in charge of regulation is to maximize social welfare. Neo-classical economics, however, suggests a theory of economic regulation which looks upon regulations as goods. That is to say, regulations are provided by regulatory authorities – for example, politicians and bureaucrats – who seek to maximize their political support from the interest groups intending to maximize their own interests (Stigler 1975: chs 7–8). The Kim Young-sam government advocated this position of the economic theory of regulation. It was argued that the regulation authority would not be able to acquire the information required to set the standard of regulation, to judge equity and fairness objectively in setting the target of regulation, and to maintain consistency of policy implementation in the actual regulation process (Jeong 1993: 295). With the implementation of the liberalization policy under the Kim government, economic efficiency took precedence over social and political equity.

The other factor that encouraged deregulation was the pursuit of economic 'openness'. The private sector argued that the government could not continue regulating domestic enterprises while simultaneously opening the domestic market to overseas capital, otherwise the international competitiveness of the Korean economy would be diminished in comparison. In other words, domestic deregulation was a precondition of an open economy. Under the Kim government, while the social obligations of big businesses were waived, their rights became stronger, as economic efficiency and the autonomy of capital were emphasized despite the social and political problems of economic concentration in the chaebol (Lee 1997). Deregulation only resulted in the weakening of the state's monitoring capacity, as businesses strove for the improvement of economic efficiency instead of coping with social equity problems by exercising self-regulation.

Ignoring the lessons of western experiences, especially the polarization of income and life-chances, South Korea unwisely mimicked neo-liberal reforms before it resolved the problems that emanated from mercantile capitalism. In consequence, the market order collapsed. The government attempted to create a market in which self-regulation would take place, by withdrawing protection and support bestowed upon domestic capital, and by relaxing market entry restrictions and encouraging market competition. But market competition created new problems. Market actors were able to evade government supervision and continue their unfair, oligopolistic practices. With an increase in the number of market participants and the enhancement of deregulation, the market monitoring capacity of the state weakened. The bureaucrats lobbied by market actors did not exercise strict supervision. The government did not realize that its market monitoring capacity had to be reinforced concurrently with deregulation and liberalization. This was a crucial cause of the financial crisis in South Korea.

Economic liberalization and the failure of deregulation

The Kim government's position on economic liberalization and deregulation was well stipulated in the 'New Economic Policy' (NEP). Identifying economic liberalization with democratization, the Kim government emphasized that policy for a democratic government should be predicated on liberal market competition. Kim suggested that the economic system of the past authoritarian government was dedicated to directing economic resources to strategically selected areas in accordance with the government's instruction and control. However, with the economy expanding in size and becoming more complex, and with political democratization advancing, government control was undermined. The NEP consequently wanted to relax regulations so that the private sector's participation and its creative power could be encouraged, and the reform of monetary, financial, and administrative institutions in the pursuit of market autonomy and justice could be realized (ROK Government 1993).

The Kim government's attempts to make the government small but effective enough to achieve the goals which the NEP projected were initially successful. Since it succeeded in coming into power with the support of the conservative middle class, the Kim government enjoyed a high degree of autonomy in the policy-making process over economic reforms. As a consequence, the Kim government was able to enforce the 'real name financial transaction'[3] and the 'real name real estate transaction systems'. The Chun Doo-hwan and the Roh Tae-woo governments had attempted to institute the real name financial transaction system several times, only to defer the enforcement of the system. After having deferred the enforcement in 1982, the government once again suggested it as one of the presidential election platforms in 1987, and in 1988 promised to institute it by January 1991. With the economy slowing, the stock market stagnant, and a speculative real estate boom, however, the enforcement of the system was once again deferred in April 1990 with the announcement of economic revitalization measures.

The Kim government's ability to manage the reform of the military and the reorganization of government–business relations relied on the strong support of the middle class. With no tangible benefits accruing to the middle class, however, the political foundations of the Kim government began to crumble. Financial reforms and the outlawing of former dubious practices led to a rapid increase in the bankruptcy rate of small–medium enterprises. Although macroeconomic indicators showed that the fundamentals of the Korean economy were sound, the middle class became increasingly insecure. Demand for wage increases became stronger, weakening the international competitiveness of Korean products.

In the mid-stage of the Kim government, while the middle-class support of the government decreased, the government's political reliance on big businesses increased. Consequently, it did not attempt to reform the chaebols very seriously. The Kim government tried to encourage gradual and voluntary economic reform measures, rather than imposing drastic reform. Having witnessed the political burdens the Chun and the Roh governments had had to bear as a result of the execution of anti-chaebol policies – for example, the dismemberment of the Kukche chaebol, the reorganization of ill-managed companies and the 8th May real estate measure – the Kim government preferred autonomous institutional reforms to forced changes. The authoritarian attempts at chaebol reform of the Chun and Roh governments were abandoned.

Encouraged by the political situation of the time, economic liberalization served as a foundation on which big businesses were able to recover their political influence. Above all, for the Kim government and the ruling party, it was big businesses that could best realize *Segyehwa*, the principal political goal of the Kim government. If the *Segyehwa* policy, which the Kim government announced in 1994, was to be implemented successfully, regulations on big businesses seeking to expand their foreign direct investment (FDI) in overseas countries needed to be relaxed. Second, state intervention lost its logical validity in 1995 with Samsung's semiconductor business turning out to be the most lucrative business in Korean economic history, despite the government's initial objections. The Federation of Korean Industry, representing the chaebols, mobilized business opposition to the government. Big business was able to force changes to government regulations over FDI in the interests of liberalization. Samsung's participation in the car manufacturing industry and the top five chaebols' domination of the petrochemical industry were all pardoned under the pretext of economic liberalization or democratization. Since then, these two industries have suffered from overproduction.

As the Kim government looked upon accession to the OECD as one of the principal political goals, it needed to show the international community visible achievements of an open economy. It assumed that the deregulation of big business and the financial industry would be a crucial achievement. Consequently, the Kim government actively implemented administrative deregulation, financial liberalization, and economic internationalization. Finalizing the third stage of the financial liberalization scheme by November 1995, the government liberalized interest rates on all sorts of savings except for checking account deposits and short-term savings (less than three months). It also abolished guidelines for loans to the manufacturing sector from March 1996, and relaxed regulations on the city banks opening overseas branches. With the amendment of the Act on Merchant Banks in July 1996, investment banks were converted into merchant banks, increasing the number of merchant banks from fifteen to thirty. In addition, the government went ahead with the opening plan on capital transfer and the financial industry, as a measure to facilitate accession to the OECD.

Moreover, in order to encourage the forces associated with economic globalization, the government devised measures to encourage foreign investment and to promote Korean big businesses' direct investments in foreign countries. Consequently, the rate of foreign investment grew by 97.6 percent as of January 1997 (*Economic White Paper* 1997: 580). In addition to these measures, the government abolished the equity capital self-supply ratio – minimum 20 percent of the total amount of the investment which is more than US$0.1 billion – in overseas investment.

Liberalization policy itself did not directly cause the crisis. The introduction of the policy was inevitable in order to improve the industrial structure and to introduce competition into the market. In negotiations for accession to the OECD, South Korea succeeded in complying with only 65 percent of 'the agreement on the liberalization of capital transfer' and 'the agreement on transaction liberalization in the non-trade sector', which was significantly lower than the average rate of member countries – 89 percent. South Korea secured more concessions from the OECD than Mexico and the Czech Republic (*Economic White Paper* 1997: 548–9). But the most critical problem lay in the Kim government's failure to institute regulatory/supervisory systems to guarantee the soundness of the liberalization policy. The social and political problems, e.g., economic concentration, should have been tackled first, before the government let the market operate autonomously and put priority on economic efficiency. Taking advantage of relaxed regulation, enterprises diversified their business, rather than improving financial soundness. The government, of course, had predicted such dangers. The NEP prescribed the reinforcement of the financial supervision systems to stabilize the financial liberalization process (ROK Government 1993). These institutional regulatory systems, however, were not consolidated because of the dominance of neo-liberal reformist ideas.

The government failure in managing economic liberalization served as one of the causes behind the expanding balance of trade deficit. The deficit rapidly increased from US$0.33 billion in 1993 to US$4.5 billion in 1994, US$8.95 billion in 1995, and US$23.7 billion in 1996. However, accepting it as an inevitable consequence of liberalization, the Kim government failed to implement special measures to tackle it.

Owing to the NEP, a pump-priming policy in nature, the Korean economy escaped from depression in 1994, the year after the Kim government's inauguration. In November, the stock market rose on the expectation that the economy would recover. Exports also grew. In 1994, the export growth rate was as high as 17.1 percent, the highest rate in the 1990s. In particular, the export of semiconductors jumped by almost 50 percent. Despite the growth in exports, however, the trade deficit expanded after 1993. Imports grew faster than exports. The trade deficit brought about an increase in debt. However, the government refrained from taking measures to reduce the trade deficit because the depreciation of the Korean won might expand foreign-currency-based debt and constrain the chaebol's development plans.

In the meantime, the economic liberalization policy induced poor management and even the insolvency of big businesses and financial institutions. As the economy showed signs of recovery in 1994, the government's enthusiasm for economic reform began to wane. Without a systematic examination of the domestic industrial foundation, the government actively implemented the market-opening scheme. In the year of inauguration, the Kim government carried out the second stage of interest rate liberalization in the domestic sector and financial liberalization on foreign exchange in the international sector. Particularly, in the area of foreign exchange, the government extended the ceiling of foreign exchange transaction, changed the issuance system of Korean firms' overseas securities from a license system to the report system, and deregulated big businesses' investment in overseas securities and direct investment (*Economic White Paper* 1994: 174). After 1995 when the OECD accession plan materialized, deregulation of inward and outward investment flows was significantly advanced.

As the international credibility of the Korean economy was enhanced by the nation's accession to the OECD, big businesses attempted to import foreign capital on a larger scale. The foreign credit which big businesses and banks imported between 1981 and 1990 amounted to merely about 3.3 trillion Korean won. In comparison, 6.3 trillion won were imported in 1994, and more than 9 trillion won in 1995 and 1996 respectively (*Dong-a Ilbo* February 12, 1998). The supervisory capacity of the government was greatly reduced by its deregulation drive to liberalize banks' overseas business, despite the rapid expansion of imported capital. The Ministry of Finance and Economy in charge of supervising merchant banks did not apply an index of financial soundness to them, abolished the permission system on importing short-term credits, and failed to control the so-called 'mismatch' between short-term external loans that were used to finance long-term domestic obligations. The merchant banks played a decisive role in precipitating the financial crisis. Through political lobbying they obtained permission to launch international businesses, including foreign currency dealing and lease businesses, despite their poor financial resources and lack of experience in these new business areas. They attempted speculation in foreign currency dealings, which ended in a fiasco. The government, moreover, failed to supervise the stockbrokers and investment trust companies speculating in the domestic market with the international loans they obtained through their fund-managing companies overseas. In some cases, the loans were five times as much as the capital they originally put in (*Chosun Ilbo* February 20, 1998).

Big businesses borrowed foreign capital by taking advantage of unregulated overseas bond markets. The bonds they issued in overseas markets between 1981 and 1990 amounted to 800 billion won, which increased to 2.8

trillion won in 1994, 4.9 trillion won in 1995, and 8.6 trillion won in 1996 (*Dong-a Ilbo* February 12, 1998). As of 1997, the overseas credit that Korean firms borrowed amounted to US$95.5 billion (*Chosun Ilbo* March 10, 1998). And the average debt ratio of the thirty largest chaebol was as high as 518.8 percent, which was significantly higher than 347.5 percent in 1995 and 386.5 percent in 1996. Despite such a questionable financial position, the number of member companies of the thirty largest chaebol increased from 616 in 1994 to 623 in 1995, 669 in 1996 and 819 in 1997 (Fair Trade Commission).

The government-implemented liberalization policy was intended to enhance economic efficiency. Nonetheless, the management practices and logic of big businesses remained unchanged. Entrepreneurs still sought to expand the size of their business rather than increasing profits. The chaebol attempted to use financial liberalization and market opening to diversify their business interests, instead of improving their financial positions in order to face intensified international competition.

Market democratization vs. market liberalization

No logical flaws were involved in the economic liberalization policy and the NEP which the Kim government attempted to implement. In the early stages of the regime, the Kim government correctly diagnosed the impending problems of the economy of the time, and the measures it prescribed to sort out the problems were largely appropriate. Yet, why did the *Segyehwa* and the liberalization policy of the government end in a fiasco?

Generally, the East Asian countries suffering from the financial crisis (i.e., Indonesia, Thailand, and South Korea) were not equipped with an institutional capacity to oversee the market liberalization process systematically. Market liberalization implies the reinforcement of competition in the market. By contrast, market democratization signifies an increase in the citizen's public control of the monopolistic capital abusing its economic power. These two concepts have often been prone to confusion, being regarded as identical to each other. But each has its own goal. As the case of the enforcement of the real name financial transaction system showed, the Kim government was committed to economic democratization in the beginning. With the development of the OECD accession plan, however, the Kim government put less emphasis on democratization. The government accelerated deregulation of the financial sector, and attempted to apply market principles onto the labor market to make it more flexible. Liberalizing financial and industrial capital, however, led to the weakening of state capacity to regulate market actors. Moreover, with no experience of market democratization, public oversight and business self-regulation were not satisfactorily institutionalized.

The Kim government expected that liberalizing the financial and industrial sectors would improve the nation's international credibility. This, however, was not always the case. The collapse of Hanbo Steel was a consequence of liberalization, but the government let it become bankrupt in accord with market principles. Under such circumstances, overseas banks started withdrawing credit from Korean banks, taking seriously the presidential economic secretary's statement that even if a bank went bankrupt the Korean government would not save it. Japanese banks demanded that the Korean government take measures to liquidate overseas branches of Korean banks. From February 1997, the so-called 'Korean Premium' began to be appended, when Korean banks and businesses imported foreign loans (*Hanguk Ilbo* February 8, 1998).

The collapse of Kia Motors in July 1997 added critical momentum to the financial crisis. Although the collapse of Hanbo Steel was seen as the less serious consequence of a political scandal, the international community regarded the Kia case as a straightforward example of the extremely poor financial structure of big Korean enterprises. Until this incident, Kia had been considered well run, with a sound business structure. It had faithfully obeyed government instructions. Despite its problems, the Kim government waited for the market to resolve the problem, instead of intervening promptly to sort it out. The government attempted to pass a bill to unify the financial monitoring functions that had been managed respectively by the Ministry of Finance and Economy and the Office of Bank Supervision and Examination, but the bill failed to pass. On 22nd October, the government announced that it would intervene in the Kia incident dismissing the non-interventionist position it had maintained. Nonetheless, it could not stop foreign capital escaping from the Korean market. The collapse of the Hong Kong Stock Exchange market on 23rd October precipitated the Korean crisis.

The government failed to manage the liberalization process successfully despite its precise diagnosis of economic problems and prescriptions for them. While the interest articulation capacity of big businesses became stronger with the recovering economy, the government's market monitoring ability became weaker with deregulation. Moreover, the government commenced the liberalization process without a carefully prepared economic foundation for liberalization, owing to the political class's desire to achieve developed country status by joining the OECD.

In short, the Korean case shows that political liberalization does not always contribute to economic liberalization. In general, while we can accept that the demand for political liberalization grows stronger once economic growth reaches a certain level (Huntington 1991), a careful examination of developing countries reveals that the growth of economic wealth does not necessarily guarantee political liberalization, nor does political liberalization necessarily encourage economic stabilization and liberalization (for example, see Neher and Marlay 1995: ch. 11).

In Taiwan and Singapore, which succeeded in insulating themselves from a massive aftershock of the East Asian financial crisis, the extent of political liberalization is limited despite their wealthy and open economies. The middle class has acceded to limited liberalization and even cooperated with the authoritarian government, for sustained economic growth and social stability (Rodan 1996: 7). In Korea, the advancement of political liberalization weakened the state's coordinating capacity in the policy decision-making process due to active interest representation of interest groups. The capitalist group which was able to articulate its interest more effectively than labor, succeeded in transforming a hierarchical state–capital relationship into an egalitarian one. With a mounting anti-government disposition of the middle and the labor classes, the government and the ruling party's political reliance on the capitalist group deepened. In line with the overall liberalization policy, big businesses demanded further deregulation, and the government requested political support in return. Institutional apparatuses to check corrupt alliances between the government and business should have been installed while experiencing market democratization. But overly rapid deregulation caused market democratization to be a slower and more resisted process. The weakening of the state's monitoring capacity caused by badly planned deregulation was the most immediate source of the financial crisis in Korea.

Conclusion

The financial crisis of South Korea in 1997 revealed a dilemma which the developing economies, that had achieved economic growth by means of mercantile industrial strategies, are prone to face when they implement market liberalization. As market liberalization enhanced the power of the private sector, the state's capacity to correct market disorders caused by monopolistic powers weakened. The only way to prevent market disorder is to strengthen monitoring institutions so that the state can regulate the private sector. Along with the deregulation program, the state has to establish new regulatory institutions to strengthen the monitoring capacity in order to manage a liberalization process effectively. To make the state's supervision of the market redundant, major market players, namely financial and industrial capitalists, have to exercise self-regulation with honesty. However, there is always a possibility that capital will cheat in business, since it aims at the maximization of profits. Therefore, the only practical alternative to maintain market order is for the state to retain a capacity to punish the market actors that transgress rules. This is the reason why regulations cannot be defined only in an economic context or isolated from their social and political environments.

Then what sort of state is required to implement economic liberalization? The strong state that is able to carry out liberalization may be different from the East Asian developmental state, in terms of its function in the market. It is not one capable of mobilizing managerial resources in an authoritarian fashion and distributing them to strategically selected areas. A strong state for liberalization is the one independent of capital and labor so that it can enforce competition on the market, supervise market violators, and punish them. Also it is the one capable of expelling those who failed to survive competition from the market. As Karl Polanyi argued, market liberalization is the choice and strategy of the state. The power to determine the relationship between the state and the market is still with the state. The neo-liberal idea that political factors have to be removed from the market is too idealistic. South Korea demonstrates that complete liberalization without state regulation can cause market failure and social instability.

In attempting to overcome the financial crisis, the economic system of South Korea will inevitably undergo major alterations in pursuit of market liberalization. That is to say, the market will grow more independent of the state. At the current stage, one cannot determine whether the Korean economy will evolve toward the Anglo-Saxon model or its German rival, or change into a variation of the Japanese model as Singapore and Taiwan did. Nonetheless, what is more certain is that the shadow of the state over the market will not disappear for a considerable period. While Confucian–authoritarian and communitarian (or familial) values remain influential (Kim 1998b), and public pressure for economic reform remains, one cannot expect that the state will leave the market unregulated, despite the currently negative views about state involvement in the economy. With the economic reforms the government effected to overcome the financial crisis, the Korean economic system will become more transparent and the link between financial institutions and enterprises will become less direct. However, this does not imply that South Korean capitalism will become free of the influence of the Japanese model after the economic reform process. Given that capitalism is a reflection of not only the economic but also the social and political practices and historical experiences, the extent to which the nature of Korean capitalism will be transformed to incorporate the elements of liberal capitalism might be more limited than we now imagine. Moreover, until market democratization is satisfactorily achieved, the public will not stop requesting state involvement in the economy.

NOTES

1   The study does not assume that the state and society are antagonistic to each other. Nor does it consider that the state is able to insulate itself from social influences. The strong state this study assumes is one able to implement policies effectively and successfully by exercising political integrating power (Lee 1996; 1997) and coordination capacity (Weiss and Hobson 1997) to coordinate social demands and compromise inner conflicts of the state. It is also one capable of adjusting the state–market relationship flexibly in accordance with what economic situations demand.

2   For example, while benefits to save the poor were reduced and unionization of labor was oppressed, measures to regulate labor exploitation were reinforced.

3   The Kim government instituted the real name financial transaction system in 1993 to prohibit capital from being transacted under false names in the unregulated financial market. False names had been frequently used to hide secret funds and shares for the purpose of reducing tax burdens. The Chun Doo-hwan and the Roh Tae-woo governments had attempted to institute the system in 1982 and 1989, but failed owing to the objection of the chaebol and politicians.

8

A MELTDOWN WITH 'CHINESE CHARACTERISTICS'?

Lance L. P. Gore

Is China experiencing a meltdown? Riding on an admirable 7 per cent GDP growth rate in the middle of 1998 amidst the negative numbers generated by neighbouring economies, China hardly seems so. However, a deeper look at the structural forces at work in the economy reveals considerable resemblance to the East Asian roller-coaster ride from 'miracle' to meltdown.

Any discussion of China in the context of East Asia[1] that goes beyond the apparently similar economic 'miracle' confronts a formidable initial question: does China constitute a variant of 'Asian capitalism'? Or, more generally, is it capitalist at all? Judging from the 'minimal criteria' of capitalism proposed by the introductory chapter of this book, the answer is quite ambiguous. Indeed, the country has a vibrant market economy, but it is not based on private ownership and labour is not a universally marketable commodity. No wonder the World Bank refrained from including China in its 1993 study of the East Asian 'miracle', despite its acknowledgement that 'East Asia could hardly be termed an economic miracle if China were not also growing extremely rapidly' (World Bank 1993: 59), its cited reason being 'China's ownership structure, methods of corporate and civil governance, and the reliance on markets are so different' (ibid.).

It is these differences that create the particular trajectory following which China lurches from 'miracle' to meltdown. This chapter outlines this trajectory, arguing that the Chinese 'miracle' is produced by an unlikely marriage between communism and the market. In contrast to the 'acquisitive, maximizing' individual assumed in a capitalist market economy, party–state cadres, or what I call 'bureaucratic entrepreneurs', are the dominant economic players who have effectively redirected communist institutions towards the pursuit of market opportunities. As such, China's institutional mix is a potent force for economic expansion. However, bureaucratic entrepreneurialism (BE) has also helped to preserve many of the weaknesses of the communist system. As politically embedded economic actors, bureaucratic entrepreneurs are not guided solely by a market rationale, but are motivated instead by a host of political and social considerations. Their politically driven economic actions, although powerful in driving economic expansion, inevitably create market distortions that eventually lead to an economic meltdown.

The chapter is organized into five parts. Part 1 delineates the two inter-twined crises of the Asian economic meltdown and indicates China's position in it; Part 2 gives an account of the political foundation of China's economic 'miracle' as well as the institutional context in which bureaucratic entrepreneurs operate; Part 3 describes the characteristics of BE-driven growth; Part 4 depicts the Chinese meltdown in both financial and economic terms; and Part 5 draws out the conclusion as well as the implications of the study.

Part 1

Conceptually, there can be two types of 'miracle' and therefore two types of meltdown: one at the level of finance, and the other in the 'real economy'. An economic 'miracle' can result from the growth of productive capacity, increasing productivity and international competitiveness of the firms and products of an economy; these are clearly part of the East Asian story. It can, however, also be created out of speculative bubbles fuelled by foreign or domestic borrowing, as is also true of many East Asian economies. For example, during the height of the Japanese property bubble, the land under-neath the Imperial Palace in Tokyo had a price tag equivalent to the whole land value of California.

Accordingly, an economic meltdown can result simply from a burst bubble, or, alternatively, it can also be the consequence of the fundamental structural problems in the economy. Burst bubbles can disrupt an economy by creating serious cash flow and balance of payment crises for firms as well as for countries; but as long as its productive capacity and competitiveness remain, the economy may bounce back. But on the other hand, if the melt-down is caused by more fundamental structural problems, the pain can be expected to be deeper and longer lasting.

The Asian meltdown of 1997–8 is an intertwined crisis at both levels, but the two affect different economies to different degrees. Conceptually, the two may not even be causally linked. Owing to the growing power of interna-tional financial capital and the increasing velocity of its movements, a basically sound economy can suffer from speculative attacks from outside or the 'contagion' of a crisis elsewhere. Taiwan, Singapore and Hong Kong are examples in the Asian crisis. The case of China, however, stands at the other end of the spectrum: a meltdown from within, and without external assaults.[2]

It is true that China has had its due share of economic bubbles, especially the speculative craze that fuelled the boom in real estate, stock and futures markets, and the headlong rush to build 'development zones' in 1993 and 1994.[3] However, the central authorities, under the leadership of then economic tsar and now the premier, Zhu Rongji, were quick and decisive in stamping out the bubbles with a three-year programme of tight credit and tight money supply, and a stern warning to 'chop a few heads off'.[4] In early 1997, when there were signs of another stock market overheating, the central government immediately bombarded the public with warnings, news editorials and analyses to cool it down. As a result of this consistent caution with regard to market speculations, a popular joke among Chinese stock investors is that China has neither a bull nor a bear but a pig market.[5]

For all the internal caution, China's external performance is exceptional.[6] By the end of 1997, the country had a record US$140 billion foreign reserve, the second largest in the world, and was running a large trade surplus. Its foreign borrowing, while larger than any of its neighbours in East Asia, was mostly long and medium term, and its debt service ratio well below the internationally recognized dangerous levels. Its current account had been in surplus for many years; the currency market was tightly controlled; the *renminbi* was inconvertible on the capital account and therefore off limits to international currency speculators. And in 1995, after the Mexican currency crisis, the central government installed a comprehensive system to monitor foreign borrowing by both state and non-state entities.

On what grounds, then, are we justified in saying that China is experiencing a meltdown?

A 'meltdown' connotes overheating, or 'too much' of something that bursts the circuit. A financial meltdown indicates a failure of the financial system to conduct transactions properly, or a systemic imbalance. An economic meltdown, on the other hand, normally results from economic overheating that creates structural misalignments. Both, however, produce the same indicators of a crisis: a slowdown or total collapse of economic growth, massive bankruptcies, large-scale unemployment or social dislocations, mounting bad and non-performing loans in the banking system and so on. It is by these same indicators that we determine whether China is experiencing a meltdown. But let's examine how the Chinese 'miracle' is created in the first place.

Part 2

China's near double-digit growth for the past twenty years is nothing short of stunning. However, even more remarkable is that it has happened in a communist institutional context. Despite nearly twenty years of reform and considerable marketization, it remains a basic fact that the bulk of the economy is still either state owned or state controlled. Figure 8.1 shows that public ownership (including both the state-owned and collective[7] sectors), while in constant decline, still dominated industrial production throughout

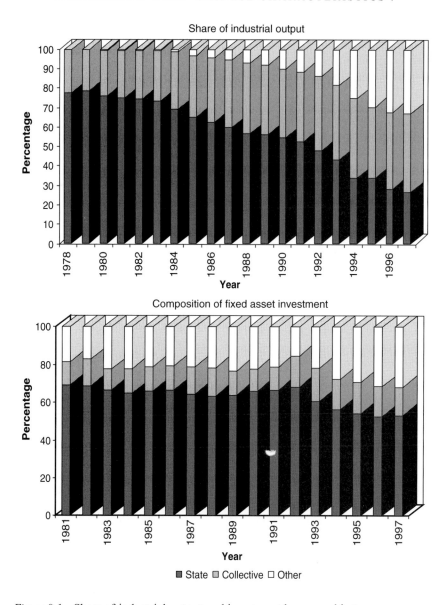

Figure 8.1 Share of industrial output and investment by ownership type

the reform period, and it is not until after 1991 that the share of the 'other' (including individual, private and joint ownership firms) category increased rapidly. It is especially so in the area of investment.

Unlike in the former Soviet Union and eastern Europe, the communist system in China has not been dismantled. The economic management and control apparatuses of the old command economy, such as the ministries, industrial bureaux, planning commission, etc., are still in place at both the central and the local levels. The economy is still organized along two chains of command inherited from the pre-reform system: the sectoral and regional structures of the party–state. The sectoral structures are called *tiaotiao* or *bumen*; these are government departments responsible for a specific industrial sector or a functional area (such as banking, taxation and business administration and regulation) of the economy. The regional structures are essentially local governments at various levels and are called *kuaikuai*, or *difang* (localities). The criss-cross of *tiaotiao* and *kuaikuai* still furnishes the basic institutional structure of the Chinese political economy.

What the Dengist reforms have done so far is essentially to decentralize decision-making power and reassign public property rights down the state hierarchy. This is achieved primarily through dismantling directive central planning, introducing the market as an alternative growth mechanism and hence the profit motives. Decentralization has empowered state actors in the lower reaches of the hierarchy to pursue economic expansion in the regions through the market, creating within the state – not outside it – a crop of powerful economic actors who effectively use state power to pursue market opportunities, with communist institutions continuing to serve as the foundation of the power of bureaucratic entrepreneurs. Bureaucratic entrepreneurs are embedded in the same communist political hierarchy and, as we will see, the macroeconomic impacts of their microeconomic choices are aggregated, not only through market mechanisms but, more importantly, through an overarching political structure that constrains their individual choices.

Bureaucratic entrepreneurs are those party–state officials who are directly engaged in business activities and activities aimed at promoting economic expansion. They are the 'leading cadre' (*lingdao gaobu*), especially the 'first hand' (*diyi bashou*), of the leadership team of the various organizations created by or under the effective control of the party–state. More specifically, they are cadres holding various appointed (or endorsed) positions, ranging from mayors to provincial governors and county executives, from industrial ministers to bureau chiefs, from enterprise managers to corporate CEOs, from village heads to township directors, from party secretaries at various levels to ordinary party members holding key positions in public administration or business management. Their common denominator is their involvement (to varying extents) in business decision making and their embeddedness in the same party–state hierarchy.

By the end of 1997, China had thirty-one provincial level units, 110 prefectures (prefectures, prefecture-level minority autonomous regions, etc., excluding prefecture-level cities), 1,693 counties (excluding county-level cities), 668 municipalities (222 at the prefecture level, 442 at the county level, 4 at the provincial level), 727 urban districts, 26,287 townships and 18,402 towns. Below the township level, there were 739,447 administrative villages (*xingzheng cun*) representing economic communities at the bottom of the party–state hierarchy in the rural areas (State Statistical Bureau of China 1998: 1 and 87). On top of these state institutions, the CCP had 58 million members that were organized into 3,487,000 party committees, branch committees, leadership groups and other types of organization both in and outside the government.[8] And under this vast party–state structure, there were 4.4 million work units (*danwei*) that were separate legal entities (*duli faren*), including 2.62 million enterprises, 620,000 *shiye* units[9] and 40,000 social organizations (*shehui tuanti*).[10] All these are either embedded in or under the effective control or influence of the party–state hierarchy, and it is at the centre of all these that bureaucratic entrepreneurs are positioned.

They are labelled bureaucratic entrepreneurs to distinguish them from their cadre predecessors in the pre-reform command economy. Whereas the pre-reform cadres were primarily implementers of state plans, policies and other directives, bureaucratic entrepreneurs of the reform era are also expected to take initiatives in the marketplace. However, unlike their envious private sector counterparts, bureaucratic entrepreneurs have at their disposal a wide range of state power and resources, and hence greater capacity to push for economic expansion. They are often able to influence the local branches of the state-owned banks to extend credits, or extract contributions from existing enterprises under their control to finance new investment (cf. Christine Wong 1997). Their knowledge and skills in navigating the complex and ever-shifting bureaucratic maze and extracting resources from it to advance their objectives are absolutely essential to their success in the marketplace (see Oksenberg and Lieberthal 1986; also Oi 1992; 1995; Nee 1992). Bureaucratic entrepreneurs are thus simultaneously economic and political entrepreneurs[11] whose economic activities reflect their imperatives as politically embedded economic actors.[12]

Part 3

The dominant political discourse in the reform era is economic development. As a result, bureaucratic entrepreneurs faced enormous pressure from above to speed up economic growth in the localities under their office jurisdictions. The national quadrupling task[13] was divided, further divided, and contracted to the localities level by level down the state hierarchy.[14] The top-down cadre *kaohe* (evaluation) system used their economic achievements (measured mainly in growth figures) as the primary criterion to determine their worth.

For example, in February 1995, forty or so leading cadres from thirteen counties of Shanxi Province were punished (by temporary pay-cuts and reprimands in the government bulletin) for failing to fulfil January's economic targets.[15] In 1991, the government of Jieshou County (Anhui Province) ordered that within one year each township government must build two–three enterprises with an output of over 30,000 yuan, and each village government must build one with an output of over 10,000 yuan, otherwise their leading cadres should resign (Haiyan Du 1992: 115–16). Many local governments openly offered promotions to bureaucratic entrepreneurs who could turn in high growth figures. For instance, the township party secretary or director would be promoted to the deputy county-executive rank if the total output value of his township reached 100 million yuan for the year (see Weiting Huang 1996: 160). In an interview in mid 1991 with reporters, a 'responsible cadre' of the State Council identified *zhengji*[16] (emphasizing 'economic growth and the improvement of people's living standard in the locality under his jurisdiction') as the primary criterion the state used to select promising cadres.[17]

The emphasis on growth, however, is driven home most forcefully by Deng when he proclaimed 'development is the hard truth' (*fazhan shi ying daoli*) during his famous 1992 southern tour. Soon after his remark, the State Council and local governments scrambled to adjust their annual growth target for the Eighth Five-year Plan period (1991–5) upward from 6 per cent to 9 per cent. Needless to say, many localities took the opportunity to set much more ambitious targets, and, as a result, the actualized GNP growth is 11 per cent for the period.

The investment rate (the portion of GDP reinvested) has increased substantially since 1978. While averaging 19.2 per cent between 1953 and 1980 (Shenmu Lin 1993: 213), sustaining a 6 per cent annual growth rate of GDP, it shot up to 29 per cent on average since 1981, and remained at a high level of 33.8 per cent in 1997,[18] generating a near double-digit growth between 1978 and 1997.

However, bureaucratic investment is characterized by what the Chinese call 'duplicate construction' (*chongfujianshe*), a phenomenon in which investors rush into the same industry at the same time, to produce the same products and target the same markets. Under decentralization, bureaucratic entrepreneurs typically strive to build productive facilities to generate growth locally. In a market economy, duplicate construction is inevitable and even necessary for the sake of forging competition. However, the nature of investors makes a crucial difference whether this neo-classical logic holds or not. If they are private investors who bear the full risk of their investment decisions, the waste of resources that results should be minimized. But if state actors make investment decisions, this neo-classical logic does not necessarily hold, for state actors follow a logic of territorial economy, not an enterprise logic of profitability. And as capital-less 'capitalists', they do not bear the whole risk of their adventures in the marketplace.

Therefore BE-driven duplication is territorially distributed and generates two consequences. The first is 'miniaturization' of investment projects. Decentralization within the communist hierarchy has resulted in devolution of financial power and investment resources to the localities and enterprises. This essentially means that the total available capital is widely scattered across the system through a process of particularistic bargaining, contracting and other decentralizing measures that divide and redivide the total available capital into ever smaller units to be held by the lower level state actors in pursuit of their local objectives. The institutional underpinning of China's dominant economic actors also means that market forces driving firms to strive for economies of scale as well as scope continue to be fettered by the political structure. As a result, in what appears to be a reversal of the trend in capitalist market economies wherein, driven by competition, firms grow into huge conglomerates or multinational corporate giants through mergers, takeovers or driving out of business smaller or less efficient firms, a 'miniaturization' of investment projects is the trend under decentralization.

While Chinese enterprises tend to be much larger than their counterparts in market economies in terms of number of employees, they tend to be 'miniatures' when the comparison is to production scale and total assets. Very few Chinese companies are large enough to be noted outside China, despite China supposedly being the third largest economy in the world. In 1996 (the year when China's total iron and steel output reached the 100 million ton mark for the first time in history), for example, there were 1,700 steel plants in China, with an average output of only 54,000 tons.[19] In comparison, most of the world's steel plants are concentrated at the 1–5 million ton and 10–20 million ton levels. In the same year, China had 325 auto manufacturers with a combined total output of 1.45 million, less than a quarter of that of Toyota Corporation (6 million).[20] Experts from the National Council of Textile Industry (formerly the Ministry of Textile Industry) believed the optimal production scale of textile firms in China was 100,000 spindles; however, among the 116 new textile projects under construction in 1995, only three had a designed capacity of 50,000 or more spindles; the other 113 had an average capacity of only 18,000 (Junbo Li 1997: 28–9).

The second consequence of the territoriality of bureaucratic entrepreneurs is a regional pattern of investment characterized by a structural isomorphism – the similarity in the structure of local economies, which in turn reflects the similarity in their investment patterns over time.

There have been a number of empirical studies of the industrial structure of China's provinces by both Chinese and foreign researchers. Shenmu Lin and his colleagues of the Investment Research Institute under the State Planning Commission measured the similarity of the industrial structure of China's provinces in 1987 by the share of output of forty main industries in each province, using the UN Industrial Development Organization's structural similarity coefficient.[21] The coefficient values are extraordinarily high:

an overwhelming majority of the provinces fall between 0.71 to 0.94, the highest being 0.98, the lowest 0.53, and the mean is 0.789 (Shenmu Lin 1993: 263). A similar study was conducted by Kumar for the World Bank (see Kumar 1994: 105). She measured structural differences of China's macro-regions (groups of provinces) in 1991 by number of employees. Her results lend support to the findings of Lin and his team four years earlier. Most of her values fall in the range between 0.118 and 0.36, with the highest being 0.425, the lowest 0.107, and the mean being 0.197.[22]

The trend has continued in the 1990s. When the figures of the third industrial census (1995) began to pour out in late 1996 and early 1997, the central authorities once again sounded the alarm about structural isomorphism of regional investment. A *People's Daily* editorial (4 December 1996) revealed that the structural similarity coefficient between the coastal provinces and the central provinces was 0.935 in 1995, and that between the central and western provinces was an astounding 0.979. If the methodology (not given) is compatible with that of Lin,[23] both would be a substantial increase from the national mean of all provinces of 0.789 recorded in Lin's study for the mid 1980s.

More significantly, this trend can be projected well into the future, for it is built into the ninth five-year plans (covering 1996–2000) and the long-term plans (up to the year 2010) of the provinces. According to the same editorial, of China's thirty provincial level localities, twenty-two have listed the automobile industry as a key industry in their future economic development; the electronics industry is targeted by twenty-four; chemical and machine-building industries by sixteen; and the metallurgical industry by fourteen. As the editorial puts it, 'There are signs of a new round of duplicate construction that extends the current trend toward structural isomorphism'.

What the above account suggests is that BE-driven growth, powerful as it is, contains some serious structural weaknesses and is prone to meltdown. In Part 4, we will examine the symptoms of a meltdown with 'Chinese characteristics' first in the 'real economy', then at the financial level.

Part 4

Certainly what China is experiencing now is nothing as dramatic as the financial crisis engulfing other Asian economies in 1997 and 1998 (hence the question mark in the title), but it is a meltdown nevertheless. The word 'meltdown' suggests overheating, and China certainly has all the ingredients for an economic overheating. The expansionary fervour of bureaucratic entrepreneurs is extraordinary because it is not only profit motivated but politically driven, and it is often reckless because bureaucratic entrepreneurs run relatively low risks in their adventures in the marketplace, and are hence less sensitive to market discipline. Decentralization has not only enhanced the capacity of bureaucratic entrepreneurs for economic expansion, but also led to the expansion being distributed in a way that compartmentalizes the economy. Both miniaturization and structural isomorphism result from duplicate construction, and growth driven by duplication is sustainable only under one condition, which has now virtually disappeared. The condition is market shortage.

The numerous sub-optimal-scale firms brought into being by duplicate construction owe their existence not only to local state protection but also to the pent-up market demand from the Maoist era of shortage. Table 8.1 indicates the unusually high returns across the board in the early 1980s. This has meant that even crude products could be sold on the market at a profit. Under shortage, BE has successfully created and protected corps of small-scale, technologically backward and organizationally uncompetitive firms whose multiplication fuelled a stunning economic expansion. However, duplication eventually builds up to overcapacity, which in turn cuts down or even wipes out the profit margins for many, and elevates market competition to such intensity that the majority of the old communist-style enterprises generated by BE find it difficult adjusting to the new business environment.

Furthermore, because bureaucratic investment is characterized by debt financing, generally poor returns are also creating huge problems for the financial system. Plummeting profit margins, heavy debt burdens, mounting bad and non-performing loans, slowdown of growth, rising bankruptcies and massive lay-offs – the key indicators of an economic meltdown – are inevitable and have already emerged in China in increasing magnitude and with mounting impacts. The emergence of a buyer's market spells the end of BE-driven growth and necessitates a complete overhaul of the growth mechanisms or the basic institutions of the economy. However, because of the way firms have been created and distributed politically, the inevitable restructuring process will be especially painful and long lasting in China. This is the basic story of a meltdown with 'Chinese characteristics'.

The seller's market of the 1980s meant that some very backward production lines, like the Great Leap Forward style of backyard steel furnaces, were still viable. Decentralization, which is the main thrust of the reform programmes of the 1980s and early 1990s, has enabled lower level state actors to utilize fully the inherent capacity of the communist system to meet effectively the huge but still unsophisticated market demand with massive duplication of production facilities. The combination of huge market demand and the institutional capacity to meet it are perhaps the most important structural conditions for the dramatic rise of the township and village enterprises (TVEs). Yingtao Deng and his research team thus characterize China's factor market in the 1980s: 'the demand for general-purpose equipment was large, for specialized equipment small; for small equipment large, for large ones small; for low-tech equipment large, for high-tech, advanced, and precision equipment small' (Yingtao Deng et al. 1990: 223).[24]

However, politically driven duplicate construction eventually leads to

Table 8.1   Profit rates by industry of all firms with independent accounting (profit + tax/total assets; %)

Industry	1980	1989	1994	1996
Tobacco processing	326.9	152.3	71.9	60.35
Petroleum processing	98.3	38.7	19.5	16.76
Rubber products	62.7	30.5	9.2	8.43
Chemical materials	22	23.1	7.4	6.99
Medical and pharmaceutical	45	22.8	10.9	9.98
Ferrous metals processing	18.3	22.1	13.2	4.81
Cultural educational and sports	56.7	21	9.5	7.91
Electric equipment and machinery	25.7	20.6	8.4	5.9
Paper making and paper products	30	20.4	6.1	7.19
Chemical fibres	32.1	20.2	9.3	5.17
Printing and record medium processing	28.6	18.8	8.4	8.48
Non-ferrous metals processing	17.2	18.4	8.2	4.81
Beverage production	48.5	18	15.1	13.8
Metal products	27	17.8	8.7	4.47
Garments	46	16.6	8.5	6.42
Non-metal minerals mining	17	16.5	10.5	8.43
Textiles	69	15.8	5.6	1.64
Logging and transport of timber and bamboo	13	15.7	7.4	4.79
Non-ferrous mining and dressing	9.7	15.3	9.7	7.73
Electronics and telecommunication equipment	14	14.9	9	7.59
Electric power, steam and hot water production and supply	20.6	13.8	–	8.84
Food processing	28.9	13.7	8	2.06
Plastic products	31.6	13.6	5.8	4.84
Ordinary machinery	13.1	12.7	8.3	4.94
Ferrous metal mining and dressing	7.3	12.1	9.2	1.36
Transport equipment	10.5	12	9.1	5.99
Timber and bamboo products	27.6	10	7.4	5.72
Leather, fur and related products	30.3	7.9	6.6	5.66
Tap water production and supply	14.7	5.4	6.6	3.14
Crude oil and natural gas extraction	55.8	−4.3	14.7	16.05
Coal mining and dressing	6	−3.8	5.3	6.43
Average	24.2	16.8	11.3	7.11

Source: China Statistical Yearbook, various issues

overcapacity. Table 8.2 shows the capacity utilization rates in 1995 in the industries in which bureaucratic entrepreneurs have invested heavily. The rates are especially low in consumer electronics and home appliances industries, which have witnessed waves of investment in 'hot' items throughout the 1980s and early 1990s.

Small scale, high debt–asset ratios, diminishing returns, backward technology and excessive competition[25] are a fatal combination that makes China's enterprises vulnerable. One implication of dwindling profit margins across the board is that they are exhausting the government's capability to

Table 8.2 Capacity utilization rates in various industries in 1995

Industry	Rate (%)	Industry	Rate (%)
VCD players	26.0	Refrigerators	50.4
VCRs	40.3	Cars	64.9
Air-conditioners	33.5	Electric fans	61.5
Microwave ovens	38.6	Motor vehicles	44.3
Electric steel	56.4	Copy machines	34.0
Rolled steel	62.0	Colour TV sets	46.1
Seamless steel pipe	68.0	Machine tools	46.2
Copper processing	51.4	Camcorders	12.0
Crude lead smelting	65.8	Dyed and printed fabrics	23.6
Electrolytic lead	64.6	Smoke ventilators	40.2
Sawn wood	41.4	Soaps	42.2
Plywood	54.8	Colour photo films	22.1
Fibre board	65.2	Vacuum cleaners	43.2
Phosphate fertilizer	60.3	Washing machines	43.4
Chemical pesticides	41.6	Motor cycles	61.6
Tyres	54.7	Radio-cassette players	57.2
Inner tubes of tyres	37.4	Sugar	65.7
Traditional Chinese medicine	34.3	Milk powder	44.1
Machine tools	46.2	Liquor	64.9
Large and medium tractors	60.6	Detergents	53.8
Mini-tractors	65.9	Household glass products	61.5
Trucks	35.9	Bicycles	54.5
Refractory material products	26.2	Sewing machines	56.0
Internal combustion engines	43.9	Cameras	57.7
Crude salt	65.8	Tape	52.0
Pulp	60.0		

Source: *China Statistical Yearbook 1997,* p. 454

protect loss-making firms.[26] As a result, large chunks of the nation's industrial capacity are in danger of being wiped out by intensified competition, especially from abroad (assuming the current 'open-door' policy continues). This is simply because many of these enterprises are too technologically backward and often of a non-viable scale. No amount of local protectionism is likely to preserve them indefinitely. A good indication that this process is already under way is that since 1990, the market share of the machine tool industry – one of China's most overbuilt industries – has been rapidly reduced to 30 per cent by foreign competitors.

As the economy turns from a supply-constrained to a demand-constrained one, China now has to wrestle with the same problems as other capitalist market economies – stimulating aggregate demand. However, beyond reckless expansion or duplicate construction, bureaucratic entrepreneurs are still very inexperienced in this. Aggregate demand (the sum of consumption, investment and export) was declining well before the Asian crisis. The Asian crisis is trimming both the export and inflow of foreign capital from the region (both accounting for over 60 per cent of the total). Investment expansion, of which China's current system is still very capable, will not be as effective as it used to be, owing to market constraints. Domestic consumption is expected to continue its current slowdown because of the uncertainties generated among the population by state-owned enterprise (SOE) reforms, housing and other reforms necessitated by the inevitable restructuring of the economy. The country may even stumble into the sort of 'liquidity trap' faced by post-bubble Japan.[27]

The total effect is an economic slowdown. GDP growth declined from a breakneck 13 per cent in 1993 to 8.8 per cent in 1997, and further to 7 per cent in the first half of 1998 (*China Statistical Yearbook*). And the trend is expected to continue. In 1997, the growth rate of TVEs – the most dynamic sector of the economy – fell for the first time since the early 1980s below 20 per cent (18 per cent in comparison with the 42.5 per cent average annual growth rate between 1991 and 1995), and a record 17 per cent of TVEs incurred a loss.[28] The Chinese authorities estimate that, to achieve the targeted 8 per cent GDP growth for 1998, the TVEs need to grow by 18 per cent, but by mid year the sector only achieved a 13 per cent growth rate.[29]

Overcapacity has also resulted in the massive underemployment of workers and productive facilities, enormous burdens to the state budget, which threaten the health of the nation's financial system. It also means that the job-creating capacity of the economy is drastically reduced, and large-scale bankruptcies and lay-offs are inevitable. The unemployment problem of China dwarfs anything experienced by the crisis-hit Asian economies. The estimate by Li Boyong, Minister of Labour, before the Asian crisis was that by the end of the century unemployment will be 16 million in urban areas, and 137 million in the rural areas (cited in Junfang Xing 1997: 379). The Asian crisis is worsening the job situation by reducing exports and inflows of foreign capital. The state has planned to lay off 3.5 million workers in 1998 (2.7 million already laid off by mid year), adding to the existing 11.5 million unemployed; however, Li Boyong warned that up to 10 million could lose their jobs in that year owing to state sector reforms.[30] Premier Zhu Rongji has repeatedly cited decades of duplicate construction as the main cause of the difficulties currently experienced by the SOEs;[31] but the unemployment problem is far from restricted to the state-owned sector, which employs only 10 per cent of the total labour force.

Figure 8.2 puts the meltdown with Chinese characteristics under a magnifying glass. The most unmistakable sign of a meltdown caused by a demand slack is deflation, which is unprecedented in the history of the People's Republic. This signifies fundamental change in the economy.

While competitive elimination is essentially a healthy market process, there are two considerations in the Chinese context that may render this neo-classical logic less straightforward. The first is whether the Chinese system really allows efficient firms to thrive on market competition rather than on collusion with the state. The second is that the social costs it exacts may be unusually high because China's peculiar investment pattern has generated a large number of enterprises that should not have been brought into existence in the first place, and because bureaucratic entrepreneurs have preserved a large number of firms that should have gone bankrupt long ago. These two factors pose special political challenges to the state and demand high leadership skills for their successful management. If not properly handled, the former may perpetuate political distortions in the economy, which are a key factor causing the Asian crisis of 1997, while the latter may lead to social unrest and political upheavals.

These structural problems in the economy inevitably have their financial manifestations. Like the rest of East Asia, China's financial system is dominated by banks. The four major state-owned banks account for two-thirds of the nation's total financial assets and 90 per cent of all banking assets. The development of equity markets has been slow and far from adequate. The overwhelming majority of the nation's investment capital is still raised through state-owned banks. In 1997, for example, total bank loans reached 7.5 trillion yuan, and the total investment in fixed assets was 2.53 trillion. In comparison with the 1.4 trillion increases in bank credits, only 30 billion

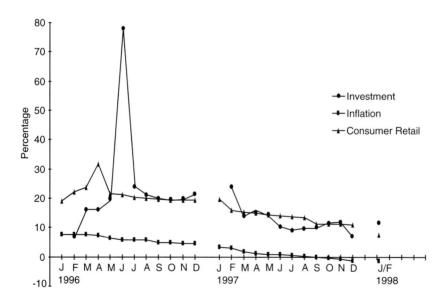

Figure 8.2   Inflation, consumption and investment trends in recent years

yuan of new stocks were issued on the market (State Statistical Bureau of China 1998: 67; Hong Ma 1998: 118). Therefore, the importance of banks in investment financing is paramount.

Banking reform has followed a similar route of decentralization and the introduction of the profit motive. However, it has also simultaneously created a situation in which the profit motive and the policy functions of the banks coexist and interfere with each other. The main problem of China's partially reformed banking system is its continued lack of autonomy from the state, especially from the local governments of the regions in which the branch banks operate. The business districts of the branch banks coincide with the administrative localities, which control crucial matters such as the personnel decisions, party organizations and the logistic support (such as housing for bank employees) and their dealings with local businesses. Officially, no local authorities should issue orders to the local banks regarding their business lending, but the latter are in fact heavily influenced by the former.

Furthermore, under BE market signals are considerably distorted by state meddling. The level of support that local governments throw behind an investment project, more than any business qualities of its own, is critical for its success; this support and the availability of loan guarantees by the local government are often better cues for banks' lending decisions. Therefore the branch banks often identify with the economic objectives of the local government, and thus become part and parcel of the local state corporatism (see Oi 1992; 1995).

The state sector has consumed the vast majority of credits;[32] the debt–asset ratio of SOEs is 84 per cent (70 per cent of which are bank loans) on average. According to Chen Qingtai, former Vice-President of State Commission for Economy and Trade, interest payment on enterprise loans was only 40 per cent.[33] Figure 8.3 indicates that the net profit of SOEs declined dramatically. Therefore, while their total loan scale has been expanding exponentially, the performance of the state-owned banks deteriorated, as shown in Figure 8.4.

Estimates of the bad and non-performing loans accumulated by the state-owned banks under decades of BE and duplicate construction vary. The official figure is around 22 per cent of total loans,[34] but experts both inside and outside China draw much higher figures. Yining Zhao and Binjie Han (1997) estimated about 40 per cent. According to *Asiaweek*, in the middle of 1997, China's banking system had $830 billion of outstanding loans (roughly 6.9 trillion *yuan*), of which $249 billion were non-performing loans, and bad loans (loan losses) were estimated at $174 billion. The two accounted for 51 per cent of total loans. To make the matter worse, the total equity of Chinese banks was only $39 billion (4.7 per cent of total loans, far less than the international standard of 8 per cent), and loan loss reserves were a meagre $8 billion.[35]

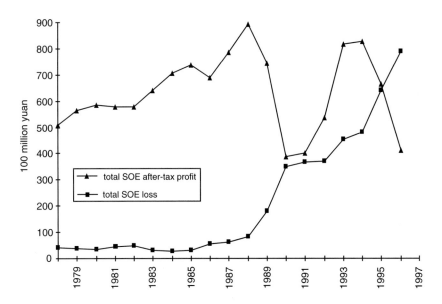

Figure 8.3 Total profit and loss of SOEs

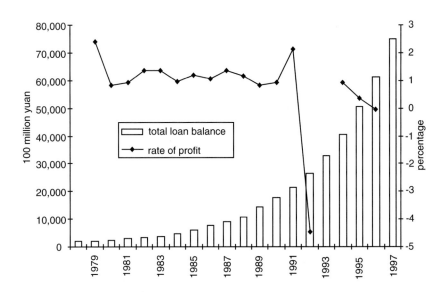

Figure 8.4 Total loans and rate of profit in the banking sector

The tell-tale signs of the deteriorating financial performance of enterprises are shown in Figure 8.5, which indicates that since 1994 total savings deposits have exceeded total loans by an ever-widening margin. This is unprecedented since the expansionary impulse of bureaucratic entrepreneurs had always resulted in an ever-ballooning loan scale, and tightening credit had always been the centrepiece of macroeconomic control by the central government. In 1997, many banks for the first time could not use up their assigned credit quotas, and began to deposit cash in the central bank for safer and in some cases even higher returns.[36] This reversal of fortune could indicate only one thing: profitable investment projects have become increasingly scarce, and lending risks have increased substantially.[37]

Thus, China has the symptoms of a meltdown in both the 'real' economy and the financial sector.

The Chinese economic woes date from far before the Asian crisis and in many aspects dwarf those haunting other Asian economies today, but they lack the drama with which the events of the Asian crisis have unfolded. This, of course, is due to China's relative insulation from the global financial market and its speculative currency attackers. The paradox of China is that in many ways it is deeper in crisis, but it has emerged as the last dry land in the rising floodwaters of the Asian crisis.

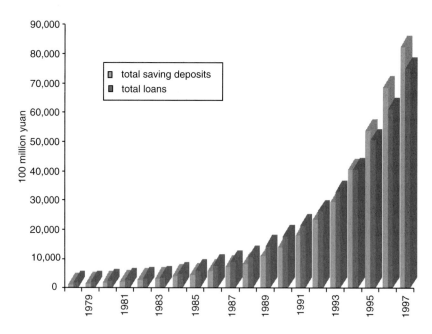

Figure 8.5   Savings and loan gap

Part 5

The paradox of China is a paradox of a marriage between the market and communist institutions. The analysis of this chapter has shown that China's high-powered growth has much to do with the communist institutions it inherits. The economy grew not in spite of communism but in part because of it, and BE is the driving force in the economy. The market has played an increasingly significant role; however, whatever benefits of marketizing reforms are gained are within the larger communist institutional context, which ties the Chinese 'miracle' right back to the weaknesses of the communist system. Stunning growth, therefore, is still associated with a Stalinist style of industrialization that will inevitably face diminishing returns,[38] and, as indicated by miniaturization and structural isomorphism, the quality of growth continues to be questionable, despite the efficiency gains brought about by marketization.

Illustrative of this point about the quality of growth is the case of the pre-reform China: its average annual industrial growth rate was 12.5 per cent between 1951 and 1980, surpassing the 11.5 per cent of Japan (State Statistical Bureau of China 1997: 485). However, at the end of the period Japan emerged as one of the world's foremost industrial powers while the Chinese economy was on the brink of collapse. It is in part because of the new awareness of its backwardness after the initial opening to the outside world in the late 1970s that China has embarked on economic reforms in earnest.

Similarly, the effects of China's continued poor-quality growth during the reform era are already being felt today, and will no doubt continue to be felt for years to come. Because much of the country's investment capital has gone into the duplicate construction of productive facilities with poor market prospects and therefore cannot be expected to count towards China's future productive capacity, China's GDP figures perhaps represent another kind of 'bubble economy' – a 'balloon economy',[39] so to speak – that will sooner or later contract. In contrast to a bubble economy that is fuelled primarily by excessive speculation in the stock and the real estate markets, a 'balloon economy' is caused by massive but fundamentally misdirected investment in manufacturing that similarly causes false prosperity. The problems it generates are likely to be more fundamental and therefore longer lasting.

The Chinese story tells us a few things. First, a market economy (therefore capitalism broadly defined) can exist in a broad range of institutional contexts, even in the most unlikely communist context. The combination of market and communism has been potent, and the BE it generates has been extraordinarily effective for initial industrialization. The accomplishment of BE cannot be erased by the problems it has accumulated over the decades that have risen to dominance only recently, just as the Asian meltdown of 1997–8 does not negate the 'miracle' the region achieved a decade ago. The common issue facing East Asian economies is structural adjustment, with the recognition that no 'miracle' is everlasting, nor can it be taken for granted.

Second, globalization has played only a marginal role in the Chinese meltdown. Although for many years China has been the second largest recipient of inflow of foreign capital in the world (surpassed only by the United States), in 1997 foreign capital accounted only for 12.2 per cent of the total fixed asset investment (calculated from State Statistical Bureau of China 1998: 45, 51). Similarly, powerful as it is, international financial capital is effectively sidelined by a closed capital account. The Asia crisis will limit China's option to pursue industrialization by an East Asia style of 'export push'.[40] But with a large domestic market and lower level of reliance on foreign capital, this will not hurt China fundamentally. The threats to China are internal rather than external. Severe as it is, the Chinese crisis lacks the element of a surprise attack from without, which allows the state effective control over the situation and the possibility of working it out over a long period of time with a series of suitably paced reform programmes. Therefore China is better positioned than any other economy in the region to pursue an independent style of market economy in post-crisis East Asia.

And it has to. While the common characteristics of a demand-constrained market economy may force China to adopt many of the policies and institutions of liberal capitalism as practised in the United States and elsewhere, the fact that bureaucratic entrepreneurs have been the dominant players in the economy and have accumulated a considerable stake in the current system suggests that any future changes will have to accommodate their interests, and they themselves together with the party–state they represent are in a position to redirect future changes. The combination of the forces of the market and forces of the state, of the benefit of a large economy and lower level of external dependency, and of a legacy of communism means that China is the most likely place in East Asia where new forms of capitalism will continue to be generated.

NOTES

1 Used here broadly to include both Northeast and Southeast Asia.
2 Among the Asian crisis-hit economies, Japan's is a similar meltdown from within, but more at the financial level, whereas, as we will see, China's is more at the level of the 'real economy'.
3 Which created liquidity problems for some banks and runaway inflation because local governments, enterprises as well as individuals withdrew or borrowed funds from the banks to invest in these areas. The Chinese authorities called this phenomenon 'external circulation' of funds (*tiwai xunhuan*). That is, funds circulating outside the state-controlled banking system, which seriously threatened the health of the state banks and the entire state sector that depended on loans.
4 Zhu's warning to CEOs of state-owned banks in case they did not obey orders to withdraw loans that were used for speculative purposes.

5 Or *zhu shi*. The Chinese surname 'Zhu' is pronounced the same as the word 'pig' in Chinese.

6 For a comparative analysis of China's external performance, see John Wong (1997).

7 The collective enterprises are under the control of local governments at various levels either because the latter start them or because their historical evolution has been such that the local governments exercise effective property rights over them. In either case local states enjoy *de facto* ownership. As Oi emphasized, 'township and village enterprises, which are the most economically significant portion of rural industry, are not privately owned, nor are they forms of hybrid privatization, but forms of government ownership' (Oi 1995: 1135), and as Walder pointed out: 'As far as property rights assignments go, the common administrative distinction between "state" and "collective" ownership is virtually without meaning' (Walder 1994: 58).

8 CCTV: 'China News' broadcast, 1 September 1997.

9 The Chinese classified as *shiye* units all schools, universities, research institutes, agencies of public administration, the health care profession, banks, the legal system and other professional services. In the tradition of the socialist planned economy, these were all financed by the state budget and were supposed to be non-profit, although this has changed significantly.

10 CCTV: 'China News' broadcast, 27 September 1997.

11 Walder (1992) and Oi (1992; 1995) provide vivid descriptions of their entrepreneurial activities in both political and economic arenas.

12 For a detailed analysis of the incentive structure of bureaucratic entrepreneurs, see Gore (1998: ch. 3).

13 That is, to double and redouble GNP between 1980 and 2000, which was accomplished in 1995, five years ahead of schedule.

14 Author's China interviews.

15 Xinhua News Agency, 7 March 1995.

16 Literally translated as 'administrative achievements'. This is a catchword among bureaucratic entrepreneurs.

17 *Wenzaibao* (Beijing), 30 June 1991.

18 Note, the figures are for investment in fixed assets only. The investment rate should be higher if other investments are taken into consideration. Sources: calculated from State Statistical Bureau of China, *China Statistical Yearbook* (various issues) and *A Statistical Survey of China* (1998: 5).

19 *Renminribao* (*People's Daily*), 9 April 1997.

20 State Statistical Bureau of China (1997).

21 Shenmu Lin (1992). The coefficient is:

$$S_{ij} = (\Sigma_n X_{in} X_{jn})/(\Sigma_n X_{in}^2 \, \Sigma_n X_{jn}^2)^{1/2}$$

S_{ij} is the structural similarity coefficient X_{in} and X_{jn} are the shares of sector n's output value in regions i and j. $n = 1, 2, ..., 40; i, j = 1, 2, ..., 28$.

22 Note that Kumar's mean, which approaches 0.2, was almost an exact fit for Lin's, which is very close to 0.8 (Lin's study measures structural similarity while Kumar's measures structural difference).

23 Which may well be the case, because Lin was the director of China's premier research institute in the area: the Investment Research Institute, under the SPC.

24 Even in 1994 I encountered roadside oil refineries set up by peasants who managed to obtain crude oil from nearby oil fields and sold the gasoline extracted using primitive technology to truck drivers passing by.

25 Owing in part to too many players and irregular means used in competition.

26 For instance, it will no longer be easy for local governments to extract resources from profitable enterprises to support the ailing ones.

27 See Paul Krugman (1998c).

28 Figures are given by Wan Baorui, Deputy Minister of Agriculture; see *Renminribao* 25 January 1998.

29 Author's China interviews in June 1998.

30 Reuters, 6 August 1998.

31 *Renminribao* 31 January 1997, and at new cabinet meetings in early 1998.

32 For example, according to *China Statistical Yearbook*, the TVEs, which now contribute close to half of the nation's industrial output, consume only 6 per cent or so of total loans.

33 *Jingjixue xiaoxibao* (*Economic News*), 18 March 1995.

34 The *New York Times* 27 November 1997.

35 *Asiaweek* 13 March 1998, p. 31.

36 Author's China interviews in 1997.

37 In fact, the 1993 bubble economy was in part caused by banks and enterprises redirecting their investment capital to speculations on the stock and real estate markets, because returns in the 'real economy' had become so disappointing. The same temptation has only increased in recent years and is kept in check by the central government with political means.

38 A similar argument is made by Krugman (1994) in his controversial (perhaps less so after the Asia crisis) article 'The Myth of Asia's Miracle'. Perhaps his argument applies more to China than other East Asian 'Tigers', especially his comparison with the former Soviet Union.

39 A Chinese scholar, Xian Gao (1997), proposes this concept.

40 See World Bank (1993). But basically when too many countries pursue this strategy, it ceases to be an option.

9

THE ASIAN CRISIS AND THE PERILS OF ENTERPRISE ASSOCIATION

Explaining the different outcomes in Singapore, Taiwan and Korea

James Cotton

The impact of the regional crisis upon Korea has been severe. Seoul was forced to appeal to the IMF for emergency credit, and is now in receipt of a $57 billion aid package with stringent conditions attached. Official statistics record that 7.5 per cent of the Korean workforce was unemployed by July 1998. Given the traditional reluctance of Korean workers to admit that they have no work, and also the understating of female unemployment, this figure should be regarded as conservative. Labour disputes have erupted across the country, with the Hyundai auto manufacturing plant at Ulsan closed for a six-week period after it was occupied with workers threatened with retrenchment. The economy contracted by 5.3 per cent in the first half of the year, and the overall performance for 1998 is expected to be around minus 7 per cent.

Within days of the IMF rescue package being negotiated in 1997, the three presidential candidates then campaigning publicly pledged to observe its conditions. The new administration has observed that pledge. Korea's present leadership has been outspoken on the causes of the crisis. These amount, in the words of President Kim Dae-jung, to 'past government failures', and especially 'collusive links between companies and politicians' (Dae-jung 1998). Officials responsible for the management of economic policy under the Kim Young-sam administration have been questioned in the legislature, and it is possible that the former president himself may be called to account for his failure to deal with a crisis, the portents of which (the record shows) some members of his administration had recognised in the first half of 1997.

The prescription for reform adopted by the present administration is a combination of 'democracy and a free market economy', though the degree of government regulation which the proposed reforms entail is reminiscent of the powers exercised by the US administrators of Japan during the era of *zaibatsu* dissolution. The Financial Supervisory Commission, which has oversight of the government's reform of the financial sector, has required the merger of five debt-encumbered banks into five healthier institutions. The Korea Asset Management Corporation has formulated a plan whereby the five largest *chaebol* will divest themselves of some of their interests and swap a range of their assets in order to concentrate on core activities – Hyundai on auto manufacturing and shipbuilding, Samsung on electronics and microchips, and so on. At the same time, the pervasive but highly opaque practice of subdivisions of the conglomerates standing surety for each other's debts is to be outlawed. At the time of writing, this, the second stage of the government's programme has been less than fully successful, with some groups reluctant to surrender control of major components of their long-term industrial strategies. Similarly, the government, having temporarily assumed its debt, has been unable to auction the assets of the bankrupt Kia group. Meanwhile, government plans to privatise major public enterprises, including POSCO (Pohang Ian and Steel Corporation) and KEPCO (Korea Electric Power Corporation), are being pursued.

By contrast, it is striking that neither Singapore nor Taiwan has suffered such dislocation and loss of confidence. Nevertheless, they have been vulnerable to some of its effects. In 1998 the growth rates of both nations have suffered, with Taiwan's growth expected to fall to 3–4 per cent, and Singapore slipping into recession in the second half of the year. But they did not suffer to anything close to the same degree from the initial contagion of the currency crisis. In the year to 30 June 1998, while South Korea's currency had depreciated by 34.1 per cent (against the US dollar), the Singapore dollar had declined by 16.5 per cent, and Taiwan's currency by 23.7 per cent. With low levels of foreign-denominated debt, international relief was not required by either economy. Though their stock markets suffered a general lowering of prices, and unemployment increased, none of these developments were so severe as to trigger social protests and political instability. At the time of this writing, they appeared to be weathering the storm, though with very strong linkages to the economy of the People's Republic of China, a devaluation of the renminbi would undoubtedly produce more pronounced effects, especially in Taiwan. Even if this were to materialise, the differences with the other crisis economies in the region would still be pronounced.

While Kim Dae-jung has blamed the ineptitude of his predecessor, and the ingrained corrupt practices that are the legacy of a generation of authoritarianism, the leaderships in both Singapore and Taiwan have claimed by contrast that their good fortune has been the result of sound governance. There are some grounds for these latter claims. Both have been committed for some time to progressive but cautious liberalisation in their financial sectors. Government policy has led to the pursuit of objectives that in the 1990s have increasingly distinguished these systems from others in the region. Both have maintained large reserves, and overall foreign debt has not been significant. Inflation has been kept low, and both governments have run current account surpluses. Gross national savings have usually exceeded investment, with the consequence that capital formation has been on the basis of local rather than external funds. Attention has also been paid to policy sequencing. In most of Southeast Asia, financial and industrial markets were opened at the same time, while in Taiwan, they were opened in sequence, with a sound industrial basis laid first.

Nevertheless, the governments in Singapore and Taiwan have introduced policy changes to cope with the new and more adverse climate. On 30 June 1998, Singapore's Finance Minister, Richard Hu, announced a S$2 billion extra-budget package to stimulate the economy, at the same time conceding that the region's economic troubles were now expected to have a major impact on the city-state (Velloor 1998). The package included measures to lower business costs, bring forward public construction projects to stimulate local demand, and offer a boost to the collapsing property market by halting government sales of land. Altogether, these measures will result in a budget deficit of S$7.3 billion, the first since the slowdown of the mid 1980s. At the same time it became apparent that the nation's growth had slowed to the point that a contraction in the economy was expected before the end of the year, thus demonstrating that earlier estimates of 3.5 per cent growth were excessively optimistic.

The cause of this slowdown can be traced directly to the Asian economic turmoil. Singapore's trade volume is expected to decline by about 5 per cent in 1998. This will be due largely to the poor performance of most regional economies. Vital markets in Malaysia, Japan, Hong Kong and South Korea for consumer and capital goods have contracted, and with Indonesia still in free fall, transportation has also been seriously affected. Nor are there any prospects of tourism rescuing the national revenues, with the number of tourist arrivals diminishing by about 20 per cent in the past twelve months.

Longer term, further steps in the continued slow liberalisation of banking and financial services can be expected, but in a nation which has prided itself on tight regulation and fiscal rectitude, more radical expedients are unlikely. Nevertheless, the full picture of the exposure of Singapore's banks to Indonesia is not yet available, and this may generate additional uncertainties. While cushioned by the absence of sovereign debt and in possession of large foreign reserves, Singapore's open economy is uniquely vulnerable to the regional and international climate.

The response in Taiwan has been similar (Siew 1998; Ruey-Long Chen 1998).[1] In 1998, Taiwan's exports to Asian markets have fallen by around 25 per cent. As these markets account for half of all exports, this has had a significant dampening effect on the economy. Unlike in Japan, Taiwan's domestic demand has remained high. The government has announced its intention to boost this demand further, by bringing forward some major infrastructure projects, including the North–South high-speed railway (Cheng-hsiung 1998). The government has remained strict in its insistence that not only all banks but all financial institutions should satisfy the 8 per cent Bank of International Settlements capital–adequacy ratio. There have been clear signals that the government is prepared again to intervene in the stock market to boost confidence, just as was done during the 1996 missile crisis. Having already experienced a property speculation boom which caused a drastic fall in the stock market in 1990, policy-makers have had some experience of the problems seen in other economies. Taiwan's biggest concern is the prospect of a devaluation in the People's Republic of China (and Hong Kong), given the island's appreciable surplus in trade with the mainland. If this happens, the Chinese market will contract, with fewer funds available for imports. Though a few Taiwan companies with joint ventures on the mainland will benefit from cheaper costs, especially labour, the overall effect will be strongly negative. With the particular structure of its industrial capacity, Taiwan finds it difficult to diversify its trade to cushion such effects, as much of its business is with TNCs.

While there is little doubt that policy has made a difference, and there is therefore some basis for the claim that Singapore and Taiwan have enjoyed unusually good governance while Korea has not, the fact that these former systems have been characterised by differences in *institutional capacity* is less noticed or analysed (on institutional capacity, see Kang 1996). The fact that these differences exist is itself a puzzle, given that there are some grounds for viewing these systems as members of a particular group, the Asian NICs/NIEs. The pursuit of this issue requires an excursus first into theory, and then into the particularities of these political and economic systems so that their superior performance by comparison with Korea can be fully assessed.

The politics of enterprise association

My argument, in brief, is that these three systems have all been constructed according to the same impulse and with the same model, that of the 'development state', in mind. The characteristics of this model have been at the centre of the regional crisis of 1997–8. In most of the NICs and would-be NICs, what was once strength has now become weakness. But particular contingencies in the trajectory of Singapore and Taiwan, though the result of other factors, have served to protect them from the worst of the regional contagion. Without these contingencies, Korea has suffered their full force.

Singapore, Taiwan and South Korea are all members of the genus, 'Asian industrialising/development state'. Theorising this state is clearly beyond the scope of this chapter, yet it is a topic that must be tackled. While there is an extensive literature on this subject, there is a good deal of disagreement as to how these states may be characterised, or indeed whether a single characterisation is appropriate. There is some agreement, however, on the distinctiveness of the policies and institutions of these states; where accounts differ regarding what scope there has been for state autonomy, and precisely what constraints and opportunities have been imposed by their positions in the world system and by the timing they have chosen for their programmes of rapid modernisation. It is generally accepted that the earlier examples – Korea and Singapore especially – were presented with unusual advantages by virtue of their security and market linkages with the dominant Cold War order in the Pacific. They were able to make effective use of their circumstances for a variety of reasons, including contingent historical and cultural factors.

The success and example of these systems shifted the focus of development studies from Latin America to East Asia. By the early 1980s, the experience of the Asian NICs came to be regarded as something of a model, not merely for the Asia–Pacific region but worldwide. This model was emulated by policy-makers in the next tier of Asian development states, which phenomenon encouraged at the same time financial institutions to invest in their markets on the assumption that they would exhibit a similar trajectory and present renewed possibilities for profit.

Meanwhile, the historical moment which had brought forth this model had passed, surpassed no less by democratisation within these systems than by globalisation without. Democratisation has fundamentally transformed the political character of Taiwan and South Korea over the past ten years. Nevertheless, the policies and attitudes that had served the 'trading states' of East Asia so well had become sufficiently part of the social and political fabric that they could not be readily abandoned, even in those instances where their inappropriateness was recognised.

A 'trading', 'development' or 'industrialising' state is clearly a state of a particular type. Theorising this type requires analysis more abstract than the approach usually taken, which generally rests upon a specification of the policies, institutions and international linkages of one or several of these states.[2] The position taken here will be to advance the view that many of the characteristics and policies of these states are best understood by regarding them as examples of 'enterprise association'. Enterprise association can be considered as a *purpose-governed community*. Such a community is to be distinguished from a 'civil association', which is a body of individuals governed by rules (legal, moral, conventional) that regulate their conduct *but which is not committed to any particular or identified purpose* (Oakeshott 1975; Cerny 1997).[3] 'Enterprise' is here understood as an undertaking: an actual enterprise association may pursue irrational or unattainable goals, such as racial purity or socialism. The purpose of the enterprise in this instance is the national equivalent of market share. To use Cerny's characterisation, the states in question have sought to become 'competition states'. These states sought, at least avowedly,[4] to follow a pattern of development that would lead them to become major trading entities, mastering the technologies necessary to produce ever greater numbers of manufactures of ever greater sophistication for world consumption.[5]

The (comparative) 'success' of Japan and Korea in this project suggests that it is a legitimate or at least a recognisable national strategy. As to its attractiveness or viability as a strategy, it is surely remarkable that the post-revolutionary Chinese state, having pursued with extraordinary assiduity the goal of socialism, should have exchanged this, by degrees after 1979, with the goal of market share. This exchange, indeed, was accompanied by conscious attempts to replicate the Asian NIC experience in China. But it is important to grasp both what is entailed and what is excluded by such a strategy.

First, what is entailed. Clearly there are degrees of commitment to a goal, and some societies are better at mobilising to this end than others. Yet if the goal really is accorded supreme or overriding importance, then institutions or policies will only be judged as good as their service to this end, and institutions and policies which serve other goals or are consistent with other – perhaps multifarious – purposes will not be established or fostered, or may even be abandoned or their functions abridged. A legislature, for example, will only be as good as its role in building national market share. If it does not make that end its prime business, it may find its operations sidelined (as in Korea in the period 1961–71) or subverted (as in Korea from 1972 to 1987). Civil servants may be required to be trained to sensitize themselves to their new responsibilities (as in the operations of Singapore's Political Study Centre after 1959), and if traditional bureaucratic offices do not discharge these responsibilities effectively, new agencies might be established (like the Economic Planning Council in Taiwan) to take the lead. Banks and bankers, newspapers and journalists, alike will be expected to serve the national purpose, and business, its owners and managers must serve as the shock troops and standard bearers of the nation's advance into the world market. In short, the dominant motif of an enterprise association is *managerialism*.

As to what is excluded, it follows that both those institutions and practices that do not accord with these goals, *as well as those social institutions and practices that are not defined in terms of particular ends*, will be extirpated, modified or stultified. Thus trades unions, by definition organisations devoted to the amelioration of the conditions of their members, were corporatised in the original NICs, their leaders often drafted into cabinets, with their functions to be cheerleaders for government 'productivity' campaigns and the like. Further, a space was not allowed to develop for those many human associations that can exist for both limited and also uncertain purposes. To the present, the provisions of the 'Societies Act' in Malaysia and *a fortiori* in Singapore, control and constrain most manifestations of interest aggregation and expression. The Lion City must be the only mature economy in which the prime minister's office appoints the leadership of the university students' society, and in which a government minister regulates the peak environmental pressure group, the Singapore Environment Council.

A more insidious process diverted or frustrated those practices from which no certain outcome could be expected. The rule of law is perhaps the supreme example of a practice that serves no end except to extend, interpret and maintain those rules that construct the network of obligations and rights owned or carried by one person in relation to others. This rule is indifferent to overriding national purpose as such, and may well find against an interfering or regimenting state. For this reason, neither legal personnel nor institutions were allowed to function without state interference or control in the original NICs. During the high tide of authoritarianism in Korea in the 1970s, even Justices were incarcerated when they resisted the bidding of the political leadership.

To recapitulate, the creation of an enterprise association can be seen at least as a recognisably coherent national project. But by travelling on one road, others are left untraversed. In pursuit of national market share, the Asian NICs neglected civil society, jeopardised the rule of law, stymied social debate and sought to control the flow of information across national borders. The business sphere was made reliant upon government, and bureaucracy became a political tool. The social and policy consequences of this pattern were those features most frequently identified by analysts and critics of the 'Asian model'.

Businesses were often allowed to enjoy local monopolies for particular goods or other forms of protection. Access to development finance bred habits of dependence, and rather than focus upon viable commercial strategies, enterprises pursued gigantism or the sure rewards that would come from captive markets. Further, as it appeared that businesses in receipt of such funds enjoyed a form of sovereign guarantee, foreign investors did not exercise the caution that should have been due when lending to them or engaging in joint ventures. With the supreme policy objective being market share, independent controls on financial institutions were actually discouraged, on the grounds that these would obstruct that policy. It was not the business of banks to maintain liquidity levels or control debt, but to support the national purpose. Korean banks, for example, were required to disperse a proportion of their funds in the form of 'policy loans' to exporting conglomerates. When, under international pressure, Asian financial systems began to liberalise, they did so hastily without the experience or institutions necessary for the proper scrutiny and control of those systems.

Even if these mechanisms could have functioned free of corruption, it is clear that the trajectory of these economies could only be maintained as long as external conditions held. If corruption and malfeasance developed, then funds that might have been put to productive purposes would instead be diverted for selfish ends. In this situation, the fact that the state was an enterprise association almost guaranteed that there would be very little check on such phenomena. An active civil sphere and an enquiring and independent media, both of which might have exposed and shamed corrupters, and mobilised countervailing political power, were lacking. And the legal system, which might have prescribed controls and punishments, was instead framed by and subordinated to the same national ends.[6]

The outcomes in the various systems concerned varied considerably, owing to the operation of (sometimes contingent) factors. Where the individuals in control of policy were genuinely committed to the national objective, and where they had the talent and support to envision the necessary social and economic programmes, impressive and (possibly) lasting results could be achieved.

Aside from timing and sequence, cultural and institutional limitations could deflect the avowed national purpose, or lead to attempts to combine development with personal enrichment, or the fulfilment of other policy goals. While the role of the Suharto family is illustrative of all these limitations and failings, the restraint of the Lee family in Singapore and the Chiang dynasty in Taiwan (though partly a consequence of other factors) demonstrates the full range of possible outcomes, functional and dysfunctional. Even in the Korean case, while it was Park Chung-hee's proud and truthful boast that he would die without significant property of his own, both his immediate successors Chun Doo-hwan and Roh Tae-woo became notorious for the immense sums they were able to divert to their own purposes. The emergence of *bumiputera* 'cronyism' in Malaysia, with the consequent distortion of business priorities, was the result of attempting to achieve increases in national market share while also pursuing policies with an avowed ethnic dimension (Searle 1998).

In this congeries of structural and political relations can be seen the seeds of the crisis of 1997. For the seeds to grow, of course, they had to receive nutrients, and this was in the form of indiscriminate finance and 'hot money' that flowed in ever greater quantities into the Asia–Pacific especially in the years 1993–7. To understand why this money was available is to ask another set of questions, relating mostly to the international system (The Asia Society 1998; Biers 1998; Gill 1998).[7]

Briefly, in the years in question, massive amounts of international capital, often in the form of short-term loans and portfolio investments, flowed into the Asia–Pacific economies. Rapid growth in the region, weak performance in Western Europe (outside Britain) and Japan, and the quest of international investors to diversify their portfolios following the 1995 Mexico crisis all impelled this trend. As this money encountered many limitations on foreign ownership, rather than being channelled into productive undertakings, it found its way into speculative concerns, including stock and property. The prices of the latter inflated, and deficits grew in the current accounts of many of the regional economies. In particular, short-term dollar- or yen-denominated debt accumulated far too rapidly (*Asiaweek* 1998). Cheap money sourced from Japan was often reloaned to enterprises and individuals at higher rates of return, which was a profitable operation so long as the domestic currency retained its value, permitting the original borrowers to repay interest and principal in dollars or yen.

Meanwhile in Japan, the erstwhile powerhouse of the regional economy, the investment of surplus funds in real estate had become an ingrained habit, a habit which was copied especially in Korea during the real estate boom of the 1980s. While it was recognised that real estate was not generally a productive asset, years of inflating real estate values led investors and banks to assume that it would always yield a generous return. This assumption was transferred to investments in Asia.

This system unravelled when doubts emerged that the loans advanced would be repaid. The first clear danger signals were seen with the collapse of the Hanbo conglomerate in Korea in January 1997, although because Korea had traditionally relied much less on foreign borrowings (a pattern which changed markedly following Korea's entry into the OECD) the markets were slow to apply this lesson to Southeast Asia. Once the international market began to doubt the ability of the borrowers to repay, credit disappeared and money flowed in the opposite direction. This caused exchange rates to fall, and stock prices and property values followed. The first noticeable manifestation of this syndrome occurred in Thailand. A liquidity crisis developed, and social unrest put regimes across the region under pressure. As the financial crisis became a currency crisis, falling currency values eroded the capacity of borrowers to repay their loans. Once the Thai government ceased defending the currency, the crisis spilled over to other systems, especially Korea, where institutions and policy were similarly tested by the market. The crisis had a regional dimension as much because of the inter-linkages of investments and trade between the systems as because there was a *perception* that they exhibited similar characteristics and problems.

Benedict Anderson and other commentators have been correct to point to the wider regional and global context in which the whole NIC phenomenon has been located (Anderson 1998). An estimate of the precise impact of these factors is difficult. However, the variable impact of the crisis, as can be illustrated from the Taiwan and Singapore cases, and also the varying policy responses of the systems – with Korea requiring support from the IMF, and Malaysia escaping the need for such a bailout – indicate that there has been some room for policy initiative on the part of the individual nations. At best, therefore, these factors comprise a broad context.

At this point, one generalisation can be advanced. The outcome of the crisis was the consequence of that very lack of social institutions which had once been the strength of the development state. Without civil society, trust and transparency, that is crucial institutional and policy capacity, formerly close business–government relations degenerated into corruption and malfeasance. The winds of globalisation then caused the Asian development states to falter at the next stage of their trajectory. But if this analysis of the Asian crisis is accurate, it ought to have been similarly manifest in Singapore and Taiwan. The reasons why they escaped the worst effects of the crisis will now be considered.

The contingencies of domestic political strategy

At first glance, Singapore and Taiwan exhibit both *policy* and *structural* differences when compared with Korea. Spokesmen from their governments have been quick to draw attention to the former, as proof of their good governance. While there are some grounds to such claims, the structural differences have received less attention. These have led to some insulation of these systems from the difficulties in the region, in a manner that will be described. Their existence, however, has had less to do with economic management, but a great deal more to do with the specific political characteristics of systems that, by any standard, are unusual and devoted to idiosyncratic (though not unsuccessful) national projects.

It can be readily demonstrated that both Singapore and Taiwan have been as much committed to the 'enterprise association' model as Korea or any of the other NICs in the region.[8] Both have pursued rapid growth through programmes of export-oriented industrialisation, and both have relied upon bureaucratic instruments to superintend this commitment to growth. During the high tide of the NIC model, both sought to corporatise labour and other interests, subordinate the legal process to the wider national purpose, and restrain the critical functions of the media. The leaderships of the two political systems were equally adept at depicting their environments as hostile and unforgiving, and thus representing dedication to the national purpose as necessary to survival. However, owing largely to its more compact size and higher level of development, Singapore's capacity to complete this project was greater.

Further, the means used by the Kuomintang until the mid 1980s to deter its political opponents have no parallel in Singapore, where an event analogous to the Kaohsiung incident of 1979 (as opposed to other instances of public disorder) never occurred. Thus, whereas detention without trial has been used in both systems to impede dissidents, the political murders in Taiwan and abroad which made the Kuomintang notorious and feared in the 1970s and early 1980s were unique.

Nevertheless, particular circumstances and inheritances required the modification of the typical enterprise association model in its application to

Singapore and Taiwan. Regarding the city-state, developmentalism was modified in several important ways by Singapore's circumstances.

From the beginnings of Singapore's industrialisation, the decision was taken to facilitate wherever possible the operation of TNCs in the city-state. This was done for a range of reasons. With little domestic market and limited capital of its own, Singapore's prosperity ultimately depended upon investments that would turn to good account its labour supply, along with its regional location and already established entrepôt status. In attracting TNCs the Lee government used all the familiar devices of the enterprise association model, with the Economic Development Board supervising the undertaking in the classic manner of the 'bureaucratic commanding agency' (Lim 1998). It is significant that in this development, nothing more than a subordinate status was envisioned for local capital. Lee and his associates were professionals, intellectuals and labour leaders with few organic linkages with the domestic bourgeoisie; their Fabian sympathies caused them to distrust a business sector which, in time and after modernisation had run something of its course, might in any case provide rival candidates for political power (Cotton 1995). By attracting TNCs, therefore, domestic capital was also kept in its place.

In time, as the best brains and resources of the city-state were absorbed into the bureaucracy, bureaucratic modes of problem identification and management became pervasive. When it was decided that the time had come to stimulate local entrepreneurship and overseas investment, state instrumentalities took on the tasks of financing, encouraging and organising these activities. Thus were developed the policy instruments whereby small companies can now turn to financial packages sponsored by the Productivity and Standards Board and the Economic Development Board, while businesses engaged in what are deemed sunrise industries, including computers and biotechnology, may also gain support from the National Computer Board and the National Science and Technology Board (Dolven 1998a).

Singapore's overseas investments, especially in such locations as the Singapore–Johor–Riau 'Growth Triangle' and the 'Suzhou Industrial Park/Singapore–Suzhou Township', have been orchestrated by concerted government action. In the latter, for example, government-orchestrated funds have assisted in the construction of a school and a medical clinic, along with roads, lighting and sewers, the very items that are last on the list in most other 'development' areas in China (China–Singapore Suzhou Industrial Park Development Co. Ltd 1995).[9] While most of these activities appear free from obvious corruption – though the delights of Suzhou help explain why young Singaporean trade officials are so keen to be seconded there[10] – the consequence for Singaporean capitalism has been to make its entrepreneurs much less flexible and more risk averse than their counterparts elsewhere in Southeast Asia. There are clearly some grounds for the argument that Singapore's continued growth in the last decade was the result of devoting an ever higher concentration of resources to its industries rather than achieving higher levels of human productivity (Krugman 1994; McDermott 1996).

If the state has been omnipresent, how has corruption and bureaucratic malfeasance been avoided? The People's Action Party regime recognised early that international business would not regard Singapore as a profitable field of investment without the protections for contracts, property and labour controls that were to be found in the system of law which had been bequeathed to the island by the British. The government was careful, accordingly, to retain those elements of this system which fulfilled significant commercial purposes. Only a section of the legal territory was thus quarantined. The subordination of other aspects of the law to government fiat is a commonplace of commentaries on Singapore's contemporary history, down to the dissolution of the Law Society when its leadership expressed reservations on the use of the law to muzzle political debate (Seow 1994; Tremewan 1994; Hong 1998). At the same time, it was recognised also that corruption was one of the greatest obstacles to the smooth and predictable functioning of international business in the region. Lee's leadership was especially fierce in disciplining official venality of any kind, and closeness to the regime was never any guarantee of immunity. Indeed, so successful has this aspect of the PAP programme been that presently many of the city-state's assets are guaranteed only by the *esprit de corps* of the elite Civil Service who superintend the various holding companies which own and control them. Accordingly, Vennewald points out that without Lee's commanding presence and single-minded devotion to these principles, Singapore may find that the absence of institutional checks – for example, the activities of government holding companies cannot be scrutinised in any critical sense by parliament – will be a hostage to fortune in the post-Lee era (Vennewald 1994). Already the merger of two major government instrumentalities – Singapore Technologies and Sembawang – if it had occurred in a system where there was greater transparency and where private capital was involved, might have been described as a bailout (Dolven 1998).

'Corruption', of course, is a value-laden term. There is some room for the contention that the very high salaries paid to politicians and officials in Singapore, though a preventive against the temptations of malfeasance in one sense, comprise an irregular reward in another. It is surely noteworthy that the president and prime minister receive higher salaries than their counterparts in Washington and Paris. Further, the veiled activities of the Singapore Government Investment Corporation in Myanmar, exposed in 1996 by the investigations of foreign media and the subject of energetic official rebuttals, might also entail corruption (Carey 1996). Both Lee Hsien Loong and Lee Kuan Yew serve on the executive board of the Singapore GIC, for which service they receive rewards and perquisites which are not a matter of public record. The business of the Singapore GIC is to invest the money of taxpayers, though because its conduct cannot be investigated by parliament or any independent body, the facts of this case cannot be determined.

The pattern of industrialisation in Taiwan was also influenced by local regime and political factors. Until the prospects of unification with the mainland faded in the late 1970s, the island was governed as a 'model province'. In order to ensure that they had no political rivals, and especially given the popular rising of February 1947, the KMT government acted to remove the influence of the landowning class. Their property was converted to bonds, many of which funded investments in industry. The Kuomintang then turned its attention to fostering industrialisation. Initially the government's response was to enter enterprise directly, but in the 1960s it was decided that attracting transnational capital would be a better strategy. Investment rules were liberalised, and in 1966 the Kaohsiung EPZ was established. The 'bureaucratic commanding agency' which oversaw these policies was the Council for International Economic Cooperation, from 1973 the Economic Planning Council, and from 1978 the Council for Economic Planning and Development (Wade 1990: ch. 7). This investment encouraged Taiwanese SMEs to develop linkages with US and Japanese companies as junior partners and component providers.

However, because Kuomintang rule was envisioned as 'temporary', the mainlander leadership left actual participation in commerce to others. Indeed, this division of labour may be interpreted as an implicit compact with the local population, which functioned with some effectiveness until at least the mid 1970s. The post-1949 Republic of China may be conceptualised as a superstructural imposition on Taiwan society. This feature was reinforced to the 1960s by virtue of its function as a distributor of externally derived largesse, mostly civil and military aid from the United States. Corrupt linkages with business were minimised, unlike in the Korea and Malaysia cases (Cotton and Van Leest 1996; Gomez and Jomo 1997), by the expedient of giving the ruling party direct and generous access to government funding.

The Kuomintang government's isolation from the general population of Taiwan was mirrored by its international position. The regime became committed to a policy of large and portable reserves. This reflected the experience of ruinous inflation which dealt a fatal blow to the Kuomintang's credibility on the mainland in the 1940s, in the handling of which the young Chiang Ching-kuo had a large personal responsibility, as well as the regime's longer term goals. At the same time, Taiwan was slow to open its financial system given the volatility of domestic opinion and international confidence as a consequence of the continued problem of recognition and identity that plagued 'The Republic of China'. The lack of convertibility of the NT dollar has insulated it from some of the region's troubles.

As it was such, it did not develop strong linkages with the local entrepreneurs. Its funds often came from elsewhere (China's transplanted reserves, US support), and it was content – having denied them effective political power – to concede to the Taiwan elite a key role in the business sphere provided they did not contest the mainlander monopoly of political power. Without government largesse, and in the absence of a government policy of fostering large conglomerates with special finance, Taiwan's SME sector was much stronger and more competitive.

The choice of SMEs, in addition to direct TNC participation, as the best vehicles for industrialisation had important implications for Taiwan's vulnerability to the recent regional turmoil (Wei and Christodoulou 1998). Taiwan's SMEs, being modestly capitalised, were never able to attract significant finance from abroad. Unlike many Southeast Asian businesses, they have thus not built up US$- or yen-denominated debt, the repayment of which has so crippled the Thai and Indonesian business sectors. These SMEs, being smaller, have generally been conducted upon more prudential financial bases, not being highly leveraged (like business in Korea and Indonesia) and often being supported by informal and family finance (Greenhalgh 1998). In addition, the bursting of Taipei's stock market bubble in 1989–90 made domestic and international investors more cautious, and led to a tighter regime of financial controls guaranteeing bank liquidity and restricting the size of loans made for the purposes of real estate purchase. Cautious progressive financial liberalisation was then pursued, with the opening of the bond market and parts of the banking sectors in 1991.

In the analysis of industry policy, the comparison with Korea is instructive (Tun-jen 1990). After 1961, the Park Chung-hee government fostered large conglomerates as their chosen vehicle for industrialisation. This was because Korea sought to emulate and rival Japan, while escaping the integration of Korean business into Japanese production networks that would have been the result had Korea relied upon small- and medium-sized enterprises. In complementary fashion, in many industrial sectors, barriers were placed in the way of foreign direct investment. This policy was, at best, a mixed success, and its legacy was to exacerbate the problems encountered in 1997. Taiwan escaped such a legacy. The Chiangs were not hostile to the trend towards symbiosis with Japan. The integration of Taiwanese companies into production networks dominated by Japan or, to a lesser extent, US companies is the pattern of this era (Bernard 1991). Unlike the policy-makers in Seoul, they saw no need to develop 'national' industrial champions – or foster 'national' capitalists – since their sojourn on Taiwan was only to be temporary, and in any case the business sphere was an area mostly left to native Taiwanese (and some émigré Shanghai capitalists) to dominate. Government-guaranteed finance was therefore, as a rule, unnecessary. This had the further effect that business–government–bureaucracy relations developed without the extensive personal networks and corruption encountered in Korea.

The mainlander/Kuomintang predominance in the political and governmental commanding heights left it exposed, once the failure of the original project of the party removed its longstanding rationale (Chao and Myers 1998). On the one hand, the neglect of the business area left the mainlanders without the extensive network of linkages that would have given them an alternative purchase in Taiwan society. On the other hand, under the leadership of Chiang Ching-kuo, the Kuomintang became committed to a policy of 'Taiwanisation' in an attempt – so far successful – to absorb (and even represent) the new social forces unleashed by democratisation. By the end of the 1980s, significant portions of the party had been successfully colonised by its erstwhile subjects. There was then a noticeable increase in the levels of corruption and crime, but these were dealt with – at least to some extent – through the exposure of malefactors in the media, and the classic expedient of electing members of the counter-elite to positions which made them responsible for dealing with these problems. It is no accident that the voters in Taipei City and Taoyuan County turned to the opposition DPP to remedy the decline in social order. Democracy has also led to the development of further transparency, specifically in the financial sector. In the era of KMT dominance, prior to around 1990, there were some instances of politically connected businesses receiving concessionary finance. Such 'cronyism' has now disappeared owing to the political scrutiny such measures would receive.

In the Korean case, comparable limitations upon the operation of the logic of enterprise association are hard to identify. Industrial champions were fostered to serve patriotic purposes in a contest which was played out upon an economic field. The policy instruments and business–bureaucratic links that evolved became the most important institutional features of the Korean political economy. The movement towards democratisation, which made a major breakthrough when competitive presidential elections were convened in 1987, led to the liberalisation of many spheres of life. The legal system began to develop the power and the confidence to regulate itself free of government interference, trades unionists and their leaders progressively dismantled the corporatist controls of the authoritarian era (Mo 1996), and non-government organisations emerged to occupy parts of the new civic space (Lee 1993).

Liberalisation did not have an immediate effect, however, on the economic sphere. Instead, the already strong regional and personal basis of political factionalism was given an additional fillip with the advent of the highly monetised politics of the Roh Tae-woo and Kim Young-sam administrations (Cotton and Van Leest 1996). To an extent, this was even an objective of government policy, with Roh Tae-woo channelling campaign funds to the rival democratic champions, Kim Young-sam and Kim

Dae-jung, in the confident expectation that they would compete with each other in the contest of 1987, thereby delivering him the presidential office. The policy linkages which had been one of the most important features of Korea heretofore took on a new aspect. The major conglomerates all sought to buy political influence with the new parties and representatives, and as three decades of policy had made them economic actors who dwarfed all others, they had the resources to accomplish this end. Money flowed freely, as the record now shows, with Roh Tae-woo in his time in office accumulating more than US$200 million in political funds. However, they extracted a price, in the form of contracts and especially concessionary loans. As state – that is, bureaucratic – direction of finance was a major aspect of the Korean model, this was easy to organise. Any oversight that the new democratic institutions might have exercised was deflected by political payments. With many players now crowding around the trough, and the patriotic foundations of the old policy now lost in the era of 'globalisation' (*segyehwa*), less viable operators also bought influence and were rewarded with loans.

The ineffective and divided administration struggled with *chaebol* reform and measures to introduce greater transparency into the banking and financial sectors. In the event, the reforms in the latter were the undoing of Kim Young-sam's credibility since they exposed corruption involving his own family, but not before the Hanbo conglomerate had been brought to bankruptcy, thus initiating the slide into insolvency of many of Korea's economic institutions. A measure of the dimensions of the problem can be gained through the Hanbo case. With 300 billion won of assets, Hanbo was able to borrow 5 trillion won in order to finance a new steel production facility, when there was already an excess in the national market and at a time of declining steel prices. Democratisation eventually allowed the political leadership of Korea to catch up with the need to reform the nation's political economy, but its slow response has been a costly failure (Mo and Moon 1998).

Nevertheless, if there have been important differences between Taiwan and Singapore, they have shared one major characteristic which has also had a parallel in the Korea case. While this argument should not be overextended, the impact of 'development shocks' on both systems should not be neglected (Haggard 1990). When the People's Republic of China staged extensive military manoeuvres during the 1996 presidential elections, the still contended nature of Taiwan's polity was highlighted. As of this writing, the semi-official public contacts between Taipei and Beijing initiated in 1992 have not been resumed; indeed, the 1998 official paper on China's defence policy makes it plain that China does not exclude the use of force in pursuit of the objective of 'unification' with Taiwan. It can be argued that there is a widespread awareness in Taiwan that treating the state as a private resource to be exploited will weaken a system still, in a sense, under siege from external forces. The 1998 Malaysia–Singapore railway war is only the latest instalment in a lengthy series of crises and altercations (including differences on rival accounts of their separation in 1965, port facilities, transport links, customs procedures, crime, media stereotypes, security cooperation and even water supplies) that have served to remind Singaporeans of their economic and geostrategic vulnerability. To be sure, this vulnerability has been exploited by the ruling party, but it has helped to constrain the inclination to corruption. South Korea's security anxieties, manifest most recently in the test by North Korea of what may be the prototype of a long-range three-stage missile, have been a continuous presence in Korean social and political affairs for five decades. This factor is clearly contingent, and therefore difficult to appropriate to any theoretical approach to state structure, but it has played its part in all three cases nonetheless.

Enterprise association and the outlook for Singapore, Taiwan and Korea

Even with its considerable reserves, Singapore's room for manoeuvre is small. With Japan in recession and the sharp contraction in Asian markets for US exports now having an adverse impact on the US economy, Singapore is hostage to the fortunes of the market. Taiwan is similarly placed. Taiwan's large trade surplus with China is presently the only hedge, though this may become a liability in the event of a devaluation of the renminbi. Ultimately, devaluation may be forced upon both, yet international linkages may prevent them from deriving any more than short-term benefits. The problems faced by Korea are somewhat different. In the earlier phases of the crisis, Korean competitiveness was enhanced by the sharp devaluation of the won. Later on this devaluation became yet another burden, as critical supplies and components (especially from Japan) became more expensive.

Regarding industrial strategies, the impact of the crisis is likely to lead to a reassessment right across the Asia–Pacific of the long-term viability of the particular form of enterprise association seen in the region. In some of the systems, including Korea and possibly Thailand as well, further liberalisation will be the order of the day. Yet it would be wrong to conclude that this will be the preferred path in every case. In Malaysia, the espousal of the notion that the financial crisis was largely a result of a foreign conspiracy to blight the country's progress to fully developed status – a position now explicit in the public musings of the prime minister – has already had policy and political outcomes (Wing *et al.* 1998). If widespread and even nation-threatening disorder results in Indonesia, similar consequences may follow. In Indonesia and Malaysia the penetration of foreign capital has always been regarded with some suspicion, and the extension of this attitude would have profound effects for the trajectory of both. Even in Korea, where official commitment towards liberalisation and transparency appears unequivocal, the popular roots of such commitment are shallow. It should be recalled that at the beginning of the IMF rescue mission to Korea, (then) presidential candidate Kim Dae-jung initially criticised the programme as yet another example of foreign interference, giving voice not only to his own long-held views (Dae-jung 1985), but to those of many of his countrymen. Taiwan and Singapore are the least likely to adopt major innovations in their social and economic models, given the relative success of their policies in these spheres.

It has been the argument of this essay that Singapore and Taiwan, while examples of enterprise association, have escaped a more severe dose of the regional affliction because of contingent structural features in their political economy. To adopt a severely summary view, these features have led to the incorporation of limited liberalisation in the first, and limited pluralisation in the second. Their relative good fortune may lead to an acceptance of the view that the fundamentals of their respective policies have been sound. In Korea, however, though liberalisation and pluralisation have made significant strides since 1987, until the crisis of 1997 this only had a limited effect on the nation's industrial structure and was also frustrated by the growth of corrupt money politics. The response in Korea has therefore been to pursue a radical break with the past, though the success of this departure has yet to be seen.

NOTES

1 Also interview with Jeremy S. C. Chen, Council for Economic Planning and Development, Taipei, 13 July 1998.
2 There is an extensive and ever-growing literature on this topic. Influential examples include: Deyo (1987), Gold (1986), Wade (1990), Haggard (1990) and Vogel (1991).
3 Cerny has recognised the applicability of 'enterprise association' in theorising the tasks of the modern state in the era of late modernity.
4 This qualification is important, since to some degree some of the leaders of the Southeast Asian states sought to combine this objective with kleptocracy.
5 For one of the most succinct analyses of states driven by market share, see Rosecrance (1986).
6 Other features could be added to this (illustrative) listing. It is important to note that the downside of the Asian development model was noticed long before the crisis of 1997. For examples, see Clad (1991), Yoshihara (1988) and Bello and Rosenfeld (1990).
7 The sources in the Roubini homepage are the biggest archive of relevant material (http://www.stern.nyu.edu/~nroubini/asia/AsiaHomepage.html).
8 The following points are drawn from the considerable literature on the two systems, including Gold (1986), Rodan (1989) and Rubinstein (1994).
9 It is ironic that Chinese entrepreneurship has undermined this project, with a more competitive park, the 'Suzhou New District', opening under government auspices next door. The sewers are undoubtedly inferior, but the labour is cheaper. See *Sunday Times* (1997).
10 Interview with China–Singapore Suzhou Industrial Park Development Company officials, seconded from Singapore EBD, 26 October 1995, Suzhou.

Part III

CRISIS OF OLIGARCHIC CAPITALISM

10

SURVIVING THE MELTDOWN

Liberal reform and political oligarchy in Indonesia

Richard Robison and Andrew Rosser[1]

Nowhere has the Asian economic crisis been felt with such devastating effect as in Indonesia. A massive speculative attack on the rupiah following the collapse of the Thai baht triggered a rush for dollars by domestic private sector corporations to cover their predominately short-term and unhedged foreign debts (*Asian Wall Street Journal* (hereafter *AWSJ*), 31 December 1997; *Forum Keadilan* (hereafter *FK*), 8 September 1997 and 12 January 1998). Driven in part by this rush the rupiah was to slump more than 80 per cent in value. Attempts in December 1997 to persuade creditors to roll over the private sector's short-term debts were unsuccessful and by late January it was apparent that most of Indonesia's conglomerates were technically bankrupt (*Bisnis Indonesia* 5 December 1997 and 24 January 1998; *Indonesian Observer* 26 January 1998). At the same time, the rupiah's collapse also generated a fiscal crisis for the Indonesian government. Contracting revenue sources and increasing demands for social sector subsidies meant that by mid July, 1998, the government was operating a budget deficit of 8.5 per cent of GDP, leaving it with little option but to reschedule its foreign debt commitments and seek increased amounts of foreign aid. In late July, total budgetary collapse was averted when western creditors pledged US$7.9 billion in loans and grants to the government (*AWSJ* 31 July–1 August 1998; *Jakarta Post* (hereafter *JP*), 21 July 1998).

Other problems were also to emerge. In an attempt to stem capital flight and maintain liquidity, domestic banks raised lending rates from around 15–16 per cent before the crisis to 60–65 per cent by mid 1998. This in turn contributed to a dramatic increase in non-performing loans within the country's banking system from around 9 per cent of total credit outstanding prior to the crisis to an estimated 50 per cent by mid 1998 (World Bank 1997: 128; *Infobank* July 1998; *AWSJ* 20 April 1998). Inflation was expected to reach up to 80 per cent by the end of 1998 while the number of unem-

171

ployed Indonesians at the end of February was officially estimated at 27.8 million, up from 13.1 million at the end of 1997 (*JP* 26 March 1998). The economy was expected to undergo a dramatic contraction, with most observers saying it would shrink by between 10 and 20 per cent of GDP during 1998 (World Bank 1998: 1; *Asiaweek* 17 July 1998). In early July, the Central Bureau of Statistics announced that the number of Indonesians living in poverty had surged to 79.4 million, or about 40 per cent of the population (*JP* 3 July 1998).

Even the most optimistic of neo-classical economists now suggested that it would take at least three years for the Indonesian economy to recover (Pangestu 1998). Other observers proposed that the currency crisis marked the end of Indonesia's economic miracle (Bello 1998). More important, the crisis signalled that the era of the highly centralised form of predatory capitalism that dominated Indonesia for over three decades may be at an end. Not only was the corporate underpinning and economic ascendancy of powerful politico-business families and Chinese–Indonesian corporate conglomerates shattered by the crisis, the structural transformation of Indonesian capitalism had become a fundamental objective of the IMF to be imposed within the terms of its US$41.5 billion rescue package. IMF reform packages required closure of insolvent financial institutions, elimination of government and private monopolies, reductions in tariffs and export subsidies, development of greater transparency in government and introduction of new regulatory frameworks to deal with bankruptcy and corporate governance (Camdessus 1997; Mussa and Hache 1998; Radelet and Sachs 1998: 26). For the IMF, the crisis came as a 'blessing in disguise', providing the opportunity to sweep away the distortions untouchable in good economic times (*AWSJ* 13 November 1997).

How can the Asian and – more particularly – the Indonesian financial and economic crisis be understood? Have Asian economies become functionally obsolete in the context of the new capital markets and systems of production that constitute modern global capitalism? Will the economic and social costs of maintaining dirigiste and predatory forms of capitalism become too great for the elites whose ascendancy is embedded in them? Or was the crisis one of global capital markets and not one of Asian capitalism? Can Asian leaders revive their economies without fundamental structural change through Keynesian policies of reflation and direct controls over exchange rates through capital controls or by pumping public funds into insolvent banks? Would a revival of the Japanese economy and a recovery of currency values allow the old orders to reorganise themselves and continue in the old ways?

The IMF agenda was predicated upon the neo-liberal proposition that the crisis was the product of factors inherent in 'Asian capitalism'. These included excessive government intervention and a system of crony capitalism in which 'cosy relationships with government' rather than impartial markets determined the allocation of resources (Roberts 1997; Fischer 1998a; Mussa and Hache 1998; Wolf 1998; Hughes 1998; Horsley 1997; *Australian Financial Review* (hereafter *AFR*), 27 October 1997). In such a system, it was argued, massive amounts of capital were directed into relatively unproductive investments because lenders perceived that the political connections of their local partners would effectively insulate them from losses, the so-called 'moral hazard' problem (Krugman 1998; Stone 1997). This in turn led to the deterioration of the country's economic 'fundamentals' and, in particular, higher levels of foreign debt, a burgeoning current account deficit, excessive non-performing loans and inflated property values.

In their policy prescriptions, neo-liberals embraced what Adrian Leftwich (1994: 364) has called 'the technicist fallacy' – that is, the idea that there is always an 'administrative or managerial "fix"' for development problems. Yet, the IMF agenda for change has been bitterly contested and highly political. Rather than being a frictionless process of adjustment in which rational actors seek greater economic efficiency, reform has always been a political process characterised by wrenching conflicts between competing groups within society (Chaudhry 1993). In the Indonesian case, the scramble to shape the post-crisis economic and political order has seen governments toppled and entrenched coalitions of power and interest thrown into conflict with liberal market reformers and various nationalist and populist forces. In this context, many attempts to impose 'good governance' in banking and financial systems, in legal frameworks and capital markets have floundered consistently. Quite clearly, 'rationality' in policy choice has been contingent upon and relative to complex sets of power and interest embedded in the social and political order.

Such dynamics, we argue, are best explained if markets are understood not as technical arrangements defined by a self-evident rationality but as political products defined by power and interest. Markets are not simply mechanisms for achieving rationality in terms of the efficient allocation of resources but are also instruments for constructing and allocating power (Bardhan 1989; Chaudhry 1993). Hence, neo-liberal reform is best understood, not in terms of a process of rationalisation, but in terms of the extent to which structural shifts in technology or in the organisation of production or global capital markets erode the power of entrenched social and political coalitions. Existing coalitions will resist liberalisation where their social and political ascendancy is threatened even at the cost of greater economic growth and efficiency. But the decay of entrenched regimes simply opens the door to new contests between contending social and political interests to define the rules that govern markets. They may be replaced by systems dominated by oligarchies or nationalist regimes, or by an era of disintegration in which gangsters and robber barons flourish. Because liberal markets, no less than any other systems of economic organisation, embody discrete relationships of power and interest they do not emerge naturally and by default but when structural change strengthens the social and political power of reformist coalitions.

Within the terms of this broad analytical framework, we argue that the crisis in Indonesia may be understood in the following terms. First, the origins of the currency crisis in Indonesia, as well as in Thailand and Malaysia, can be understood in terms of a shift of power from the bureaucratic elites of highly centralised state systems to new coalitions of political and business oligarchies (Hewison 1993; Anderson 1990; Gomez and Jomo 1997). As state power became harnessed to the interests of these oligarchies, former public monopolies were transferred to private hands and banking systems and capital markets were liberalised to accommodate the new private sector interests. Yet, the shift to markets produced a system in which general rules for the operation of corporate and financial activity such as bankruptcy laws, legal lending limits and capital adequacy ratios remained poorly developed and where political power and influence remained the currency of success. These were ingredients for a fatal embrace with the new global capital markets.

The new interests now enjoyed undreamt-of access to huge funds from global capital markets and flows of credit that had grown from negligible levels in the 1950s to more than US$6 trillion by the mid 1990s (Perraton *et al.* 1997: 265). These were, however, also more mobile, volatile and potentially destructive. As John Plunder has pointed out, it has become increasingly difficult to impose controls on the free flow of capital. 'Any attempt to clamp down on imprudent financial practices', he argues, 'risks driving business and jobs away to other more lightly regulated centres' (cited in Gill and Law 1988: 188). Because of the extremely mobile nature of portfolio and commercial bank investment they were liable to dramatic swings in sentiment that result in widespread panic among investors and a scramble for the exit (Eichengreen 1997: 379; Winters 1997; Radelet and Sachs 1998). In the case of Asia, a series of bank and corporate failures in South Korea and Thailand and the prospect of political instability in Indonesia set in train a dramatic reversal of capital flows (see Table 1.1 in the introductory chapter).

As the crisis struck, there developed a bitter struggle between social and economic interests to define the new economic and political institutions. While governments and international agencies attempted to organise bank recapitalisation and the closing of insolvent banks, to impose bankruptcy laws and commercial courts, corporate moguls sat tight. By defaulting on loans, refusing to participate in debt renegotiation schemes and stalling on bank recapitalisation they hoped that a revival of the currency would wipe out their debt problems without the need for structural change. At the same time, the collapse of Soeharto's New Order was to precipitate a dramatic realignment of power within Indonesia's elites and a search for a new political format within which their ascendancy might be reorganised and institutionalised. The outstanding feature of all this was the relative absence of the factors necessary for the rise of liberal markets and systems of governance defined by transparent and accountable processes. No powerful civil society or public sphere was in existence, no autonomous institutions of middle-class social and political power, no entrenched business interests independent of political patronage and favour. It is the degree to which the crisis will strengthen these forces rather than releasing populist and nationalist agendas that will be decisive in determining the future shape of Indonesian capitalism.

The origins of the crisis in Indonesia

Since the emergence of Soekarno in the late 1950s, Indonesia has been dominated by a highly centralised form of state power unmatched outside the communist world in its pervasive control of economic and social life. Within this leviathan, the authority of power-holders and officials was entrenched economically through a massive apparatus of state enterprises and trade, investment and finance regimes set within the context of nationalist economic policies. It was a system bound together by a powerful military and security apparatus and a set of organic ideologies that legitimised the *de facto* possession of the apparatus of the state by its corps of officials and denied rights to political opponents.

Despite Indonesia's re-entry into the international capitalist economy in 1965 and its opening to foreign investment, the system of state capitalism was to reach its peak only in the oil-boom years of 1973–82 when petrodollars were to fill the state coffers (Winters 1996: 120–1; Robison 1988: 58–66). Funding to the state-owned sector increased from Rp.41 billion in 1973 to Rp.592 billion in 1983 (Hill 1996: 102–3). According to one estimate, by 1980, the state controlled almost 60 per cent of the equity in all domestic investment and a further 9.2 per cent of the equity in foreign investment projects (*Tempo* 14 March 1981). At the same time, monopolies in oil and energy, commodity trade and public infrastructure together with protective trade regimes and programmes of state investment in upstream industries like steel, petrochemicals and paper allowed officials to secure control of the strategic gateways to the economy. Officials and political power-holders also exercised authority through the state banking sector, controlling the allocation of credit to particular industrial sectors and private corporate clients (MacIntyre 1994: 250–1; Hill 1996: 99–116; Pangestu 1996: 157).

By the mid 1980s this system of state capitalism had incubated a large number of highly diversified private sector conglomerates, mainly Chinese owned but increasingly involving members of the Soeharto family and other indigenous business and political interests. Protected from international competition by restrictive trade, licensing and investment policies and guaranteed privileged access to state funds and facilities, these conglomerates extended their activities from forestry and trade into the manufacturing industry, property, oil distribution and forest products (Robison 1988: 64–65; Shin 1989). Yet these giants remained excluded from an important range of potentially lucrative industries in banking, television and telecommunications, transport, electricity generation and public infrastructure that continued to be the preserve of state-owned corporations.

In the early and mid 1980s, the collapse of oil prices caused a disastrous deterioration in Indonesia's tax base and foreign earnings, producing substantial deficits in the budget and current account and reducing severely the capacity of the state to provide the engine for investment. Such developments increased the government's need to mobilise alternative sources of investment capital, new tax revenues and new non-oil industries to produce foreign earnings. As a result the government embarked on an extensive programme of reform in the following decade, abolishing public sector monopolies in trade and public infrastructure, relaxing restrictions on foreign investment and ownership, lowering trade barriers and deregulating the banking and finance sectors. The capital market was expanded, resulting in the public listing of a range of large state and private sector companies.

The reforms produced a dramatic increase in the role of the private sector in Indonesia's economy. Whereas the private sector accounted for only 51 per cent of total investment in 1980 according to World Bank estimates, by 1990 it accounted for almost 65 per cent of investment (Bhattacharya and Pangestu 1992: 7). Government projections suggest that this figure increased further to around three-quarters of total investment during Repelita VI (1993–8). While these reforms were widely applauded at the time by liberal economists in the World Bank, the IMF and other institutions, they also contained the seeds of Indonesia's present economic crisis. Deregulation created the opportunity for a sudden and extensive growth in the private sector but it was not to take the form of a flowering of business within liberal markets defined by common law and regulation. Instead, deregulation provided the mechanism whereby the new politico-business interests pushed aside the formerly dominant managers within the ministries and state corporations and seized the newly deregulated public monopolies in public utilities, road and port construction, television broadcasting and telecommunications. Public monopoly was to become private monopoly dominated by the Soeharto family and large Chinese-owned conglomerates. In several highly public struggles, a number of prominent public sector directors were removed from office in the context of disputes over allocation of trade monopolies and tenders for supply (*JP* 17 and 18 January and 10 and 12 October 1992; *Matra* 7 August 1992; *Prospek* 22 June 1992).

In the petrochemical industry, foreign investors and lenders rushed into partnership with well-connected licence holders who were guaranteed protection from foreign competitors, subsidised inputs from the state oil company, Pertamina, and the state electricity company, PLN, as well as guaranteed markets with downstream producers (Robison 1997: 54–5). Despite a growing oversupply of electricity, selected investors continued to gain licences to establish themselves in the booming power generation industry. These were able successfully to attract credit from international banks and foreign partners on the basis of guarantees that electricity would continue to be purchased in US dollars by the state power company, PLN, and that the government would accept the risks of currency falls (World Bank 1995: 71; 1996: 56; Robison 1997: 40; *FK* 29 December 1997).

While the entry of the Soeharto and associated interests into the petro-chemicals and electricity industries and into forestry, telecommunications, road building and other areas of public infrastructure was supported with large state bank loans and injections of capital from state pension funds, they also attracted large loans from international banks. Within this context, although the economy grew strongly, so too did the current account deficit, the foreign debt burden and the level of non-performing loans at state and private domestic banks (see Figures 10.1 and 10.2).

At the same time, the deterioration of these variables also reflected the inability of the technocrats to enforce much-needed regulatory reforms in the face of strong opposition from the conglomerates and politico-business families. For instance, the central bank's attempts to impose stronger legal lending limits in a bid to counter the growth in non-performing loans foundered because it was unable to enforce them adequately. Most private

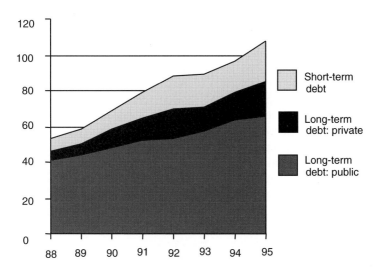

Figure 10.1 Indonesia's foreign debt, 1988–95 (US$ billions)
Source: World Bank (1997a)
Note: Figure does not include use of IMF credit

177

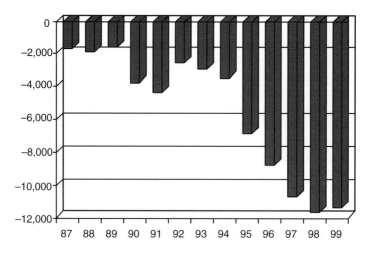

Figure 10.2 Indonesia's current account (US$ millions)
Source: Agency for Research and Development, Partai Demokrasi Indonesia, based on World Bank data
Note: Figures for 1997–9 are forecasts, not actual figures

banks totally ignored capital adequacy requirements and the legal lending limits, dispersing up to 90 per cent of their loans to companies within the same business group (*JP* 18 November 1997; *Panji Masjarakat* 19 August 1998). State banks were just as imprudent in their lending decisions, in many cases extending massive amounts of credit to well-connected borrowers for dubious projects. At the end of the day, the central bank simply lacked the political authority that was needed to tackle these problems head on.

Similarly, the technocrats' attempts to stem the growth of Indonesia's foreign debt through the establishment of a special team (Team 39 or COLT) to regulate foreign borrowings were stymied by the ability of well-connected conglomerates to circumvent the team's restrictions on private sector loans. This was clearest in the Chandra Asri case where well-connected capitalists who were behind the giant petrochemicals project were able to sidestep attempts to block their enormous overseas borrowings by reconstituting the project as a foreign investment. The technocrats' protests over this decision were met with the announcement in 1994 that the existing team, which was headed by Finance Minister Mar'ie Muhammad, would be abolished and replaced by another one under the Minister of Industry, Hartarto, and including the nationalist head of BKPM (Robison 1997: 54). Finally, in 1996–7, the government dramatically reduced the team's authority by eliminating its ceilings on private borrowings. Thereafter, the

178

team was to be restricted solely to regulating state-related foreign borrowings (World Bank 1997b: 14–15).

The crisis and the struggle over economic policy

In a desperate attempt to protect its sliding currency, the Indonesian government called in the IMF on 8 October 1997. As a *quid pro quo* for its assistance the IMF demanded a series of reforms striking at the heart of politico-business and conglomerate power. Foremost among these were the postponement of several large industrial projects, the abolition of state trading monopolies in various agricultural products, reductions in tariffs, the liquidation of insolvent banks, and the adoption of tighter fiscal measures including the removal of a range of subsidies. Other demands included the elimination of taxation privileges for the controversial national car project, the abolition of the clove trading monopoly, and the scrapping of a controversial jet aircraft project being pursued by the state-owned aircraft manufacturer, IPTN. A US$43 billion rescue package was announced on 31 October in which the government agreed to a range of measures involving fiscal austerity and trade reform although it refused to abolish the national car project, the clove monopoly or IPTN's jet aircraft project (*JP* 1 November 1997).

It was clear that Soeharto had expected the mere announcement of IMF assistance would restore confidence and avoid the need to undertake fundamental structural change. When this expectation did not eventuate, he was to prove resistant to implementing the conditions of the packages. A few days after the package was announced, it was revealed that Soeharto had reinstated fifteen large and expensive infrastructure projects previously postponed. Particularly irritating for the IMF was the fact that many of these projects were of dubious economic value. Five of them involved the construction of power plants in Java at a time when electricity on that island was already in oversupply. Business groups associated with the Soeharto family were prominent among the beneficiaries of this policy reversal (*JP* 8 November 1997; *AWSJ* 7–8 November 1997; *Far Eastern Economic Review* (hereafter *FEER*), 4 December 1997).

Strong resistance was also to emerge to the implementation of the IMF's financial sector reforms. On 1 November, the Minister of Finance, Mar'ie Muhammad, announced that sixteen ailing private domestic banks would be liquidated immediately in accordance with the IMF package. Among the banks to be closed were three partially owned by members of the Soeharto family. Soeharto's second son, Bambang Trihatmojo, responded angrily to the closure of his Bank Andromeda, accusing the finance minister of plotting against the Soeharto family and threatening to take the government to court. At the same time, the president's step-brother, Probosutejo, also refused to close his bank (*JP* 2, 5 and 6 November 1997; *AWSJ* 5 November

1997). Whilst Trihatmojo was eventually persuaded to drop his court case, it appears that he did so only because he was guaranteed that he would later be allowed to re-establish Bank Andromeda under a different name (*JP* 26 November 1997; *AWSJ* 13 November 1997). Similar efforts by Probosutejo to keep his bank alive through complicated legal manoeuvres confirmed a general view that the family still considered itself immune from demands for structural reform (*JP* 31 December 1997; *AFR* 5 January 1998; *AWSJ* 6 January 1998).

The IMF also confronted resistance to its demands for fiscal austerity. Running a budget surplus meant cutting into large state-funded projects critical to Indonesia's corporate moguls. Perhaps more important, the rapid spread of poverty in the regions and urban centres made current levels of spending on items such as food and fuel subsidies even more essential. Failure to embrace fiscal austerity in the January 1998 budget and to base its estimates on realistic predictions of currency movements was further evidence to financial markets that the Indonesian government was not serious about fiscal reform. As a consequence, the rupiah collapsed to more than 10,000 to the US dollar, driving companies with large foreign debts into technical insolvency and provoking a wave of panic buying as Indonesians attempted to stock up on commodities before inevitable price rises kicked in. By the next day, most basic food products had vanished from supermarket shelves and traditional markets. The collapse on the Jakarta Stock Exchange was just as severe. By 9 January, the market index had fallen to 340 points after having been more than 700 points six months earlier (*AFR* 8 and 10–11 January 1998; *JP* 10 and 12 January 1998; *AWSJ* 9–10 January 1998).

In a second package of reforms negotiated between the Indonesian government and the IMF in mid January, Indonesia's increasingly desperate situation allowed the latter to secure a far greater range of reform commitments than in the previous October. Among the new reforms were: greater independence for the central bank; the withdrawal of taxation privileges for the national car project; the elimination of cement, paper and plywood cartels; the withdrawal of credit privileges as well as budgetary and extra-budgetary support for IPTN; the removal of restrictions on investment in the retail sector; the introduction of revisions to the budget; the elimination of the clove monopoly; the abolition of state trading monopolies in flour, sugar, soybeans and other basic commodities; and the phased elimination of subsidies for fuel and electricity (*AFR* 16 January 1998; *AWSJ* 16–17 January 1998; *JP* 16 January 1998).

As with the first IMF package, however, it soon became clear that full implementation would continue to be frustrated by resistance from the major politico-business families and conglomerates. For instance, although the government officially abolished the plywood cartel, Apkindo, it appeared that the cartel continued to exercise authority over exporters through its control of plywood shipping. Timber companies found it difficult to operate outside and continued to pay fees and adhere to its pricing policies (*AWSJ* 10 February 1998). A range of disingenuous devices were also put in place to keep the national car project and clove monopoly alive (*AFR* 26 February 1998; *AWSJ* 24 February 1998).

By far the main concern for the IMF, however, was that the government would proceed with a controversial plan to form a currency board to manage the value of the rupiah. Despite the introduction of the second IMF package, the value of the currency continued to fall, at one point trading at around 17,000 to the US dollar. Within this context, Soeharto lashed out at currency speculators, accusing them of trying to destroy the Indonesian economy, and announced that the Indonesian government would 'soon fix a certain exchange rate' in order to bolster the currency and assist local companies with hefty foreign debts. On 11 February, the minister of finance announced that the government was 'preparing steps toward the setting up of a currency board system, including legislation to support the board' (*AFR* 11 February 1998; *Sydney Morning Herald* 12 February 1998; *AWSJ* 10 February 1998).

A currency board was attractive to a cornered Soeharto because it offered a possible way out of the dilemma without the radical structural surgery demanded by the IMF. Cynics also suggested that a currency board, even established for a short time, might also allow well-connected business groups to cover their foreign debts and Soeharto to be re-elected as president in March. Given the involvement of Soeharto's eldest daughter and prominent businessman, Peter Gontha, in arranging the visit of Professor Steve Hanke to organise the board, such observations were not without substance (*AWSJ* 10 February 1998; *AFR* 11 February 1998).

In the face of heated opposition from leading figures within the IMF, including Camdessus and Fischer (*AWSJ* 17 February 1998; *JP* 14 February 1998; *Suara Pembaruan* (hereafter *SP*) 11 March 1998), Soeharto pressed ahead with the proposal. On 17 February, he sacked the governor of the central bank, Soedradjad Djiwandono, a move many observers believed was in response to Djiwandono's opposition to the currency board proposal. In early March, Soeharto appealed to the IMF and foreign governments to help Indonesia find 'a more appropriate alternative' to the existing IMF programme. What Indonesia needed, he said, was an 'IMF Plus' programme, which, besides the IMF's reforms, would also include measures specifically designed to stabilise the rupiah, including the adoption of a currency board system (*AWSJ* 2 March 1998, 16 and 18 February 1998; *The Australian* 16 and 17 February 1998; *JP* 18 February 1998).

In response, the IMF announced on 7 March that it would delay the second US$3 billion tranche of its bailout package until a full review of the package was completed during April. On 10 March, the World Bank and the Asian Development Bank followed suit, withholding US$1 billion and US$1.5 billion respectively (*Bisnis Indonesia* 8 March 1998; *SP* 11 March

1998; *Asiaweek* 20 March 1998). By now, Soeharto was clearly in a desperate situation. On 8 March, he declared that the IMF package could not be implemented because it was 'unconstitutional'. 'The IMF package will impose a liberal economy, which is not in line with Article 33 of the Constitution', he was quoted as saying (*Straits Times* 9 March 1998). Other senior government and business figures also joined the fray. Tanri Abeng, a leading businessman and a member of Soeharto's economic advisory council, reportedly said: 'The IMF may not understand the mechanism of our economy'. And Soeharto's daughter, Siti Hardiyanti Rukmana, was quoted as saying: 'If the funds sacrifice and degrade our nation's dignity, we do not want them' (as quoted in *Asiaweek* 20 March 1998).

Forced to choose between economic disaster and political suicide, Soeharto and his associates predictably opted for the former. In selecting his new cabinet and his vice-president, Soeharto was to retreat to the most trusted and closest of his political, family and business associates. He nominated as vice-president his long-time supporter, B. J. Habibie, in spite of well-known antipathy towards him within the international finance community and in the IMF (*Green Left Weekly* 4 March 1998; *AFR* 16 February 1998). A few days later, Soeharto announced the composition of his new cabinet. Gone were the technocrats who previously had controlled such portfolios as finance and trade and industry. In their place were one of Soeharto's main business cronies, Bob Hasan, his daughter, Siti Hardiyanti Rukmana, and several family associates including Fuad Bawazier and Tanri Abeng. Hasan was given the key trade and industry portfolio, Bawazier the finance portfolio, Abeng the state enterprises portfolio, whilst Rukmana was made minister for social affairs (*FK* 6 April 1998; *The Australian* 16 March 1998; *FEER* 26 March 1998).

At the same time, the Indonesian government took advantage of a rising tide of social unrest to persuade the IMF to be more flexible in its approach. With the prices of basic commodities and unemployment rising, millions of Indonesians found it increasingly difficult to maintain their livelihoods. In a range of cities and towns – Jakarta, Bandung, Pamanukan and Ende among them – outbreaks of rioting and looting targeted ethnic Chinese. Although facilitated by military involvement, the riots were driven by long-held resentment amongst indigenous Indonesians because of their dominant economic position and suspicions that they were hoarding food and deliberately inflating prices. In addition, student groups became increasingly active, with major demonstrations in Jakarta, Bandung and Yogyakarta. Within this context, the Indonesian government claimed that the implementation of further IMF reforms – and in particular the reduction of government subsidies on basic commodities – could pose a severe threat to political and social stability in Indonesia (*AWSJ* 16 February 1998; *JP* 20 March 1998; *FEER* 26 March 1998).

A third round of negotiations between the IMF and the Indonesian government began on 17 March, confirming a more flexible approach on the part of the IMF (*AWSJ* 18 March 1998). It was to approve the Indonesian government's plan to continue subsidies on imports of basic commodities and to keep BULOG in existence (*JP* 21 March 1998). As a result of this concession, when a third IMF agreement was signed in early April, the IMF was also forced to agree to a budget deficit of 3.2 per cent of GDP (*South China Morning Post* 8 April 1998). At the same time, the IMF also retreated from its earlier warning to the Indonesian government not to take part in debt-rescheduling negotiations for fear of encouraging local companies to ask for a government bailout rather than repay their debts. In late March when the government announced that it favoured an approach similar to the 'ficorca' programme that had been used successfully in Mexico in 1995, the IMF reacted positively (*AWSJ* 25 March 1998; *Asiaweek* 10 April 1998).

However, the IMF was also able to force other concessions from the Indonesian government in this third round of negotiations. These included: divestiture of state-owned shares in six listed companies, privatisation of seven other state-owned enterprises within twelve months, an end to the allocation of monopoly privileges, the introduction of a new bankruptcy law and commercial court, and reductions in foreign ownership and trade restrictions in areas such as wholesale trade and palm oil exports (*JP* 13 April 1998; *AWSJ* 13 April 1998). Perhaps the most significant concession made by the Indonesian government, however, was the scrapping of its currency board proposal. On 20 March, the new Finance Minister, Fuad Bawazier, stated that a currency board was no longer 'feasible' in Indonesia. So, rather than pursue this option, he said, the government would begin 'studying other alternatives' (as quoted in *The Advertiser* 21 March 1998).

In general, it appeared that the government's commitment to the IMF's reforms was much stronger this time. On 22 April the government announced that it had met the first deadlines for the implementation of reforms agreed to under the third package. Most significantly, these reforms included the removal of the ban on palm oil exports and its replacement with an export tax of 40 per cent. This was the firmest indication so far that the authority of such figures as the new Minister for Trade and Industry, Bob Hasan, one of Soeharto's closest business cronies, was in eclipse. It was an impression reinforced by a declaration from Coordinating Minister for the Economy, Ginandjar, that Indonesia would 'fully adhere' to the IMF package and that the government would become increasingly transparent (*AWSJ* 15 and 23 April and 1–2 May 1998; *JP* 23 April 1998).

Such protracted struggles were to be overtaken by the fall of Soeharto on 17 May 1998. His inability to deal with the crisis had become increasingly apparent as the recession continued to deepen. Not only was he now seen by foreign investors and funds managers as the critical element in political instability and policy inaction, he had become the target for domestic critics. It was anti-Soeharto sentiment, not any coherent programme of action, that held together the student opposition and the continuing demonstrations against the government. For Indonesia's civil and military elites it became clear that his departure was a prerequisite to reviving international investor confidence and ending escalating domestic political unrest. In other words, the survival of the system of power and interest he had created over the past three decades was now contingent upon his departure. As student demonstrations became more intense and as anti-Chinese violence in Jakarta and elsewhere escalated into mass murder and widespread arson, Soeharto announced his resignation after discussions with the military commander, Wiranto, and other political leaders.

The fall of Soeharto and the reform process

Does the fall of Soeharto also signal the collapse of the New Order and the apparatus of power and interest embedded within it? At one level, many of the important political, bureaucratic and military offices in the new Habibie government continue to be staffed by the same people who ran the New Order. Most of these, including Habibie himself and Coordinating Minister for the Economy, Ginandjar Kartasasmita, have been long-time advocates of nationalist economic policies and deeply involved as economic gatekeepers presiding over the allocation of state contracts to private corporate oligarchies and close political allies of Soeharto. It is also evident that the military remains, for the time being, a central pillar of the new government, not only in terms of maintaining public order but in the context of intra-elite struggles for power. It was the military under the new armed forces commander, General Wiranto, that put an end to the riots and civil unrest. Wiranto was also to play a central role in ensuring that Habibie retained control of the state political party, Golkar, in the face of a challenge by a faction of former generals under Edi Sudradjat (*JP* 10 and 12 July 1998).

Within an intact and powerful state bureaucracy and the military there remains apprehension over the direction of change and the prospect of instability. In a recent interview, ABRI's Chief of Social and Political Affairs, Lt.-Gen. Susilo Bambang Yudoyono, reputedly the most progressive of the senior officers, claimed that a western-style multiparty democracy remained inappropriate for Indonesia (*Christian Science Monitor* 28 May 1998). The base of support for conservatism extends beyond the civil and military apparatchiks of the state. Generally well treated under the New Order, important elements within the middle classes and business are fearful of the prospect of social chaos as the regime begins to lose cohesion. Such fears have been heightened in the riots of May 1998 and the increasing activities of gangsters, often in collusion with conservative political forces, and the more recent incidents of unilateral seizure of property by peasants and urban poor (*Swa* 19 August 1998). In particular, the Chinese business community has clearly expressed its requirement for strong state protection in the wake of the May experience and the emerging proliferation of political parties with nationalist and religious agendas if they are to return and reinvest (*Panji* 19 August 1998).

Despite these continuities, the political and economic fabric that constituted Soeharto's New Order is now fundamentally and irrevocably damaged. Habibie cannot impose the same highly centralised and unchallenged system of authority that characterised Soeharto's rule. In particular, the cohesion and standing of the military has suffered. It has been embroiled in a struggle for power between the armed forces commander, Wiranto, and the army chief of staff, Prabowo, a Soeharto son-in-law and former commander of the Special Forces Regiment, Kopassus. This struggle ended in Prabowo's dismissal and an investigation into his involvement in the disappearance of critics of the New Order. A further split in the unity of the 'great ABRI family' was revealed as the manoeuvring to decide the next presidency intensified. An influential group of retired generals has formed an organisation, Barisan Nasional, which favours the emerging opposition alliance of Megawati Soekarnoputri and Abdurahman Wahid, rather than President Habibie. Most important, the role of certain military units in the anti-Chinese riots of January and May, 1998, and in the killing of students at Trisakti University has provoked calls for investigations, not only into these incidents but also into military involvement in past atrocities in Aceh, Timor, Irian Jaya and Tanjung Priok (*FK* 10 August 1998; *Asiaweek* 3 July 1998; *FEER* 20 August 1998; *SP* 18, 20 and 24 July 1998).

To an important extent, the social base of the ruling coalition is also altered. Many of the big conglomerates are now insolvent with little likelihood of returning to their previous position of dominance now that their access to privileged bank loans, forestry concessions and state contracts and licences is gone. For example, the largest of these conglomerates, that of Liem Sioe Liong, has seen its Bank Central Asia taken over by the government after panic by depositors, while his giant Indofood noodle maker, with reported debts of US$1 billion has had to suffer the removal of the wheat subsidy that was formerly at the heart of the operation (*AWSJ* 18 May and 24 August 1998). So, too, the Soeharto family has been struck a mortal blow. Not only have the family enterprises been amongst the most important corporate casualties of the crisis, the family has lost all control of political office and the influence that depends upon it, removing the keystone of the business, military, political alliance that sustained the New Order.

Important shifts are in progress within the coalitions of power and interest that had dominated Indonesia for three decades. Despite his long association with Soeharto, Habibie has much to gain politically by distancing himself from a family synonymous with the nepotism, corruption and collusion widely seen as the cause of Indonesia's current difficulties. In the reorganisation of membership of the Peoples' Consultative Assembly (MPR), and the establishment of a new Golkar Board, Soeharto family members have been removed (*Australian* 24 July 1998). Moves are under way to unravel the Soeharto family business empire. The minister of mining and energy cancelled several long-standing distributorships and other contracts for supply and transportation previously established between the state oil company, Pertamina, and companies associated with the Soeharto family. Further cuts to the estimated 120–150 contracts and insurance agreements awarded to Soeharto-related companies were in process (*JP* 2 July 1998; 1 and 3 August 1998). As the struggle to reorganise the banking sector has progressed, banks associated with Soeharto and his cronies have not been immune from attention. In fact, it has been Bank Andromeda, a joint venture between Soeharto's son, Bambang Trihatmojo, and two of the regime's leading business cronies, Prajogo Pangestu and Henry Pribadi, that has been the subject of most intense scrutiny. In September 1998, ten officials of the bank were arrested in what may prove to be the beginnings of a wider assault on the Soeharto business empire (*Kompas* 4 September 1998).

Not only is the internal composition of the ruling coalitions undergoing change, the new alliances must secure different institutional frameworks within which their interests might be secured. Habibie has little alternative but to appropriate the mantle of reformism, pre-empting more radical agendas for a fundamental dismantling of the regime and its institutions. Controls on the press have been relaxed, allowing unprecedented criticism and comment in the public arena. Proposed changes to the laws governing the formation of political parties and elections had seen the emergence of fifty-six parties by 9 August (*JP* 9 August 1998). New parliamentary elections have been scheduled for May 1999 to be followed by a presidential election in December. With the departure of Soeharto and the immediate prospect of elections, the energies of opponents of the government and leadership aspirants within it have been at least temporarily diverted from attacks on the government to the organisation of alliances and coalitions with the forthcoming election in mind.

As well, Habibie has been forced to adhere more fully to the path of reform as determined by the IMF as a consequence of the sheer weight of fiscal pressures. If Soeharto's fall demonstrated one thing it was the futility of attempting to deal with the crisis by political fiat through such instruments as a currency board or through various schemes suggested by various business leaders to abolish debt unilaterally (*Business Times Online* 15 August 1998). As the government's fiscal base has effectively collapsed, the financial support of the international community through CGI, the World Bank and the IMF has become essential to Indonesia in a way that it is not to Malaysia. As Indonesia's poor increased from 22 million to 80 million in the past year foreign sources of funding became essential to sustain fully the 8.5 per cent GDP budget deficit used primarily to fund the growing cost of food and fuel subsidies. Such subsidies expanded from Rp.12.3 trillion in January 1998 to Rp.55.47 trillion in August (*JP* 11 August 1998).

Combined with these fiscal pressures, the government is also forced to address the problems of recapitalising and reorganising a state and private corporate sector that is effectively insolvent and a banking sector weighed down by non-performing loans and unable to provide effective financial services and credit. In doing so, institutions that had been essential to the structure of power under the former Soeharto regime are threatened. The new government has begun to move against old collusive arrangements established between state officials and private interests in the use of state corporations and departments as conduits for the allocation of credit, contracts for supply and distributorships. As noted earlier, a range of Pertamina contracts are being renegotiated. Allegations by former banker and leading PDI figure, Laksamana Sukardi, of mark-ups of contracts with foreign contractors worth US$2 billion per month that reached up to 100 per cent of the original contract, provide a glimpse of the real extent of the problem (*Kompas* 1 August 1998). Similar arrangements between the airline, Garuda, and its suppliers are also being investigated and the current system of allocation of forestry concessions is under review.

Perhaps the most significant case is that of the state electricity company, PLN, which had entered contracts with twenty-six private producers, despite an oversupply of electricity in Java, most of which were highly leveraged companies associated with the Soeharto family. Under the terms of the agreements, PLN had agreed to pay for electricity in US dollars while being required to sell to domestic consumers at subsidised rates in rupiah, thereby bearing an effective differential cost of US$1.50 per kWh before the currency collapse (*Sinar* 11 August 1998). Not surprisingly, the currency collapse resulted in disaster for PLN which will announce a Rp.14 trillion (US$1 billion) loss in 1998 and expects further losses of Rp.10 trillion in 1999. It is estimated that a further Rp.117 trillion in investment is required if PLN is to become viable once again.

Most important, the government is also forced to address the problem of recapitalising the country's banks. With non-performing loans estimated to be at least 50 per cent of total outstanding credit, most Indonesian banks are now insolvent (*Infobank* July 1998). Initially addressing the question by providing cash injections eventually reaching Rp.140 trillion (US$10 billion), the government found itself owner of 70 per cent of the assets in a banking system that continued to deteriorate. Complicating the issue further was the fact that most of the banks had misrepresented their assets, meaning that their own capacity to recapitalise was less than believed. For example, the large Bank Dagang Nasional Indonesia owned by corporate tycoon Sjamsul Nursalim was revealed to have received Rp.27.6 trillion from Bank Indonesia on reported assets of Rp.33.6 trillion that proved after checking to be no more than Rp.5.8 trillion. Other banks, including the former market leader Danamon and Bank Umum Nasional, were found to have shortfalls of Rp.28.3 trillion and Rp.10.4 trillion respectively (*Panji*

Masjarakat 19 August 1998; *JP* 8 August 1998). On 21 August, the Indonesian Banking Reconstruction Agency (IBRA) announced a major shake-up of the banking industry, effectively nationalising four major private banks and freezing the operations of three others. At the same time, it also announced that four state banks would be consolidated into one large bank called Bank Mandiri (*AWSJ* 24 August 1998).

In an important sense, the problems of the banks are driven by the broader problems of corporate debt. Operating in a system without rules, large conglomerates and family business interests have amassed over US$70 billion in foreign debt, of which US$34 billion is due in 1998. Recapitalising Indonesia's private sector has become a priority. A government-sponsored agreement reached with creditors in Frankfurt provided for US$64 billion to be rescheduled over an eight-year period at an exchange rate capped by the government at Rp.13,233 (*JP* 4 August 1998). Yet such a solution offers little to most of Indonesia's cash-strapped companies. Their recapitalisation appears to rest on the introduction of bankruptcy laws that allow for debt to be converted into equity. Without such mechanisms, insolvent companies simply continue to trade and there is no means of calling in assets within the same group to facilitate the recapitalisation of individual insolvent companies. Newly promulgated bankruptcy laws that came into effect on 20 August, if effectively implemented, represent a major departure from a system where political influence and predatory relationships prevailed over regulation and law as the currency of commercial activity.

Yet, implementing such reforms presents difficulties. In the case of PLN, unilaterally cancelling the unfair contracts is not so easy. Such retrospective action threatens complications with the seventy foreign banks involved in financing the projects, potentially damaging international confidence in Indonesia. Hence, PLN director Djiteng Marsudi, who unilaterally cancelled the contract with P.T. Cikareng Listrindo, owned by Soeharto's stepbrother, Sudwikatmono, was replaced. Given that PLN simply cannot repay the loans as presently constituted, there is no other answer, in the view of Mining and Energy Minister Kuntoro Mangkusubroto, than to begin the process of renegotiation (*JP* 1 August 1998; *Indonesian Observer* 1 August 1998; *AWSJ* 31 July–1 August 1998).

In the case of the state banks, converting state ownership into equity is proving difficult. While some banks, including Liem's BCA and Nursalim's BDNI, have agreed to hand over equity in companies within the conglomerates, other banks have argued that they are unable to pay (*Kontan* 5 October 1998). Clearly, the recovery of government funds used in bailing out the troubled banks is going to be a long and inconclusive process. At the same time, dispersal of the assets is contested. Cooperatives Minister Adi Sasono has argued for such assets to be allocated to the 'poor' via the cooperative system. Some domestic businessmen are pressing for the assets to be used to bolster indigenous business (*Suara Pembaruan* 18 September 1998 and 28

August 1998). Progress in debt renegotiation also appears to be slow and inconclusive. In particular, the new bankruptcy laws and commercial courts are having little success. An initial case led by American Express Bank to recover debts against an Indonesian company was dismissed. Fears that strict application of bankruptcy provisions would delay further the return of Chinese-owned capital to Indonesia and provoke nationalist backlash against increased foreign takeovers have been expressed (*FEER* 22 October 1998).

While the crisis has indisputably affected the existing systems of power and wealth, the establishment of a liberal market economy and effective systems of public and private governance based in law remains enmeshed in a continuing process of struggle. The economic crisis has given opportunities for technocrats to implement reforms in banking and administration not possible previously, and provides the prospect for increasing foreign investment, binding Indonesia closer to the global economy and replacing the old Chinese family conglomerates. However, efforts by the World Bank and the IMF to impose by deliberate policies of technical reform, institution building, training and policy formulation from above still have little base in the existing architecture of social or political power in Indonesia or in the reality of its politics.

Indonesia's disintegrating political, economic and bureaucratic elites remain a formidable force. Under Soeharto, their power was secured by the military and by the state party, Golkar, which was used to secure majorities in parliament and form the backbone of powerful patronage systems. With the active support of the military and the bureaucracy, and the funds to dispense patronage and careers, Golkar had regularly achieved around 70 per cent of the vote. With its funding now under question and abolition of the requirement that members of the state bureaucracy and their families support Golkar in elections, its potency is diminished. Several of Golkar's founding member organisations have severed their ties with the organisation (*JP* 9 August 1998). Yet, in the attempt to stop the drift from Golkar, Habibie is being forced to go beyond its reconstitution as the party of the state bureaucracy, the military and the various regional clients formerly attached to such a system. In the reconstitution of Golkar, the regime is shifting towards the cultivation of a populist base.

A central figure in these projects is the new Cooperatives Minister, Adi Sasono, former secretary-general of the Islamic reformist association, ICMI. His reformism is both nationalist and populist. It is based on a determination to unravel the trading and distribution monopolies formerly allocated to large (mainly Chinese) conglomerates, and opening opportunities for indigenous small business and co-operatives (*JP* 11 August 1998; *Swa* 19 August 1998). As Cooperatives Minister, he has been energetic in championing subsidies and assistance to a suffering indigenous population that will be an attractive asset for a government going to elections in addition to achieving longer term ambitions in relation to changing the structure of economic and social power in Indonesia. Connected with these agendas, Sasono is a driving force behind the transformation of Golkar from a party reliant on the old state-sponsored functional groups led by former military officers to one in which the cadres more closely reflect the sorts of middle-class/propertied and Islamic attachments that characterised ICMI.

Such a shift in Golkar towards a party of social interest based on Islamic populism threatens the reconstitution of centralised state power. It does so because it potentially drives a wedge between the regime and its existing social base amongst the regional and local clients of state power and the propertied interests of Indonesia, particularly the Chinese.

What, then, of the emergence of new, secular reforming forces? While most of the newly emerged political parties claim the mantle of reform in terms of their opposition to the corruption and arbitrary repression of the Soeharto era, and their demands for the dismantling of the old monopolies and business groups, they are not parties of the free market, nor even democratic parties in the liberal sense. Ironically, the economic distress induced by the crisis has made appeals to the tough medicine of the market less attractive than policies based in economic nationalist and romantic populist sentiment and in appeals to Muslim support.[2] Liberals remain a small element within the new political parties that have emerged to contest the 1999 elections, bound together in complex alliances with nationalist and religious groupings. In this environment, democratic reform, in so far as it occurs, is most likely to take the form of money politics as in the Thai model, characterised by a highly volatile parliamentary system in which contending economic and social interests bid for the favour of parties. In some ways, this is a return to the Indonesian politics of the 1950s and is entirely within the Indonesian experience.

At the same time, the crisis has brought the very real spectre of disintegration and unravelling of state cohesion. Hence, another possibility is the descent into a political system ruled by gangs or the growth of social disturbances and chaos, a development already evident to a small degree with the increasing incidence of land seizures and overthrow of local village heads and town mayors. At another level it may result in ever-greater regional autonomy, the rise of local notables and the increasing power of local political institutions. Calls for greater autonomy in Kalimantan, Aceh and other areas are already being made and considered by the government. The Indonesian experience demonstrates the reality that the transfer of liberal markets and political systems are not technical matters that may be aided by sudden shocks to the economy which bring 'rent-seeking' elites to their senses. Liberalism is, no less than any other system, embedded in structures and relationships of social and economic power. To a large extent, the crisis in Indonesia has released the constraints upon the political and social coalitions that might sustain a liberal revolution. But with various other interests also vying to shape Indonesia's post-crisis political and economic order, it is by no means certain that these coalitions will prevail.

NOTES

1 We wish to thank Robert Roche for his research assistance in preparing this paper.
2 Of the major new parties, the mass-based organisation, Nahdatul Ulama, draws on rural Islam in Java and supports Abdurahman Wahid's Partai Kebangkitan Bangsa. At the same time, Amien Rais' new Partai Amanat Nasional appeals to the more urban Muslims and elements within the Muslim intelligentsia. Similarly, Megawati Soekarnoputri's party, PDI, exploits populist and nationalist sentiment and the nostalgia for the former president, Soekarno.

11

THAILAND'S CAPITALISM BEFORE AND AFTER THE ECONOMIC CRISIS

Kevin Hewison[1]

The Asian economic crisis came as a great shock, especially to those who saw Asia as carving out a 'new' path to capitalist development.[2] After all, the crisis had its greatest impact in some of the economies that had previously been applauded as part of the Asian economic miracle. This is particularly true of Thailand, where the crisis first struck. Indeed, in mid 1998, Prime Minister Chuan Leekpai admitted that the country was broke (*Bangkok Post* (hereafter *BP*), 19 July 1998). The social consequences of this are dire, and have led to a process of 'de-development' , in which many of the income and other gains of the 'boom' decade (1986–97) are threatened by recession.

Clearly, it is important to understand the processes at work. My intention here is to make some tentative observations about the impact of the 1997–8 crisis on the domestic capitalists, noting that the current crisis represents the most substantial restructuring of that class since the Second World War. This analysis will begin with a background to economic development for, as indicated in the introduction to this book, the historical context of political and economic power is central to understanding the current situation. This will be followed by a discussion of the crisis, its outcomes, and an attempt to assess the impact of the crisis.

Crises and Thailand's recession

Until mid 1998, when the Asian financial crisis became a recession and, then, came to look like a crisis of global capitalism, there was an emerging consensus among orthodox economists and policy-makers on the causes of the Asian crisis – exchange rate misalignments, weak financial institutions, export declines and 'moral hazard' (see Noland 1998). The emphasis placed on each of these factors varied, but the crisis was, in the words of Paul

Krugman (1998d), 'punishment for Asian sins, even if the punishment was disproportionate to the crime'. The sins were corruption, lack of transparency, collusion and cronyism.

World Bank and IMF analysis centred on two explanations of the crisis. First, so-called weak policy environments and, second, macroeconomic imbalances. These weaknesses were said to reveal that there were further 'hidden' problems in domestic political economies–governance issues. For example, Bankers Trust economist Chris Caton (1998: 1) argues that, 'Asia's ... model contained the seeds of its own destruction. Mutually supportive relationships corroded into moral hazard and corruption.' From this perspective, the crisis reaffirms the critical difference between 'right' and 'wrong' policies, and the need for sound macroeconomic management (see Shirazi 1998; Ouattara 1998).

A problem with this analysis is that it allocates considerable blame to domestic factors, while absolving international investors who chose to ignore risks when lending to Asia. There is evidence that both domestic and international investors were seduced by the longevity of the boom, forgot the risks, and believed that 'endless growth would ... bailout all errors' (Thomson 1998: 2). In Indonesia, a pre-crisis survey showed that

> many international investors were very optimistic. Bureaucratic strings, corruption, insider trading and the weak financial system did not deter investors. ... Almost all business players truly understood the weakness of the legal system, the lack of transparency in decision-making and the role of political forces. ... But there were still no signs of hesitation on the part of investors.
>
> (*Kompas Online* 22 July 1998)[3]

That is, a 'let the good times roll' mentality led the way into the crisis.

Others argue that measures put in place during the mid 1980s' downturn promoted the boom, but also had a role in the 1997–8 crisis. For example, financial deregulation and increased competition encouraged banks to search for more marginal investments, making the management of risk more complex. Meanwhile, the rapid rise in international liquidity fuelled huge lending to Asia (Bank of International Settlements 1998: 118–21). International lenders, caught up in the optimism of the boom, were unwilling to acknowledge any signs that the booms would not continue, and actually increased their lending to Thailand through 1996 and in early 1997 (Wade and Veneroso 1998: 9; Bello 1998a: 9–11).

However, explanations focusing on problems of investment and its supervision during the credit boom miss several significant issues – overexpansion, overproduction and declining earnings (Beams 1998: 3–8), and as Falkus (1998) points out for Thailand, declining real wages. The Bank of International Settlements (BIS) (1998: 33–4) notes the irony that some of the factors praised as fuelling economic and export dynamism also provoked the loss of confidence. These included the development of over-capacity in various sectors, including electronics, auto construction, electricity generation and household appliances, in a number of countries in the same markets (Caton 1998: 1; Garnaut 1998: 3). Real estate was another sector where heavy investment and speculation led to overcapacity and the financial downturn. The BIS (1998: 35–6, 117) states that overcapacity led to a 'price collapse', an erosion of 'the rates of return on new capital invested', and 'unprofitable industry capacity'.

For Thailand, Chalongphob (1998: 3) points to overinvestment in real estate and heavy industry. Others have argued that the fundamental problem was overcapacity in heavy industries (especially cement, petrochemicals and steel), and consumer goods (electronics, textiles and garments, footwear, and electrical goods). This overcapacity was mirrored in many of the Asian miracle economies (*Nation* 18 June 1998). Finance companies were the conduit for 'hot money' pouring into unproductive areas and sectors with overcapacity (US Embassy 1998: 1).

As noted in this collection's introduction, crises are normal in the capi-talist system. Sachs (1998b) has suggested that rapid development, based on huge capital flows, will *inevitably* lead to overinvestment and speculation. While Sachs sees crises resulting from irrational market behaviour, Marxists argue that crises are unavoidable, being a part of the logic and contradic-tions of capitalist production (Bottomore 1985: 11–17). Essentially, the cyclical nature of capitalist production means that there must be periodic – and often generalised – crises.[4]

Marxists also recognise that a crisis is often a starting point for a recom-position of capital and new phase of investment (Marx 1978: 264, 358). This reflects the tendency for competition between capitalists to become more intense, and for capitalists to turn on each other in times of crisis. O'Connor (1984: 28) observes that 'Crises and their aftermaths ... invariably resulted in the growth of the largest capitals through internal expansion and acquisition and merger'. Some non-Marxists agree, arguing that crises propel globalisa-tion (Sachs 1998a).

Thailand's problems are part of a global cycle of capital accumulation. This cycle has always included periods of slump and crisis. The boom emerged from the aftermath of an earlier crisis, and the country is consumed by crisis again. While domestic capital did exceptionally well during the boom, it is now suffering, and restructuring and competition will mean that the immediate victors will be international capital and some elements of Thailand's banking capital. In line with this, the IMF responds to the need to restore the profitability of capital-in-general rather than a particular national capital. Hence, much 'blame' has been directed to national govern-ment, elements of domestic capital, and their relationships. What, then, is the IMF attempting to achieve? The basic aim is to make the Asian regulatory environments more like those of the West. Why?

At the end of the 1990s, it is clear that the era of global manufacturing has arrived (see *The Economist* 20 June 1998). To be fully entrenched, global manufacturing requires open markets and an increasing homogeneity of regulatory environments. Sachs (1997a: 19–22) argues that a globalised world requires a convergence of policies. He argues that the world has to learn to operate a *rules-based* system with *shared* principles. A raft of reforms is being pushed, and the Asian crisis – like the fall of communism in eastern Europe – is an opportunity to promote these.

This is not simply a US conspiracy. Globalising capital will inevitably seek reforms that enhance their cross-border investments and profitability by providing investors with greater certainty regarding the 'rules of the game'. Global manufacturing needs global financing, and there is an attempt to 'institute a world-wide regime of capital mobility that allows easy entry and exit everywhere' (Wade and Veneroso 1998: 19–20). This requires increased international transparency through harmonised legal, accounting and disclosure standards. The IMF concurs on the need for: greater transparency; stronger banking systems; avoiding cronyism; further liberalisation of capital flows; a level playing field for the private sector; reductions in unproductive government spending; strengthening domestic and international financial systems; higher, but cost-effective, spending on health, education, the poor, unemployed and the environment; and more effective 'dialogue' with labour to prevent 'opposition' to reform (Ouattara 1998; Camdessus 1998). In the words of Henry Kissinger, 'If the definition of a revolution is fundamental change in the economic and political system ... then what we are trying to engineer in some of these countries is clearly a revolution' (cited in Beams 1998: 10).

The result of the 'revolution' and the crisis is likely to be a massive transfer of ownership from Asia to its creditors. The social costs will be enormous. But, the point is, regardless of the cost, the freeing of the market and the drive to secure profits will be given priority, requiring a sweeping aside of national rules and regulations considered restrictive to these goals (see Beams 1998: 11).

The argument here is that the Asian recession is a part of a wider crisis of world capitalism. This is a crisis of overproduction and falling profitability, but it is also a part of the consuming capitalist versus capitalist competition that is at the heart of the capitalist mode of production.[5] It is thus appropriate to examine the impact of the Asian recession on Thailand's capitalist class.

Before the crash

Thailand's economic success was well known. From the late 1980s, it was one of the world's fastest growing economies, and the darling of economists and journalists. It attracted enormous foreign investment (see Table 11.1), especially from East Asia, and the economy boomed (Jansen 1997). The boom brought rapid change. Confidence brimmed, employment opportunities grew, absolute poverty declined, wealth inequalities increased, and fabulously wealthy magnates were created.

The driving force for change was industrialisation. Academics argue that the country's industrial path has gone through two broad phases characterised by, first, import substitution industrialisation (ISI) and, second, export-oriented industrialisation (EOI).

The industrial revolution

Thailand's industrial revolution grew out of a political revolution. General Sarit Thanarat's government came to power following twin coups in 1957 and 1958. Establishing an authoritarian political system, Sarit's government, with World Bank and US support, decided to make Thailand progressive and 'civilised' (Hewison 1989: ch. 4). The private sector was pivotal, having

Table 11.1 Flows of private financial account (selected data), 1986–95 (billions of baht)

	1986	1987	1988	1989	1990	1991	1992	1993	1994	1995
Bank	−22.0	5.9	21.5	−7.7	40.8	−6.6	49.1	91.0	349.9	279.7
Commercial bank	−22.0	5.9	21.5	−7.7	40.8	−6.6	49.1	−102.2	96.4	77.2
BIBF*	–	–	–	–	–	–	–	193.2	253.4	202.4
FDI	6.9	9.0	28.0	45.7	64.7	51.4	53.7	43.8	33.2	49.7
Other loans	−3.3	−16.0	4.6	46.9	114.9	143.7	69.2	−61.2	−146.7	35.3
Portfolio investment	2.5	12.9	11.2	36.7	11.5	3.8	14.1	122.6	27.5	84.9
Equity securities	2.5	12.9	11.2	36.7	11.5	0.9	11.5	67.8	−10.3	53.6
Debt securities	–	–	–	–	–	2.9	2.6	54.8	37.8	31.3
Non-resident baht accounts	9.7	10.6	21.7	28.1	34.3	52.4	44.5	67.8	51.1	87.9
TOTAL	−9.4	22.4	95.6	152.2	279.4	262.2	237.2	260.9	301.9	523.6

Source: Chittima and Mathee (1996: 48)

* BIBF data first reported in 1993

the lead role in industrial development, with the state limited to infrastructure development.

Manufacturing expanded through incentives for foreign and domestic investment. While the export-oriented agriculture remained dominant, development plans and investment promotion laws directed resources to industry. Local manufacturers gained protection, and local business gained space to invest, free of state competition. Meanwhile, foreign manufacturers established themselves behind protective barriers (Hewison 1985: 280–1). Industrialisation was funded through foreign investment, agricultural taxation and the movement of household savings into the banking sector (Jansen 1990). Manufacturing's contribution to GDP rose significantly during the ISI period (see Figure 11.1).

Despite its success, ISI came under attack from technocrats wanting a change to EOI. However, there was resistance to dismantling ISI. In fact, under pressure from domestic capitalists, protection for import-substituting manufacturing increased through the 1970s and into the 1980s (Pasuk and Baker 1996: 144–5). It was the economic downturn in the mid 1980s that saw EOI fully established. The downturn had a substantial impact, indicating problems for manufacturing policy, and for the state's fiscal and monetary position (Hewison 1987: 61–9).

Growth predictions were the lowest for years, bankruptcies mushroomed, investment dropped, unemployment increased, and even the largest

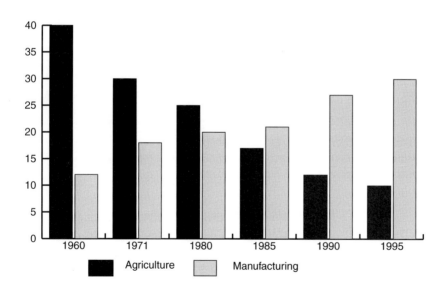

Figure 11.1 Percentage contributions to GDP, 1960–95 (selected years)
Source: Thailand Development Research Institute

companies reported flat profits or losses. The IMF was called in, implemented stabilisation and structural adjustment programmes, and urged increased liberalisation (Hewison 1987). As Pasuk and Baker (1996: 65–6) note, technocrats were unsure of the appropriate response to the downturn, and even entreaties from powerful domestic banking and textiles interests, and from the World Bank, brought few decisions. The recognition that commodity prices were not going to salvage growth brought devaluation and the fuller adoption of EOI. The devaluation immediately made Thailand's manufactured exports more attractive, especially for manufacturers from Japan and the East Asian NICs.

The results were spectacular. Exports expanded rapidly, investment rocketed, and the economy was transformed (see Figure 11.1). In 1960 agriculture accounted for almost 40 per cent of GDP, most exports, and employed the bulk of the population. However, industrial growth has seen manufactured exports expand from 1 per cent of total exports in 1960 to 80 per cent by the mid 1990s (Mingsarn 1998: 3–4). In 1960, agriculture accounted for the employment of 82 per cent of the economically active population. By 1997, just 48.4 per cent were employed in agriculture, either full or part time (Economic Section 1998: 9).

As a foreign investment boom began, the sources of foreign direct investment (FDI) changed. By 1986 Japan had become the leading investor, and the levels of net inflows from Japan increased nine-fold between 1987 and 1990 (Thailand Development Research Institute 1995: 17). The boom pulled the domestic market along. While this was especially noticeable in Bangkok, urban centres nationwide experienced an investment spurt. According to Jansen (1997), domestic savings were insufficient to finance the economic boom. However, as Pasuk and Baker (1996: 35) explain, 'Foreign investment may have sparked the boom … [but] Thai investments made it a big boom'. The huge growth of domestic investment was made possible by the liberalisation of the finance sector that allowed Thai companies to borrow from overseas banks.

Yet industrialisation brings substantial social change. By the mid 1990s Thailand, like much of Asia, was undergoing a remarkable socio-economic transformation – a capitalist revolution – but at a pace that far outstripped similar transformations in Western Europe and the United States.

Profiles of the capitalist class

One result of this transformation was the emergence of a significant domestic capitalist class. By the mid 1990s, Thailand had become an industrially oriented capitalist economy. In order to appreciate the changes brought by the crisis, it is useful to examine the contours of this class, and explain the changes that took place during the boom.

Thailand's capitalist class has had a long period of development.[6]

Capitalism emerged under the absolute monarchy, through an alliance between a diminutive, mainly Chinese, domestic capitalist class, powerful royals, and a small foreign business community. These groups cooperated in commerce, trade and in processing agricultural products, and the royal state implemented reforms – including the control of labour and the peasantry – that established the conditions for capitalist accumulation.

Early capitalist development saw many economic crises, with the Great Depression culminating in the 1932 overthrow of the royalist regime. This was the first reorganisation of the small capitalist class, as royals lost state power and had their business activities curtailed. The Second World War saw a further reorganisation as Thailand entered the war as Japan's ally, and most western businesses closed. This had a major impact on banking as Thai banks were established to provide services previously provided by western banks. The 1940s and 1950s saw steady growth of the domestic capitalist class, with strong links between business and government.

The 1960s and 1970s, at the beginning of a long period of uninterrupted growth (1958–97), saw strong private sector growth. Increases in aid and investment saw foreign investors becoming more significant. However, domestic capital was dominant, especially in the financial sector. Those capitalists who established links to political and military leaders – especially bankers – did well. Banking's extensive financing of industry saw a kind of finance capital begin to emerge (Hewison 1989: chs 7–8).

The economic downturn of the mid 1980s saw finance and banking squeezed, while overcapacity in the domestic market meant difficulties for ISI-based industrial capital. Despite problems, the owners of the big banks remained the predominant capitalists. However, the downturn saw some technocrats decide that the bankers' economic dominance was too great, and they moved to dilute the family control. Before these regulations could have a significant impact, however, changes in international competitiveness saw growth surge, and the technocrats' challenge seemed insignificant.

While foreign capital became more important during the boom, the local capitalist class expanded and diversified, with a deepening of business, especially in the provinces. Political change saw business further establish its dominance over the state (Hewison 1993). Thailand's business became increasingly internationalised, and as EOI expanded, so did the financial sector. This saw 'old' banking capital challenged by 'upstart' and aggressive business groups in media, communications, electronics, manufacturing, retailing, finance, securities (see Pasuk and Baker 1997; Handley 1997).

The challenge posed to the financial dominance of the big banks was significant.[7] The commercial banks had controlled the supply of funds to the domestic market (Jansen 1997: ch. 3). In part, the challenge emerged because the boom saw foreign investors seeking local partners. This demand went beyond the boundaries of the bank-dominated fraction. Simultaneously, changes to financial policies allowed borrowers to go beyond the domestic banks, seeking overseas loans. In addition, more foreign banks were established, and were aggressive in their lending. Merchant banking also expanded, allowing finance companies to expand, free of their reliance on the big banks; third, the long-established but small Securities Exchange of Thailand (SET) took off following the 1987 Wall Street crash. While still volatile, and something of a surrogate casino, the SET became attractive to both local and international investors.[8] It mobilised considerable capital for the private sector, loosening the grip the banks had on finance and industry.

The expansion of the SET was symbolic. For new capitalists, it was liberating, allowing a range of new companies to emerge. Handley observes that

> the new capitalists were particularly confident. These were business people who found that, for the first time, they could thumb their noses at the big banks, which they saw as part of the control apparatus of the old elite, monopolising capital. The changes in the economy allowed them to tap non-bank resources. ... This included investment funds from foreign lenders and investors, from the disposal of newly valuable assets like land, cashing in on the exports boom and, most importantly, from the SET.
>
> (Handley 1997: 98)

Many new business people saw the SET as an expression of the freewheeling spirit of capitalism and an unlimited source of funds. Manipulation was not unusual, and regulation was slack. It was this laxity which fuelled confidence and investment. Handley (1997) shows that fluctuations of the SET index became a barometer of government performance. It was felt that the SET should be 'loose', and the state facilitated this. Regulatory interventions were rare, unwelcome and were denounced as the 'bureaucratic elite trying to prevent the new generation from enriching itself' (Handley 1997: 104–5).

Banking and industry, while still significant, were no longer the areas where the dominant capitalist groups were concentrated. The broader financial sector, telecommunications, real estate, tourism and a range of services produced remarkably wealthy capitalist groups (Pasuk and Baker 1996: ch. 3). Huge profits were made, and while much was reinvested, consumption also increased in the late 1980s and early 1990s, expanding the domestic market.

The accumulation regime of the ISI era saw a small capitalist group develop, bolstered through close relationships to officials. The growth of the EOI period and the internationalisation of the economy disrupted this. The expansion of electoral politics, where success depended on access to massive funding, saw business and elected politicians establishing relationships that were at the centre of Thailand's pre-crash expansion and euphoria.

The crash

It should be remembered that almost everyone praised Thailand's boom before the crash. IMF Managing Director Michel Camdessus (1998: 1) opined that, 'We have all admired the "Asian miracle" based on saving, prudent fiscal policies, investment in physical and human capital, and ... liberalization and opening up'. The World Bank observed that Thailand provided 'an excellent example of the dividends to be obtained through outward orientation, receptivity to foreign investment, and market-friendly philosophy backed up by conservative macro-economic management and cautious external borrowing policies' (cited in Bello 1998a: 12). Not only orthodox economists were excited by the changes in Thailand. Public intellectuals like Chai-Anan Samudavanija (1997) argued that the forces of globalisation were unstoppable, and that they would sweep aside much that was anachronistic in Thailand's economy, society and politics. So the crash, when it came, was all the more shocking.

The crash unfolds

That something had gone wrong with the success story was signalled by the Bank of Thailand's (BoT) expensive and ill-fated venture to shore up the baht in mid 1997 (see US Embassy 1998: 1; Bangkok Post 1998). With hindsight, the confidence that the boom would continue appears naïve, yet even when the crisis had begun, there was disbelief. For example, the BoT (1997: 5) referred to the first nine months of 1997 as 'subdued', and used words such as 'slowdown', and claimed 'substantial gain[s] on the stability fronts'. A few weeks later, the Bank's annual report was forced to concede 'severe difficulties', 'unproductive and speculative investment', and a 'sharp economic slowdown' (BoT 1997a: 5–6).

The baht crisis began with a series of speculative attacks on the currency in 1995. While the BoT's efforts to protect the baht were initially successful, speculators moved in when the BoT was seen to be maintaining the peg. Concerted attacks in May and June 1997 depleted official reserves from about $38 billion to just $2.8 billion by the 2 July float of the baht (Chalongphob 1998: 3–4, 8; BIS 1998: 136). The result was that by August 1997 the government had no choice but to go to the IMF. The 'alternative was total collapse' (US Embassy 1998: 3).

The boom had coincided with Thailand's increased attractiveness to Japanese investors after the 1984 baht devaluation. While the crisis might be seen to have begun because the baht was pegged to the dollar, it simultaneously became overvalued against the yen (Chalongphob 1998: 3). When combined with the competitive impact of Chinese devaluations in 1990 and 1994 (Wade and Veneroso 1998: 10), this became more than simply a financial crisis. There is a deeper economic malaise. Some of this was reflected in the SET, where price/earnings ratios peaked in 1993 (BIS 1998: 122). The significant declines that followed suggest that investors were already factoring in lower returns. Other problems were also evident: increasing debt in the private sector and related unproductive investment, and contracting domestic and international demand. The problem was that few took notice of such changes when the economy was apparently humming.

Thailand's external debt had grown to more than $70 billion (about 38 per cent of GDP) by the time of the crisis, with more than half borrowed from Japanese institutions. Almost all was in the private sector, and about two-thirds of it was of less than one-year maturity (Caton 1998: 5; IMF 1997: 7). European banks had lent $19.2 billion, and US banks just $5 billion. Much of this lending had been for productive activity. However, the length of the boom also encouraged investment in conspicuous consumption and unproductive areas such as real estate. Property had been highly profitable and was a convenient investment for borrowers and lenders alike, for as asset prices rose, borrowing continued, because banks remained willing to lend as the value of their collateral kept rising (BIS 1998: 120).

There was a concentration of investment in property, banking and finance, with up to 70 per cent of the SET's capitalisation in these sectors (Nuntawan 1997). This led to overproduction in residential and commercial property. In 1996, the unsold stock of property units amounted to $20 billion, and about half of annual GDP growth was in the property and construction sector. Some suggested that half of all investment was property related. By early 1997, the sector was fragile, and when Somprasong Land and Finance One collapsed, 50 per cent of loans to property developers – up to $32 million – were non-performing (Bello 1998a: 12–13; 1998c).

An earlier warning regarding the fragile finance sector was the late 1995 crash of the struggling Bangkok Bank of Commerce (BBC). The trigger for this collapse was undercollateralised loans, many to influential politicians 'to allow investment in stocks and land, which were then leveraged for further loans' (Handley 1997: 108–9). The BoT took over BBC in early 1996, putting up an estimated 100 billion baht in a bailout (US Embassy 1998: 3). Rescuing BBC did not, however, result in action against corrupt owners and managers. Handley (1997: 108–9) argues that this may have been related to alleged credit from the BBC to BoT managers, and to the Chart Thai Party's successful 1995 election campaign. Even so confidence had been dented. In the first half of 1997 there were several runs on finance company deposits, and the authorities pumped huge amounts into these companies. In fact, these companies were already insolvent (Chalongphob 1998: 4). When this was realised, investor confidence crashed.

The proposed rescue vehicle was the government's Financial Institutions Development Fund (FIDF), established in 1985 to bail out troubled financial institutions. When fifty-six finance companies were closed in mid 1997, the FIDF was their largest creditor, having extended them about 430 billion baht. In August 1997, the government announced that the FIDF would guarantee the deposits and liabilities of all financial institutions (Economic Section 1998: 7). By early 1998 the FIDF had committed 800 billion baht to struggling financial institutions, and it was estimated that 1.1 trillion baht would be required (US Embassy 1998: 3). When the crisis bit, as foreign investors shifted their funds, residents with unhedged foreign liabilities rushed to cover them, putting tremendous pressure on the baht (see BIS 1998: 128; *The Economist* 20 June 1998).

Given that the contraction of the economy has been spectacular – estimates are for negative rates of up to 9 per cent (*BP* 28 July 1998) – it is significant that the economic crisis has seen no military intervention. There has been political instability, a change of government from the bumbling Chavalit Yongchaiyudh's New-Aspiration-led coalition to that led by Chuan Leekpai's Democrat Party, and a reshuffle of the Chuan coalition in October 1998. However, this has all been through constitutional means. There were demonstrations against Chavalit, led by business and middle-class groups, but the military stayed in their barracks.

Recession and the capitalist class

While no detailed analysis of the impact of the crisis on the capitalist class is yet possible – the outcomes are still being determined – it is clear that the pre-crisis structure, and wealth, of the class has been devastated. Individual firms and business empires have been crushed.

The crisis is a significant moment in a competitive reorganisation of banking capital that began during the boom. A number of banks, and the families who controlled them, had found it difficult to recover from internal conflicts and competitive pressures in the 1980s. They included Siam City Bank (Mahadamrongkul family), First Bangkok City Bank (Tejapaibul family) and the Union Bank of Bangkok (Cholvicharn and Penchart families). The BBC (Jalichandra family) collapsed in 1995. At the same time, the boom demonstrated the competitive disadvantages faced by family-based banks, acting as family treasuries and investment brokers, in the era of globalised finance. The Laemthong Bank (Chansrichawla family), Nakornthon (Wanglee family) and the Bank of Asia (Phatraprasit and Euachukiarti families),[9] for example, were all revealed to be weak when the crisis hit (*Nation* 13 August 1998).

The crisis brought more change to the banking sector than a decade of government efforts to dilute the power of the families and restructure the small banks. The Bangkok Metropolitan Bank (BMB), First Bangkok City, Siam City and the BBC have been nationalised. The Tejapaibul family stake in BMB was lost, and the family was found to owe the bank 4.42 billion baht (*BP* 9 April 1998). Three banks (Thai Dhanu, Laemthong and Bank of Asia) sold majority stakes to interests in Singapore, Kuwait, Hong Kong and the Netherlands (*BP* 1998). The Ratanarak family sold 25 per cent of its Siam City Cement to Swiss investors in order to support its holdings in the Bank of Ayudhya (*BP* 12 August 1998). Siam Commercial, a conservative bank with a large Crown Property Bureau (CPB) shareholding, also became 49 per cent foreign owned – mainly by Japanese interests – as it raised 34 billion baht. Shareholders were to forgo dividends for a number of years. The CPB pledged to maintain its holdings and to keep the bank in Thai hands (*BP* 30 May 1998). Essentially, this amounts to a bailing out of the CPB. Ratings agencies responded to the bank's unwillingness to bring in more outsiders by downgrading its rating (*Nation* 8 October 1998).

Thailand's biggest commercial banks, the Bangkok and Thai Farmers, were able to raise new capital quickly, but this meant moving to 49 per cent foreign ownership. Both banks have long had strong international connections, especially with US investment banks (*Nation* 13 August 1998). The shareholdings of the powerful Lamsam (Thai Farmers Bank) and Sophonpanich (Bangkok Bank) families had already been diluted during the 1980s, but these families have been able to maintain management control.

However, a number of smaller banks failed to attract new capital, as required by the BoT (*Nation* 7 July 1998). Coupled with this, banks announced record losses of 155 billion baht for the first half of 1998. The liquidation of fifty-six finance companies and the government takeover of four banks wiped out about one-third of the financial system. The remaining finance companies reported first-half losses of 48 billion baht (*Nation* 2 October 1998). By mid 1998, Moody's had downgraded the financial strength rating for Thai banks to below E+, the level of Mexican and Pakistani banks (*BP* 12 June 1998). Non-performing loans at the nationalised banks ranged from 30 to 55 per cent (*Nation* 16 July 1998), and even the strongest banks were affected, with the Bangkok and Thai Farmers rates estimated at 40–44 and 38 per cent respectively (*BP* 19 August 1998). Non-performing loans were valued at over 1.78 trillion baht, with $20 billion required for recapitalisation (*BP* 23 September 1998). When the dust settles, only four of the fifteen commercial banks – Bangkok, Thai Farmers, Krung Thai and Siam Commercial – are likely to remain in majority Thai ownership (*BP* 24 June 1998).

On the fringes of big banking capital, the rout has been devastating. Only a handful of finance and securities companies are likely to survive (*BP* 1998). The insurance industry experienced its worst result for five decades (Charoen and Walailak 1997). Foreign buyers have been active in these sectors (*Nation* 7 October 1998).

In industry, restructuring will also be significant. One of the stars of Thailand's corporate capitalism has been the Charoen Pokphand (CP) group. CP is a giant in Thailand, and has 280 subsidiaries in sixteen countries (Bangkok Post 1997). CP's management was considered conservative, and the group was not expected to suffer too much from the crisis. However, it was found to have cash flow problems, with up to $1 billion in offshore debt, much of it unhedged and short term. Five of its six listed companies reported 28 billion baht in 1997 losses (Bangkok Post 1998). Massive restructuring got under way, and foreign investors were sought (*BP* 13 and 19 May, 9 June 1998).

Another giant industrial corporation, the Siam Cement Group (SCG), also known for its conservative management, was found to have $4.2 billion in foreign loans, three-quarters of them short term, and mostly unhedged. About 60 per cent was owed to Japanese institutions. The crisis caused SCG to sell overseas assets and shelve a large number of proposed projects. Recapitalisation has been difficult for SCG because the group's major share-holder, the CPB, would have been adversely affected (Bangkok Post 1997).

More broadly, industrial investment has crashed, with up to 400 billion baht in approved investment cancelled or delayed by the end of 1997. Domestic demand plunged. All manufacturers appeared to be struggling, with overcapacity in many sectors. There have been contractions of 80 per cent in auto parts, 50 per cent in construction materials and 40 per cent in electrical appliances (*BP* 25 September 1998). Profits in telecommunications plummeted, with only two of the eleven major firms being profitable in 1997 (Vivat 1997: 3). Majority stakes in a range of the giant Metro Group's companies were being offered to foreign investors to offset a 16 billion baht debt (*Nation* 4 October 1998). One of the country's biggest textiles plants, Thai Melon, closed, laying off 8,000 workers (*Nation* 17 July 1998). Survival became the aim as bankruptcies doubled in early 1998, with some 5,000 companies closing by June 1998, and hundreds more were expected to follow (*Nation* and *BP* 21 July 1998).

Retailers also faced serious problems as local demand dropped. Daimaru, the pioneering Japanese department store, sold its 26 per cent stake in Thai Daimaru, established in 1964, expecting a loss of more than 1.75 billion baht (*BP* 26 June 1998). The country's largest retailer, the Central Group, sold stakes in subsidiaries to foreigners (*Nation* 1 September 1998). Robinson Department Stores, with 1996 sales of 10.8 billion baht, suspended its loan repayments in June 1998, with more than $200 million in outstanding loans (*BP* 11 June 1998).

Land developers, the first to be affected by the downturn, have fared particularly badly. For example, the Kanjanapat family's Bangkok Land, once the most prominent developer, reported losses of almost 18 billion baht and debts of almost 45 billion baht (*Nation* 7 October 1998).

On top of corporate collapse, unemployment is expected to top 2 million by 1999 (*BP* 25 September 1998). Thus, in addition to the obvious economic problems faced, there are also significant political implications that will shape attempts to manage the crisis.

Responses to the crisis

After dithering by the Chavalit government, the Chuan government announced its 'full commitment' to the IMF's economic programme. In its November 1997 Letter of Intent to the IMF, the Chuan government announced that it would 'strengthen the policy package' (Thailand 1997). However, domestic, populist opposition to the IMF programme has emerged. The government has adopted a dual-track political strategy, keeping the IMF satisfied while deflecting local criticism.

The IMF approach has emphasised the restoration of confidence through: tight monetary policy; restructuring the financial system; deepening the role of the private sector; a return to international capital and finance markets; and a social safety net (Thailand 1997: 1; 1998: 1). The IMF argued that restoring confidence required 'deepening the external openness ... and *increasing* foreign direct investment flows' (Thailand 1998a: 4). While admitting the difficulties associated with the programme, the Thai government has accepted the IMF medicine.

The government has been careful to satisfy the IMF and its western supporters, despite local criticism. Foreign Minister Surin Pitsuwan explained the Thai position (in *Thai-Oz News* 30 July–11 August 1998: 11). He admits mistakes, a lack of discipline, and a failure to maintain balanced growth. The task, he says, is to 'win the trust and confidence of the international business community', adding that this requires international standard regulations and a transformation of corporate governance. The aim is to make international business 'more comfortable' and to have rules 'acceptable to international investors'.

Finance Minister Tarrin Nimmanhaeminda has repeatedly stated that the government will do all that is required to get foreign investors back. This includes addressing long-standing complaints from foreign investors regarding: alien business laws; customs duties, taxes and procedures; privatisation; and transparency, deregulation and an end to corruption (*BP* 18 June and 1 August 1998). The US Embassy believed that, despite 'resistance from indigenous business and political interests', the crisis will move the government to adjust its 'legal and regulatory regime with the objective of creating a more competitive climate for foreign investment' (Economic Section 1998: 1).

While the government's approach has received significant support, this has not been universal. Much has been made of the fact that domestic 'culprits' for the crisis were not being held responsible, while innocent bystanders are paying a heavy economic price. Prime Minister Chuan has been compared with the captain of the *Titanic*, allowing only first-class passengers into the lifeboats (*Nation* 8 June 1998). While Chuan agrees that 'the real problem did not originate from the poor or working classes', he argues that the impact of the crisis will be on 'all sectors of society' (*Time* 23 March 1998).

He has argued that 'we must prove to the world that, despite their occasional problems and pitfalls, free trade and market liberalisation remain the most effective and efficient means of ensuring ... sustained growth' (*BP* 4 April 1998). The government has relied on the World Bank and Asian Development Bank for its 'safety net' support (Thailand 1998a). While the Fifth IMF Letter of Intent (Thailand 1998b) put more emphasis on welfare, the government has socialised some private sector debt.

While there have been charges laid against some of the culprits (see *BP* 21 and 22 August 1998; *Nation* 3 September 1998), there are also examples of bailouts. FIDF support of Finance One, which at one time had 102 billion baht in assets, and was the first finance company to collapse, required 40 billion baht of public funding (Nuntawan 1997: 3). At the same time, Finance One executives reportedly sold 455 million baht of shares and warrants during the second half of 1996 (*BP* 12 June 1998). In order to avoid panic in 1998, the BoT announced measures to support the Union Asia finance company. The Bangkok Bank was the principal shareholder, but was reluctant or unable to provide additional capital. The BoT, having already guaranteed all depositors and creditors, intervened to 'avoid additional burden' for the banks (*BP* 15 May 1998). This occurred when action was mounted against the Bangkok Bank's Sophonpanich family, for insider trading over Union Asia (*BP* 12 June 1998).

The socialisation of debt and the relationship between big business and the state has been most clearly demonstrated in the bailout of the banks. Following the huge bank losses announced in mid 1998, foreign analysts predicted another financial crisis, with more banks to go (see *BP* and *Nation* 22 July–1 August 1998). The major bank shareholders would not or could not raise further capital, and were also refusing to allow any further dilution of their shareholdings.

Foreign investors had been buying up cheap assets in the financial sector. For example, foreign firms took control of the securities industry (*Nation* 3 August 1998). So powerful was the position of foreign capital that it could demand exactly the government guarantees that it identified as having contributed to the crisis. One bank, considering a stake in the Nakornthon Bank, demanded that the BoT protect it against any unforeseen circumstances. The BoT initially agreed because such measures were considered necessary to attract investors (*BP* 29 July 1998).

However, these demands appear to have played a part in the launch of the government's bank rescue – the alternatives were to guarantee foreigners or save local bank shareholders. As the editor of the *Bangkok Post* (17 August 1998) observed, 'there was no other choice' but to support the local bank investors. With representatives of banking capital calling for action, the government's rescue plan was announced on 14 August (Ministry of Finance 1998). Chuan stated that the rescue was in the public interest, regardless of cost or political consequences. Explaining that the survival of the entire banking system was at stake, Chuan argued that this was 'not to help capitalists', but to rescue the institutions. The cost of the bailout is estimated to be at least 1.5 trillion baht or 30 per cent of GDP (*Nation* 10 August 1998).

This approach is not surprising, being in line with previous government approaches to financial crises (see Warr and Bhanuphong 1996: 41–2), although the scale of this bailout is beyond anything contemplated in the past. Further, while there has been a love–hate relationship between government and the big banks, the government has generally protected them. Indeed, one commentator has observed that the bailout represents a further victory for 'vested interests' (*BP* 19 August 1998), and press reports indicate that 'crony' deals continue in the finance sector (see *Nation* 29 August 1998). It is likely that the bailout will privilege the biggest and best-connected banks – Bangkok, Thai Farmers, Thai Military and Siam Commercial – and foreign investors.

A surprising aspect of this action, however, has been the political impact. Some of those who had opposed the IMF package saw the bank rescue as a victory for proposed alternative approaches to the crisis and a step away from the IMF. This populist perspective is misconceived, for the government had few alternatives, and the package was reasonably congruent with the revised line developed between the government, the IMF and the World Bank.

This is not to say that the alternative views on the crisis are unimportant. Many see the crisis as revealing fundamental weaknesses in the country's development and social and political make-up. Social critic Nidhi Aeusrivongse has observed that the 'fundamental reasons for Thailand's ... crisis are its shaky social foundations, misplaced development policies – which put economic growth before human resource development – and skewed distribution of wealth' (cited in Gill 1998). A Forum of the Poor spokesman has argued that the IMF–Chuan government approach is a form of slavery (*BP* 7 October 1998), and the Forum has demanded that the IMF protect the poor, with assistance based on principles of 'social justice, morals, sustainable society, global concern and equality' (*Watershed* 1998, 3(2): 21).

There is a search for alternatives. This has included campaigns to raise local funds to buy state enterprises, attacks on the United States for insisting on the forfeit of a deposit for fighters not taken by the armed forces, and 'patriotic movements' to save the country through, among other things, 'buying Thai', collecting gold and foreign exchange donations from citizens, a return to agriculture, and demanding Thai solutions rather than those of the West. Others see the crisis as an opportunity. Pasuk (1998: 23) argues that the ... crisis is a great opportunity for rural people to be left alone to think up their own sustainable solutions to ... the problems that they now face. In this sense, it presents a huge opportunity for the growth of local community groups, and for them to push forward debates about local democracy and participation.

Bello (1998a; 1998c) and many Thai academics argue that neo-liberal approaches are the root cause of the crisis, enhancing the dominance of international capital. Bello calls for more control over financial markets, the establishment of the centrality of the domestic market, 'selective globalisation', progressive taxation, equity, ecological sustainability, self-reliance and democratic control over capital. He sees this control lodged in democratic decision making by communities, civic organisations and people's movements. This approach draws considerable support from NGOs and populist groups, many of whom have called for a rejection of 'foreign approaches' (*BP* 12 July 1998).

Some Thai NGOs promote crude populist solutions. For example, Project for Ecological Recovery Director Srisuwan Kuankachorn (1998) argues that macroeconomic management is not the problem, but the model of development chosen – 'rapid, large-scale development, ... totally dependent on foreign capital, is wrong.' The United States, during the Cold War, foisted this model on Thailand. Those who studied in the United States, 'mostly members of the Thai elite and high-level technocrats, were brainwashed,' and willingly implemented the US model. The 'trickle-down' approach meant natural resource destruction, with few benefits to the majority. The IMF reinforces this model, at the expense of people, families and communities. It is 'local and foreign corporations, the media, and the IMF and World Bank ... [who] have changed the cultural values of the people in society'. It is these consumerist values that must be challenged.

Populism is a common response to industrialisation and to the vagaries of the capitalist market. But it is limited politically because it is a reaction. Pollack (1962: 2–3) observes that 'agrarians often aligned with conservative groups in the vain attempt to turn back history. ... Whether radical or conservative, agrarianism ... takes on the shape of a retrogressive social force'. In Thailand, populist reaction is to industrialisation, the triumphalism of the capitalist boom, and the glorification of globalisation this involved. But Thailand's populism has yet to wrench itself free of the issues which have bedevilled populist politics everywhere: it sees conspiracies, it is reactionary, romantic, anti-urban, and includes an intolerance of outsiders (see Unger 1964). Populists offer a political response to the irrationality and exploitation of the market, but do not offer a viable economic solution. Even so, the political impact of such responses to the crisis should not be overlooked.

Conclusion

In seeking 'culprits' for the collapse, an accusing finger can indeed be pointed at central bankers, bureaucrats, poor policy, and the like, but the fact remains that those responsible for the crisis are domestic *and* international capitalists. There is no escaping this conclusion. It is these groups who, for a variety of reasons – greed, overconfidence, ignorance, competition – made bad investment decisions. However, the fact that they have done this is a normal element of capitalist development, national and global. Thailand's crisis is a part of a global process of capital accumulation and cycles of crisis. In the Introduction, Beeson and Robison provide a useful approach to markets, as relations of power and interest, and involving political struggle. In the context of this crisis, the real struggle is not so much political as economic. Corporations – in fact, all capital in the globalised capitalist system – produce and invest themselves into a crisis of overproduction, speculation and boom. The inevitable crisis rearranges the architecture of capital. While domestic capital did well from the boom, it is now restructuring, and there will be some winners and many losers. The immediate victors will be expanding international capital and elements of Thailand's banking capital.

Outdated political and social arrangements must also be transformed, and this will inevitably involve political struggle. As the Introduction notes, this struggle may result in a range of political outcomes, not all of which will be capital enhancing (and populism may have its day). States and the ability to influence them will continue to matter, especially as capitalists realign in the aftermath of the crisis.

NOTES

1   Earlier versions of this paper were presented at the Asia Research Centre's Workshop on the economic crisis in Asia and at the 12th Conference of the Asian Studies Association of Australia, University of New South Wales, September 1998. The paper has benefited from conversations and criticisms from Andrew Brown, Paul Healy, Pasuk Phongpaichit, Malcolm Falkus and Dick Robison. The financial support of the Asia Research Centre is gratefully acknowledged.

2   Thailand does not easily fit the East Asian 'model'. The contradictions between the Thailand country paper for the *Miracles* report (Christensen *et al.* 1993) and the *Miracles* (World Bank 1993) report itself indicate this. Suggestions that there is a singular East Asian capitalism should be rejected. While *The Economist* (1998c: 7) is correct to note significant diversity, the 'biggest myth of all is that of a single Asian economic model. These economies differ hugely', capitalism now dominates almost everywhere, and every capitalist economy will have commonalities. But each capitalism emerges in particular social and historical contexts, meaning that there cannot be a single path to capitalist development, politically or economically (Hewison 1989: 214).

3   A translation of this report is provided by the electronic list, Forum on Labor in the Global Economy *LABOR-L*

4   Many of Marx's observations show that little has changed in 150 years. Marx emphasised the 'ten-year cycle of modern industry' and 'distortions and overcapacity' during booms (Bottomore 1985: 11–12). He saw nineteenth-century crises as international, and involving contagion (Marx 1978a: 623). Speculation during the boom following the 1843 Opium War showed the frenzy of speculation that develops in such periods. Marx (1978a: 533–5, 618) also pointed to 'boundless fraud' in the East Indian trade as having much to do with the 1847 crisis, and observed that 'the entire world of commerce [was provoked] into meeting the outbreak of a crisis by putting aside a reserve stock of banknotes, thereby accelerating and intensifying the crisis' (Marx 1978a: 689).

5   For details regarding the global nature of the crisis, see Tabb (1998).

6   For details see Krirkkiat (1983), Suehiro (1989) and Hewison (1989).

7   Big bankers did not oppose the direction of the boom, and did well from it (Pasuk and Baker 1996: 38).

8   By 1995, foreign investors became net buyers on the SET, and Thais net sellers (Bello 1998a: 12).

9   For information on these banks and families at the beginning of the 1980s, see Hewison (1989: ch. 8).

12

ECONOMIC NATIONALISM AND ITS DISCONTENTS

Malaysian political economy after July 1997*

Khoo Boo Teik

There was no miracle, just sheer hard work and doing the right thing. A miracle is something that comes from heaven. What we did was build up the economy, create wealth through the right policies, the right incentives, the right direction of development. And why is it that suddenly it seems to have disappeared? It has not disappeared; it is still there. The sad thing is that now we have some power which stops us from doing what we have been doing all the time, which created all this very real growth and development.

(Mahathir Mohamad, in *Asiaweek* 27 March 1998)

The markets also want Malaysia to recognize that Asia's old, government-directed economic model no longer works. The country needs to open the banking sector to foreign investments, bring bankruptcy laws and accounting practices up to international standards and improve corporate governance. All of these moves would help bring back foreign investment.

(Christine Hill 1998: 71)

The economists, by dint of their refusal to see that economic choices are practicable only if the political and social compromises that they imply are acceptable, are encouraging a utopian economism.

(Samir Amin 1993: 7)

Introduction

In the aftermath of the currency crisis which began in July 1997, and laid prostrate several Asian economies, foreign observers made much of Dr Mahathir Mohamad's 'anti-western vociferations'. But mainstream western media, including regional magazines based in Asia, have expressed their share of 'anti-Mahathirist vociferations' to the point of calling for Mahathir's resignation from the premiership of Malaysia (Wain 1998). It is unnecessary to recall the tirades launched by each side against the other. Yet, the divide between their different portrayals of the crisis has been so stark that a summary of their main points of disagreement may be instructive.

Mahathir insists that the proximate cause of the crisis was the rapacity of western currency traders who mounted a speculative attack on Asian currencies beginning with the Thai baht in mid 1997. More broadly, he views the crisis as an outcome of the uncontrolled operations of an international financial system which leave weaker economies defenceless against foreign exchange volatility and speculative manipulation. In other words, 'unnecessary, unproductive and immoral' currency trading, dominated by enormously powerful funds, has subverted the control that governments of sovereign countries ought to have over their national economies (Mahathir 1997: 64). Consequently, the global 'paper economy' and the international financial system, and not individual Asian governments, require stiffer restrictions and stricter policing.

However, the 'market consensus', largely voiced by mainstream western media, depicts the crisis as the result of economic mismanagement which provoked a 'loss of investor confidence' in the 'East Asian miracle'. The market consensus indicts Asian dirigiste regimes for having violated the principles for efficient, that is to say, 'free market', resource allocation and capital deployment by pursuing an 'East Asian model' of development that was riddled with non-transparent business practices. The leading practitioners of what might crudely be labelled 'Asia Incorporated' were accused of protecting favoured coalitions of commercial and political interests in ways that reeked of inefficiency, cronyism and corruption. Thus, East Asia's presently moribund 'tiger economies' can only be nursed back to health on a strict regime of 'good governance', 'economic reform' and 'market discipline' (*The Economist* 7 March 1998).

This outline of the differences between Mahathir, on the one hand, and the market and mainstream western media, on the other, sets aside various changes in the 'discourse of the crisis' as it has developed since July 1997. But it shows the lines that have been drawn in the battle between the state in Malaysia and international finance capital. It captures the tensions, exposed by the crisis, present in the economic nationalism of a small nation when forced into confrontation with the global money market.

213

The term 'economic nationalism' is used advisedly, because there are views, academic and otherwise, which hold that nation-states, national boundaries and nationalism have no real place anymore in the global economy of a borderless world (Ohmae 1995). But one cannot hope to understand the crisis in Malaysia without appreciating that the Malaysian political economy has been propelled by a state-directed developmental programme since 1970, but especially since the 1980s.

At one level of comparative argument, one can reduce that developmental programme to an intricate mix of macroeconomic policies loosely associated with the East Asian model (World Bank 1993), whether one casts that model in terms of development, modernization, late industrialization, or capitalism, or, miraculously, all four of them.

At another level of understanding, however, one can characterize this developmental programme in Malaysia either as a capitalist project imbued with nationalist aspirations, or as a nationalist project driven by capitalist impulses. Either way, the project was undertaken not only to contain the class and ethnic contradictions of Malaysian society but also to respond to the pressures of an accelerating globalisation.

The project was *capitalist* in several senses. Historically, it built upon an economic structure and social formation begun and bequeathed by colonial capitalism between the British founding of Penang in 1786 and Malaya's independence in 1957. Strategically, it succeeded by defeating the putative anti-capitalist alternative posed by the Communist Party of Malaya when the latter mounted an insurrection fifty years ago. And, given the multi-ethnic peculiarities of Malaysian political economy, much of the project was bound up with the rise of Malay capital.

The project was *nationalist* in two senses. It began in 1970 under Malay nationalists who used the New Economic Policy (NEP) to recompose the Malaysian class structure in ethnic terms so as to social-engineer a *Bumiputera Commercial and Industrial Community* – a combination of a Malay capitalist class and a Malay middle class. (In the process, they created a Malay industrial working class, too.) In the 1980s the project fostered the consolidation of a Malaysian capitalist class which, Mahathir envisioned, would lead a unified *Bangsa Malaysia* (Malaysian nation) towards parity with the developed nations of the world (Mahathir 1991).

That it was a historical and social *project*, and not the accidental outcome of a *laissez-faire* economy, was indicated by the high degree, expansive scope, and strong purpose of the state interventionism which arose to implement it. Successive post-1970 regimes in Malaysia performed three critical roles. They acted as a provider of opportunities for the Malays, a regulator of (principally non-Malay and foreign) economic activity, and an entrepreneur with substantial investments in strategic sectors (Khoo 1995: 106).

One should neither reify this project, nor suggest that it was monolithic in its design, uncontested in its implementation, or inexorable in its progress. Even so, the project had its overarching policy manifestations in the NEP, the National Development Policy of 1991, and what has been popularised among Malaysians as *Wawasan 2020*, or Vision 2020.

The nationalist–capitalist project 1970–97

What were the domestic and external factors which made this project feasible?

The NEP, with its ethnic targets and quotas, ruptured the old alliance between the state and domestic non-Malay capital. But, after May 1969, the consolidation of Malay political power enabled the NEP state to overcome residual non-Malay challenges to its agenda of restructuring the Malaysian political economy and society via economic planning, legislative regulation, and bureaucratic enforcement. Consequently, the rise of Malay capital – which assumed a variety of statist and bureaucratic forms (Jomo 1986; Mehmet 1986) – was relatively weakly opposed by domestic non-Malay capital. In the post-1969 political economy, the former had been sidelined, and subjected to ethnic restructuring which wrested control of certain corporations from domestic Chinese capital in particular (Jesudason 1989).[1] But the NEP compensated domestic non-Malay capital by enlarging its share of corporate wealth, at the expense of foreign capital. Foreign capital itself disliked the nationalistic aspects of the NEP and balked at the regulations contained in the Industrial Coordination Act (Jesudason 1989). Yet foreign capital was mollified in at least two ways. The old foreign capital of the established banks, plantation houses, and import-substituting industries was never threatened with nationalization even if NEP-inspired equity-restructuring and state-backed acquisitions, at market or negotiated prices, 'Malaysianized' the ownership of several leading companies in those sectors (Mahathir 1986). The new foreign capital of the MNCs was favoured with pioneer status incentives and only constrained by the NEP's target of inducting Malay workers into the modern sectors of the economy which the MNCs were only too keen to meet.

The NEP state was administratively well equipped. During the first decade of NEP implementation, state revenues were vastly expanded by rising commodity prices, not least from petroleum exports after Malaysia became a net oil exporter in 1970. Hence, the state was able to finance its economic intervention without imposing undue stress on the national budget or the country's balance of payments (Jomo *et al.* 1996: 74–5). At the same time, the Tun Abdul Razak government instituted an effective shift of power to an enlarged corps of Malay technocrats and bureaucrats who determinedly pursued the NEP objectives. Indeed, a whole generation of Malay technocrats, bureaucrats, and professionals were trained at state expense and provided with the resources to embark on a wide range of economic and social projects in the name of increasing 'bumiputra economic participation'.

Economically, the NEP political economy interfaced with the global economy in what was then described as the 'new international division of labour'. A marriage of domestic priorities (mass employment, which import-substitution industrialization could not generate) with external requirements (the MNCs' search for politically stable offshore production sites and cheap labour) at this critical conjuncture allowed the traditionally open Malaysian economy to be integrated into what would now be called the globalization of industrial production. As a result of a concerted effort to attract the MNCs by offering the comparative advantages of lower wages, the prohibition of unionization among a new industrial labour force, sound physical and social infrastructure, and fiscal, tax, and other incentives, the state was able to launch Malaysia's first wave of export-oriented industrialization and transform a previously commodity-export-based economy into an industrialized economy (Rasiah 1995).

The nationalist–capitalist project took a different turn when Mahathir became prime minister in July 1981. Mahathir had been the NEP's chief ideologue, but he was no longer content with merely achieving the NEP's ethnic restructuring goals. He had promoted the MNC-based export-oriented industrialization, but he was no longer satisfied with Malaysia's remaining a Third World producer of 'industrial commodities' (Mahathir 1986a). Inspired by the performance of kindred nationalist–capitalist projects in Japan and South Korea, he set out to industrialize Malaysia to developed country status.

Mahathir planned a heavy industrialization drive based on the production of steel, automobiles, motorcycle engines, and cement. Domestic capital was reluctant to be involved because of the heavy costs, high risks, and long gestation periods. Consequently, this heavy industrialization programme was realized via state investment (represented by HICOM, or the Heavy Industries Corporation of Malaysia), 'East Asian technology' (sourced from Japanese and South Korean firms through joint ventures), and indigenous (i.e. Malay) management (Machado 1989–90, 1994). The programme began with a pronounced import-substituting character: HICOM's infant industries were supported with credit and other subsidies, and protected by tariffs. Its intermediate objectives included technological mastery and upgrading, and the creation of extensive linkages with other sectors of the economy. Its eventual goal was export competitiveness.

Politically, Mahathir meant to re-establish a state–capital alliance but on a different footing. One decade of state economic intervention had not quite created an independent class of Malay capitalists, but it had produced numerous Malay entrepreneurs and technocrats with varying degrees of experience in business. One decade of state regulation had rendered non-Malay capital grudgingly receptive of the necessity of ethnic restructuring

216

for social stability. In Mahathir's view, the time had arrived to heal the rupture between state and (non-Malay) capital by forming a new alliance, but one in which Malay capital could play a major role. Mahathir's twin 'Privatization' and 'Malaysia Incorporated' policies were intended to achieve that goal (Khoo 1995: 129–36). Privatization was presented as the means to reduce state expenditure on unprofitable public enterprises by handing them over to a presumably more efficient private sector. Simultaneously, the assets held under 'Malay trusteeship' would be redistributed to capable Malay entrepreneurs as a reward for performance and as a boost to advancement. In the long run, privatization would reduce Malay dependence on the state by making the private sector the primary generator of investment, growth, and employment. Malaysia Inc., however, promised cooperation between the state and a national capital that was not automatically dominated by its non-Malay segment. This Mahathirist plan for the emergence of a unified and externally directed Malaysian capitalism found its mature form in the so-called post-1990 *Wawasan 2020*.

In 1985, after fifteen years of high growth, the Malaysian economy contracted by 1.0 per cent. In 1986 it grew by 1.2 per cent. Three major economic factors led to this unexpected situation – huge declines in commodity prices,[2] an escalation in public debt,[3] and the reduction in the government's development expenditure at the same time that total private investment declined.[4]

Between 1983 and 1985, Mahathir's administration had been rocked by financial scandals and political crises. The recession intensified the political battles. In 1985–6, Mahathir and his Finance Minister, Daim Zainuddin, introduced a regime of austerity and structural adjustment, and even suspended the NEP's requirements in a bold if desperate move to attract private (especially foreign) investment. The Malay-dominated bureaucracy and the Malay business community became polarized between a 'pro-growth' camp (supporting a temporary suspension of the NEP to boost investment and growth) and a 'pro-distribution' camp (wanting a continuation and even extension of the NEP's restructuring targets). By 1987, Mahathir and Daim were opposed by half of the cabinet members appointed from their party, UMNO. In April 1987, Mahathir barely survived the combined challenge of his former deputy prime minister and his former finance minister. By October, relations between the Malay and Chinese communities had deteriorated to the point of almost sparking a repeat of the May 1969 violence.

Then was when the nationalist–capitalist project came close to collapse. But, evidently, Daim's austere response to recession, and Mahathir's authoritarian reply to opposition gave it time to recover in the late 1980s. Between 1985 and 1987, Mahathir and Daim liberalized the investment regime, initially for foreign capital, but later for domestic (ethnic Chinese) capital as well. They relaxed the limits on foreign equity ownership, suspended the NEP's restructuring requirements, and offered fresh investment incentives. These measures coincided with moves by Japanese and the East Asian newly industrializing countries to relocate part of their production to Malaysia (and other Southeast Asian countries). The combination of the appreciation of the yen, an anticipated loss of the Generalized System of Preferences (GSP) privileges, and escalating domestic labour and production costs brought a wave of Japanese and East Asian NIC investment that began a new period of rapid economic growth in the Malaysian economy.

Malaysia Inc. and the origins of the present crisis

Evidently, the experience of recession and recovery convinced Mahathir of the virtue of privatization, and that Malaysia Inc. showed 'the way forward' (Mahathir 1991). Yet the subsequent consolidation of Malaysia Inc., under a widening privatization programme, had several consequences for the economic structure, power alignments, 'governance', and political ideology, which laid some of the conditions for the present crisis.

Mahathir's original rationale for privatization rested on curbing public sector expenditure and dismantling unprofitable state enterprises in favour of a more efficient private sector. But privatization increasingly encompassed the sale of profitable state monopolies (in energy and telecommunications, for example), the award of large-scale infrastructural works (the North–South Highway and the Bakun Dam being the largest), and the opening of new areas (social services such as health care and tertiary education) to the vanguard of domestic capital – Malay, non-Malay, and interethnic joint ventures. Hence, privatization promoted a new category of Malaysian conglomerates. They tended to congregate in sectors offering the competitive advantage of state support or protection, that is banking, resource exploitation, construction, property and real estate, tourism, transport, utilities and services, and selected import-substituting industries. Critically, these were not sectors in which success depended on indigenous technological innovation, advancements in research and development, and international competitiveness – unlike, say, manufacturing for the world market (which was under MNC control), primary commodity production (with its capacity dating back to colonial times), or resource-based industries (where local sourcing was an obvious strength). These were areas where licensing restrictions, policy preferences, and state approval made a real difference between success and failure.

Not every conglomerate started out with a privatized project. Many big corporations had made their name in their chosen fields (with varying degrees of state patronage) before they became candidates for the large privatization projects. But the typical conglomerate was inclined to adopt a familiar strategy (not necessarily in the following order of activity): deal in property and real estate, build up construction capacity, lobby for infrastructural and utility works, secure a banking or finance arm or a brokerage licence, buy up plantations, diversify into tourism, and enter newly privatized areas like telecommunications and social services. Justified by arguments about synergy, conglomerate after conglomerate demonstrated this form of expansion: beginning with a 'flagship' in one area, they would, by takeovers, acquisitions, or applications to the government, build up a 'fleet' of companies. In effect, they evolved into a privileged league of private oligopolies which benefited from the fragmentation of state monopolies. These conglomerates were remaking themselves into erstaz *zaibatsu*, *sogoshosha*, and *chaebol* – with the critical difference that the typical Malaysian conglomerate was not known for industrial strength (Yoshihara 1988; Gomez and Jomo 1997). To put it another way, there were few captains of *industry*, and too many captains of *commerce*.[5]

This limited form of corporate expansion drew much of its financial support from two sources: external borrowings, and capital raised on the Kuala Lumpur Stock Exchange (KLSE). Between 1988 and 1990, the private sector's medium- and long-term external debt stood at just under RM5 billion (Table 12.1). Thereafter, this debt grew at an average annual rate of 33.8 per cent or from RM6.723 billion in 1991 to RM38.650 billion in June 1997 (Bank Negara February 1998: 103).[6] The non-bank private sector's external short-term debt also grew from RM4.404 billion in 1994 to RM4.911 billion in 1995, RM7.256 billion in 1996, and RM6.347 billion in June 1997 (Bank Negara February 1998: 103).

Between 1992 and 1996, the private sector debt/GDP ratio rose from 7.0 per cent to 13.2 per cent (IMF 1998: 78).

The second major source of funds for corporate expansion was the KLSE

Table 12.1 Private sector medium- and long-term debt, Malaysia, 1987–97

Year	Medium- and long-term debt (RM billion)
1987	5.559
1988	4.855
1989	4.613
1990	4.943
1991	6.723
1992	10.471
1993	15.498
1994	24.203
1995	28.080
1996	33.474
1997 (June)	38.650
1997 (total)	61.089

Source: Bank Negara (February 1998: 103)

which, for the purposes of this essay, grew as a direct result of a deluge of portfolio investment entering Malaysia between 1991 and the second quarter of 1997. As Table 12.2 indicates, incoming foreign funds invested in shares and corporate securities increased from RM13.645 billion in 1991 to a high of RM127.950 billion in 1996. Just the first two quarters of 1997 showed portfolio investment receipts of RM69.797 billion (Bank Negara February 1998: 117).[7]

Except for the beginning and end of 1991–7, Malaysia received a net inflow of funds invested in shares and corporate securities. These capital inflows greatly boosted the KLSE's market capitalization (Table 12.3) which peaked at RM888.66 billion in February 1997 (compared with RM131.6 billion in 1990) and RM744.47 billion in June 1997 (Bank Negara February 1998: 72).[8] During the 1990s, the KLSE composite index rose from 506 in 1990 to 644 in 1992, and then almost doubled to 1275 in 1993, before declining to 971 in 1994, and 995 in 1995 (Bank Negara February 1998: 72). In 1996, the composite index increased to 1238 before falling to 1077 in June 1997, and a low of 545 in November 1997 (Bank Negara February 1998: 72).

Since the late 1980s, there had been 'reforms' of the financial system, but these were typically made to liberalize the capital market, support its growth, and introduce some competition (Ariff 1996: 328–31; Awang 1994: 147–52). New legislation giving Bank Negara broader powers of supervision (Banking and Financial Institutions Act 1989) and establishing the Securities Commission in 1993 were attempts at regulation and institutional reform (especially after the 1986 'deposit-taking cooperatives' débâcle) (Awang 1994: 152–6). But the conglomerates largely escaped the scrutiny and regulation that should have accompanied liberalization. That was partly because the power of the technocrats and bureaucrats had been curtailed under Mahathir's administration. Under the Razak government, the technocrats

Table 12.2 Portfolio investment in shares and corporate securities, Malaysia, 1991–7

Year	Receipts (RM million)	Payments (RM million)	Net inflow (RM million)
1991	13,645	15,524	−1,879
1992	33,324	26,481	6,843
1993	116,743	92,076	24,667
1994	129,953	115,521	14,432
1995	90,987	85,642	5,345
1996	127,590	120,899	6,691
1997 (to June)	69,797	78,279	−8,482
1997 (total)	113,212	138,675	−25,463

Source: Bank Negara (February 1998: 117).

Table 12.3   Kuala Lumpur Stock Exchange, selected indicators, 1990–7

Year	Composite index	Turnover (RM billion)	No. of listed companies	New share issues (RM billion)	Market capitalization (RM billion)
1990	505.92	29.522	285	8.6496	131.66
1991	556.22	30.097	324	4.3914	161.29
1992	643.96	51.469	369	9.1815	245.82
1993	1,275.32	387.276	413	3.4326	619.64
1994	971.21	328.057	478	8.5479	508.85
1995	995.17	178.859	529	11.4376	565.63
1996	1,237.96	463.265	621	15.9244	806.77
1997	594.44	408.558	708	18.2247	375.80

Source: Bank Negara (February 1998: 68–9, 72)

and bureaucrats in such agencies as Bank Negara, the Treasury, and the Economic Planning Unit played key roles in planning, implementation, and regulation. Under Hussein Onn, the non-financial private enterprises and state economic development corporations enjoyed their status as 'social enterprises'. Even if one were sceptical about their actual performance and their ethnically coloured motives, the technocrats and bureaucrats who regulated capital under NEP probably did so with a sense of mission. Under Malaysia Inc., however, they were instructed to cooperate with the private sector, or, more crudely, serve capital (not least, Malay capital).[9] Thus the power balance between bureaucracy and business shifted: 'With increasing Malay hegemony in the 1970s, the role of the predominantly Malay bureaucracy was significantly enhanced, only to give way to an increasingly assertive executive and a more politically influential rentier business community in the 1980s' (Gomez and Jomo 1997: 179).

Regulation or 'good governance' could not mean very much against the growing power of the conglomerates.[10] Their power was reflected not just in their multiplying assets, or their political connections, but also in the influence they wielded by being part of several high-level fora (the Malaysian Business Council being the most important) which institutionalized government–business consultations within Malaysia Inc. Particular corporate leaders were reputed to be especially influential, but, on the whole, Malaysia Inc. gave big business an almost equal footing with government so that, according to former Deputy Prime Minister Musa Hitam, 'it got to the stage when the private sector was dictating terms, telling government what to do based on their links to leadership' (Jayasankaran and Hiebert 1998: 14). The notable exception was the prime minister who had so centralized if not personalized decision and policy making that business circles took it as a truism that gaining Mahathir's confidence was a necessary part of good business practice.

The conglomerates progressively assumed characteristics which have been variously described as *rentierist* (Gomez and Jomo 1997), *distributional–coalitionist* (Mehmet 1986), or simply *cronyist*. As corporate figures and their political allies joined to secure privatized projects, they intensified the politicization of commerce, and the commercialization of politics (locally derided as 'money politics'). Privatization, if conceived in terms of 'rolling back the frontiers of the state', might have retarded that tendency had it been conducted scrupulously. But the peculiarly Malaysian mode of privatization – the secretly negotiated contract justified by Mahathir himself as rewarding 'those who come to us with good ideas' – only became conspicuous for its lack of transparency. Malaysia's ethnically defined, dual-track, meritocracy exerted its influence over this process of 'picking winners'. Despite the presence of new Chinese capitalists who profited from close associations with Malay politicians, most Malaysians held that capable Chinese entrepreneurs rose on their own merit. There were numerous Malay conglomerates, but even those who headed them did not seem to exude the confidence of a self-made class. Among them, those who had proven themselves capable of 'performance' – the ability to win, manage, and finish projects – and not necessarily judged by the 'performance criteria' of South Korean industrialization, for example – were the ones to be rewarded with even more projects.

Thus an intensifying concentration of wealth and power in the 'politicized oligopolies' (Gomez and Jomo 1997: 180) created various problems: the absence of a strong regime of corporate governance, lack of transparency in government–business relations, and rentierism. To those could be added a persistent current account deficit, the threat of 'overheating', the probability of declining export competitiveness, mounting indebtedness, and an emerging asset bubble, both in the property sector and the stock market (Kitamura and Tanaka 1997: 42–6) – the kinds of structural problems which ranked among the primary reasons initially offered for the speculative attack on the Southeast Asian currencies in mid 1997.

Even so, the high-growth situation before July 1997 brought real socioeconomic gains: the rise in income and fall in employment, to take the most important examples for the majority of the people. Those gains were real enough to garner a high degree of legitimacy and popular support for Mahathir's administration. Contrasted with the dismal experience of recession, recovery was enthralling. Most Malaysians could not remember a time of greater prosperity or lesser interethnic recrimination than the mid 1990s. Economic indicators alone would not have captured the pride that Malaysians had discovered, perhaps for the first time, in being Malaysian. In the popular imagination, economic success, under Mahathir and Malaysia Inc., had resolved some of the almost intractable political problems. There was a sense, no doubt fostered by the ruling elite, of limitless possibilities

offered by an economy that 'could not overheat', that could show 'zero inflation', and succeeded because 'nothing about it was fortuitous'.[11]

July 1997 and after

With hindsight, not even the cynical could have foreseen that it would fall to
the lot of the international money market to show that the Malaysian
nationalist–capitalist project was living on borrowed time and not just
borrowed money. The 'East Asian crisis' which began in July 1997 and its
spiralling fallout now threaten the continued viability of that project from
two principal directions.

Global (money) market forces, manifest in a 'loss of investor confidence'
among currency traders and fund managers, drastically depreciated the
Malaysian ringgit and reduced the KLSE's market capitalization. From its
peak exchange rate of RM2.493 to US$1 in April 1997, the ringgit fell to
RM2.636 in July, and to RM4.545 in January 1998.[12] The KLSE's market
capitalization declined from RM806.77 billion to RM375.80 billion between
1996 and 1997 (Bank Negara February 1998: 72). Within a short time, therefore, the leading Malaysian conglomerates, already dependent on external
borrowings and market capitalization, were exposed to external loan repayment pressures, severe asset reduction, loss of profits, and, ultimately, the
threat of insolvency. At home, an abrupt end to two decades of high growth
compelled the state to confront the agony of IMF-type 'structural adjustment' and 'market reform', and the urgency of preserving the Malaysia Inc.
state–capital alliance spearheaded the capitalist–nationalist project. The
economic growth of the 1990s turned into recession in 1998. Rather than
heady performance, survival became the concern of the conglomerates (but,
of course, not just them).

Where was the international money market in this unanticipated turn of
events? Matters would be simple if one could counterpose the international
capital market's lack of confidence in the Malaysian economy against
domestic confidence in the period prior to July 1997. But the market was
evidently no less enthralled, as seen by the external borrowings and capital
inflows which boosted corporate expansion in Malaysia before July 1997. It
would be naïve to think that the pre-crisis corporate practices and government policies and measures in Malaysia were so lacking in transparency
that the international fund managers and their research analysts had no
hint of potential problems in the Malaysian economy. The problems were
known, whether stated in the form of 'fundamentals', or 'governance'. On
the one hand, the feared loss of export competitiveness arising out of a
high exchange rate, tight labour market and intra-Asian competition, and
the not unusual concern with the current account deficit had occasioned
cautionary statements about the feasibility of maintaining a high growth
rate and the likelihood of overheating. On the other hand, the seamier sides

of privatization, burdens of 'mega projects', and the swelling of the share- and property-based asset bubble prompted other warnings about a need for good governance. These problems did not prevent the fund managers from partaking in the bounty they thought the economy had to offer. Much of the inflow of portfolio investment arrived as part of the international money market's euphoric dalliance with 'emerging markets' across the globe (Fox 1998). For instance, as late as November 1997, twenty-four European and American institutional investors still held a total of 55.3 million shares in just one UMNO-controlled company – United Engineers (Malaysia) (UEM) (Fox 1998).[13]

None of this foreshadowed the events that followed the depreciation of the Thai baht on 2 July 1997, and the subsequent depreciation of other Asian currencies (Bello 1998b; Krugman 1994; Radelet and Sachs 1998; Wade and Veneroso 1998). Initially, Bank Negara tried to defend the ringgit but its short-lived and unsuccessful attempt cost several billion ringgit. When further defence risked depleting the country's reserves, Bank Negara removed the ringgit's quasi-peg to the US dollar, and the ringgit slid to an average July 1997 rate of RM2.636. At the time, that scale of depreciation of the ringgit, alongside other Southeast Asian currencies, was not alarming, compared with the fall of the yen (from about 80 to US$1 in mid 1995 to 130 in 1997), and an earlier devaluation of the Chinese renminbi. Some observers even expected the ringgit to trade between RM2.70 and RM3.00 to US$1 (Lim 1998: Preface). Whether the ringgit could have averted its subsequent plunge in value – to RM4.88 to US$1 in January 1988 – had Mahathir not said the wrong things at the wrong time is unanswerable now given the 'contagion' impact of the unravelling of the Thai, Indonesian, and South Korean economies. Many fund managers would probably have departed East Asia's 'submerging markets' on their own to avoid share and foreign exchange losses.

However, Mahathir's responses – in deed and not just in word – turned what might have been an orderly departure of international capital from Malaysia into a sudden flight. In a number of speeches and interviews, Mahathir urged an overhaul of the international money market to curb currency speculation so as to arrest its debilitating effects on developing economies. Some of the criticisms Mahathir made then about trade in money he had made years ago (Khoo 1995: 59–60), only this time, during a generalized crisis, he was abusive towards the currency traders, speculators, and hedge fund managers. Mahathir had no illusion that small or weak economies could on their own preserve sovereign control over the value of their currencies. Hence he argued for an international effort to regulate the global money market. Mahathir's arguments never received more than a curt dismissal by the IMF, or a mocking rebuttal by mainstream western media, both of which interpreted the 'East Asian meltdown' as a failure of state interventionism, and a confirmation that markets are ultimately right (*The Economist* 27 September 1998).

In practice, Mahathir acted to impose what control he thought the government retained over international capital within Malaysia's borders. On 27 August 1997, the KLSE banned the short selling of 100 index-linked blue-chip stocks, hoping to halt the decline in stock prices (Hiebert and Jayasankaran 1997). On 3 September, the government announced the formation of a RM60 billion fund to support the stock market by selectively buying stocks from Malaysians but not foreigners (Hiebert and Jayasankaran 1997). This conversion of 'nasty words [and] mere bluster ... into economic deeds' (*The Economist* 6 September 1997: 14) failed as a remedy: the stock market plunged as foreign fund managers feared being locked into a falling market. Within days, those government decisions were reversed or modified, but 'investor confidence' had vanished and capital had taken flight.

Mahathir's confrontation with the market eased between October and December 1997 when the Minister of Finance, Anwar Ibrahim, and former Minister of Finance Daim Zainuddin (appointed executive director of the newly established National Economic Action Council, NEAC) temporarily took charge of economic and fiscal policies. The 1998 budget, presented in October, showed fiscal restraint, made budget cuts, and adopted some IMF-type structural adjustment measures. The salient anti-crisis points of the budget were:

- reducing federal government expenditure by 2 per cent;
- postponing several 'mega projects';
- reducing the current accounts deficit (beginning with reductions in imports);
- reducing corporate tax by 2 per cent;
- limiting credit growth to 15 per cent by the end of 1998; and
- consolidating the prudential standards and regulations covering non-performing loans, liquidity, and disclosure within the banking system (Malaysia 1998: ch. 1).

Still, the budget forecast a growth rate of 7 per cent which the market considered wholly unrealistic (RAM 1997a). In early December, Anwar announced a new set of more stringent austerity measures, the most significant of which were:

- a reduction of the current account deficit to 3 per cent of GNP in 1998 (from about 5.1 per cent in both 1996 and 1997);
- an 18 per cent reduction in federal government expenditure in 1988 – consisting of an immediate across-the-board cutback of 10 per cent on

operating and development expenditure, and an additional, more selective 8 per cent cutback;

- a lowering of the projected 1998 growth rate to between 4 and 5 per
  cent;
- deferment of non-strategic and non-essential projects;
- stricter criteria for approvals of 'reverse investment'; and
- enhanced information disclosure by corporations and closer regulation
  of corporate restructuring (Malaysia 1998: ch. 1).

This December package seemed to restore some 'confidence' (*Business
Times* 9 December 1998).

But by January 1998, the implementation of 'buyout' plans for some
conglomerates, by changing takeover rules (Fox 1998; Lim 1998: 45–7;
Subramaniam 1998) and using public funds (Lim 1998: 48–51), sent the
ringgit and KLSE down to their lowest levels (Shameen 1998; Tripathi
1998). From the market's point of view, those decisions, Mahathir's ultimately, were a setback, a confirmation that Mahathir suffered from a 'denial
syndrome'. The capital flight turned into a capital strike: the market would
not return if the state, under Mahathir, could not be disciplined.

Some have said that Mahathir's actions bordered on inanity if not
insanity, and were cynically directed at saving several conglomerates
belonging to his party (Renong), children (Konsortium Perkapalan), and
cronies (Malaysian Airlines System). One need not be a Mahathir apologist,
or overlook the bailout character of Mahathir's moves (Subramaniam
1998), to argue all the same that critical issues of political economy lay
behind them. In the one year following July 1997, those issues included
subtle and low-level policy skirmishes between Mahathir and Anwar that
brought the political economy of the crisis back home.

On the one hand, Anwar seemed more prepared to heed the views and
positions of several non-unified constituencies: the technocrats, small business, and part of the Malay and non-Malay middle classes. The technocrats,
notably in Bank Negara and the Treasury, generally sought economistic
solutions to the crisis by strengthening 'economic fundamentals', exercising
fiscal restraint, and tightening monetary policy – that is, by imposing
budgetary cuts, reducing credit growth, raising interest rates, controlling
inflation, and stabilizing the ringgit. Others performing regulatory functions,
in the Securities Commision, for example, hoped to make 'corporate governance' a reality (Chandra 1998). Together, the technocrats and regulators
hoped to restore investor confidence. Small businesses – especially small
Malay businesses having their ties to UMNO, hurt by the market conditions,
and given no assurance of protection – were more prepared to fasten on the
'cronyism, nepotism, and lack of transparency', associated with Mahathir
and big business, as the reasons for the economic disaster.[14] From this point
of view, small business was not indifferent to arguments for disciplining the

conglomerates, for instance by withholding the public funds needed for their rescue. At least part of both the Malay and non-Malay middle classes were offended by the lack of accountability in privatization, the rentierism and money politics rampant under Malaysia Inc., and Mahathir's refusal to admit any government failure (Spaeth 1998a).[15] The more disillusioned, or even the more self-confident, among them thought that perhaps only IMF intervention, or a full blast of globalization, could really cleanse the Malaysian political economy of its ills (RAM 1997: 2–7).

On the other hand, Mahathir's position, while obviously crucial to the survival of big business and strategic commercial interests, gained the support of other social groupings, some more 'patriotic', but others simply more 'realistic'. The more established businesses (those represented in chambers of commerce, for example) and the more nationalistic of social groups found little comfort in IMF intervention, further economic liberalization, or 'market reform' which promised a spate of closures, bankruptcies, and an eventual transfer of control of corporate assets to foreign equity. The businesses saw in credit loosening, a lower interest rate regime, and even asset sales, short of a transfer of control to foreign hands, the means to help business operations weather the economic crisis (*The Star* 1 July 1998). Others, patriotic or realistic, were prepared to reduce imports and 'buy Malaysian products'. Even if these groups did not necessarily accept a 'western conspiracy theory' of the origins of the East Asian crisis, the far from satisfactory experiences of Thailand, Indonesia, and South Korea had proven to them the dangers posed by IMF's conditionalities for intervention, and full 'market discipline' (Khor 1997). Home-grown alternatives to an outright transfer of domestic equity to foreigners were to be preferred: for example, tapping the resources of cash-rich corporations in the name of 'national service', selling non-Malays a part of Malay equity (Jayasankaran and Hiebert 1998), and, for that matter, using public funds, such as the Employees Provident Fund.

These were indicative positions often tentatively expressed in a multitude of fora, including the Internet, rather than fixed battle lines behind which were arrayed definite classes and ethnic groups. They gave a sense of the narrowing of choices, options, and solutions available to the political leadership. Not to accede to market demands for 'reform' would invite a capital strike until 'market forces are at last being allowed to work' (*The Economist* 7 March 1998: 7). To accede to radical reform, deregulation, and liberalization would mean 'the total opening of national capital markets', a 'resulting predatory rush to take over absurdly depreciated assets' (Godement 1998: 28).[16] Mahathir despaired of knowing what else to do to restore confidence (*New Straits Times* 13 June 1998), when market demands, over the course of a year, had changed from proper management of economic fundamentals, to the implementation of IMF conditionalities, to the forced closures of domestic financial institutions, to the opening up of domestic corporations to foreign equity and control, and, ultimately, to changes in government.[17]

It was equally difficult to reorient economic planning towards slower growth, lower consumption, and stricter regulation since both the NEP and *Wawasan 2020* had been predicated upon high-growth-supporting redistribution. The austerity budget and structural adjustment measures adopted between October and December had not prevented the economy from slipping into contraction during the first quarter of 1998.[18] The familiar route of inviting the first wave of foreign direct investment to carry out long-term productive activities in the 1970s took time, and could not be of much use in rescuing the economy from impending disaster. The other route of welcoming the second wave of (predominantly East Asian) foreign direct investment in the late 1980s was impracticable now. Initial hopes of an 'Asian solution' to an 'Asian crisis' by creating an 'Asian Monetary Fund', perhaps more sympathetic than the IMF, were dashed when Japan could not assert the regional economic leadership it had been urged to assume for many years (*The Economist* 27 September 1998: 84).[19]

In that context, the 'policy debates at the top of government [which] have slowed radical reform' – a 'policy gridlock' (Saludo and Shameen 1998: 44) – provided a tentative understanding of the contradictions which beset Malaysian economic nationalism when it confronted the international money market. The 'conflicting signals' from the leadership, which market analysts complained about, were evidence of political uncertainty over the tradeoffs that had to be made, roughly between 'national interest' and 'market confidence'. By August 1998, the Mahathirist position had strengthened. Just before the UMNO General Assembly of mid June 1998, Anwar's allies in the party tried to provoke a public criticism of Mahathir's policies, precisely over issues of 'cronyism, nepotism and lack of transparency'. But they were defeated, and Mahathir reclaimed 'full control of the economy', in his words (Khoo 1998a: 7). After the UMNO General Assembly, Mahathir's appointment of Daim as a minister of special functions (for economic development) cast Anwar in a subordinate role as far as policy making for economic recovery was concerned.[20] It was not a political development calculated to restore confidence since the international money market, institutions, and media had warmed to the idea that Mahathir should be replaced by Anwar as prime minister soon (Khoo 1998a: 5–6).

Economic nationalism and its discontents

The aggrandizement of Mahathir's Malaysia Inc., and the profligacy of the new Malaysian capital – Malay *and* non-Malay – had much to answer to in this crisis. Their predilection for easily and cheaply accessible funds, which the one tolerated and the other indulged, at the very least smacked of incompetent management and corporate adventurism. Their self-righteous expectations of a public acceptance of 'moral hazard' (Lim 1998: 125–9, 142–5) would financially encumber Malaysian society for a long time to come.

Yet, there was always more to the refusal of Malaysia Inc. to bow to market discipline than mere cronyist calculations. Behind the objectionable aspects of Malaysia Inc. stood an entire social compact, constructed and accepted over almost thirty years, that made possible a peculiar configuration of political stability, interethnic acceptance, and social progress. To a large degree, the ability of this social compact to remain intact under the present crisis allowed Malaysia to avoid the kind of interethnic recrimination that occurred in the form of anti-Chinese pogroms in Indonesia. It even allowed the government to make policy changes to permit Chinese capital to buy out its Malay counterpart, if selectively and temporarily. As Mahathir revealed at the UMNO General Assembly, partly out of immediate political motives, more than a handful of 'cronies' benefited from the nationalist–capitalist project (*New Straits Times* 21 June 1998; *The Star* 22 June 1998).[21]

Characteristically, Mahathir pushed a kernel of truth to its logic. The NEP-engineered Bumiputra Commercial and Industrial Community (BCIC) now comprises a large mixture of Malay capitalists, professionals, and other middle-class groups. A majority of them remain dependent on state assistance and patronage. Is their dependence truly unavoidable because they are still not self-reliant, as is often suggested? Or is it habitual in that it reflects the refusal of entrenched classes to surrender privileges they have been accustomed to receiving? The ideal answer would come from distinguishing broadly accepted forms of affirmative action from political patronage for the powerful. For the moment, though, hardly anyone (outside the market) would risk dismantling Malaysia Inc. if that meant subjecting the BCIC to the 'fundamentally unappealable judgements of The Market' (Henwood 1997: 199).

The architects of the NEP and *Wawasan 2020* never pretended to practise egalitarianism aside from attaining an ethnically more equitable redistribution of wealth in Malaysian society. Even so, the state in Malaysia did not pursue a nakedly predatory path of socio-economic development that marginalized entire subordinate classes and social groups. Development projects were undertaken which reduced the incidence of poverty, promoted social progress, and opened up unprecedented opportunities. But all that marked the limits of a social compact that rejected radical land reform at the beginning of the nationalist–capitalist project and the installation of welfarism during its late stages. By comparison with the social democratic compact achieved in western capitalist societies after the Second World War, the corporatism begun by Razak and consolidated by Mahathir privileged capital – domestic and foreign – over labour – organized and unorganized, domestic and migrant. Before the present crisis, state and capital revelled in a novel amiability, while labour was given no more meaningful role in this incomplete corporatism than to supply the comparative advantages of low wages and industrial peace. What kept the post-1970 social compact intact was essentially the 'trickle down' from high growth and state interventionism which made crucial differences to the lives of most Malaysians.

Under the circumstances, it is one thing for internal pressures and political struggles to loosen the subordination of Malaysian society to Malaysia Inc. (Lim 1998: 81–2). It is quite another to undo the social compact on behalf of a global market in money that has 'no heart, soul, conscience, homeland' (cited in Henwood 1997: 113). Nothing of Malaysia's post-colonial record of achievement could be credited to a 'free market'. The only period in modern Malaysian history to have had a political economy approaching *laissez-faire* capitalism was the Alliance period (1957–69). That period ended in the violence of May 1969. Neither the NEP nor Malaysia Inc. invented state interventionism in Malaysia. There was no free market under the colonial state which made its own alliances with capital, produced its own cronies, conducted its plunder, and remained far less responsive to social restructuring either of an ethnic or class nature. None of those who upheld the sanctity of the market during this crisis was troubled by history, or objected to the interventionism of the nationalist–capitalist project when it meant material incentives, subsidies, and policies (including authoritarian anti-labour measures) which directly benefited a more stable form of foreign capital, that is the FDI of the MNCs. Or, as Mahathir said, 'Hoping for market forces to create a stable currency exchange, a stable economy and stable politics is the same as doing nothing and leaving everything to fate' (Mahathir 1998).

Benedict Anderson observed that the crisis could turn more than one East Asian nation into a place 'where capitalism has been and gone' (Anderson 1998: 3). If so, that would only prove that capitalism's triumph over communism ironically drew its 'collateral damage' in East Asia not long after the region had ceased to be the Cold War's bloodiest cockpit. During the Cold War period, it may be useful to recall,

> the Asian NICs [were] not the only countries to try to use state power to direct private capital. They [were] unusual, however, in that the United States did not undermine their efforts. Governments in South Korea and Taiwan, for example, nationalized private commercial banks with no serious objection from the United States. In fact, in the name of anti-communism, the United States extended significant financial support to both for economic restructuring. Moreover, until recently, all three countries (including Singapore) enjoyed relatively free access to U.S. markets.
>
> (Hart-Landsberg 1991: 59)

In the wake of the crisis, what annoyed the free marketeers, neo-liberals, or bearers of the 'IMF–Washington consensus' was the hubris of a historical form of economic nationalism which, having achieved 'East Asian competitiveness', wanted globalization, but still wanted to 'govern the market'. That sense of economic nationalism had been evoked before, by Samir Amin when he cast the East Asian path of development as 'the project of Bandung … a national bourgeois project of "catching up" in a context of circumscribed independence' (Amin 1993: 1–2), and by Manuel Castells when he argued that the East Asian 'developmental state' pushed 'a fundamentally political logic, directly expressing a nationalistic project' (Castells 1992: 24).[22]

In light of those descriptions, the 'East Asian model' may be said to have manifested certain nationalist anxieties and capitalist aspirations. The anxieties of nationalism will not be assuaged even if the global money market imposes its discipline on the East Asian states. The aspirations of capitalism will be unfulfilled even if the historical period which gave East Asia its niche in a globalizing capitalism has come to a virtual end. In fact, and whether or not the market cares any more for his pronouncements, Mahathir alluded to this 'East Asian dilemma' when he warned of a breed of 'new capitalists' who, in seeking global domination, could provoke a 'new war of national liberation' in an Asia that might become prosperous again but only under non-Asian control (*New Straits Times* 5 June 1998c).[23]

Postscript[24]

On 1 September, Bank Negara instituted new 'exchange control mechanisms' that effectively ended the free convertibility of the ringgit (*New Straits Times* 2 September 1998). The ringgit, traded at RM4.0960 to US$1 on that day, was pegged at RM3.800 to US$1 the next day. Holders of offshore ringgit accounts were given a month to transfer their funds back to Malaysia: beginning 1 October, the Malaysian currency could not be traded overseas, and licensed offshore banks could not trade in ringgit instruments. The exchange controls included the following provisions:

- domestic credit facilities to non-resident correspondent banks and non-resident stockbroking firms were no longer permitted, while residents were not allowed to obtain ringgit credit facilities from non-resident individuals;
- non-residents were required to deposit their ringgit securities with authorized depositories, and to hold the proceeds from any sale of such securities in external accounts for at least one year before converting them to foreign currency;
- all export and import trade settlements were to be made in foreign currency;

- except with Bank Negara's approval, Malaysian residents were limited to making a maximum payment of RM10,000, or its equivalent in foreign currency, per transaction to non-residents for meeting general, non-trade, or overseas investment purposes;
- resident travellers could import or export ringgit notes not exceeding RM1,000, and import any amount of foreign currency, but could only export foreign currency not exceeding the equivalent of RM10,000; and
- non-resident travellers could import or export ringgit notes not exceeting RM1,000, and import any amount of foreign currency, but could only export foreign currency up to the amount of foreign currency they brought into Malaysia (*New Straits Times* 2 September 1998).

Bank Negara stressed that it only intended to curb 'hot money' and currency speculation. The exchange controls would not affect the 'general convertibility of current account transactions' as well as 'free flows of direct foreign investment and repatriation of interest, profits and dividends and capital' (*New Straits Times* 2 September 1998). Bank Negara's defence of the exchange controls was strident ('to regain monetary independence') yet diffident (to 'insulate the Malaysian economy from the prospects of further deterioration in the world economic and financial environment') (*New Straits Times* 2 September 1998). In reality, the imposition of these exchange controls reaffirmed the economic priorities of Mahathir and Daim (as noted under the section 'July 1997 and after', above) – briefly, to reflate the economy and resuscitate local business by making credit available again at much lower interest rates. Hence, it was critical, in Bank Negara's acting governor's words, to 'bring the ringgit back into the country' (*New Straits Times* 2 September 1998a) so that reflation, relaxation of monetary policy, and rescue for domestic businesses would not lead to the ringgit's immediate collapse.

Mahathir and Daim's political priority was to preserve Malaysia Inc. by domestic initiative without waiting for 'normalisation in the global financial environment' (*New Straits Times* 2 September 1998). Whether or not the strategy of 'temporary' exchange controls would work, Mahathir and Daim, and the conglomerates which stood behind them, had nothing better. The capital strike remained. The Malaysian government abandoned its attempt to issue new bonds when Moodys, and Standard and Poor, responded by downgrading Malaysia's creditworthiness. Hence, the controls were, collectively, a 'measure [of] last resort', as Mahathir put it (*New Straits Times* 2 September 1998b), the obdurate stance of a state which would reject market demands for domestic reform so long as the 'international community' denied its call to reform the global money market (*New Straits Times* 2 September 1998a). But implementing the exchange controls required battle on two fronts – against the external orthodoxy of the 'free market', and internal dissent rallied tentatively around Anwar Ibrahim.

Free marketeers predictably poured scorn on Malaysia's exchange controls. Some dismissed them as being impracticable by citing China's and India's capital control problems of 'bureaucratization and leakages, leading to corruption and capital flight' (Tripathi and Saywell 1998: 52). Others warned that 'even if controls on capital outflows can buy time in a short-term panic, it is time bought at a high long-term price', and that 'even if the controls are explicitly designed to exclude foreign direct investment, as are Malaysia's, history [!] suggests investors shy away nonetheless' (*The Economist* 12 September 1998a: 93). But as gambles go, Mahathir's was made under not unfavourable global circumstances. The orthodoxy of the global money market was discredited even by supporters of global capitalism – as the self-serving dogma of an 'IMF–Treasury–Wall Street Complex' (Bhagwati 1998), or 'a phony Washington consensus' (Sachs 1998c: 19). In Indonesia, South Korea, and Thailand, IMF intervention had become synonymous with arrogance *and* failure. Instances of sudden currency depreciation in Russia, South Africa, and Latin America were openly blamed on 'contagion' from the 'speculator's disease'. With Russia defaulting on its external debt, Hong Kong defending its currency peg and its stock market, and China and Taiwan appearing exemplary in their maintenance of currency controls (*Asiaweek* 18 September 1998a), East Asian states seemed to hedge their bets on the Malaysian experiment. Not many would go along with it, but not all wished it ill. 'Call me a heretic', or 'a pariah, if you like', said Mahathir (Mahathir 1998), but he had seized upon a regional 'resentment' at a western-dominated money market (see Richard Higgott's essay in this volume) to speak for East Asian economic nationalism.[25]

The domestic situation turned out to be more turbulent. On 2 September, Mahathir dismissed Anwar Ibrahim from the cabinet; one day later, UMNO's Supreme Council expelled Anwar from the party. No official reasons were given beyond suggestions that unproven allegations of sexual misconduct, corruption, and 'anti-national' actions against Anwar rendered him 'not suitable' to remain in his official and party positions (Hiebert and Sherry 1998). Leaving aside the details of the allegations, and now formal charges, made against Anwar (as well as background on the differences between Mahathir and Anwar, for which see Johnson (1998) and Khoo (1998; 1998a)), the latter's dismissal is relevant to the discussion here in at least two ways.

One critical dimension of Anwar's sacking involved policy differences between him and the Mahathir–Daim combination. For several months beginning in December, Anwar and his advisers in Bank Negara tried to limit the damage Mahathir had inflicted on 'international investor confidence' by reassuring foreign capital that firmer regulatory measures and prudential standards would be adopted to reform the financial system. Anwar's December austerity package, followed by Bank Negara's tighter monetary policies (prior to Daim's announcement of the *National Economic Recovery Plan*), however, ran counter to Mahathir–Daim's inclination towards restimulating the economy, restoring credit, and lowering interest rates (Keenan *et al.* 1998: 11).[26] Those policy differences intensified with negative economic growth in the first half of 1998, and were complicated by political events in Indonesia in May. Mahathir had already curbed Anwar's scope in financial and economic management by recalling Daim to head the National Economic Action Council. For the June UMNO General Assembly, Anwar's allies had planned to provoke an open criticism of Mahathir for cronyist and nepotistic practices. That line of criticism took a cue from the slogan of the Indonesian movement (*korupsi, kolusi, nepotisme*) that forced Suharto out of office in May. It was an ill-disguised preparation for a challenge to Mahathir's leadership at the 1999 UMNO General Assembly, when the triennial party election would be held (Khoo 1998a: 7). Mahathir responded by forcing the resignation of the editors of two Malay-language newspapers (*Berita Harian* and *Utusan Malaysia*), and the managing director of one television station (TV3) reputedly allied to Anwar.

The 'anti-cronyism' of the Anwar camp also echoed the global money market's call for an end to 'East Asian crony capitalism', not least in Malaysia. Especially after the May events in Indonesia, Anwar himself had publicly spoken of East Asia's need for 'reforms', and even 'creative destruction'. Increasingly it appeared as if Anwar, and the combination of mainstream foreign media, and institutions such as the IMF, were using each other to signal Mahathir to give way to Anwar (Khoo 1998a: 5–6). But Mahathir's confrontation with the money market was coming to a head by late August. The Bank Negara Governor, Ahmad Don, and his deputy, Fong Weng Phak, resigned in disagreement over Mahathir's decision to implement exchange controls (Keenan *et al.* 1998: 11). A few days later, Anwar – 'a former Muslim radical who became the West's model for appealing leaders in the world's emerging-market nations' (Spaeth 1998: 17), whom the money market and the 'international community' might have wistfully regarded as their last influential voice in Malaysia – was sacked. It is perhaps in the context of Mahathir's willingness to push his economic nationalism to its logic, and his suspicion that Anwar – with 'his regard for global market efficiencies' (Johnson 1998) – would desist, that the otherwise bizarre insinuations of Anwar's 'anti-national' conduct might be understood.[27]

The second critical dimension of Anwar's dismissal concerns the future of Malaysia Inc., about which it is difficult to be conclusive presently (2 November, the first day of Anwar's trial in the High Court in Kuala Lumpur). Few doubt that Mahathir–Daim's exchange controls, ringgit stabilization, credit loosening, and lower interest rates would principally benefit the conglomerates close to them. After his fall, Anwar claimed he opposed Mahathir–Daim's plans for bailing out their 'cronies' (*Asiaweek* 18 September 1998a; Elliott 1998: 15; 1998a: 25) but any serious evaluation of this claim must await the availability of reliable evidence. Since 2 September, however, Anwar has fought back by reactivating his former activism, and unexpectedly tapping a deep vein of anti-Mahathir disaffection at that. Not all the dissent which has been expressed in largely spontaneous anti-Mahathir protests and marches had its roots in the economic crisis. Nonetheless, a 'reform movement' (*Reformasi*) has begun, the goals of which are as yet inchoate, and the directions for which depend as much on whether Mahathir's current economic policies succeed rapidly enough, as on Anwar's eventual personal fate. If the policies fail, for reasons global and/or domestic, Mahathir's Malaysia Inc. will lose whatever is left of its appeal of economic nationalism against the money market, and manifest itself merely as a 'camp of privilege' against which stands a populist front.

NOTES

*   This paper is part of a project, 'Discourses and Practices of Democracy in Southeast Asia', conducted by the Research and Education for Peace Unit, University Sains Malaysia (REPUSM), jointly with the Göteborg Centre for East and Southeast Asian Studies (GESEAS). Funding from Sida, Sweden, which supported the research and preparation of this paper is gratefully acknowledged. I also wish to thank Chang Yii Tan, Chua Soo Yean, Halim Salleh, Khoo Khay Jin, Francis Loh Kok Wah, Loo Peng Peng, Ong Hooi See, and Subramaniam Pillay for their comments and assistance.

1   See Gomez and Jomo (1997: 53–74) for case studies of such takeovers in various economic sectors.

2   The price of crude petroleum fell from US$36.50 per barrel in 1980 to US$14.70 per barrel in 1986. Palm oil earnings fell from RM4.5 billion in 1984 to RM3.0 billion in 1986. By 1985, the tin market had collapsed and the value of tin exports in 1986 barely exceeded 25 per cent of the 1980 figure. Commodity export earnings were RM37.6 billion in 1985, instead of the RM63.1 billion forecast by the economic planners after a three-fold increase in earnings between 1975 and 1980 (Jomo *et al.* 1996: 79–80).

3   Public debt rose from RM34.16 billion in 1981 to RM87.06 billion in 1986, because of NEP-based deficit spending, the HICOM projects, and the post-1985 Plaza Accord yen appreciation (Jomo *et al.* 1996: 80).

4   Government development expenditure for 1985 and 1986 was RM6.756 billion and RM7.521 billion respectively compared with RM11.189 billion for 1982, the first year of Mahathir's premiership. Total private investment fell from RM13.3 billion in 1984 to RM10.1 billion in 1986, while foreign corporate investment alone fell from its peak of RM3.26 billion in 1982 to RM2.93 billion in 1983, RM2.14 billion in 1984, RM1.73 billion in 1985, and RM1.26 billion in 1986 (Jomo *et al.* 1996: 80–1).

5   Gomez and Jomo (1997: 179–80) observed of the 'contemporary conglomerate style of growth' that it has increasingly involved 'mergers, acquisitions and asset-stripping, with scant regard for relevant experience and expertise' and that it reflected 'the greater attention to financial accumulation rather than the difficult

but ultimately necessary development of internationally competitive productive capacities'.

6 In comparison, from 1987 to 1997 (June), the government's external debt never exceeded the 1987 level of RM44.767 billion; public sector external debt totalled RM41.530 billion in June 1997 (Bank Negara February 1998: 103). This was due to the government's holding down its debt since the 1985 recession, and not to any lack of international lender confidence.

7 For 1996 and the first half of 1997 respectively, there were, additionally, RM14.995 billion and RM18.627 billion for bonds, money market instruments and financial derivatives (Bank Negara February 1998: 117).

8 New private sector share issues amounted to RM8.6496 billion in 1990 but declined to RM4.3914 billion in 1991. The figure rose to RM9.1815 billion in 1992 but again fell to RM3.4326 billion in 1993. After that, it rose from RM8.5479 billion in 1994 to RM15.9244 billion in 1996, and RM18.2247 billion in 1997 (Bank Negara February 1998: 68).

9 Mahathir was fond of reminding civil servants that private sector profits, translated into government (tax) revenues, paid their wages.

10 The persistent use of cheap foreign labour in sectors like construction despite numerous injunctions and warnings to employers to switch to capital-intensive methods is a case in point. Few instances of the failure of regulation can match the fragmentation of the environmental impact statement which Ekran was permitted to submit for its Bakun Hydro-Electric Project.

11 Stung by foreign criticisms that the economy might overheat in the 1990s because of its high growth, Mahathir was known periodically to sneer that his critics had never run an economy before. In reply, he rejected the likelihood of overheating, launched an *inflasi sifar* ('zero inflation') campaign and proudly declared that there was nothing 'fortuitous' about the (planned and directed) performance of the economy.

12 The rates quoted are the monthly averages of buying and selling rates at noon, as quoted by Bank Negara (Bank Negara May 1998: 65). The lowest rate at which the ringgit traded was RM4.88 to US$1, in January 1998.

13 Many Malaysian punters on the KLSE based their decisions, to buy or sell, on rumours forever circulating about the comings and goings of foreign institutional investors, who, it was assumed, had the real financial power to move the markets significantly.

14 An UMNO delegate to the party's general assembly said, 'There's a lot of unhappiness against the prime minister. Small traders blame him for mismanagement of the economy and selective bailouts. People are getting fed up with his constant attack on foreigners. It's beginning to hurt us' (Hiebert 1998: 14).

15 See http:\\www.pathfinder.co...malaysia_interview1.html for the full text of the *Time* interview with Mahathir. The abridged printed version omits several criticisms Mahathir made of the IMF, and financial bailouts in the United States.

16 Which, Godement added, 'will be viewed by many as a form of thievery'. Even the opening of the financial system to foreign penetration was being contemplated: see the deputy minister of finance's tentative statement about the need to reconsider raising the limit on foreign equity in financial institutions beyond 50 per cent (*New Straits Times* 30 July 1998).

17 Mahathir put it thus: 'Anything we do in the direction of recovery is seen as wrong and will cause a loss of confidence' (*Time* 15 June 1998).

18 From Mahathir:

What the IMF wants us to do is to increase the interest rates, to reduce credit, to increase taxes. Now all of these things would bankrupt our companies. ... If you cannot top up, our regulations say you will be considered to have a non-performing loan after six months – the IMF says no, it must be three months. But in three months they cannot pay. But if we do not follow the IMF, the result will be a loss of confidence and down goes our currency.

(*Time* 15 June 1998)

19 'The crisis has been mismanaged from the start by the world's two largest economic powers, the United States and Japan, both of which wield influence in the region dwarfing that of any other country' (Godement 1998: 28). See Anderson (1998), too, about Japan having missed its opportunity of exerting leadership.

20 Few things showed more clearly Anwar's subordination to Mahathir and Daim this time around than the *New Straits Times* of 24 July 1998, which reported Daim's announcement of the *National Economic Recovery Plan* on its front page, and Anwar talking about solutions to 'social ills' on the second page.

21 At the assembly, Mahathir declassified lists of (mostly) firms and individuals who benefited from privatized contracts, government projects, preferential share allocations, and award of business licences.

22 'even if, in the same moment, the leaders of the new nation did personally benefit from their power, by ransacking the society and the economy as all nondemocratic states do' (Castells 1992: 24).

23 For a different assessment of the present situation, but one which also recognizes that the regional if not world order has changed significantly, see George Yeo, 'Crisis and Confidence: Building a New Asia', Speech at the Business Week Asia Leadership Forum, Singapore, 23 June 1998.

24 This 'Postscript' was completed on 2 November. The rest of the chapter is only slightly different from the original paper presented, on 21 August 1988, at the Asia Research Conference mentioned in the introduction to this volume.

25 Even if Malaysia did not exemplify the 'East Asian model' partly because Malaysia, unlike South Korea or Taiwan, never scaled the heights of late industrialization, and partly because its class and ethnic complexities were alien to the other Asian NICs.

26 Note the following report:

at a cabinet meeting late last November, Dr Mahathir acquiesced to a 'virtual IMF' plan, accepting all the IMF's policies without the national disgrace of having the IMF then approve the plan, a step the fiercely nationalistic Dr Mahathir couldn't stomach.

(Johnson 1998)

27 'Anwar counts as friends U.S. Secretary of State Madeleine Albright and Defense Secretary William Cohen. Not long ago, he planned to co-author a book with Michel Camdessus, managing director for the International Monetary Fund' (Spaeth 1998: 17).

13

THE PHILIPPINES

The making of a neo-classical tragedy

Walden Bello

In the latter half of 1997, the actors in Southeast Asia's economic drama were cast in unfamiliar roles. The Philippines, once tagged the 'sick man' of Asia, appeared to be weathering the financial crisis better than its formerly supercharged neighbors, Thailand, Malaysia, and Indonesia. Not without a slight swagger to his voice, President Fidel Ramos attributed the reversal of fortune to the Philippines allegedly having 'sounder economic fundamentals' than the former Tigers.

Not everyone agreed. Indeed, critics claimed that Ramos and his technocrats were underestimating the depth of the crisis. The assertion that the Philippines had better fundamentals, they said, was merely a smokescreen for the administration's lack of a strategy for dealing with the financial crisis.

By the second half of 1998, it was no longer possible to sustain the illusion of a relatively unscathed economy. From 5 percent in 1997, the growth rate for 1998 was expected to be just 1 percent, if, that is, the country was lucky. Indeed, on a number of key indicators, the Philippines was faring worse than its neighbors. A greater proportion of the work force – 13.3 percent – was now unemployed in the Philippines than in the deep crisis economies of Thailand, Korea, and Malaysia. The fall in stock market value in the first nine months of 1998 was steeper – at 37.2 percent – in Manila than in all the other East Asian exchanges with the exception of Jakarta. And while the peso and the Thai baht – the original crisis currency – were approximately equal in value at the start of the crisis at 25 or 26 baht to the dollar, the baht had strengthened, by September 1998, to 37:1 from around 54:1 at the beginning of the year while the peso had remained stuck at 44:1.

Assuming office in late June, the newly elected president, Joseph Estrada, asserted that he was inheriting not Asia's latest tiger economy, but a 'puppy', and promptly declared the government 'bankrupt'.

To many in government, business, and academic circles, the Asian financial crisis was an unfortunate external event that put an end to a promising economic recovery that had put the Philippines on the road to the prosperity

238

enjoyed by its neighbors. To others, however, the unraveling of the Philippine economy was not simply brought about by external circumstances but was the natural consequence of a model of economic development that had been gradually institutionalized over a decade: a liberal, free market economy that was greatly dependent on foreign capital inflows and foreign markets.

Liberalization and depression

An adequate understanding of the current Philippine crisis can only be achieved by situating it in the context of the dramatic shifts in Philippine economic policy making since the early 1980s. In the three or four years before 1980, a partnership between the regime of Ferdinand Marcos and the World Bank to develop the country along export-oriented lines within a liberal economic policy framework had unravelled – a victim of the fateful conjunction of severe government indebtedness to foreign banks, a subversion of market-oriented initiatives by insider, 'crony capitalist' interests, continuing strong protection of the domestic market, international recession, and the political crisis of the dictatorship.

The limited results of the liberal, export-oriented policies pushed by the World Bank and its technocrat allies during the Marcos era were summed up by one observer thus:

> In fact, trade reform efforts revealed the limits on the power of the liberal technocrats and their multilateral supporters. ... The incentives to export promotion were hardly dismantled, and the government's commitment to export promotion was limited. Export enclaves remained just that; enclaves within an inward-oriented economy.
>
> (Haggard 1990a)

It was to accelerate the liberalization of the economy that the World Bank and the International Monetary Fund (IMF) inaugurated a period of structural adjustment in the Philippines in 1980, a move that was facilitated at the political level by the installation of a cabinet dominated by technocrats close to the two multilateral institutions (Bello *et al.* 1982).

Adjustment unfolded in roughly three phases, the first from 1980 to 1983, when the emphasis was placed on trade liberalization; the second, from 1983 all the way to 1992, when owing partly to severe economic crisis, the focus shifted from liberalization to stabilization and debt repayment; and the third, from 1992 to the present, when all-sided free market transformation marked by rapid deregulation, privatization, and trade and investment liberalization was the order of the day.

During the first phase, a process of liberalization was pushed on a hesitant government where close associates of the Marcos regime were waging a rearguard war to protect their privileged positions and local firms were seeking to preserve their preferential access to the domestic market. Despite this resistance, structural adjustment, which was implemented with two loans from the World Bank (Structural Adjustment I and II), forged ahead. Between 1981 and 1985, quantitative restrictions (QRs) were removed on more than 900 items, while the nominal average tariff protection was brought down from 43 percent in 1981 to 28 percent in 1985.[1]

But liberalization slowed down significantly in 1983, when international recessionary trends combined with the structural program's liberalization component and its tight fiscal and monetary policies to create a vicious cycle that plunged the economy downward. 'Whatever the merits of the SAL', noted one analyst, 'its timing was deplorable' (Lindsey 1992). The program failed to adjust to the onset of a world recession, so that instead of rising, exports fell, while imports, taking advantage of the liberalized regime, severely eroded the home industries. Instead of allowing the government to push countercyclical mechanisms to arrest the decline in private sector activity, the structural adjustment framework intensified it with its policy of high interest rates and tight government budgets. Not surprisingly, the GNP shrank precipitously two years in a row, contributing to the deepening of the political crisis that resulted in the ousting of Ferdinand Marcos in February 1986.

The 'model debtor' strategy and economic stagnation

By that time, the Philippines' foreign debt had risen to over $26 billion, from $20 billion in 1981, when the process of adjustment began. This led the World Bank and the IMF, under strong pressure from the big commercial creditors, to put the emphasis on debt repayment in their agenda for the new administration of Corazon Aquino. The choices for the new administration immediately boiled down to this: either limit debt service payments in order to get the country to grow or fully comply with debt obligations in order to preserve creditworthiness even at the risk of throttling growth.

The first position was espoused by Solita Monsod, who became director of the National Economic Development Authority (NEDA), and her colleagues at the University of the Philippines School of Economics, who wrote: 'The search for a recovery program that is consistent with a debt repayment schedule determined by our creditors is a futile one and should therefore be abandoned'.[2] The Central Bank and the Department of Finance, dominated by figures with links to international finance, lined up behind the second position. The so-called 'model debtor' strategy won out (Lindsey 1992).

A financial hemorrhage marked the succeeding years, with the net transfer of financial resources coming to a negative $1.3 billion a year on average between 1986 and 1991.[3] The outflow was particularly heavy in

1986–8, with payments on interest and principal coming to $3.3 billion a year. To service the debt, the Aquino administration was forced to borrow heavily from domestic financial resources, forcing it to channel much of its budgetary expenditures to repaying domestic and foreign debt obligations. Some 50 percent of the budget was allocated to servicing the debt in 1987 and the figure did not go below 40 percent until 1992 (Freedom from Debt Coalition 1997). *What all this meant was that the priority of economic policy was effectively the repayment of the foreign debt, not development.*

While liberalization took a backseat to debt repayment, it was nonetheless pursued. In the first year of the Aquino administration alone, some 994 items were liberalized. In the succeeding years, key commodities were liberalized, such as crude oil in 1987, cement in 1989, and motor vehicle spare parts in 1990 (Chavez-Malaluan 1996). Nevertheless, the pace of liberalization did slow down, partly due to fears of a repeat of the 1983–4 crisis, partly because of the strength of key business elements within the Aquino administration who had opposed Marcos and his cronies but whose enterprises depended on a protected domestic market – like the influential Concepcion family, one of whose members, Jose Concepcion, served as the secretary of trade. This continuing influence of domestic-market-based industrialists within the administration was revealed in 1990, when an executive order mandating a swift and deep reduction in tariff levels was reversed by the famous Executive Order 470, which phased a more gradual reduction over five years.

While some growth was registered from 1987 to 1989, stagnation again overtook the economy in 1990, a consequence of the limits of recovery with a weak private sector, a state channeling much needed capital and expenditures to foreign debt payments, and the absence of significant foreign direct investment.

Japanese foreign investment: the missing link

The role of direct foreign investment in differentiating the Philippines' performance *vis-à-vis* its neighbors must not be underestimated. It was during this period that a massive inflow of investment into Southeast Asia occurred as a result of the Plaza Accord of 1985, which forced the Japanese government to allow the value of the yen to appreciate drastically relative to the dollar in order to relieve the US trade deficit with Japan by 'cheapening' US exports to that country and making imports from Japan more expensive in dollar terms for American consumers.

With production costs in Japan rendered prohibitive by the yen revaluation, Japanese firms moved the more labor-intensive phases of their production to cheap-labor sites in East Asia. And within the region, Southeast Asia became the key recipient of Japanese direct investment. What occurred was one of the largest and swiftest movements of capital to the developing world in recent history. Between 1985 and 1990, some $15 billion worth of Japanese direct investment flowed into Southeast Asia.[4] In the case of Thailand, for instance, the Japanese direct investment that flowed into the country in 1987 exceeded the cumulative Japanese investment for the preceding twenty years.[5] When one includes in this inflow of capital Japanese bank capital and bilateral aid, both of which were usually in support of Japanese direct investments, then one was probably talking about $50 to $70 billion financial inflow from Japan into the region over a five-year period.

The inflow of Japanese capital not only allowed Southeast Asia to rise from the deep international recession of the mid 1980s and propel it into a decade of high growth. It also allowed countries which were under either IMF or World Bank structural adjustment programs, such as Thailand and Indonesia, or self-imposed ones, like Malaysia, to avoid implementing the core adjustment policies of trade and investment liberalization, tight spending, and tight money. Had these governments stuck faithfully to these programs, which they had entered during the recession of the mid 1980s, they would most likely have been propelled into a decade of stagnation, as were the Philippines, Latin America, and Africa.

Being skirted by Japanese capital, the Philippines had no choice but to implement adjustment since being stamped with the IMF–World Bank seal of approval was the only way to regain access to world capital markets. Between 1985 and 1990, the Philippines received only $748 million in investment from Japan while Indonesia received $3.1 billion and Thailand received $3.7 billion.[6]

Why did the Japanese avoid the Philippines? Part of the explanation undoubtedly resides in the perception of political instability as the country was rocked by six coup attempts on the way to a more consolidated democratic political structure. In any event, while the Philippines, wracked by the combination of structural adjustment, political crisis, and foreign investment deprivation, was registering a 1.4 percent average growth between 1980 and 1993, its Southeast Asian neighbors, unhampered by adjustment and buoyed by Japanese investment, were flying high: 8.2 percent average growth for the period for Thailand, 5.8 percent for Indonesia, and 6.2 percent for Malaysia.

Not surprisingly, stagnation led to a worsening of social conditions in the country. Filipino families living below the poverty line in 1991 reached 46.5 percent – a marginal reduction from the 1985 figure of 49.3 percent.[7] Income distribution actually worsened with the share of income going to the lowest 20 percent of families falling from 5.2 percent to 4.7 percent, while that going to the top 10 percent rose from 36.4 percent to 38.6 percent.[8] The Philippines also provided one of the best documented studies of the correlation between environmental destruction and structural adjustment, with the now famous Repetto study concluding that adjustment

created so much unemployment that migration patterns changed drastically. The large migration flows to Manila declined, and most migrants could turn only to open access forests, watersheds, and artisanal fisheries. Thus the major environmental effect of the economic crisis was over-exploitation of these vulnerable resources.
(Cruz and Repetto 1992: 48; Broad and Cavanagh 1993)

Radical liberalization under Ramos

This was the 'sick man of Asia' that Fidel Ramos inherited upon winning the presidency in 1992. Ramos's response was even more adjustment, even more free market orientation, with the next years marked by a comprehensive program of liberalization, deregulation, and privatization pursued with almost Messianic zeal.

The ideological character of economic policy making during the Ramos period can only be understood partly as a reaction toward the Marcos regime, which many in the urban middle and upper middle classes had identified not only with dictatorship and the loss of human rights but also with cronyism, protectionism, and rent seeking. Academics or political figures with advanced academic training were a key in this process, and many of them had done their graduate work in the late 1970s and 1980s, when state-oriented Keynesianism lost its luster, and neo-liberalism came into vogue not only in the economics departments of US universities but also in key local institutions such as the School of Economics of the University of the Philippines and the School for Research and Communications (now University of Asia and the Pacific).

The 'neo-classification' of the Philippine technocracy reached its apogee under Ramos not as a result of an intellectual coup but as a gradual capture of the strategic heights of the bureaucracy by these free-market-oriented policy-makers coming from the academy, government, and business. As one pivotal figure pointed out, she and her colleagues who played prominent roles in the country's free market turn acted not only out of external pressure from the World Bank and the IMF but out of belief: 'Imposed, maybe in one way, but on the other hand the mainstream decisionmakers – [the] technocracy and policymakers – also internally believe in that. So there's a confluence of policy direction' (quoted in Chavez-Malaluan 1996: 9). Another figure stressed the emergence of a broader 'consensus' among the elite and middle class around free market reform: '[No] policy reform becomes credible, workable policies, unless the people accepted. Yes, there were researchers and economists pushing for that, yes there were donor communities pushing for that ... but ultimately it is a question of whether the public accept that policy' (ibid.).

In any event, the 'neo-classical revolution' had achieved a critical mass by the time Ramos came to power, and its hegemony was consolidated during his administration. 'It's the dominant sector', one player put it. 'It's the president; it's his chief economic advisers, both formal and informal; the house of representatives; the senate – the mainstream. The mainstream is pushing for liberalization' (ibid.). This player, Gloria Macapagal-Arroyo, is now vice-president in the government of President Joseph Estrada.

Ramos and his allies in government, business, and the academy were all impatient with getting the Philippines out of the rut and joining the ranks of the Asian Tigers. Their view of how their neighbors achieved success was, however, filtered through their neo-classical ideological prism. Against much evidence, they saw the high growth rates of the East Asian and Southeast Asian economies as products of free market policies instead of strategic state interventions in the market. Typical of this selective interpretation of the Asian miracle was the following comment of Jesus Estanislao, Aquino's secretary of finance, and a Ramos supporter:

> Government takes very good care of macro-economic balances, takes care of a number of activities like for example infrastructure development, and leaves everything else to the private sector. And that is exactly what Singapore, Malaysia, Indonesia, and Thailand have done, and that is what the Philippines should be doing, and we are beginning to do it.[9]

These considerations account for the speed with which initiatives aimed at deregulating, liberalizing, and further privatizing the economy unfolded and the relatively little controversy they elicited.

Profitable government enterprises like the oil-refining and marketing firm Petron, considered the crown jewel of the state sector, were handed over to the private sector, as were some vital services like the management of the water supply. In energy and infrastructure building, government managers became enthusiastic promoters of 'build, operate, and transfer' (BOT) schemes in which projects were contracted out to the private sector with payment in the form of rights to manage the finished facility and rights to part of a stream of the expected future income it would generate.

Nationality restrictions on foreign investment were loosened considerably, with 100 percent foreign equity allowed in all but a few sectors on a short 'negative list' and the government determined to open up even the retail trade sector – long a sacred cow – to foreign firms. This was a far more liberal foreign investment code than those of most of the Philippines' neighbors.

Trade liberalization was a central concern, and here, interestingly enough, the administration's technocrats used Chile as a model, going so far as to invite the finance minister of the Pinochet regime, Rolf Luders, to speak before many Filipino audiences. In Chile, Luders and other radical free marketeers had reduced tariffs across the board to 11 percent. Believing they could outperform the Chileans, the Filipino technocrats produced an executive decree that would reduce tariffs on all products (except on sensitive agricultural commodities like rice) to a uniform 5 percent by 2004 for all trading partners. The administration also made sure to build external constraints that would, among other things, bind future governments to a liberal trade regime by entering the ASEAN Free Trade Area (AFTA), bringing the Philippines into the Asia–Pacific Economic Co-operation (APEC), and, most of all, ratifying the Uruguay Round of the General Agreement on Tariffs and Trade (GATT), which, among other things, obligated the country to reduce its tariffs and ban import quotas.

Together with financial liberalization, these measures elicited the much desired seal of approval from the IMF and allowed the Philippines to re-enter world capital markets in the early 1990s. With the country starved of capital in the years of draconian structural adjustment in the 1980s, the aim of the Filipino financial managers was to attract significant amounts of foreign capital to drive a high level of GDP growth that would allow the Philippines to join the ranks of the 'tigers' to 'become a NIC by the year 2000', as the administration's slogan put it.

Attracting foreign capital

To make up for the Philippines having been skirted by the region-wide boom generated by Japanese capital in the late 1980s and early 1990s, Ramos's technocrats were on the lookout for foreign capital flows that could come in significant quantities and do for the Philippines what Japanese capital had done for its neighbors. Japanese capital itself came in increasing amounts to the Philippines, but the focus of Philippine technocrats like Bangko Sentral Governor Gabriel Singson and Finance Minister Roberto de Ocampo was on the vast amounts of personal savings, pension funds, government funds, and corporate savings that were deposited in mutual funds, hedge funds, and other investment mechanisms that were designed to maximize their value. These funds were often placed under the management of big international banks or investment houses and they were played as portfolio investments by fund managers that were experienced in spotting investment opportunities that combined high yields with a quick turnaround time. In the early 1990s, noted an Asian Development Bank report, 'the declining returns in the stock markets of industrial countries and the low real interest rates compelled investors to seek higher returns on their capital elsewhere' (Tang and Villafuerte 1995: 10) .

But just like Japanese capital in the late 1980s, these funds were not simply going to walk in. They had to be invited in by creating the appropriate policy environment. To create this environment, the Filipinos looked at the strategies of other financial managers in Southeast Asia that had begun to successfully attract northern finance capital. And here, the Thais, who in the early 1990s were seeking alternative sources of foreign investment to make up for the tapering off of Japanese direct investment, seemed to provide a good role model. Ironically – and, as events would later show, tragically – the one place where the Filipinos borrowed heavily from their neighbors was not in those areas where state intervention and regulation was prominent but in that area where significant liberalization had indeed occurred: the capital account and the financial sector.

Borrowing the Thai formula

To attract portfolio investment and massive credit flows from the international banks, the Thais had evolved a strategy with essentially three key elements: capital account and financial liberalization, maintenance of significant differentials in interest rates in Bangkok and northern money centers to suck in foreign speculative capital, and 'pegging' of the local currency to the dollar at a stable rate to insure foreign investors against foreign exchange risk.

To Manila's technocrats, the Thais' great success in attracting portfolio investment was the best proof of the correctness of their policies, and they proceeded to replicate the Thai experience.

In the area of financial liberalization, the government moved to create one of the most foreign capital-friendly systems in the region. The capital account was almost fully liberalized, with most foreign exchange restrictions lifted, making the peso virtually fully convertible; full and immediate repatriation of profits, dividends, and capital; and the free utilization of foreign currency accounts. Significant liberalization was also imposed on the financial sector. After being closed for fifty years, the insurance sector was opened up to 100 percent foreign-owned companies in 1994. Especially critical in facilitating capital flows was the liberalization of the banking system by Republic Act 7721, which opened up the banking system to foreign banks, resulting in twelve of them setting up operations by September 1996.

Like the Bank of Thailand, the policy of the Bangko Sentral ng Pilipinas (BSP) was to keep local interest rates high – some 12 to 15 percent – in order to suck in foreign capital. Prime lending rates in the Philippines in the last few years were kept about six percentage points above US rates, on average (Samonte and Garcia 1997). This policy transformed the view of high interest rates in financial circles; as one analyst has written, '[b]eing endowed with high interest rates turned out to be a "virtue" that attracted external capital whereas it was once nothing but a brake upon economic activity as it served as a barrier for businesses to acquire capital' (Esguerra 1997).

And like the Thais, the Ramos administration pegged the peso to the dollar at a stable rate of exchange, so that in the whole of 1996, for instance, there was only a 2 percent fluctuation in the peso–dollar rate. The consequent inflow of dollars caused the peso to appreciate relative to the dollar, and the BSP intervened in the foreign exchange by buying or selling dollars to keep the peso within a certain band.

Finance capital's vote of confidence

The country re-entered the international bond market in 1993 and was able to successfully float about $1.3 billion that first year (Tang and Villafuerte 1995: 13). Portfolio investors were attracted to Philippine Treasury bills and their relatively high yields. Foreign exchange liberalization also drew them to the reorganized Philippine Stock Exchange, where publicly listed local firms sought to sell equities as a means of raising capital. In 1993, the first year of the Ramos presidency, the stock price index in the Philippine Stock Exchange rose by 154 percent – the highest among all major stock exchanges in Asia and the third best in the world (Tang and Villafuerte 1995).

The Philippines was on the way to becoming a darling of foreign portfolio investors, and between 1993 and 1997, some $19.4 billion worth of net portfolio investment flowed into the country.[10] These flows dwarfed the foreign direct investment inflows, with estimates of their size ranging from 75 to 90 percent of total investment (Bondoy 1997).

Foreign capital also flowed in the form of loans made abroad by the private sector or as capital raised by local banks through the issuance of debt instruments like floating rate certificates of deposit (FRCDs). Contracted at relatively low interest rates, a great portion of these funds were registered as time deposits at the banks, then relent via foreign currency deposit units (FCDUs), a facility dating back to the Marcos era that enabled local and foreign banks to extend dollar loans to local borrowers. With the wide spread – some 600 basis points – between US interest rates and interest rates on peso loans in the local markets, local banks could borrow abroad and still make a clean profit relending to local customers at lower rates than those charged to peso loans. In 1996, the average interest rate for FCDU loans came to 7.41 percent compared to 12.8 percent for peso loans (Samonte and Garcia 1997a).

Financial liberalization brought more foreign banks into the local scene by late 1993 and brought about a greater competition for customers. This translated into a rapid build-up in FCDU deposits and loans over the last few years, with deposits coming to $14.4 billion by the end of 1996 and loans coming to $9 billion, according to BSP data (Samonte and Garcia 1997). In 1996 alone, new foreign currency loans totalled $4.9 billion.[11] Other estimates showed an even sharper increase, with the investment analyst Deutsche Morgan Grenfell (DMG) asserting that dollar loans had risen to $11.6 billion as of March 1997 – or almost five times the level of $2 billion in December 1993 (*Philippine Daily Inquirer* 1997).

In other words, the FCDU facility played the same role as the famous – or, in the current view, notorious – Bangkok International Banking Facility: that of providing cheap dollar loans to domestic customers. As an HG Asia study put it, with the exchange rate 'padlocked' for two years at 26.2 to 26.3 pesos to the dollar, 'They are not fools in Manila. They were offered US dollars at 600 basis points cheaper than the peso rates along with currency protection from the BSP. They took it' (ibid.).

Overheating and overbuilding

For the most part, this inflow of foreign investment and foreign capital was hailed as a vote of confidence in the management of the 'new Philippine economy'. By late 1996, however, worried looks began to be cast by fund managers as the Philippine banks' net foreign liability reached close to $14.6 billion or close to 35 percent of the Philippines' foreign debt of $42 billion. The private debt was equivalent to 13 percent of GNP and rising – a position which bore comparison with that of their models, the Thai banks, whose net foreign liability position at the end of 1996 was equivalent to 20 percent of GNP.[12] This picture led one investment analyst to warn:

> The Philippines has not yet had to pay its reckoning for copying Thai Practices. It adopted them much later than Thailand. But its reckoning is likely to come earlier than Thailand's. The BSP does not have the resources of the Bank of Thailand and the game is heating up faster than it did in the early stages in Thailand.[13]

The Philippine banks had gone on a borrowing spree, but this would not have been that worrisome had the money gone to the right places. Unfortunately, much of the lending of banks had gone not into the really productive sectors of the economy but into the speculative areas, like the financing of consumption and property development. A clear indication of lending going to the wrong sectors was that while construction had been booming, industrial growth dropped from a 17 percent annual rate in 1996 to −2.3 percent in 1997.[14]

Manufacturing and agriculture were not attractive sectors to lend to because they would demand strategic commitments of large chunks of capital that would only bear fruit in terms of decent returns over the medium and long term. Moreover, their future was uncertain since the radical liberalization of trade and investment that paralleled financial liberalization was making production less and less profitable for domestic producers. Duty-free shops were flooding the country with cheap imported manufactures, and cheap rice and corn imports were coming in volumes that far outstripped the minimum access volumes committed by the country under the GATT–WTO Agreement. Indeed, with the prospects for profit making being much brighter in real estate, it is not surprising that many manufacturers were making dollar loans not for reinvestment or for research and development, but to play the stock market and the property market.

In any event, in the wake of the much publicized real estate problems in Bangkok and the suspected high exposure of Philippine banks to the real estate sector, rumors about the imminent collapse of a highly indebted developer, Megaworld, early in 1997, forced people to look more closely at the Philippine real estate sector. The result was a consensus that a glut would emerge in 1998, though analysts differed on how big it would be. All Asia, one local investment house, predicted that, owing to overbuilding, by the year 2000 the supply of high-rise residential units would exceed demand by 211 percent, while supply of commercial developments would outpace demand by 142 percent (Oviedo and Oviedo 1997). In any event, fears of a coming glut were so widespread that the property index of the Philippine Stock Exchange fell by 40 percent on fears that developers would be saddled with unsold condominiums (*Business World* 1997).

Overbuilding was forcing developers, according to one account, to 'become creative in search of new markets'. More and more companies, it noted, apparently without irony, 'are spending billions of pesos to develop resorts, golf courses, and other special projects' (Oviedo and Oviedo 1997).

Stats wars

To calm public worries about bank exposure in the real estate sector, the BSP, in June 1997, declared that no more than 20 percent of the total exposure of commercial banks should be in property loans. But as a DMG study found, this tightening, which paralleled similar moves by other Asian central banks, was 'probably too late' (*International Herald Tribune* 1997). The BSP announced that lending to the property sector in mid 1996 amounted to only 9.2 percent of the exposure of banks, going up to about 11 percent by December (*Philippine Daily Inquirer* 1997a). BSP officials in that same survey admitted, however, that the property loan exposures of individual banks ranged from 'negligible' to as high as 28.6 percent (*Asian Wall Street Journal* 1997a).

Under pressure from a skeptical public, Finance Secretary Roberto de Ocampo upped the figure of the banks' real-estate-related exposure to 14 percent in September 1997 (*Business World* 1997a). But even this figure was considered low by foreign analysts, some of whom saw the real exposure of the banks at around 15–25 percent (*Asian Wall Street Journal* 1997a). These analysts felt that the higher estimate would take into account property-related loans that could be classified under other categories such as services, hotel, construction, and even manufacturing.

The huge capital inflows and the banks' real estate exposure did begin to worry BSP officials, but this was at a rather late stage in the game. In May 1997, one BSP official warned that funds could be easily moved globally 'at the tap of a finger' and there was the possibility of facing 'abrupt reversals of capital flow' (*Business World* 1997b). And it was only in early June, shortly before the July 11 *de facto* devaluation of the peso, that the BSP issued 'pre-emptive measures … aimed at curbing the growth in foreign currency lending'.[15]

Foreign investors took much earlier notice of the massive debt build-up of local banks and the crisis of the real estate sector, and they saw these in the context of serious structural flaws that were glossed over by the growth rates of 5 to 6 percent GDP per annum that the Philippines registered from 1994 to 1997. For them, the two most sensitive indicators became the trade deficit and the current account deficit, which, among other things, indicate if a country would have the capability in the long term to pay for its imports and service its foreign debt obligations. The trade deficit in 1996 stood at $12.8 billion, or a doubling in just three years! And a key reason for this was that even as exports continued to rise, imports rose even faster owing to the high cost of imported components that went into the Philippines' prime export, electronic products, the import content of which was 70–80 percent (*Philippine Daily Inquirer* 1997b).

Moreover, traditional Philippine mainstays had a lackluster performance, with garment exports, for instance, falling by 27 percent in 1996, contributing to foreign investors' perception that despite its 24 percent export growth rate that year (owing mainly to import-intensive electronics and machinery exports), the Philippines was facing the same difficulties of declining export capacity as Malaysia and Thailand, which registered no export growth, and Indonesia, which registered only 7 percent.

The slowdown in the growth of traditional exports was related to the very policies that had encouraged foreign capital inflows. For the only way that portfolio investors would be encouraged to come in was to tie the peso to the dollar at a stable rate, at 25 or 26:1. But with the appreciation of the dollar in the mid 1990s, many Philippine exports became increasingly non-competitive pricewise. This led to increasing conflict between two schools of free marketeers: the central bank lobby, who favored foreign capital inflows by keeping the peso strong, and the University of the Philippines School of Economics, who wanted a devalued peso to promote Philippine exports.[16] This conflict did not, however, preclude their broader consensus around rapid liberalization of trade and investment, accelerated deregulation, and continuing privatization of government enterprises.

In any event, to many foreign direct investors in the Philippines and other parts of the region, the export slowdown indicated, not a temporary blip, but the ending of the export-led 'Southeast Asian Miracle' and dampened their enthusiasm to commit new funds. Many began, in fact, to consider shifting their investments to China, whose low-wage-based export machine was going into high gear, displacing higher-cost Southeast Asian exports in many key markets, including that of the United States.

But not to worry, said Philippine government analysts, and please don't compare us to our neighbors. For instance, they claimed that the country's current account balance, which brought to bear on the positive side of the ledger the remittances from the Philippines' vast army of overseas workers, was manageable; and the current account was, more than the trade deficit, what foreign investors, analysts, and speculators allegedly looked at in assessing the strength of the peso. But even if one were to grant this argument, things looked shaky. In 1996, according to estimates based on official figures, the current account deficit of $3.5 billion stood at 4 percent of GNP. Worrisome but not alarming, said some.

However, when one tightened up the methodology for calculating the figure to account for unexplained errors and omissions in the balance of payments (which now add up to almost 6 percent of GNP), as one prescient investment house study did, one came up with the realization that the real current account deficit was around 7 percent of GNP for 1996 – or uncomfortably close to the 8 percent deficit experienced by Mexico and Thailand before their economic meltdowns began. With a deficit of that size, investors speculated, the pressure would increase on the Philippine financial authorities to close the deficit by devaluing the currency, a move which would allow the country's exports to remain competitive.

Uneasiness on the part of foreign investors over the possibility of a peso devaluation and over the parallels between Thailand and the Philippines led them by the beginning of 1997 to significantly scale down their commitments, with foreign equity inflows to banks dropping by 97 percent in the first quarter of the year relative to the first quarter of 1996. With the jitters over property, a possible devaluation, and the massive private debt build-up, the stock market began its downward plunge – not surprising since 70 percent of the trading activity was accounted for by foreign investors (Francisco 1997). Indeed, instead of being parked in peso-denominated paper, awaiting new opportunities in the domestic market, foreign investors began to demand dollars for their pesos and move out, adding to pressures for depreciation of the peso.

'Stampede Tramples Tiger Cub'

It was this escalating exit of foreign investment in response to the strong possibility of a devaluation that would reduce the value of their peso holdings that attracted the attention of currency speculators looking for opportunities to cash in on large-scale foreign capital movements through the well-timed sale and purchase of dollars and pesos. In June and early July, the BSP worked mightily to contain the stampede of foreign investors to change their pesos to dollars and leave. It intervened in the foreign exchange market to maintain the peso at roughly 26:50 to the dollar, but, after spending almost $1.6 billion of its $11.3 billion reserves, it gave up the fight and let the peso float freely against the dollar.

To stem the outflow of dollars, the BSP, on the advice of the IMF, moved to raise local interest rates to stabilize the peso and continue to make investment in the country attractive to foreign investors. Interest rates doubled, from 15 to about 30 percent, but capital continued to flow out. The expected fall to P29:$1 was rapidly breached, and exporters, who had initially felt that devaluation would serve their interests, started to get worried as it pushed past the P30:$1 mark since this could significantly raise the value of their imported inputs that would more than wipe out any gains from the devaluation.

The impact on the local economy of the expected inflation owing to higher peso import prices, higher interest rates, and the sudden rise in the peso cost of servicing dollar obligations by local borrowers was expected to lead to an economic downturn and a string of bankruptcies, but Philippine officials continued to characterize the crisis as an external event, 'a storm passing through', as Finance Secretary de Ocampo put it.[17] Manila's 'economic fundamentals' were sound, in contrast to Bangkok's, and investors would see that.

But the IMF was unconvinced, and in its Capital Markets Report released during the IMF–World Bank Annual Conference in Hong Kong in the third week of September 1997, the Fund said that 'commercial banks in the Philippines have a high exposure in the property sector' (Garcia 1997). The big credit rating agencies concurred, with Standard and Poor's Corporation downgrading its outlook for the Philippine economy from 'positive' to 'stable' and warning that 'aggressive' lending by banks 'has exposed the banking system to potential asset-quality problems'.[18] It estimated the total exposure of Philippine banks to the real estate sector at 20 percent.[19] And, with the onset of the currency crisis, the 'asset quality' problems of loans to this sector had most likely intensified. It seemed only a matter of time before such heavily indebted firms would surface in newspaper reports.

Rumors began to circulate in Manila that the creditworthiness of a number of banks had been damaged by loans to the real estate sector, including Westmont Bank, Banco de Oro, Traders' Royal Bank, Urban Bank, China Banking Corporation, and International Exchange Bank. To quell the rumors and avoid a bank run, the BSP directors threatened to unleash the National Bureau of Investigation on people making those claims. But the threat dissipated when a member of the monetary board that governs the policies of the BSP admitted that five banks had indeed overshot the cap on real estate loans to 20 percent of the banks' total exposure (*Business World* 1997c). Moreover, threats could not conceal the surfacing of a succession of victims of the weaker peso and higher interest rates seeking government protection from their creditors. Among them were Vitarich, a major food processor, the big milling company Victorias Milling Company, and the EYCO Group of Companies, which had started as an appliance maker but diversified into real estate with dollar-denominated loans as well as peso loans from twenty-two banks. More key companies fell as the year wore on.

Meanwhile, the value of the local currency went down to 44 pesos to the dollar in early January 1998 – a figure unimaginable just a few months earlier – prompting importers and local industrialists to call for currency controls. At this point, it could no longer be concealed that the Ramos administration had no other strategy for dealing with the crisis than to keep interest rates high to discourage an outflow of capital and stabilize the peso. These rates, which went from 15 percent prior to the crisis to as high as 30 percent by January 1998, were killing local business, while allowing the banks and whatever foreign capital remained in the country to make a killing.

More proactive measures were precluded by the Ramos administration's *laissez-faire* ideology, which held that the best way to manage an economy was not to try to manage it at all. What came to substitute for policy was the slogan, constantly repeated, that the Philippines was not hit as badly as its neighbors because of the 'better economic fundamentals' the Ramos policies had given it. As a number of commentators rightly saw it, the administration continued in a 'denial mode'.

Instead of innovating in economic policy, when things began to really look desperate in early 1998, the Ramos administration ran to the IMF, entering into an agreement to access a $1.37 billion standby facility as part of the precautionary arrangement. Not only did the move contradict the administration's much trumpeted claim that, after thirty-six years, the Philippines was exiting the IMF. It also bound the administration to a regime of high interest rates, the achievement of fiscal surpluses, and continuing the liberalization of the capital account.

This formula, however, was increasingly dubious: the liberalization of the capital account had, of course, been pinpointed as the major culprit in the Asian crisis, having facilitated the entry and exit of massive amounts of hot capital. And high interest rates and the prohibition against running a budget deficit – which the Ramos technocrats proceeded to implement by decreeing a cutting back of non-personnel expenditures of government agencies by 25 percent – were guaranteed to put a damper on any recovery. Further, it would worsen the long-term structural problems of the country, including the massive poverty which, at the end of Ramos's term, still engulfed over 32 percent of Filipinos.[20]

Neo-classical continuity from Ramos to Estrada

The transition from the Ramos administration to the presidency of Joseph Estrada, who won the presidential elections in May 1998 by a landslide, was accompanied by the acceleration of the crisis. As of April 1998, unemployment had reached 13.3 percent of the work force – the highest since the recession year of 1991. Inflation, showing the effects of the 38 percent plus devaluation of the peso in the form of higher priced imports, rose to a sixteen-month high of 10.7 percent in June. Manufacturing registered an astonishing 14 percent decline in May 1998 from its level a year earlier. Non-performing loans as a percentage of commercial banks' total exposure had risen to 9.2 percent by mid year, with the level projected to rise to 20 percent by 1999 (*Business World* 1998).

Hopes were high that the new administration would initiate a more activist and innovative policy on the crisis. The rhetoric of emergency was certainly there, with the president telling the country that the government he inherited was 'bankrupt', in the sense that it would not be able to cover many planned and normal expenditures.

Yet, expectations of innovative action were quickly dashed. Even prior to the elections, Estrada had declared that he would continue the free market reforms of greater deregulation, privatization, and liberalization initiated by the Ramos administration. An advance team had also been dispatched to the IMF and the World Bank, consisting of close Estrada advisers such as Cesar Espiritu and Ronnie Zamora, to assure the Bretton Woods institutions that there would be no reversal of free market policies should Estrada be elected.[21]

Upon his election, Estrada put in place a decidedly neo-classical economic team. Singson was kept at the BSP – out of deference, said a close Estrada adviser, to 'his 40 years at the Central Bank'.[22] Cesar Espiritu, head of Westmont Bank, which profited greatly from dollar inflows that were relent to local borrowers, was appointed secretary of finance. And two avowed free marketeers, Philip Medalla and Benjamin Diokno, were recruited from the University of the Philippines School of Economics, the bastion of neo-classical thinking, and were named secretary of planning and secretary of the budget, respectively. Summing up the character of the cabinet, Diokno declared that 'a protectionist has no place in Mr. Estrada's cabinet' (*Business World* 1998a).

Not surprisingly, one of the first acts of the Estrada team was to affirm the P580 billion budget of the Ramos administration for 1999. While special expenditures for congresspeople ('pork') were cut out, the budget affirmed the previous administration's 25 percent cut in non-personnel expenditures for government agencies. The budget was essentially a 'hard times' budget that was hardly appropriate to the rapid decline in private sector activity, which necessitated a more expansionary fiscal policy to serve as a counter-cyclical mechanism.

This course of action would, however, have entailed significant deficit spending. Deficits, of course, have always served as a tool to reignite demand to spur an economic recovery. But Estrada's technocrats were not Keynesians. The view of deficits of the Estrada team was succinctly expressed by Planning Secretary Medalla: 'If the government runs deficits, it will be a source of macroeconomic instability' (quoted in *Business World* 1998a).

Due to a decline in revenue collections, there was no way that the Ramos administration's commitment to the IMF to produce a budget surplus could be achieved by his successor. But if a deficit had to be sustained, it had to be as small as possible. Thus, to project an image of fiscal responsibility to the middle class and prepare the poorer classes for cutbacks in government expenditure that would impact mainly on them, the Estrada team projected a deficit that could come to as high as P70 billion, without putting this figure in the larger context of an economy that was facing severe economic contraction.

When the IMF came in August to review Philippine performance on the new standby agreement, the result was a Letter of Intent, the main points of which were the following: maintenance of the high interest rate regime; deficit spending that would be strictly limited to P40 billion or 1.4 percent of GDP; and a continuation of capital account and financial liberalization through abolition of key taxes on initial public offerings (IPOs) and securities transactions like the documentary stamp tax.

This fairly orthodox package must be seen in the context of the departures from IMF policy that were occurring at around the same time elsewhere in the region. In Thailand, the government had gotten the IMF to agree to a deficit to the tune of 3 percent of GDP; brought down interest rates to around 10–13 percent; and brought about the virtual nationalization of the banking system through a government bailout of local banks instead of allowing them to pass to foreign hands through their recapitalization by international banks. And even more dramatic, of course, was Malaysia's imposition of tough currency and capital controls in early September.

It cannot be said, of course, that the conditions laid out in the Letter of Intent were imposed on unwilling technocrats. Indeed, one might say that there was a meeting of minds among ideological confrères, or even that the Estrada team used the IMF as an excuse to impose a classic stabilization program on the country. Both the IMF and the Estrada technocrats had a horror of budget deficits. And both greeted Malaysia's moves with strong disapproval, with the latter vowing that the new administration would never resort to them.

The administration's other moves evinced the same ideological consistency. Despite mounting evidence that local manufacturers were suffering from lower priced imports coming into the country from neighbors whose currencies had devalued more radically than the Philippines, the Estrada team rejected a plea from the Federation of Philippine Industries to impose a 10 percent duty on locally produced commodities where sudden surges of imports were taking place. Instead, the administration affirmed its commitment to reduce tariffs to a uniform 5 percent across all commodities by the year 2004. In neo-classical parlance, the planning secretary justified this stance by saying that: 'If we put more distortions in the economy, all the more that we are really vulnerable to external shocks' (quoted in *Business World* 1998a).

Again, acting as though there did not exist a state of economic emergency, the administration's technocrats affirmed as one of their priorities the further liberalization of the foreign investment code by repealing the forty-year-old law that had nationalized retail trade. Revealing a 'beggar-my-neighbor' approach to the regional crisis, Budget Secretary Diokno justified this and other moves at foreign investment liberalization thus: 'The name of the game is investor confidence and it's important for investors to differentiate the Philippines from the rest of Asia'.[23]

A local industrialist captured the frustrations of a large number of small, medium, and big manufacturers that were tired of continually being dismissed as protectionists for seeking government support against unfair competition.

> We are up against an ideology, a school of thought. These people seem to be happy when we fail, for that only proves that we were not competitive in the first place. On the other hand, if you're barely surviving but go to them for help, the fact that you're surviving means you really don't need help. It's a catch-22.[24]

By the last months of 1998, it was, of course, not just local businesses that were being impacted negatively by the high interest, tight budget, free market policies of the administration. With economic contraction, the ranks of the unemployed were sharply increasing in both the city and countryside. Neo-classical policies were making a mockery of President 'Erap' Estrada's presidential campaign's key thrust of commitment to the poor (*Erap para sa mahirap*). Yet, in the eyes of his economic team, there was no contradiction between the market and a 'commitment to the poor'. In classic Friedmanite language, Planning Secretary Medalla said:

> One might say that those seem to be contradictory principles because the market is not well known for kindness. It is well known for being impersonal, for being Darwinian. But in the long run, those two are actually consistent. ... Only by opening up to the rest of the world can the Filipinos use the best inputs.
>
> (Quoted in *Business World* 1998a)

To which the many Filipinos who were going under in the deepening recession could very well have responded, like Keynes, that 'Yes sir, but in the long run, we are all dead'.

NOTES

1 Mario B. Lamberte, quoted in Chavez-Malaluan (1996).
2 Florian Alburo *et al.*, 'Towards Recovery and Sustainable Growth', School of Economics, University of the Philippines, September 1985.

3 Freedom from Debt Coalition: Philippines, 'Revisiting Philippine Debt', Paper presented at National Debt Conference, Innotech, Commonwealth Avenue, October 9–10, 1997.
4 Japanese Ministry of Finance figures.
5 Japanese Ministry of Finance figures.
6 Japanese Ministry of Finance figures.
7 Leonor Briones and Jenina Joy Chavez-Malaluan, 'New Social and Political Challenges within the Framework of the Structural Adjustment Process in Southeast Asia (with Focus on the Philippines): Effects on New Population Trends and Quality of Life', Paper prepared for the Population and Quality of Life Independent Commission, Manila, May 1994, unpublished.
8 Ibid.
9 Interview with Jesus Estanislao, by Marco Mezerra, Manila, November 13, 1996.
10 Figures provided in Esguerra (1997).
11 Central Bank data cited by Solita Collas-Monsod, 'Calling a Spade', *Business World* September 30, 1997.
12 HG Asia Ltd., *Communique: Philippines* ....
13 Ibid.
14 Calculated year over year on a six-month average basis. HG Asia Ltd., *Asia Communique*.
15 BSP memo, quoted in Solita Collas-Monsod, 'Clutching at straws', *Business World* September 30, 1997.
16 The position of the University of the Philippines School of Economics' faction on the exchange rate is articulated in Emmanuel Dios *et al.*, 'Exchange Rate Policies: Recent Failures and Future Tasks', *Public Policy* 1(1): 15–41 (August 1997).
17 Statement in *Public Forum*, talk show on Channel 7, Quezon City, September 11, 1997.
18 Quoted in *Business World* September 29, 1997.
19 Quoted in 'Rating Agency Paints Bleak Outlook on RP Banks', *Business World* September 29, 1997: 11.
20 Cited in Solita Monsod, 'Para sa Mahirap', *Business World* October 20, 1998: 5.
21 Reported in a number of Philippine newspapers and admitted by the Estrada team, this was revealed at a press conference on April 15, 1998, by the political party, Akbayan.
22 Antonio Lopez, *Morning Show*, Channel 9, October 12, 1998.
23 Quoted in *Manila Bulletin*, undated.
24 Personal communication from an official of Federation of Philippine Industries, anonymity requested, Makati, September 23, 1998.

Part IV

REGIONAL AND INTERNATIONAL CONTEXT OF THE CRISIS

14

THE INTERNATIONAL RELATIONS OF THE ASIAN ECONOMIC CRISIS

A study in the politics of resentment*

Richard Higgott

Introduction

The currency and market turmoils and their impacts in East Asia since July 1997, as even economists now accept, are every bit as much *political* crises as they are economic ones. Indeed, the political manifestations of these events will linger long after the necessary reforms have been introduced to return at least a semblance of economic normalcy to the region. This chapter assesses some of these longer term political implications. It attempts to do so through Asian-tinted lenses rather than Anglo-American ones. This is deliberate. The chapter offers an alternative reading of the East Asian economic crisis to that which prevails in the mainstream of western policy analysis. It does so because perceptions matter in politics and the perceptions presented here appear closer to the hearts of many influential members of the East Asian public and private sector policy-making elites than is often assumed amongst their American and European counterparts. As such these perceptions, and the politics they spawn at elite levels – and increasingly at civil society levels – will be crucial to understanding future national and international policy in the region.

In the first section, while accepting that detailed explanations must apply on a country-by-country basis, the chapter outlines those aspects of the crises that appear common to all the countries – notably, Thailand, South Korea, Indonesia and to a lesser extent Malaysia and the Philippines – affected to date. It also highlights the importance of the silent but fundamental role of Japan as a long-term and ever-present factor in the crisis. In addition, and notwithstanding the real, material explanations of the crisis, it argues that it also needs to be interpreted in an ideological fashion reflecting a western conceptual inability to deal with the resistance of the Asian model

261

of economic development to converge to, and conform with, an Anglo-American form of capitalism.

The second section looks at the policy remedies that have emanated from the IMF and suggests that while the medicine has been, and will continue to be, swallowed in the short run, it will not be appreciated in the long run. A major implication of the experience of Asian states at the hands of the IMF doctors may well be the enhanced development of an 'East Asian' as opposed to 'Asia–Pacific' understanding of region. The desire for national decision-making autonomy in the face of economic crisis and the enhancement of a greater collective regional understanding in the wake of the crisis are not incompatible. The third section offers evidence of regional social learning from the crisis that may well consolidate the trend towards the enhanced economic policy coordination – that gathered pace (albeit often more rhetorical than real) since the 1980s – but now with a stronger East Asian, as opposed to Asia–Pacific, flavour. This assertion is demonstrated by discussion of the limits of APEC after the crisis and regional discussion of a putative Asian Monetary Fund.

The fourth section and the Conclusion speculate about longer term Asian responses to the intervention of the international financial institutions in the context of the debate over the prospects for continued global economic liberalisation on the one hand versus some form of re-regulation of international capital on the other. They demonstrate the tension between dominant Anglo-American understandings of global liberalisation on the one hand and the emergence of East Asian sites of resistance to some aspects of it on the other. Asian interests, it is argued, will test further the viability of the 'APEC consensus' as an element in the wider neo-liberal enterprise in the early stages of the twenty-first century.

The events in East Asia represent – at two levels – the first 'crisis of globalisation'. At an obvious first level, it has been a series of economic crises that have altered the economic and socio-political fortunes of several hitherto rapidly developing states. Second, at a more abstract though no less significant level, the East Asian economic crisis represents a setback for the inexorable process of international economic liberalisation that has come to be known as 'globalisation'. On the eve of the twenty-first century we are experiencing the first serious challenges to the hegemony of neo-liberalism as the dominant form of economic organisation since the end of the Cold War. This resistance is not uniform, nor is it restricted to one site or group of actors. Moreover, in many instances, resistance is more often to practice as much as it is to principle. As this chapter will argue, events in Asia represent less the final ideological triumph of liberalism in a post-Cold-War era than a context for rethinking significant aspects – especially continued capital deregulation – of the neo-liberal project (see Higgott and Reich 1998).

'Common sense' and 'not so common sense' explanations of the crises

The broad outlines of a general explanation of the currency free fall in several East Asian states are now well known and reviewed elsewhere in this volume (see Beeson and Robison; Winters). From late 1997 on a full-blown Asian crisis has seen several of the affected states facing record unemployment and social and political upheaval (actual and prospective). What is worth emphasising is that the financial fallout in East Asia is distinguished from earlier Latin America crises because it occurred in a disinflationary environment tied to the increasingly integrated nature of East Asia as an interdependent *region of production* (Hatch and Yamamura 1996), and the interdependent nature of the international economy as a *global market*. Rapid regional economic growth in the 1970s and 1980s hid the sloppy, inefficient and at times corrupt business practices (especially in the financial and banking sectors) of the region that had prevailed during this period. That which was not hidden was often tolerated in the context of the accommodatory alliance politics of the Cold War when the United States, in addition to providing the necessary security architecture, was also willing to play the market of last resort for East Asia's increasingly good and cheap manufactured goods – and tolerate (explicitly even) a manipulated 'exchange rate' solution on its trade imbalance with Japan.

This, in shorthand, is the 'common sense' explanation of the currency crises in East Asia. This explanation – especially the 'discovery' that all was not what it should be in the banking system – has made it difficult for many western analysts to disguise a certain *Schadenfreude* at the situations in which these states now find themselves. Chalmers Johnson (23 February 1998) in classic style calls it 'obscene jingoism' and 'malicious pleasure'. If pride cometh before a fall, then even the most saintly found it difficult to ignore the discomfort that Dr Mahathir – and other high-profile exponents of the superiority of the 'Asian Way' that had accompanied high East Asian growth in the 1990s – now faced.

Such readings, however, are superficial. Keen to capture the urgency of the economic crises – and the supposedly simple neo-classical economic reforms that needed to resolve them – the 'common sense' explanations downgrade the manner in which the crises are not simply the result of a failure of 'rational' economic management. They are part of the wider processes of structural change that have gone on in the region. Those states that did not appear *directly* involved in, or affected by, the immediate crisis – especially Japan – are integrally interwoven into it and, in the longer run, will be increasingly significant in how it is resolved. Indeed, Japan has been central to the crises from the outset. Notably, the Japanese model of economic development has acted as a template for the manner in which the other Asian miracle economies have developed. The 'developmental state' is very much a product of a reading of Japanese development after the Second World War. Yet at the core of the recent economic crisis in East Asia is an incompatibility between the developmental statist and the Anglo-American model of capitalist economic development.

This is not to suggest that Korea, Thailand or other Asian states are facsimiles of the Japanese economy. Indeed, it is well understood in the literature that it does not apply in uniform fashion anywhere in Asia (see Weiss 1998). Rather, Japan has been a source of inspiration – especially in the replication of the Japanese incentive structure – in the pursuit of policy (both implicitly and explicitly) over the last several decades (Wolferen 1998: 109).

While for all states of the region North America was the major destination for exports, throughout the late 1980s and early 1990s, Japan had become an increasingly important market. But the 1995 devaluation of the yen against the dollar severely curtailed this market for East Asian exporters. Japanese capital created overcapacity in the region without fulfilling the role of a market of last resort to absorb it. This factor was largely ignored in the initial 'common sense' explanations of the crisis. Only as the yen became increasingly devalued in the second half of 1998 did this fact appear to register more strongly with the analytic community in North America and Europe. In effect what we have seen in the second half of 1998 is a realisation that the crisis is an evolving, multi-stage, multi-dimensional process with no simple one-stop approach to resolution.

The 'common sense' explanation also ignores the manner in which the policy reforms emanating from the international financial institutions are highly political in nature. The initial popular, western view of the behaviour of the United States and the IMF in the wake of the economic crisis in East Asia is that the IMF has effectively bailed out these newly industrialising economies (NIEs) – especially South Korea, Thailand and Indonesia – that got themselves into trouble largely by acts of their own making. That the acts that led to the immediate crisis may, in part, have been self-inflicted by the policy elites of the region is not contested. That the major powers and the international financial institutions have saved the day – and will be duly recognised and appreciated for doing so in the region – is. In so doing, this chapter – seeing crisis in the Chinese sense as both danger and opportunity – argues that the crisis may lead to an increasing desire on the part of regional policy-makers to enhance their collective as well as national policy-making capabilities.

International policy reform in East Asia: initial regional responses

IMF prescriptions for the Asian rescue were not new. They were tried and tested initially in Latin America and Africa where the principal economic ills were large budget deficits, high inflation and massively indebted public sectors. In Asia, where budget deficits have been largely non-existent and inflation relatively low, the problems have emanated from excessive private as opposed to public sector borrowing (*Far Eastern Economic Review* 25 December 1997: 5). Deregulation of the financial markets allowed Asian firms to engage in massive overseas borrowing.

In the absence of government control – on domestic companies, banking supervision, or even any policy coordination on borrowings and investment – those governmental conditions that had given stability to Asian development in the first instance now gave rise to the real problem, illiquidity not insolvency. Corporations began borrowing overseas more cheaply than at home. Devaluations and enhanced productivity growth in China between 1991 and 1994, and the pegged East Asian currencies to a rising US dollar, led to the sharp decline in their value. Massive increases in debt and the rush of foreign investors to call in loans – many of which were short term – led to the crisis.

This process undermined what Robert Wade and Frank Veneroso (1998a: 1–4) call the 'High Debt Model of Asian Development', central to which has been a 'strong financial rationale for co-operative long term reciprocal relations between firms, banks and governments'. Often referred to in the western press as 'crony capitalism',[1] this misleading aphorism belies the degree to which this relationship intermediated the functional connections between the high domestic savings (characteristic of Asian NIEs and often as high as a third of GDP compared with an OECD average of about 15 per cent) and the high corporate debt/equity ratios (equally characteristic of the Asian NIEs). The analysis of Wade and Veneroso is not offered here as a defence of the grosser infelicities of Asian business culture, nor of the seriousness of high debt to equity ratios in times of currency devaluation (when it is much more serious than for countries with low debt to equity ratios). Rather, it is offered as a starting point for thinking about likely regional political responses to the 1997–8 economic crisis in East Asia and especially Asian longer term responses to the neo-liberal (IMF) approach to reform.

Viewed through Wade and Veneroso's lenses and, indeed, even those of some senior officials from the World Bank (Stiglitz 1998a), IMF remedies – domestic austerity and financial restructuring based on a western understanding of liberalisation[2] – are more likely to erode rather than boost investor confidence. There is a world of difference between the liberalisation of the exchange of goods and the liberalisation of trade in money. IMF policies aimed at cutting demand and liquidity have had the effect of causing bankruptcy and slashing the value of companies that are not only inefficient and unprofitable but also among those which are not so afflicted. In so doing IMF strategies have undermined the advantages inherent in the high-debt model without putting in place a viable 'western-style' alternative

– which cannot take hold without the removal of the debt mountain in the first instance.

If debt cannot be repaid or whittled away by inflation then only by bankruptcy or debt for equity swaps can it be controlled. For either to happen, large sections of the economies of the Asian NIEs would disappear or end up in foreign control. Both are theoretically possible and the latter most likely in any circumstance given that devaluation offers knock-down bargains for cashed-up foreign buyers. US, European and Japanese investors can move, are moving and will move easily from minority to majority share-holders in Southeast Asia by the tactic of writing down Asian partner debt. Countries hit hardest by the crisis – Thailand, Indonesia, Malaysia, South Korea and the Philippines – have little alternative but to relax restrictions on foreign ownership in sectors traditionally difficult for outsiders to access, such as services, property and retailing.

Prospects of a socio-political backlash against these activities, when coupled with the imposed reforms of the IMF, are all too evident. At the popular level, the currency devaluation and demand-restricting austerity measures of the IMF (laxer labour laws in South Korea, higher petrol prices in Indonesia, new bankruptcy laws in Thailand) have led to riots in all three countries. At the elite level, increased foreign ownership of the corporate sectors of the East Asian NIEs will, later if not sooner, call forth a height-ened nationalist response, although the exact form it will take is not yet easy to identify.

If the United States and the IMF have their way, then a western model of liberalisation, replacing the Asian 'high-debt model', may eventually come into place. Alternatively, it could also see a hardening nationalist resistance to neo-liberalism. For what has been challenged in the crisis of the East Asian NIEs in the late twentieth century is the very model on which they have built their success. It should be seen not only as an economic crisis, but as an 'ideas battle' or an ideological battle. Having 'won' the Cold War against Soviet-style collectivism, no sooner is one bout of triumphalism over than liberalism is now gleefully protesting its superiority over the 'develop-mental statist' approach towards capitalist economic development. The long-standing critique of statism inherent in the neo-classical economic liter-ature and language of the established policy community is seen to be vindicated by the crisis. The speeches of senior US policy-makers and opinion-formers have been peppered with references to the need to jettison the remaining vestiges of the developmental statist model. This does not play well in East Asia in the short run. It will not play well in the long run either.

During the Cold War, US willingness to supply official capital and to open its markets for an initial one-way flow of exports was predicated heavily on the security consideration of containing communism. In a more benign security environment, US concerns that it was becoming a 'normal country', or that many of its former junior partners in the Pacific alliance were continuing to free-ride when no longer necessary, have seen an increasing clamour in the US policy community for change in the region. Thus regional economic trade liberalisation *and* financial deregulation were the payoffs for a continued US security presence in the region. Those socio-political practices of the so-called Asian model that were acceptable for security reasons during the Cold War – exclusionary politics, nepotism and the blurred lines of authority between political and economic power – now clash more violently with the interests of private capital in search of greater market share and profits in an era of deregulation.

Yet as important as such factors are in impeding domestic structural reform, to lay the blame for the economic problems in East Asia solely, or even primarily, on the seamy side of so-called Asian values would be to miss the point. The essence of Asian values – if indeed there be any – are thrift, hard work, respect for one's parents and priority for the community over the individual. These are unlikely to be the source of economic failure. On the other hand, corruption and cronyism – deemed to be crucial factors – are not peculiarly Asian in their origins. Moreover, the importance of crony capitalism – corruption, nepotism, bureaucratic sweetheart dealing – would appear, except in Indonesia, to be overstated. Rather, it was a '*potent mix* of globalisation, poor governance and greed that brought about the crisis' (emphasis added) (*Far Eastern Economic Review* 12 February 1998: 47).[3]

Most East Asian political elites accept that their current problems are unlike those of the mid 1970s and mid 1980s – both of which were mainly externally derived – and from which Asian economies bounced back quickly. Contrary to the initial arguments of the kind advanced by Dr Mahathir, the current crises have been recognised as largely internally driven and much deeper than anything hitherto experienced. Regional leaders understand that the currency and stock market collapses (excessive as they might be) arose from a combination of property booms and other bad investments on the one hand and mismanagement, corruption and inefficiency in both public and private decision-making sectors – especially the cosy relationship between governments and business – on the other. Crony capitalism may be an insufficient explanation of the magnitude of the crisis, but Asian middle classes hold their political and economic elites 'accountable'.[4]

Adjustment will be painful and necessitate much Schumpeterian 'creative destruction' (Ibrahim 1998: 18). Banks and business houses will fail. Thus the real question, in both the short and longer term, is the degree to which regional economic and political leaders will be willing, and/or able, to grasp the nettle of economic adjustment in an era of potential political instability that will inevitably accompany the generational transition processes in train in many countries. This remains an open and multi-dimensional question, but there is one aspect of this process that has been given scant attention to date. The next section looks at a range of circumstantial evidence that has emerged throughout the crisis that points towards a need for a 'regionalisation of thinking' on how to mitigate the kinds of economic problems visited on Asia since 1997.

The limits of regional cooperation: the USA and the aborted AMF

The abortive exercise, led by Japan in late 1997, to set up an Asian Monetary Fund (AMF) is instructive for the argument of this chapter. The proposal was given impetus by the need to bail out Thailand and the US refusal to participate in the initial $17 billion fund. Contrasting its support for Mexico in 1994, Asian leaders were critical of US policy. They argued that US reluctance to support Thailand made the spread of the crisis to other countries all the more likely.[5] The main donors for the initial financial adjustment package were Japan (US$4 billion), Korea and Taiwan (US$2 billion), Australia and the PRC (US$1 billion). All were from the region. Their motives may have been mixed but this is less important than their demonstrable desire to be involved in the process. All states, in their own ways, were attempting to consolidate their regional positions in both an economic and political fashion.

Not only did the United States refuse to support the package, however, it also opposed calls to set up a regional fund to do so. To be capitalised initially at $100 billion, this was to provide emergency support in a regional way and avoid what many leaders saw as the humiliation of the IMF telling them how to readjust to the new circumstance. The initiative was always a long shot but with an initial Japanese agreement to underwrite it, it even led to talk of a permanent regional fund. The proposal for an AMF made up only of East Asian states was in many ways an exercise in 'thinking East Asian' not dissimilar to the setting up of the East Asian Economic Caucus (EAEC) within APEC (Higgott and Stubbs 1995). According to the Japanese plan, the AMF would have to be more flexible and perhaps less strict in its disbursements of funds (Altbach 1997).

Interestingly, and in contrast to the development of the EAEC proposal, Japan was willing to lead the proposal for an AMF. It took the initiative in trying to persuade the United States that it was additional to, not incompatible with, the IMF. Japan's strategy, with the benefit of hindsight and contrary to some readings of the exercise at the time, does appear to have been genuine rather than merely rhetorically symbolic. Currency crashes in Southeast Asia were of considerable economic significance for Japan. In addition to the well-understood nature of Japanese export concentration in Asia (40 per cent of Japanese exports went to Asia overall) Southeast Asia was also the destination for the largest share of Japanese FDI and its banks held large proportions of Southeast Asian foreign debt (nearly 50 per cent in

Thailand and 40 per cent in Indonesia). This contrasted with the smaller role of US banks (at 6 and 8 per cent respectively).

It was also felt in Japanese foreign policy circles that support for an AMF offered the chance to demonstrate a long-called-for leadership role commensurate with its economic importance in the region. Moreover, this could be done by developing a policy of its own rather than – as is traditionally the case with Japanese policy towards the region – as part of the US's Asian policy.[6] Although not explicitly stated, there was also the question of the degree to which an AMF might, in the longer run, building on the strength of the yen, act as the basis for the creation of a common currency in Asia.

The proposal was, however, insufficiently thought out, naïve and, with the benefit of hindsight, destined to fail. It was underwritten by, and verbally accompanied by, a large dose of 'Asian way' hubris amongst its ASEAN supporters. The proposal, in the minds of some regional leaders at least, was underwritten by an assumption that the existing international institutions did not necessarily know what best suited Asians and that they could produce regional solutions to the management of their own financial affairs. In this regard, they had still not understood the power of the global financial markets, but the proposal's most naïve failing was to underestimate the strength of the opposition from the United States and IMF, the full force of which was felt in September 1997 at the inaugural joint IMF–World Bank meeting in Hong Kong.

The proposal was seen by US policy-makers and senior figures in the two institutions not only as likely to undermine their ability to impose tough conditionality on loans, but as a veritable threat to US interests and influence in Asia. The United States, as Chalmers Johnson notes:

> correctly sensed that Japan was about to try its hand at long promised, but never delivered, leadership. If the Japanese had succeeded, they would have slipped the leash of the US cold war system. Moreover, they would have started using their capital to help countries in Asia rather than continuing to send it to the world's number one debtor nation, the United States.
>
> (Johnson 1998: 16)

Other factors were, of course, salient. Mounting Japanese financial problems were also a major factor in the *démarche*. Indeed, some argue that Japan's real interest was in protecting its own banking system – with the highest exposure to regional risk (Haggard and MacIntyre 1998: 389). In the end, Japan also conceded US and IMF assertions that the AMF might duplicate the activities of the existing international institutions and that there was a danger that any adjustment funds not under the direct or indirect control of the IMF might not be 'properly used'.[7] By November 1997, the proposal was aborted. The US desire for the IMF to control adjustment funding prevailed and its dominant role in the process was endorsed at the Vancouver APEC in late 1997. Thus APEC backed an IMF-led response to Asia's problems. Any idea of a special (regional) assistance programme was scotched by the United States, as were Dr Mahathir's attempts to tighten currency regulation. In effect APEC endorsed a standard model of macro-economic policy reform – with all the accompanying implications of painful restructuring processes for most countries of the region.

This may, however, be a turning point for the organisation. By opposing the proposal (more) seeds of polarisation in the relationship between the Asian and Caucasian members of APEC have been sown. Subsequent arguments about the role that the IMF should play in the rescues in the region, especially in Indonesia and South Korea, were only resolved in favour of the IMF taking the lead role after considerable argument. The exhortatory liberalisation rhetoric of the Vancouver APEC meeting only superficially concealed a deeper schism between the two edges of the Pacific. The economic turmoil reinforced the notion that the Asia–Pacific is an artificially constructed region, the long-term salience of which may well be affected by the economic downturn, or more specifically by the prospect of longer term regional resentment at the US- and IMF-led responses to the crisis.

Added to the problems now facing APEC, the failure of the AMF leaves us with an open question. Is it more or less likely that there will be further initiatives to provide some kind of regional economic cooperation in general and financial policy coordination in particular? The answer is two-fold. In the short run, no grand regional strategies are likely to be proposed. In the longer run, however, the international responses to the Asian crises may make the prospect of the greater management of East Asian (as opposed to Asia–Pacific) economic affairs all the more likely.

Indeed, both short-term practical and longer term conceptual avenues of regional financial cooperation are being explored. Even the AMF idea is not dead. At the practical level ASEAN finance ministers (meeting in Manila, 1–2 December 1997) inspired and agreed a framework whereby member states would engage in the mutual surveillance of each other's economies. Such an agreement, unthinkable prior to the crisis, demonstrates a desire to enhance regional policy-making capabilities – especially in a period in which regional states will provide financial aid to each others reform processes. This is a significant exercise in the recognition of the 'East Asianness' of the region. The crisis has been a spur to it. While it is anchored within the existing international financial institutional context, the Manila Agreement, as per its full title, is intended to 'Enhance Asian Regional Cooperation to Promote Financial Stability'.

The framework was supported by all at Manila – the ASEAN core, plus the East Asian economies of Japan, China, Hong Kong and Korea and the Caucasian members of APEC. Also present at the meeting were officials from the IMF and the World Bank Group (WBG). The Manila framework will operate on an 'ASEAN plus' basis (East Asia without Australia and New Zealand). For obvious reasons, the United States will be present and the Asian Development Bank will provide a secretariat. The framework will offer a process of enhanced mutual, IMF-style, surveillance and Asian-style 'peer pressure'. In short it represents a contribution to the regional institutional economic architecture that does not currently fit with any existing model.

The formula adopted at Manila was portrayed in certain sections of the US media as a US defeat of Japanese attempts to establish a fund without IMF-style conditionality. While at one level this is certainly the case, it is also an incomplete reading of Japanese behaviour. The offer came as a response to widespread regional disappointment at the US failure to support the IMF package for Thailand (*Asian Wall Street Journal* 12–13 December 1997: 6). At a more exploratory and conceptual level, the idea of an AMF continues to resurface, as indeed do other ideas, as regional states seek ways to stabilise their currencies.[8] There is a growing recognition in the region that Asian currency fluctuations do not accurately, or fairly, reflect economic fundamentals. Asian policy communities are now fully sensitised – in a way that they were not prior to 1997 – to the degree to which small open economies are vulnerable to the global financial markets and the need to guard against this vulnerability.

Whether endeavours to secure greater regional financial policy coordination are contested or supported by the global financial markets will depend on the nature of the institutional architecture envisaged. It will require a major Japanese leadership role, both intellectually and by the internationalisation of the yen. This, in turn, will be dependent on the successful restructuring of the Japanese financial system. It will also need support from the United States, which is not currently forthcoming; and from Europe which, while less important, is more likely if the Asia–Europe Meeting Process (ASEM) can develop and the euro can become an important international currency (Higgott 1999). These discussions are for the realm of future policy analysis. But whether the Asians will be successful or not in their endeavours, there can be little doubt that the exploration of some form of AMF-style cooperation as a way to combat vulnerability will be an item on the regional policy agenda in the twenty-first century.

US policy during the crisis

US policy towards an incipient AMF reflects a private sector desire for continued financial liberalisation on the one hand and a political/bureaucratic (both domestic and international) institutional desire not to cede the power of the international financial institutions – in which the United States is dominant – to regional institutions over which it would certainly have less ideological/philosophical and practical control, on the other. This two-prong strategy emanates from a wider policy context – what Jagdish Bhagwati (1998) calls the 'Wall Street–Treasury Complex'.

Bhagwati provides a compelling demonstration of how the actors, values and interest of the group he identifies have been at the heart of the US and IMF policy response to the recent crises in East Asia in general and in opposition to an AMF in particular:

> Wall Street's financial firms have obvious self-interest in a world of free capital mobility since it only enlarges the arena in which to make money. It is not surprising therefore that Wall Street put its powerful oar into the turbulent waters of Washington political lobbying. ... [Moreover] ... Wall Street has exceptional clout in Washington for the simple reason that there is ... a definite network of like minded luminaries among the powerful institutions – Wall Street, the Treasury Department, the State Department, the IMF and the World Bank. ... This powerful network ... is unable to look much beyond the interest of Wall Street, which it equates with the good of the world. Thus the IMF has been relentlessly propelled toward embracing the goal of capital account convertibility.
>
> (Bhagwati 1998: 11)

This should come as little surprise to the student of modern policy analysis. In the application of values to policy, the Wall Street–Treasury complex, as with many other issue-oriented policy networks, exhibits the now well-understood epistemic-like characteristics of a public and private sector policy community with strong, shared normative values and common causal, problem-solving methodologies (Haas 1992). The Asian crisis, more than any other recent example, demonstrates the influence of Washington over the international financial institutions.

Wall Street's concern was that an AMF-style organisation would slow down the liberalisation of Asian financial markets. The US response towards the crises, inherent in IMF policy, has been to liberalise trade, deregulate financial markets and enhance disclosure rules.[9] All, by happy coincidence, coincide with the broader aims – both before and after the crises – of US economic diplomacy in the region. As President Clinton's first Secretary of Commerce, Jeffrey Garten, noted in an article entitled 'Worsening financial flu lowers immunity to US business' (!!) Asian economies were passing through a 'dark tunnel ... [b]ut on the other end there is going to be a significantly different Asia in which American firms have achieved much deeper market penetration, much greater access' (*The New York Times* 14 January 1998).

There were also more general foreign policy reasons why the United States did not wish to see an AMF realised. Two are germane. First, in foreign economic policy terms, the utilisation of 'impartial' multilateral agencies has long been seen as an important way to 'put at one step remove' or 'depoliticise' US policy interests in the imposition of economic conditions on developing countries (Cohen 1986; Kahler 1990). This is important to secure international acceptance of a given policy recommendation, not to mention the opportunity to share the costs of such policies with other donors. It also helps sell such policies to a national political community, increasingly obsessed with domestic politics and less interested in wider US foreign policy questions. Most importantly, notwithstanding the declining share of its quota in the organisation, the United States is still the dominant actor in the IMF (Leech 1998). The development of viable alternative organisations would diminish its influence.

Moreover, US policy towards Asia over the last decade, in both the economic and security domains, has seen a gradual shift from hub and spoke relationships towards a greater multilateralisation of its regional relationships. These were initially resisted by the United States but gradually came to be accepted in the context of a broad definition of region as the *Asia–Pacific*, as opposed to the narrower definition of *East Asia* (see Mack and Ravenhill 1994). APEC, in the economic domain, became acceptable as a vehicle for US interest. Similarly, the ASEAN Regional Forum was acceptable in the security domain because it was always secondary to the still dominant bilateral security structure.

Viewed through American eyes then, a successful AMF was not consistent with overall US interests. It would have reinforced the trend, following the strengthening of the yen from the time of the Plaza Accord through to the first half of the 1990s, of the Japanese replacement of the United States as the major source of FDI, the major force for production and principal aid donor in the region (Hatch and Yamamura 1996; Rix 1993; Stubbs 1994). For many in the US foreign economic policy-making community the AMF seemed like a potential first step toward a yen zone.

With hindsight, US fears that an AMF would have weakened its hold over the policy process in Asia, especially *vis-à-vis* the Japanese, appear grossly overstated. The AMF was never viewed by the Japanese as a competitor to the IMF, although it may have been by others such as Dr Mahathir. Japanese unwillingness to push the AMF in the face of US opposition represented a failure to break the 'occupation psychology' (Bello 1998: 437) in its relationship with the United States and, as a consequence, left other, more desperate regional elites no alternative but to acquiesce in the IMF conditions imposed by the IMF programmes. However, such is the perversity of international politics that US opposition to the proposal may well make a further attempt to initiate such a body – in less frenetic times – all the more inevitable.

Asia, the IMF and the politics of resentment

The ambivalent relationship that has always existed between the states of East Asia and the United States, and the US-led international institutions, has been brought into sharp relief by the collapse of the East Asian currencies and the subsequent process of international financial institutional intervention. As time progresses, the nature of the bailout seems increasingly ambivalent and problematic for many Asian policy-makers. They do not like it, but it is difficult to know what they would have done without it. The authority of the IMF would have been accepted more readily by the state policy elites of East Asia if the interventions had indeed rapidly restored market confidence and stability. But they have not. Rather, for many in the region, the crisis appears to have presented the IMF with the opportunity to force open East Asian economies in two ways.

First, conditionality attached to the bailout packages has allowed, and will continue to allow, international banks to make major inroads into the region's banking sectors. It has happened already in Thailand, where Citibank has taken a majority share in a major Thai bank. In South Korea, where IMF adjustment package support was contingent on a range of 'reforms' in the financial sector, including the prospect of majority foreign ownership of Korean banks and the establishment of subsidiaries and brokerage houses by December 1998, the way is open for a major foreign stake in the Korean financial sector (Khor 1998).

Second, liberalising conditions – going beyond 'normal' macroeconomic targets – have paved the way for US firms to achieve unprecedented market access. Indeed, there is mounting evidence to suggest that this is already happening. In the first four months of 1998 there were 479 mergers and acquisitions in Asia to the tune of US$35 billion (*The International Herald Tribune* 20–21 June 1998: 5). These buyouts have been dominated by US and, to a lesser extent, European banks, MNCs and money managers. Moreover, cash-rich foreigners are the major beneficiaries of the bargains that are to be had from the various regional 'fire sales'. This can be seen from the first auction of seized assets from bankrupt Thai finance companies (conducted by the Thailand Financial Sector Restructuring Authority in June 1998) where one US company – GE Capital – snapped up US$1.2 billion of vehicle instalment purchases for less than US$530 million (Bardecke 1998). The average discount on book valuations at this auction was 47–50 per cent.

The economic troubles have caused many Asian political leaders to rediscover the rhetoric of popular nationalism as a way of deflecting domestic criticism. Across the most affected states a discourse of 'robbery', or a 'new imperialism' – not heard since the years of the immediate post-colonial era – is very strong. This is not only in Malaysia, where Prime Minister Mahathir has gone as far as to argue that western governments and financiers have deliberately punished Asia for its arrogance and refusal to converge more quickly towards Anglo-American, liberal, approaches to democracy, market opening, labour standards and human rights. Similar themes can also be heard in Thailand, the Philippines, South Korea and Indonesia.

The implications of this for the global economy are precisely the opposite of what liberal(isers) would wish. Western political elites have underestimated the influence of scapegoat explanations of the crisis within the region. Asians were coming to understand and accept the workings of markets, but this understanding is less than one generation deep. There is no strongly socialised or cognitive belief in the market. Most Asians have only an instrumental feeling for the market. What Linda Lim (ironically?) calls 'the lightly regulated' international financial markets stand in sharp contrast to the 'visible hand' that moves domestic markets in Asia (Lim 1998a). The treatment of East Asia by the financial markets in 1997–8 will have ambiguous results. While it may make Asian states more responsive to 'market disciplines' in the short run, it may also in the longer run make them more suspicious of them and it will certainly lead Asians to prefer tighter, rather than looser, market regulation.

It is not necessary to subscribe to a financial market conspiracy – to drive up Asian companies' external indebtedness only to then depress asset values in order to make these assets available to international buyers – to recognise that the crisis in Asia has given a crucial advantage to international (especially US and to a lesser extent European) investors in Asia. There are several sets of losers in this battle. In addition to the obvious domestic Asian players in those economies that are now the sites for these contests, the principal corporate losers, as one senior market analyst[10] has noted, are the Japanese *vis-à-vis* corporate America in the global competitive fights in many industries (*The International Herald Tribune* 20–21 June 1998: 5).

Equally resented in the region, however, is a widely held view that a double standard is present in the IMF insistence that regional governments not rescue local financial institutions while at the same time insisting that they guarantee the repayment of international loans, thus alleviating foreign lending houses from any 'moral hazard'. To the educated populations of the crisis-hit countries of the region this is seen as local entrepreneurs paying for their mistakes while the mistakes of foreign investors are underwritten at local expense. Judging by demonstrations in Bangkok, Seoul and Jakarta in the latter parts of 1997, there can be little doubt that the populations of East Asia are keen to see their own leaders held accountable for their mistakes.

But there is also a strong belief that foreign banks are escaping the costs of their commercial mistakes thus undermining the legitimacy of the externally coerced policy recommendations from the IMF. In short, IMF policies are seen in the region as designed to save western investors, not to save Asian economic development. As J. K. Galbraith notes: 'the peculiar genius of the

IMF is to bail out those most responsible and extend the greatest hardship to the workers, who are not responsible' (*The Observer* 21 June 1998: B4). Going further, one Malaysian analyst noted:

> What the rich could not do through bilateral and multilateral pressures, they are now extracting by using the IMF loans as leverage. ... No wonder the IMF's main role in Asia is increasingly seen as chief debt collector for international banks.
>
> (Khor 1998: 29)

It might be all well and good for western analysts to say that this is a partial reading of these processes. It may be, but perceptions count and this perception prevails in East Asia in 1998. For sure, some of the more enthusiastic investors in Asian stocks have paid heavy prices, but to many Asians the real bailout has not been of their economies but of the foreign banks and investment houses which lent the money and that are thought to be as much responsible for the problem as the local business that borrowed from them.

In addressing their obligations, Asian governments have been extremely good international citizens and not necessarily with much to show for it. In Korea, for example, notwithstanding that the government has undertaken to honour private foreign debt, capital is not flowing back. This is because the failure to sort out domestic debt questions, especially which banks and firms are viable and which are not, is not yet clear. This does nothing to stem the resentment that is developing in the Korean public and private sector policy community.

By contrast, the banks that lent so freely have worn little of the cost of their policies. How to allocate wealth losses remains a key political problem emerging from the crisis and around which future policy adoptions turn. Almost all actors within the region think that the policies advanced by the IMF have favoured the international investor at the expense of the domestic creditor. Moreover, it is argued by some that the strategies advanced – especially an insistence on tighter monetary policies – have worsened rather than enhanced the creditworthiness of indebted companies (Stiglitz 1998a: 4–6).

In this regard, the Asian crisis is a contest of ideology between Asian and Anglo-American ways of organising capitalist production. Alan Greenspan, of the US Federal Reserve Bank, has publicly argued that the crisis in East Asia's currency markets will have the effect of moving East Asian economic practice closer to that associated with the US model (Greenspan 1998a). In this regard, for many western analysts, the crisis is a weapon in what they see as the normatively laudable process of convergence. Only time will tell if Greenspan is correct or not. One does not have to accept the cruder versions of this analysis – which suggest that the IMF is merely an instrument of US policy doing Treasury Secretary Rubin's bidding in attempting to bring

Asian economic policy making into line with the dominant approach of the United States – to recognise an important test of intellectual will is in train.

This chapter does not wish to deny, in theory at least, the role of the IMF as a valuable instrument to bring short-term stability to economies in distress. Indeed, Asian leaders recognise the importance of the IMF in this role. The IMF did not cause the crisis and, as senior figures in the regional policy communities note, it is appropriate that the IMF should play hard ball to secure some aspects of policy reform in the region – especially in Indonesia. What is questioned by regional leaders – of all political stripes – is the role of the IMF as an instrument of ideological change. Many of the adjustment packages are thought to have gone beyond traditional structural reform strategies, designed not only to restore stability to the regional financial markets and reform banking sectors, but actually to contest the nature of the political process and the power base of the political elites of the region.

Whether this was normatively a good thing is of little concern to the argument presented here. What is clear is that a figure like Suharto, an important ally against communism during the Cold War, had in 1998 become a liability for his erstwhile western supporters. What had been tolerated then, could not be tolerated now (Kane and Passicousset 1998: 8–9). It is more important to note that the policy communities in most affected states of East Asia believe that the IMF and its major members have taken a more intrusive role in their economic affairs than at any time in the post-colonial era. It is a role that Asian leaders resent – from Jakarta to Tokyo – and often feel obliged to resist. It is seen as part of an attempt to secure a convergence towards the dominant Anglo-American form of economic development at a time of Asian weakness. As even the *Nikkei Weekly* (27 April 1998: 18) notes, this is as much the case in Japan as anywhere else in Asia where 'there exists an undeniable, if hidden undercurrent of nationalism ... against the prevalence of the Western system'.

Conclusion: convergence? What convergence?

Whether western analysts like it or not, Asian explanations of the crises do not privilege the same factors as they do. Asians appreciate that there are flaws in their economic system that do not serve it well under contemporary capitalism. But uncontrollable movements of money are deemed to be as responsible for their current problems as are the idiosyncrasies of Asian political and social systems. In the first wave of the crises, it was easier to target the problems of crony capitalism, and accept that these needed to be addressed. But continued violent movements of capital in the second half of 1998, a full twelve months on, are causing more and more members of the Asian public and private sector policy-making elite to resent the ineffectiveness and the inability of any existing international institutions to offer solutions other than to demand dramatic domestic structural adjustment within Asia.

Liberal economic internationalism is on trial in Asia at the end of the twentieth century. The crises, and western responses to them, demonstrate the danger of interpreting Asian political and economic practice through western-elite images. These kinds of analyses represent the unthinking assumption that the dynamics of globalisation – defined as economic liberalisation and political liberalism – will prove as attractive to Asian policy elites as they have done to western policy elites. In so doing, the likelihood of 'convergence' around an idealised western system of economic management, political practice or an understanding of the culture of modernisation as a homogenising category is always going to be overstated. While there is some evidence of liberal influences finding their way into the elites of states such as Thailand, Korea and Taiwan, the often wholesale generalised assumptions of western policy elites that a convergence 'embodying universal interests which will create an Asia more like the liberal stereotypes: more rational, more individualist, democratic, secular and concerned with human rights', are lacking sound empirical foundations (Robison and Goodman 1996: 2–3). At present, authoritarianism, nationalism and fundamentalism are as likely as internationalism, secularism and free markets.

A crucial lesson to be learned is that the Asian crisis, contrary to triumphalist arguments, is not the vindication of the convergence hypothesis that much neo-classical economic analysis would like to assume. The crisis confirms the differences in systemic capitalist organisation rather than refuting them. Asian leaders may parrot the language of neo-liberalism within the context of APEC gatherings, but much of it is still opposed in practice. Unlike those non-governmental members of the transnational political community within the regional organisations such as PECC – especially Caucasian members – Asian political leaders have always been more instrumental than cognitive in their commitment to neo-liberalism. This general assertion has specific political implications.

For many Asians the feeling that there was an exploitative element in the Pacific economic relationship was never eradicated from fora such as APEC over the last decade. The nature of the IMF reform packages, and especially the overt power politics manner in which they have been imposed, has brought a north–south divide back into the open in the relationship between the Caucasian and East Asian members of APEC. Indeed, the downsizing of the economic status of the Asian states has rendered redundant the discourse of the 'miracle NICs' and reconstituted a 'Third World', 'us–them', 'haves–have-nots' dependency discourse not too dissimilar to that which prevailed in the 1970s when a call for a new international economic order dominated north–south relations.

Such feelings give rise to resentment and resistance not only within the domestic polities and societies of the region – where 'mass politics with a class edge' is set to make a comeback (Bello 1998: 442) – but also at the level of the transregional policy-making communities that had supposedly been making strides towards greater economic dialogue and harmonisation of economic policy across the Asia–Pacific within bodies such as APEC. The crisis demonstrated the limits of APEC. As a body capable of making decisions of regional utility it was paralysed by the crisis. The United States drove through the IMF reform packages at the Vancouver Summit. In so doing, the crisis has made the gap across the Pacific greater rather than smaller and the inherent tensions more transparent. As a consequence, putative regional economic cooperation – through groupings like the East Asia Economic Caucus and the exploration of regional monetary cooperation – may prove more conducive to the longer term interests of regional policy elites than APEC. Unlike APEC, the EAEC is unambiguously 'regional' and may prove a more comfortable ideological venue for East Asia's political leaders in the era of the new economic reality.

Competing IMF and Asian views of how to manage the regional economic order are delicately balanced. For many of the region's policy communities the crisis confirms the dangers of too much economic liberalisation. Asian policy elites may not have solutions, but it is clear to them that there is a problem with the management of the international economic system. To Asian leaders it appears that no one is in charge of the financial markets. This lack of order does not sit well with them. Notwithstanding the recent intellectual battering of the 'Asian Way' in the international media (especially *The Economist* and the *International Herald Tribune*) Asia's greater permissiveness towards state intervention may not have yet run its course. We may see Asian governmental structures becoming leaner, more transparent and less receptive to rent-seeking behaviour and cronyism, but it is unlikely that all elements of the 'developmental statist' model will be torn up in the interests of a purer Anglo-American neo-liberalism. State capacity will remain an important element of the developmental equation in Asia in the twenty-first century.

What the Asian crisis tells us is that there is no consensus on how to manage international capitalism in the closing stages of the twentieth century. The major financial institutions are caught between nationalists and liberals with competing views of how the world should work. These institutions have proved leaden footed by comparison with the speed at which markets operate. The IFIs have been found wanting in both theory and practice by the events in East Asia. At the most basic levels, such as economic surveillance, the IMF has been inadequate. This was especially the case in Korea and Indonesia, if less so in Thailand. Policy advice on structural reform to the financial system has been inadequate, intrusive, often wrong and raises questions about the legitimate role of the international institutions. Exactly what, asks Martin Wolf of the *Financial Times*, is the IMF and the international community it represents entitled to demand of a sovereign government? Providing advice is one thing, insistence that presidential candidates all sign the agreement with their country in blood, before an election ... [as in Korea] ... is surely another.

(Wolf 1998: 8)

In short, the IMF programmes have had only limited success, and aspects of them have undoubtedly enhanced the sense of panic within countries and, by making real incursions into the sovereign autonomy of the political processes of several countries (for better or worse), they have generated long-lasting resentment.

The desire to enhance supervision of private cross-border flows, especially FDI in emerging markets, can be expected to grow in the wake of the recent experiences in East Asia. Capital markets (domestic political explanations of the crises notwithstanding) have been a major cause of the problems in East Asia. Nothing is likely to shake the view – held in many Asian capitals – that the market's punishment of the weaknesses in Asia's financial systems, real as they are, far exceeded the crime. We must expect not only Asians but others to ask what good openness to global capital markets might serve. If the economic crisis in East Asia is to provide a positive learning experience at the multilateral level – as opposed to a negative, resentment-generating, learning experience at the regional level – it must trigger a discussion of how to combat the knee-jerk assumption that the unfettered movement of capital (especially short-term lending) is axiomatically a good thing.[11]

Globalisation requires the development of institutional capability for prudential regulation in these areas. If not, speculative portfolio capital will continue to wing its way around the world as part of the underregulated global competitive game. While most policy analysts recognise regulation – or more appropriately, re-regulation – is best pursued at the global level, regional-level initiatives of the type outlined in the Manila framework and in the discussion of an AMF will evolve. In a post-hegemonic era there is no 'lender of last resort'. Asian policy elites – those on the way out and those on the way in – will have learned that they must look to self-help at the regional level as much as to the institutional resolution of these issues at the global level.

The events of 1997–8 have been the most traumatic experienced in Asia since decolonisation and the Cold War confrontations of the 1950s and 1960s. They have triggered a fundamental rethink on a range of issues. They have also side-tracked policy elites from the regional dialogue activities – trade liberalisation and security – popular throughout the first half of the 1990s. In this context, ASEAN as the leader of wider Asian regional dialogues has lost its way since 1997. As the immediate crisis recedes and policy elites begin to think again more constructively about the regional cooperative agenda, the events of 1997–8 will need to be put into clearer analytical perspective.

We can expect the development of multi-level regionalism to continue. In one way or another, East Asia will be a pillar of it. In addition to the role of the United States, the future of the region after the crisis is also now more firmly tied to the role of the two indigenous Asian superpowers than at any time in the past. Specifically, the future of the region is dependent not only on Japanese economic reform, but also on a willingness of the PRC to continue the new-found regional economic role that it has been so keen to consolidate since the return of Hong Kong and advent of the economic crisis in 1997.

The Asia–Pacific, as constituted by the membership of the APEC, may continue to form an outer regional shell. Broad economic philosophies, principally liberal in nature, will continue to underpin both the rhetoric of inner core and outer shell – especially a commitment to a broadly defined multi-lateral trading system. The economic crisis will continue to ensure reform of a market-opening nature in the trade arena. But there will be a different regional spin towards these global issues in East Asia that will reflect more strongly Asian political, cultural and economic experiences and which will lead to enhanced Asian policy responses to the major global economic questions of our time. East Asian policy-makers may be less willing in the early stages of the next century to subscribe as unreflectively to the tenets of neo-liberalism – especially in the financial sector – than they have been in the closing stages of the current one.

NOTES

* An earlier version of this paper was delivered at the conference on 'Business Challenges in the Asia Pacific', The Royal Institute of International Affairs, London, 30 March 1998, and will appear in *New Political Economy* 3(3), 1998. It has been considerably revised and updated for this conference.

1 'Cronyism' was originally used to describe the politics of Ferdinand Marcos' regime in the Philippines. It has now come to be used as a generic term in the region. This, to my mind, illustrates a considerable intellectual deficit on the part of contemporary analysis of the political economy of East Asia.

2 Measures proposed for Korea, Indonesia and Thailand aimed at financial deregulation and liberalisation and domestic demand containment include abandoning crippled financial institutions, making provision for international purchase of domestic financial institutions; internationalising domestic accounting and auditing activities – in both theory and practice; the elimination of government-directed lending and non-intervention in commercial banking; removal of government assistance, including tax privileges, to domestic corporations as well as more rapid liberalisation of the trade regime and the labour market.

3 While it is no defence of Asian values, similar instances of corrupt cronyism can be found in non-Asian societies, as for example in the Savings and Loans scandal in the United States; in arms dealings between the United Kingdom and several

Arab states; and in Germany, where bribes to foreign officials in the hunt for contracts are still tax deductible. But the essence of the Savings and Loans scandal in the United States – a private sector insulated from the costs of its decisions because banks lent money while government assumed the risk – is very similar to the problems that beset Asia. The difference is not one of style but one of substance. While no exact estimation is possible, bad loans in East Asia can count for anywhere between 15 and 25 percent of total loans. This contrasts with a figure of 1 per cent in the United States. The Savings and Loans crisis took about 2 percent of US GDP to sort out. Estimates for Southeast Asia in late 1997 were that about 13 percent of regional GDP will be required. This figure is rising throughout 1998.

4 Although the nature of 'accountability' remains a problem. For example, 'accountability' in Japan often means little more than 'the responsibility to explain' rather than being accountable for the results of one's actions. See *Nikkei Weekly* 27 April 1998: 18.

5 See reports in *The Business Times* 3 October 1997.

6 See the arguments of Yoichi Funabashi (1995).

7 See the discussion in *South China Morning Post* 16 November 1997.

8 A South Korean delegate to the Asia Neighbours Forum in Tokyo raised again the idea that Asian countries needed to think about an AMF, led by Japan, to maintain currency stability in the region. Similarly, the Head of the Asian Development Bank Institute, Jesus Estanislao, has suggested that a system not unlike the EMS – in which Asian currencies would move against a currency basket consisting of the dollar, the yen and the euro – is not impossible in Asia (see Fujii 1998: 23). The Japanese Institute for International Monetary Affairs, along with Thai and Korean research organisations, is also conducting a feasibility study for a single-currency system for Asia. The crucial point of these avenues of exploration is not their immediate significance. Nor is the point to underestimate the difficulties of such policy coordination in the region. Rather it is to suggest we would be naïve not to think that at some stage Asians will not introduce greater regional institutional mechanisms for the common management of financial questions.

9 As the US Treasury has made clear all along, support for bailouts, especially in Korea, was and is contingent on continued financial opening.

10 Michael Koeneke, Chairman, Global Mergers and Acquisitions, Merrill Lynch.

11 As even the *Financial Times* (16 January 1998: 18) noted, 'the wisdom of over-hasty integration of emerging economies into global financial markets must be reconsidered'.

15

MORAL (AND OTHER) HAZARDS

The IMF and the systemic Asian crisis

Richard Leaver

Let me begin with a tricky two-part question and a number of clues that suggest an answer. The question is this: about which country in the Asia–Pacific, and during which decade, am I talking? There are four leads to follow.

First, the major corporations from this country are amongst the most dynamic in cutting-edge technologies. Global trade outcomes have therefore run very strongly in this country's favour for some time. In addition, and more recently, this trading state has also assumed the status of financial creditor to the world economy. Although this combination of positive trade and capital balances goes against the grain of historical experience, great hopes are invested in its ability to use these capital surpluses in ways that help solve extant 'world order' problems.

Second, because of its evident economic dynamism, others seek to emulate the development model of this country. There is a steady stream of trade missions and inquisitive visitors from other places searching for the secrets of its success, ultimately hoping to renovate their own lagging industries. However, while this tribute is enjoyed politically, one of the most pronounced themes in the intellectual life of this commercially dominant country emphasises that the totality of its development experience is culturally and historically unique, and therefore not amenable to wholesale export. 'Inward-looking exceptionalism' is a theme much bandied about.

Third, the country in question has, in recent times, profited greatly from major wars, without ever being keen to enter into them. Its national budgets only commit a low level of resources to the preparations for conflict. In place of self-help, it has derived a good portion of its physical security from close association with the country formerly regarded as the hegemonic power of the international system. It attracts a broad range of criticisms

283

from that quarter for being something of a sleeping partner, a consumer rather than a producer of international order. But in extreme emergencies, it will usually buy into geopolitical disputes on its side, and when it does so, the economic and technological resources it brings to the ring have proved vital.

Fourth, its diplomats appear to have raised into an art form the practice of not provoking anyone. The foreign policy it has constructed is regionally rather than globally focused, and dominated by the commercial interests of its corporations. In part, this reflects an unresolved tension amongst its citizens about whether or not their state should have any active role in global affairs at all. Critics of this foreign policy style accuse it of chequebook diplomacy, while its supporters regard it as the prototype of a new and superior kind of world power, a civilian power.

The answer that I am hoping you will have arrived at is that the country in question is Japan in the decade after 1985 – that is, after the Plaza Agreement marked the beginning of the yen's most rapid period of ascent, but before its equally rapid descent began in 1995. A number of markers were deliberately left lying around amongst the clues to point in that direction; phrases like 'inward-looking exceptionalism' (Funabashi 1993), 'trading state' (Rosecrance 1986) and 'civilian power' (Maull 1990–1) would ring loud bells to observers of the international debates about Japan during that decade.

The trick in the question is that there is also a second answer, equally legitimate save (perhaps) for the attempt to confine the quiz to the age of Asia–Pacific consciousness – namely, the United States in the decade after the Great War. As with the Japan of the late 1980s, the United States was then an immature creditor to the world economy. Its governments were uncertain about what, if any, role they should play save for a regional and commercial one. It, too, was a practitioner of cheap and effective 'dollar diplomacy' close to home, often in the service of corporate interests. And like many Japanese of more recent times, Americans were then captivated by the native theme of 'American exceptionalism'.

There was also a fifth clue that might have been provided, but it was held back to shield the concealed answer. For the final and most profound export from the United States of the roaring twenties was not the Model T Ford. The export which brought that period of American self-absorption and conceit to an end was the deflationary impetus of financial collapse and economic depression that the United States imparted to the world economy after 1929 – much as Japan has been doing to the Asia–Pacific region in more recent times.

This is not meant to suggest that the Asian currency crisis is just the preamble to a rerun of another Great Depression, although that theme has increasingly been bobbing up in recent commentary (WuDunn and Kristoff 1997; Hartcher 1998a; Walsh 1998; Colebatch 1998; Johnson 1998a). The

American economy of the early twentieth century loomed much larger in relation to the total world economy than Japan or anyone else has since or is likely to again. Likewise, the world economy of our time has infinitely better developed and more resilient structures than the rather fragile formations of the 1920s. But neither should these differences be any cause for complacency about where the current crisis might ultimately lead.

For even twelve months after the current downturn began, there is still no country in the region where an actual quarterly growth outcome looks rosier than the estimate it replaces. This trend is officially corroborated by significant changes in the tenor of the most recent performance-monitoring Letters of Intent struck between the IMF and its more compliant regional supplicants, where the importance now being given to stimulating domestic economies through lower interest rates and larger budget deficits implicitly acknowledges the seriousness of this deepening process (see Mehta 1998): in Indonesia, for instance, a budget deficit of 8.5 per cent is now being sanctioned by the IMF (*The Business Times* 1998). Absent China, all regional economies outside Japan display falls in imports (UNCTAD 1998), with the collapse close to 40 per cent over the last year for most of the IMF's clients. And with the exceptions of the Philippines, China and (only just) South Korea, exports are also down, although by much smaller percentages (Saunders 1998). Hence export surpluses are virtually universal, but their real foundation lies upon growth-reducing import reductions. Applied on a regional scale, this pattern of 'distress surpluses' suggests the export of recession rather than sustainable recovery. Small wonder, therefore, that Alan Greenspan found time in his July 1998 Congressional testimony to depart from his main theme about 'the virtuous cycle' of economic fundamentals driving American economic performance to note that many Asian economies 'have been spiraling in quite the opposite direction' with 'the risk of further adverse developments ... remaining substantial' (Greenspan 1998b). Consequently, no one can yet say with any great conviction exactly when or how the phase of descent will cease, let alone how the path to a regional recovery might be recharted. Nothing quite seems to be following the expected script.

Systemic crises of the simple and complex kinds

There is, however, one thing that these depressing and somewhat counter-intuitive fragments of evidence ought to confirm – namely, that the crisis is systemic in nature. The idea of a systemic crisis has a simple meaning. Where the degree of economic interdependence has developed to the extent that everything becomes connected to everything else, the label 'systemic' suggests that the totality of the event exceeds the sum of its isolated national parts. The condition of systemic interdependence in this simple sense carries a nasty corollary – namely, that the very definition of what is rational becomes contingent upon the actions of others. What appears to be an appropriate course for corrective action in the face of an economic down-turn in any one nation can turn out to be a sustaining cause that maintains its downward momentum. Hence formulae and designs worked out in advance through prevailing criteria of theoretical correctness therefore have the unnerving capacity to induce negative feedback rather than alleviate it. This was certainly true of the Great Depression, where the depth and dura-tion of the experience was compounded by continued obeisance to prevailing theory, and the elements of meaningful national solutions eventu-ally emerged more from exogenous chance (the Second World War) and the exhaustion of endogenous tinkering (Roosevelt's eventual embrace of Keynesianism) than anything else (see Gourevitch 1984).

For an increasing number of analysts, this gloomy argument about the unintended consequences of remedial actions under systemic conditions offers a particularly apt description of the IMF's own involvement in the crisis. Despite putting together successively larger rescue packages for Thailand, Indonesia and South Korea, critics coming from different ideolog-ical corners increasingly agree with the assessment authoritatively articulated by Martin Feldstein (1998) and Jeffrey Sachs (1998d) – namely, that long-established IMF deflationary medicines intended to deal with structural current account deficits have been widely but wrongly dispensed, while the Fund's more recent penchant for making extensive financial support conditional upon wide-ranging institutional reforms has been inap-propriate. Hence, despite financial rescues on a regionally unprecedented scale that statistically offer partial compensation for the flight of private capital (see IMF 1998), many now conclude that the IMF's double mandate of deflation plus institutional reform made the exit option of private capital doubly attractive, so destabilizing rather than stabilizing regional currencies. Consequently, those on the Left primarily concerned with economic injus-tice, and those on the Right worried about the creation of moral hazard, increasingly find common cause in criticising the IMF's combination of 'old' conditionality and 'new' mission creep into institutional reform. In the words of the high republican Senator Lauch Faircloth, the IMF has 'priva-tized profits and socialized losses' (Longman and Ahmad 1998) – or, as Michel Camdessus has chosen to couch the accusation, been 'too soft on lenders, too hard on people' (Stokes 1998). Even worse, as is now evident in Indonesia, the Fund's successive visitations are widely regarded as having established the preconditions for another draw of that political lottery known in other regions as 'an IMF revolution'.

No one from Latin America or Africa would be particularly surprised about this kind of critique, even if it sometimes comes from unusual quar-ters. In those continents, bitter experience has long suggested that the IMF is something other than the politically neutral tool of disinterested multilat-eral adjustment (see Swedberg 1986), and that its standard mode of operation entails the combination of deflationary 'overkill' (Dell 1982) with structural adjustment that imposes significant long-term reductions in real living standards (see Ramirez 1991). For an organization whose first Article of Agreement commits it to attaining high levels of employment and income through expansion of the balanced growth of international trade, the experience of other places about IMF adjustment has long raised discomforting questions about its methods and purposes (see e.g. Stewart 1987). These homespun truths from other regions are therefore being recycled as new and melancholy appendices to the largely self-congratulatory debates of recent decades about Asian economic success. In so far as future Asian development debates will, in that respect, move back into the orbit of mainstream peripheral experiences, then this sad example of Asian catch-up should be welcomed.

But in one very important sense, the 'new' Asian critiques of the IMF's role cannot afford to be content simply to assimilate lessons from other places. This is so because the systemic crisis that now confronts the Asian economies is critically different from those of Latin America and Africa in previous decades. For the Asian crisis is not just systemic in the simple, organic sense outlined above. It is also systemic in a second and more complex sense which differentiates it from all previous post-war debt crises. Those crises all grew out of a network of interdependence between economies with current account deficits. By contrast, this crisis envelops – indeed, centres upon – the world's most important structural surplus economy, Japan. In that sense, as our quiz question sought to demonstrate, the Asian crisis is morphologically more similar to the Great Depression than anything we have seen for seventy years.

One worrying difference, however, concerns the role of the IMF. The act of creating the IMF in 1944 was an important element in a conjunction of policies that capped the possibility of some future return to the deflationary spiral. The fact that the Fund figures within most accounts of today's crisis as a catalyst rather than a suppressant of that kind of spiral is a matter of considerable concern. At the very least, it underscores the pertinence of analyses that pose fundamental questions about its purpose and modalities under contemporary conditions.

The power to dispose

Amongst those many fundamental questions, one long-neglected issue seems particularly important precisely because the double complexity of the current crisis nods unambiguously towards it. As James Tobin and Gustav Ranis (1998) have recently observed, 'the architects of the IMF ... did not presume that currency difficulties were the victim's fault'. They did not make this presumption because they thought that an international institution tasked with achieving currency stability through balanced current accounts should treat both deficit and surplus nations relatively equally. According to their implicit notion of moral equivalence, and despite the commonplace verdict that current account surpluses were good, Keynes in particular regarded countries that accumulated structural surpluses on the current account as being every bit as guilty as deficit nations of creating pressures to realign the relative value of currencies. In a global economy that is ultimately a closed circle, every surplus induced a corresponding deficit. Keynes therefore sought, and thought he had obtained, disciplinary powers for the Fund to exercise against surplus economies. The 1944 Articles of Agreement for the IMF included a 'scarce currency clause' that enabled sanctions to be applied against surplus economies, thus forcing their government to reflate, increase their volume of imports, and gradually eliminate both their tendency to surplus and the forced march of others towards deficit.

The scarce currency clause, however, hardly figures at all in the history of the Fund's operations. Since 'special decisions' within the Fund – including decisions about its *modus operandi* – initially required a super-majority vote of 80 per cent, and the American original share of votes was more than 30 per cent, Washington had an effective veto sufficient to determine what the Fund would *not* do. It drew upon that power to dispose at the first substantive meeting of the Fund to gut the operation of the scarce currency clause – a highly convenient gutting, since the United States was then the world's surplus economy *par excellence*. Twenty years later, however, the relatively much smaller US economy had firmly embraced current account deficits, while the locus of surpluses and increased economic throw-weight was shifting towards Japan and East Asia. But despite these two shifts, American power to dispose remained undiminished.

After the first oil shock, things both changed and remained the same. Washington's vote had already slipped near to the critical 20 per cent threshold, and now the new importance of oil producers meant that their voting rights within the Fund should be doubled, largely at the expense of the aggregate vote enjoyed by industrialized nations. In addition, Japan, by virtue of its own growing economic mass, also sought to raise its IMF quota from fifth to third largest. The combination of these two adjustments seemed to dictate a sharp reduction in the US quota from 23 per cent to 19 per cent, so depriving Washington of its veto power. But in the face of American opposition, Japan and the Europeans eventually settled on a compromise. Washington's voting power was indeed pushed under 20 per cent, but the super-majority hurdle was racked up to 85 per cent, so preserving its veto (Yoshiko 1992: 296–8).

This deal – repeated in its essentials within the World Bank a decade later (see Rapkin *et al.* 1997: 177) – gave us the essential structure of the implicit political bargain that still drives the IMF today. It spared the world's largest deficit economy both from the rod of any possible IMF intervention and from any unrequited redefinition of the IMF's purposes. In return, it gave the world's largest surplus economy immunity against the application of the scarce currency clause, both through the existing convention of neglect and through the implicit understanding that Japanese surpluses would serve American-nominated purposes (of which the purchase of US Treasury bonds has been the most important). Hence, although Washington never tires of lecturing Tokyo about the necessity to reflate its surplus-ridden economy – and no more so than during the current crisis – its own self-interest dictates that these demands be routed around the IMF. Weaker bilateral conduits necessarily carry that message.

For interested third parties, the main consequence of having the world's largest surplus and deficit economies outside the disciplines of multilateral principles is that the Fund necessarily operates in a vastly sub-optimal way. Nonetheless, the incentives to preserve this private game and the mutual indulgences it confers find clear expression in the debates of the last twelve months about the possible reform of the IMF. Of these, the most important centred on the possible creation of an Asian Monetary Fund (AMF), an issue that first figured prominently in the agenda at the back-to-back meetings of the IMF and the G-7 at Hong Kong in September 1997 (see Altbach 1997).

As Richard Higgott's analysis in this volume notes, the idea of a well-backed regional fund capable of acting quickly and with minimal conditionality was well within Japan's capability, especially since Taiwan and China were sympathetically disposed. Narrowly defined calculations of self-interest – Japan's increasing integration with the ASEAN area through trade, foreign direct investment and bank loans – suggested compelling reasons for the Hashimoto government's proposal. But if self-interest was indeed the primary factor driving the AMF float, then one might have expected that Tokyo would ultimately have battled much harder to defend the proposal. In the end, it did not – and this suggests other motivations.

The critical point in this episode lies in the American absence from the second line of government financiers who stood behind the IMF during the Thai rescue. The Japanese government took this absence to mean that, in financial matters, Asia was Japan's responsibility (Masahiko 1997). However, a combination of political and legal reasons largely accounted for this absence. Washington was considerably less sensitive to worries about contagion than Tokyo, as Clinton's casual assessment of the crisis as 'glitches on the road' (Dejevsky 1998) clearly showed even two months later. Along the legal front, the instrumentality through which the United States might have involved itself in the Thai rescue, the Exchange Stabilization Fund (ESF), had been reined in and capped by Congress after extensive drawings were made from this largely unknown fund during the Mexican crisis of 1995. Since the Clinton administration was about to enter the Congressional fray to renew the president's authority for fast-track trade negotiations, it wanted to avoid being doubly presumptuous and conserve its political capital for that higher priority campaign.

In so far as Washington's capacity for independent financial action was low, then its opportunities for voice in the management of the crisis depended almost totally upon its ability to hold court through the IMF. An AMF that opened possibilities for what Treasury Secretary Robert Rubin (1998) later called 'reform shopping' could see Washington shut out altogether. Consequently, under the vigorous leadership of US Treasury Under-Secretary Larry Summers, the United States spared no energy to retain an 'IMF-centric' configuration for the adjustment process, and to kill off the possibility for creating a floating pool of pre-positioned funds capable of dousing fears of contagion. Governments, he argued, might occasionally want to pay ransom, but 'no government should set up a ransom fund in advance to make sure they can pay it efficiently' (cited in Muehring 1997).

The end product of this unrelenting opposition was, as Higgott notes, 'the Manila framework', subsequently endorsed at the Vancouver APEC in November and at the Kuala Lumpur summit of East Asian leaders in December. This channelled regional cooperation along four avenues: greater economic surveillance of the region; strengthened domestic financial systems and regulatory mechanisms; improved capacity for response for the IMF; and supplementation of IMF resources. Nonetheless, two aspects of this framework still represented a minimal kind of concession towards the regionally popular argument that the most pressing problem was the lack of confidence *per se*.

First, the idea that there should be some kind of time-urgent financial disbursing facility provided a focus for further IMF discussions, eventually resulting in agreement behind an American proposal for a Supplemental Reserve Fund (SRF). Without adding to the overall level of IMF resources or short-circuiting the process of conditionality, this innovation now promised quick action through loans with shorter terms and higher interest. The harsher terms, it was argued, were necessary to avoid moral hazard; they encourage borrowers to keep their attentions fixed on the reforms necessary for the full restoration of confidence. But on the other hand, it might be argued that the finite backing and high interest rates on SRF disbursements would have the effect of neutering the attractiveness of the new instrument during the early stages of a crisis. Second, enhanced processes of mutual surveillance centred on the IMF's new regional office in Tokyo were also agreed. These could be seen as providing the means for bringing a modicum of Asian peer pressure to bear upon somewhat mechanical IMF approaches. But in the first instance, what they certainly did do was pose a first-order challenge to the ASEAN principle of non-interference. As Lee Kuan Yew reportedly argued, if someone had to tell

Thailand how to reform its economy, he would prefer that the IMF carried the bad tidings (*The Economist* 1997).

There are, then, two political morals lurking within the account of the rise and fall of the AMF, for at the end of the day, two essentially cultural processes characteristic of the broader architecture of international policy had been reaffirmed. Early American disinterest had provided the opportunity for a seemingly forceful Japanese assertion of regional leadership. This, in turn, produced the expected backlash of American (and ultimately regional) opposition, clearing the way for Washington's subsequent involvement in the Indonesian and South Korean rescues, while watering down the Japanese proposals. In that sense, this reaffirmed the continuing relevance of the long-established rules in the highly privatised game of Japanese–American relations on questions of monetary order, most particularly the American power to dispose.

Second, at the conclusion of that process of debasement, some Japanese commentators were left wondering whether this was not, after all, an example of the growing maturity of the region. Had they not played the United States and Japan off against each other, so preserving the idea of regional trust and 'the Asian way'? (Yoshihiro 1997) That would be a more convincing reading if 'the Asian way' showed signs of surmounting its long-standing inhibitions about domestic sensitivity. But Lee's above comment led directly into a reaffirmation of this principle at the next ASEAN summit, albeit not without opposition. This, then, has the makings of a sub-optimal outcome when viewed from almost any direction.

Consuming the Fund: Congress and IMF recapitalization

The 'crude arithmetic' of the power to dispose within the Fund began to matter from another quarter. By the end of 1997, after committing US$35 billion of its own monies to its three Asian rescues, the IMF's working capital shrank to around US$15 billion. New rescues on a South Korean or Indonesian scale looked beyond its immediate capacity. The idea for New Arrangements to Borrow (NAB), conceived in the aftermath of the peso crisis but massively underfunded, and the September 1997 increase in quotas of 45 per cent, presented the Clinton administration with the challenge of appropriating a total of US$17.9 billion for the Fund. And since the standard super-majority of the Fund's contributors need to approve this recapitalization, the ability to dispose was passed from the administration into the hands of the US Congress. Hence, despite all the talk about the power of 'the Washington consensus' manifest in the management of the crisis, one paradoxical outcome is that it created the political conditions within the American polity for a fusion of left and right that might yet consume the Fund altogether.

Although the Senate approved refunding with only minor amendments in

March 1998, this led House Speaker Gingrich to opine that the chances of passage were dwindling away in his Republican-dominated chamber. In part, that was because many representatives, in particular majority leader Dick Armey, bore a personal grudge against Rubin for what they regarded as his excessive deviousness in previous budgetary dealings (Dunham and Foust 1998). Since Rubin's Treasury functioned as the phalanx for the administration's recapitalization case, this complicated matters somewhat. Moreover, the routine amendment of the moral majority – an anti-abortion amendment – was threatened, with Gingrich saying the two issues should forever be linked. Administration concerns about the quite predictable attacks from this quarter were more serious than usual. For unlike the Latin crisis, the enthusiasm of economic libertarians was not offset by any prudential concern for the high exposure of American banks, which stood in aggregate at roughly one-quarter that of Japan's banks (see Marshall 1998). Think tanks such as the Cato Institute and the Heritage Foundation could therefore afford to be unusually uninhibited in presenting their case. They duly obliged (see Niskanen 1998; Vasquez 1998; Feulner 1998).

From the progressive side, a coalition of twenty-seven non-governmental organizations entered the fray. Intellectually speaking, the action centred on the Catholic organization Center for Concern and its well-established *Rethinking Bretton Woods* project (see Griesgraber 1997), but in organizational terms, the environmental group Friends of the Earth was more to the fore (Franke-Ruta 1998). While, however, the size of this anti-IMF coalition looked impressive, it was not simply a copy of the bloc that frustrated fast-track authorization in late 1997. Organized labour was notably less interested in this issue, with minority leader Richard Gephardt supporting the administration (Miller 1998). In addition, the sheer size of the coalition inevitably meant they were not totally united. At one extreme, some wanted more than 'economics-only' conditionality, but conditionality nonetheless. So, for example, Sidney Jones, Executive Director of Human Rights Watch, observed that 'Indonesians [after Suharto] have had more freedom in the last two weeks than they have had in the last three decades', and went on to argue that 'continued conditioning of IMF and donor assistance on following through with political reform is crucial' (Jones 1998). At the other end, consumer advocate Ralph Nader sounded more like an economic libertarian, arguing that the IMF got in the way of less expensive and superior market solutions such as debt renegotiation and bankruptcy procedures (Nader 1998).

Despite active and early involvement for the Treasury's case from Defense, the Federal Reserve Board, and export-oriented American business – supported from the sidelines by a higher-than-usual public profile of the IMF's own senior staff (see Stokes 1998; Fischer 1998) – exhaustive House investigations into the refunding question nonetheless provided a convenient forum for spreading the general message, if not the specifics, from the new consensus. If there was a single vector outcome from all these tensions, then an emphasis upon greater public accountability looked a likely part of their resolution. This, indeed, was partly suggested by the process of the House inquiry itself; after an initial refusal from the Treasury (see Bachus 1998: 4–6), the threat of subpoena elicited the first-ever appearance before a Congressional committee from the incumbent American Executive Director of the IMF, Karin Lissakers. She went on to reveal that more than 2,000 decisions had been made during her five years on the Board, primarily by consensus rather than a formal vote, with the United States voting 'no' on three occasions and abstaining on a further nine (Lissakers 1998). The United States, she assured, 'worked behind the scenes' inside the IMF to improve the human rights and labour rights of member states, and had occasionally held up or blocked loans to governments with poor records in these areas. However, the fact that it had done so only occasionally, and not during the Indonesian rescue, led her inquisitors to argue that US law was being flouted (Sanger 1998). It therefore seemed highly probable that greater transparency in the Fund's own decision-making processes – transparency at least before the eyes of the Congress – would emerge from its inquiries.

Stand by your man: Russia

In mid May, well before the House was within sight of a final decision, 'contagion effects' spread to Russia. The stock market collapsed, and interest rates were moved up to defend the rouble, quickly reaching 150 per cent. Negotiations with the IMF commenced, but made little headway. The Fund held the attitude that Russian governments were really not interested in those politically difficult reforms involving a changed relationship between taxing and spending, and therefore not worthy of its assistance. In addition, the disinterest of capital markets in all things Russian was confirmed when, on two separate occasions, there were no bids at all for a majority share in the seemingly lucrative prize of the state-owned oil company, Rosneft. Later that month, talks between Russia and the IMF broke up after disagreements about the nature of conditionality.

After a period of mutual recriminations, Yeltsin proceeded to conscript Anatoly Chubais back into diplomatic service, dispatching him to Washington to deal over the head of the Fund directly with the Clinton administration about the terms of a new rescue package. An experienced hand, Chubais focused his efforts inside the beltway, working senior officials from the State Department and the Treasury (see Gordon and Sanger 1998). By the second week in July, and after a period of particularly rapid depletion in Russia's currency reserves, his personalised diplomacy brought home the IMF bacon – new loans of US$17.1 billion over two years, bringing Russia's cumulative total of credits from the IMF to US$22.6 billion. Subsequent reports indicated this was three times the level of support that the Fund had previously contemplated (Wessel and Davis 1998). One important result of this enlarged standby facility was that it pushed the Fund's own liquidity ratio into dangerous waters. Despite setting various new records in Asia, the Fund's own monies never amounted to more than 37 per cent of any single package. In Russia, however, nearly half of the credits came straight from its own coffers. In addition, there was no American participation this time, with the administration appearing to fear that this could swing the House against the Fund's replenishment.

At first, all of this appeared like wise politics in regard to the House debates. The clear demonstration that the Fund would go well out along a financial limb to help Washington stand by its most important bilateral relationship was thought likely to impress the House. And, for a time, it did. By July, both Gingrich and Armey were conceding that the requested appropriations would probably be approved (Seelye 1998). This was helped along by the first signs that the contagion was spreading to the United States through collapsing agricultural exports. For a brief period, therefore, Rubin appeared confident of a positive outcome.

However, the politics of this package soon swung back the other way. Precisely because the IMF's working capital stood at its lowest level since the early 1980s, 80 per cent of the Russian credits from the Fund had to be raised through IMF borrowings from the central banks of the industrialized nations under the General Agreement to Borrow (GAB). This rarely used mechanism dated from 1961, but was last invoked in 1978 to help the Carter administration stabilize the dollar. The knowledge that GAB borrowings did not have to be routed through any political screening process was therefore reminiscent of earlier Congressional opposition to the ESF. Despite increasing division within Republican ranks, Armey therefore reverted to his *ex ante* position, with the GOP leadership taking a new and narrow bead on the head of Camdessus. Other House critics appeared quite content to see the Fund stretched thin, arguing that it should resort to issuing bonds or selling its US$30 billion in gold reserves to raise future working capital (*Inter Press Service* 1998). This line was underscored by a report from the General Accounting Office which estimated the Fund's resources at US$75 billion. By August, the rout looked complete when, in spite of its agreement with the Fund, the Russian rouble nonetheless collapsed. The internal and external debt moratoriums that followed re-emphasized before the House the continuing relevance of the prudential argument that good money ought not be thrown after bad.

However, the whole question of IMF recapitalization was now one of a large number of back-logged issues that had to be considered in the highly politicized context of Clinton's possible impeachment arising from the Lewinsky scandal and the looming mid-term Congressional elections. As American appreciations that the crisis was not just an Asian affair began to rise quite sharply, Clinton was able to recast his image as a reforming internationalist in advance of the G-7 and IMF meetings of October 1998. After the minor appropriation of US$3.4 billion for the NAB passed through the House, the Republicans appeared increasingly likely to cut a deal for the residual around three reforms: increased IMF transparency, a one-year time line on credits, and non-concessional interest rates (Shenon 1998). Further tactical concessions along these fronts seemed likely as political resources were concentrated along others. The IMF, then, may well escape the undivided attentions of the House, though not without a severe mauling. And if the Republicans proceed to do well at the polls, then there is always the prospect of more to come.

Conclusion: Keynesianism through inadvertence?

Because the crisis continues both to deepen and spread, it is much too early to talk about eventual solutions. What is clear is that the interim solution of an IMF-centric adjustment process leading to an export-led recovery is looking totally discredited. The recent developments previously mentioned – the spread of the crisis to Russia and beyond; the 'distressed' nature of regional export growth – are best regarded as two symptoms of a further phase in the development of the crisis. Taken in conjunction with the abrupt slowdown of the US economy in the second quarter of 1998 and the continued pressure on the yen, it seems entirely appropriate to speak of the arrival of 'the second wave' of the crisis. A substantial deflationary spiral on a scale much larger than just Asia is now in the offing. And for this, we can largely thank the actions (and inactions) taken under the mandate of the IMF.

There are nonetheless some positive signs emerging in a piecemeal fashion around the region that offer some hope for an outcome that is better than a compound spiral of depression. Across the East Asian region, an increasing number of governments are being drawn towards recovery strategies based on domestic stimulation through lower interest rates and larger domestic deficits. In addition, Yeltsin's moratorium on Russia's foreign debt repayments may well provide the precedent for breathing space that others will want to follow, especially since foreign capital generally shows no sign of returning to the most affected regions. This generalised inward-turning process is, however, a double-edged sword. Over time, it can lead either towards a hardened form of economic nationalism – or towards a solution that is broadly Keynesian and internationalist in inspiration. The choice of which fork will ultimately be taken depends in large measure upon revisiting the question of an appropriate framework for international monetary cooperation.

Strangely enough, the rise of an LDP government in Japan run by 'Dad's Army' fits into the more positive of these two scenarios, partly because Finance Minister Miyazawa appears to be rekindling interest in

Hashimoto's AMF proposal (see Hirano 1998). It also bears remembering that Miyazawa, in his former incarnation as finance minister, was regarded as the most Keynesian in the large LDP stable of post-war finance ministers, and as a staunch opponent of both the 'money politics' of his party and the dictatorship of the Ministry of Finance (Hiroaki 1987). In addition, Prime Minister Obuchi was the foreign minister who ushered the AMF onto the Hong Kong stage. While the interest of regional debtors in this rekindling process is predictable, less so is that of those with deep pockets of foreign reserves such as Hong Kong (Rowley 1998), where the interventions of monetary authorities in the stock market have been quite unprecedented. Given, however, that the total currency reserves of East Asian states are three times larger than those of Europe and the United States combined, there is considerable scope in principle for collective action by Asian states on a regional or international scale.

These disparate elements of a Keynesian solution could well coalesce over time, especially as it becomes increasingly clear that the crisis is unlikely to end in an export-led recovery, and that the run-down of the IMF has crippled its capacity to dictate the terms of future efforts at currency stabilization. It is not totally inconceivable that a future US government will, after the companion bubbles of Wall Street and US economic arrogance have both been pricked, begin to think about its interests in the Fund more from the point of view of the deficit and debtor nation that it is. And at that point, its political stranglehold over the Fund is likely to make multilateral discussions of 'the architecture' of international finance something more satisfying than the back-of-the-envelope sketches made during the first year of the crisis.

16

AUSTRALIA IN THE SHADOW
OF THE ASIAN CRISIS

Mark Beeson and Stephen Bell

Over the past couple of decades Australian policy-makers of all political persuasions have made developing closer relations with East Asia a central part of foreign, and by extension domestic, policy. Although Australia has not been as badly affected by the crisis as its northern neighbours – or not yet, at least – the current crisis in the region is, nevertheless, a seminal event. Domestically, the rationale of attempting to harness Australia's economic future to a region that now looks a lot less dynamic than it once did has already been subjected to new, and potentially divisive, criticism. Of possibly more enduring significance, however, is Australia's somewhat surprising role as regional exemplar. Over the last twenty years or so, Australia has adopted precisely the sorts of reforms that are being encouraged or imposed upon the region by external agencies like the International Monetary Fund (IMF). Australia therefore provides an extremely useful comparative case study with which to contrast the experiences of the troubled East Asian economies. If the orthodox neo-liberal model that is currently being promoted throughout the region really is the answer to the supposed perils of 'crony capitalism', excessive state intervention or the repression of market forces, then Australia might be expected to demonstrate its efficacy unambiguously.

Despite the claims of the current Liberal–National Party coalition government that Australia is now the 'strongman of Asia', and that the Australian economy is effectively 'fireproofed' from the worst effects of the crisis, we shall argue that such claims are premature, Panglossian, and demonstrate little appreciation of the long-term trajectory of economic activity in Australia. A more sober reading of recent economic and political history suggests that Australia is far from immune to the intensifying crisis. Moreover, Australian policy-makers have made little progress in addressing underlying structural economic problems and appear to have few answers to the troubling social effects the economy and orthodox policy are increasingly generating. Whenever economic recovery does occur in the region, it is

likely that Australia will remain relatively marginalised and with comparatively little control of its economic destiny. In essence, we shall argue that
not only has Australia's own experience with neo-liberal reform been of
questionable efficacy, but attempts by Australian policy-makers to export it
throughout the region may backfire, especially in the event of what Richard
Higgott (this volume) calls the 'politics of resentment' becoming more
widespread. Indeed, we shall demonstrate that even within Australia itself,
there is growing opposition to the sorts of neo-liberal policies that have
become the bilaterally supported orthodoxy, making Australia's own continuing adherence to such policies increasingly problematic.

The first part of this chapter presents a brief overview of Australia's
conversion to neo-liberalism, the political forces that coalesced behind it,
and its overall efficacy. Following on from this, we look at the direct impact
of the crisis in Australia, and assess the validity of the government's claims
to have 'fireproofed' the economy. Finally, we consider the implications of
the crisis on Australia's overall policy framework, paying particular attention to the tension between Australia's ambitious external agenda and a
rising tide of domestic discontent.

Neo-liberal reform in Australia

At the outset, two aspects of Australia's relations with the region and the
policy framework that has informed it of late merit particular emphasis.
First, Australia's relationship with 'Asia' has undergone a profound change,
from one characterised by fear and suspicion, to one in which proximity to
Asia has come to be seen as an asset, especially economically. If one act
symbolised this transformation, it was the 'watershed' decision in 1972 of
Australian Labor Party (ALP) leader, Gough Whitlam, to recognise China
(Stephen FitzGerald 1997: 3). Despite some subsequent vacillations along
the way, successive Australian governments have made closer economic
engagement with Asia an increasingly central component of overall policies.
Indeed, 'Asian engagement' has become such an important and unchallenged part of Australia's foreign – and by extension domestic – policies
(Beeson and Firth 1998) that the only real disagreement between the major
parties is over their respective contributions to furthering this process
(Gurry 1998). For both the ALP and the current Liberal–National Party
coalition government, it is not so much a question of whether the engagement process should continue, but of its manner.

The other point to emphasise is that the engagement process, particularly
its economic aspects, has occurred within the overarching context of a neo-
liberal policy framework. From being a fairly insular, protected and
regulated economy for much of the post-war period, successive ALP governments during the 1980s self-consciously attempted to 'open up' Australia's
economic space to the supposedly efficacious effects of international

competitive pressures. The policies of the 1960s and 1970s came to be seen as discredited and responsible for the declining position of the Australian economy (see Bell 1993), particularly in comparison with the emerging 'tigers' of East Asia. A sense of mounting anxiety about Australia's position culminated in the 'banana republic' episode, in which a currency crisis provided the catalyst for a decisive break with the policies and thinking of the past (Kelly 1992: 197). This major shift in Australian policy was articulated and given further momentum in a seminal report by Ross Garnaut (1989), which effectively set Australia's economic agenda in the years that followed.

Significantly – and in contrast with most of their East Asian neighbours – Australian policy-makers actively embraced market-oriented reforms and *voluntarily* tried to loosen governmental control over the economy. Yet it is important to note that despite this enthusiasm, Australia's experience with financial liberalisation in the mid 1980s led to precisely the same sorts of effects as those which precipitated the current crisis in the region. Indeed, the impact of financial sector liberalisation in Australia is similar in many respects to Japan's experience – a phenomenon that led directly to the 'bubble economy' and the debt overhang that continues to plague both Japan and the region. As Australia's domestic banking sector was exposed to increasing amounts of unaccustomed competition in a newly deregulated environment, Australian bankers embarked on a reckless round of lending to 'entrepreneurial' investors who used easily accessible capital to fund corporate takeovers (Davidson 1992). Much like the experience of the troubled Asian economies, the result was the emergence of a speculative bubble in the stock market and property sectors, and a concomitant series of corporate collapses (Sykes 1994). By the early 1990s, in the banking sector alone, total write-offs amounted to over A$28 billion. More tellingly still, despite all the claims about the possible benefits of competition in the financial sector, there was little benefit as far as investment job-creating manufacturing investment was concerned (Hawtrey *et al.* 1991). On the contrary, one of the principal effects of Australia's liberalisation experience was to consolidate the influence of the financial sector and a policy agenda that even former supporters of deregulation suggested discriminated against high employment and threatened the cohesiveness of Australian society (Argy 1996: 2). More immediately, the growing influence of 'rentier' capital has actually had the effect of maintaining high real interest rates in the new deregulated environment, placing further pressure on economic activity in the 'real' economy (Bell 1997a: 173; see also Beeson and Robison in this volume). This did little to address underlying structural problems in an economy that remains reliant on the production of commodities which are worth less and less on world markets. The current downturn in world commodity markets stands as a stark reminder of Australia's vulnerability at times of economic crisis and externally driven changes in its terms of trade.

The issue of the strategic provision of capital to industry through mechanisms such as 'guided' credit is one of the most important characteristics that distinguish East Asian political economy and is a key point of contention in both understanding the crisis and attempting to resolve it. As Beeson and Robison point out in Chapter 1, the predominantly credit-based systems of East Asia have a very different logic from those of the Anglo-American economies like Australia. Yet financial liberalisation and the impact of the crisis has reduced ability to direct credit or control financial flows within national economic space and this has clearly been a central element in the unravelling of the Japanese-inspired Northeast Asian model in particular (Leyshon 1994). To judge from the Australian experience, however, there would seem to be little obvious benefit to be gained from the transition to a market-centred system. In the absence of a wider policy framework intended to encourage productive development, there is little reason to suppose that useful economic restructuring will occur in response to market signals alone (Bell 1997a: chapter 10).

The other important comparative issue between Australia and some of the East Asian nations revolves around the closely related question of state capacity. Weiss and Hobson (this volume) claim that state 'strength' is defined by a 'transformative capacity' or the ability to 'intervene' effectively in pursuit of specific objectives. For the reasons mentioned above we are less sanguine about the ability of the 'strong' states of East Asia either to withstand the crisis in tact, or utilise it to their advantage. Hence whilst it is true that a number of East Asian states have played an effective and important role in shaping the trajectory of economic development in the past, and that this has been a central element of the 'East Asian miracle' (see Bell 1995a), the question remains whether this is any longer a feasible model, or whether the Anglo-American, neo-liberal alternative is a more useful contemporary alternative.

Again, the Australian experience offers important comparative lessons. One of the most important distinctions to make in respect of the past performance and future prospects of the ideal–typical developmental state is between the capacity of states to influence the direction of economic development, and their capacity to exert an influence in particular circumstances. In countries like Japan, not only did the desire to influence the course of development exist, but there was also the requisite technocratic competence and – crucially – institutionalised linkages between government and business that permitted such plans to be implemented (Krauss 1992). Whatever the long-term problems of such institutionalised relationships may be, particularly after they have achieved their initial ends, there is no doubt that such policies *were* instrumental in transforming Japan and a number of other East Asian countries.

In Australia, by contrast, not only was there an absence of such institutionalised transmission mechanisms with which to implement various industry policies (Bell 1993; Beeson 1997), but there was little political support to encourage governments to adopt anything other than the sorts of market-centred policies that reflected the priorities of powerful economic players like the mining sector (Bell 1995b; Kaptein 1993). When considering the lessons to be drawn from the current crisis, therefore, it is important to distinguish between those elements of policy that may have actually been successful in the past, and those which may no longer be feasible or appropriate. Whatever the future of the developmental state model may be, there is no doubt that major transformations in a number of the underlying 'real' economies of East Asia *have* occurred – transformations that will not simply disappear, but which have permanently altered the structure of domestic economies and their place in the overarching international economic order. In Australia, by contrast, there has been no such thoroughgoing transformation. Consequently, whenever 'normal' economic activity returns to the region, and even if Australia emerges comparatively unscathed from the current trauma, Australia will begin the next phase of global economic expansion with exactly the same sort of unsophisticated, resource-dependent economy that appears structurally incapable of avoiding recurrent, autonomously generated crisis, or of providing its citizens with adequate numbers of jobs.

Even in the short term, however, there are substantial grounds for treating with caution the present coalition government's claims about insulating Australia from the crisis. Even if the crisis remains relatively contained within East Asia and does not trigger a global recession or depression which will inevitably savage Australia's terms of trade, there are grounds for expecting that the crisis will have a greater impact on Australia than we have seen thus far.

Australian economic fallout

The damage caused by Australia's most recent exposure to the vicissitudes of financial instability – via the Asian crisis – is still being assessed. The severity of the effects will be determined by the degree of integration between Australia and key Asian economies and on future economic developments in Asia. Even in the short term the latter is still hard to predict. At present the current account crisis in the worst-hit Asian economies is being corrected through export growth but especially through weak imports. Export performance is being assisted by the large competitive advantages wrought by currency depreciations, whilst weak imports reflect IMF deflationary medicine and the collateral damage wrought by the crisis on domestic demand and the real economy. Most economists predict Asia will one day bounce back, though at this stage there is greater concern about Indonesia. Table 16.1 provides recent figures and forward *estimates* of GDP growth in the troubled Asian economies.

Table 16.1   Historical data and consensus forecast for Asian GDP

Country	Historical data					Consensus forecasts for 1998–9						
	95	96	97e	Sept.	Oct.	Nov.	Dec. 98	Jan.	Feb.	Mar.	Apr. 99	GDP
China	10.5	9.7	8.8	9.9	9.8	9.1	9.0	8.5	8.2	7.9	7.8	8.2
Hong Kong	4.5	4.9	5.2	5.4	5.3	4.0	3.7	3.1	3.3	2.7	3.0	3.9
Japan	1.4	4.1	0.9	1.9	1.7	1.6	1.1	0.2	0.1	0.1	−0.3	0.8
South Korea	8.9	7.1	5.5	6.4	6.2	5.4	1.8	−0.1	−0.2	−1.3	−1.6	1.6
Taiwan	6.0	5.7	6.8	6.6	6.5	6.4	6.3	6.1	6.0	5.8	5.9	6.1
Indonesia	8.2	7.8	4.6	6.5	5.2	4.2	3.0	−0.6	−3.3	−4.9	−6.3	0.5
Malaysia	9.5	8.6	7.8	6.6	5.9	5.4	3.9	2.6	2.7	1.5	1.1	2.3
Philippines	4.8	5.7	5.1	5.2	4.4	4.3	3.7	3.0	2.9	2.3	2.2	3.9
Singapore	8.8	7.0	7.8	6.7	6.4	5.9	5.1	4.6	3.9	3.0	2.7	4.0
Thailand	8.7	6.4	0.0	1.9	1.2	0.0	−1.3	−2.0	−2.7	−3.5	−4.1	1.7

Source: Consensus forecasts

There are, however, many wild cards, especially in terms of Asia's ability to export its way out of trouble. For example, will China devalue its currency and impact on the export competitiveness of other Asian economies? Will the growing protectionist mood in the United States stymie the absorption of Asia's exports? And what of Japan? A high proportion of Asian trade occurs within the Asian region and if Japan continues to slide, it will further damage Asia (Thurow 1998). The seriousness of Japan's plight and the spiralling down of regional trade has led some officials in the World Bank to speak openly of a looming Asian 'depression' (Wood 1998). In contrast to the IMF's deflationary policies, the Bank has recently advocated expansionary policies – along Keynesian lines – to kick-start the region. Talk of an Asian depression contrasts with the IMF's somewhat more optimistic model of Asian recovery along Mexican lines where there was a sharp 'V'-shaped slump followed by an upswing. As Grenville (1998: 17) points out, however, the Asian context is different from that found in Mexico. In Mexico, substantial bailout funds were administered quickly. This has not been the case in Asia. Mexico also had a booming US market at its doorstep to absorb exports, whilst Asia is afflicted by weak regional trade and a beleaguered Japan.

All this clouds the outlook for Asia and Australia. The emerging situation in Russia further clouds the picture. In terms of the economic fallout from Asia in Australia, there are a number of factors to consider. Australia is heavily integrated economically with Asia. Before the crisis, this was unequivocally considered a good thing. For example, 60 per cent of Australian exports go to Asia, equivalent to almost 10 per cent of domestic

GDP (*The Economist* 13 June 1998). Comparatively, then, Australia is more exposed to Asian ills than any other advanced economy.

Australia's level of Asian exposure, plus weaker commodity prices, has certainly worried financial market players. Since late 1996 the Australian dollar has been sold down 25 per cent, hitting a low of US$0.56 in September 1998. Not since the 'banana republic' crisis of 1985–6 has the dollar been sold down to such a level. This is an especially important consideration for the incumbent coalition government as it has staked much political capital on its claim to have 'fireproofed' the domestic economy from the impact of the crisis. By this logic, macroeconomic fundamentals, particularly the budget surplus and low inflation, were expected to shield Australia from adverse market sentiment. In the event, a key market concern has been that weaker exports will widen Australia's current account deficit (CAD), something which is already happening. In 1996–7 CAD was 3.4 per cent of GDP. In 1997–8 it was 4.25 per cent and Treasury estimates in the 1998 budget papers predict it will worsen in 1998–9 to 5.25 per cent. Some analysts are predicting an even worse outcome (Hopkins 1998). The first quarter CAD result was 33 per cent worse than for the 1997 December quarter. A CAD anywhere near 6 per cent is potentially dangerous as far as market sentiment is concerned.

Officials in Canberra and the Reserve Bank, however, are keen to point out (especially to the markets) that Australia's CAD situation is in hand. The argument is that Australia has sounder macroeconomic fundamentals than those prevailing in the 'banana republic era' of the mid 1980s, that the banking system has been strengthened, that Australia's debt to GDP ratio is relatively modest compared with many other countries (Table 16.2) and that our foreign debt to GDP ratio, after rising rapidly in the 1980s, has stabilised in the 1990s.

The Reserve Bank's Ian Macfarlane (1998) has also argued that Australia's exports to many Asian countries (especially Japan and Korea) are essentially 'inputs into exports', and so Australian export levels have not been as badly affected by the Asian downturn as might have been expected. 'I would be a lot more worried if Australian exports consisted of consumer products', Macfarlane comments. Macfarlane also argues that most of Australia's commodities exports are 'fungible' and can be sold wherever demand is. 'If Korean demand for base metals falls, Australia will still probably sell the same amount of base metals as before, but with more sales to countries other than Korea.' The structural diversification of Australian exports to non-Asian economies is also a factor that will help cushion the impact of the Asian crisis on Australia. In this regard there has been strong export growth in recent years to 'other' economies, principally the Middle East, New Zealand, former Eastern Bloc economies and South America.

For these reasons the Treasury estimates that the impact of the Asian slowdown on export volumes is likely to be substantial but not necessarily

Table 16.2   Comparative national debt levels: external debt as percentage of GDP

Net debt		Gross debt	
New Zealand [1996]	64.2	Ireland [1996]	143.1
Sweden [1996]	45.2	Sweden [1996]	101.7
Canada [1996]	44.8	Switzerland [1995]	96.0
Australia [1996]	**40.2**	Denmark [1995]	89.0
Greece [1993]	33.3	Netherlands [1994]	88.3
Finland [1996]	31.6	Canada [1996]	77.7
Denmark [1995]	29.9	New Zealand [1996]	75.6
Ireland [1996]	29.8	Finland [1996]	74.0
United States [1996]	20.2	Austria [1996]	73.4
Austria [1996]	12.3	Greece [1993]	62.4
Italy [1996]	6.0	France [1995]	57.2
Spain [1995]	3.8	Germany [1995]	57.2
Norway [1993]	3.7	**Australia [1996]**	**55.9**
Germany [1995]	−2.1	Italy [1996]	54.0
France [1995]	−2.8	Norway [1993]	49.0
Portugal [1993]	−6.7	Portugal [1993]	48.6
Netherlands [1994]	−19.7	Spain [1995]	44.3
Japan [1996]	−19.9	United States [1996]	42.6
Switzerland [1995]	−99.0	Japan [1996]	33.0
United Kingdom	n.a.	United Kingdom	n.a.

Source: IMF, *Balance of Payments Statistics Yearbook*, 1997

catastrophic. So far exports have not fallen and (on the last three quarter averages) have actually improved on comparable periods over the last few years. However, this will not last. The May 1998 budget papers estimate that commodities exports will show modest growth in the coming year but that the previous strong growth path of elaborately transformed manufactures (ETMs) and services exports will slow. Overall, it is estimated that goods and services export volumes will slip from a growth rate of 5.25 per cent in 1997–8 to 2.5 per cent in 1998–9. This compares with an average rate of growth over the previous decade of around 7 per cent. Treasury estimates of GDP growth in Australia for 1998–9 will be 3 per cent, down from 3.75 per cent in 1997–8. Increasingly, as the crisis drags on and the situation in Japan worsens, most market economists are lowering growth expectations down to as low as 2 per cent, with almost a third of economists in a recent poll now expecting a recession in 1999 (Kohler 1988).

Australian policy implications

The most immediate and fundamental implication of the crisis as far as Australia's overall policy direction is concerned centres on the changed status of the region itself. If the 'Asian miracles' are – in the short term, at least – unlikely to generate the sorts of economic spin-offs that sheer propinquity seemed to guarantee, then the direction of much of Australia's post-war foreign economic policy becomes potentially contestable by those with little enthusiasm for the process (Grattan 1998). It needs to be remembered that the perceived preoccupation with 'big picture' public policy issues by one of the principal architects of closer Asia ties – former Prime Minister Paul Keating – was directly implicated in the ALP's loss of government (Williams 1997). The coalition's electoral success was in large part attributable to a fundamental disenchantment with what is taken by many Australians to be an unresponsive and elite-driven political process.

If one institution encapsulates both the overall direction of Australia's economic policies and the disjuncture between 'political elites' and the general public, it is the Asia–Pacific Economic Cooperation (APEC) forum, the centrepiece of Australia's economic engagement with the region and Australian policy-makers' principal mechanism for encouraging regional neo-liberal policies in general and free trade in particular. APEC was established in 1989, the culmination of a long-standing process of regional diplomacy and policy networking in which Australia played a conspicuous part (Funabashi 1995). Encompassing the key economies of East Asia, the United States, Canada, Australia and New Zealand, and now an increasing number of South American countries, APEC's principal goals, as outlined in the Seoul Declaration in 1991, are to sustain regional growth and development; to encourage the flow of goods, services, capital and technology; to strengthen the multilateral trading system; and to reduce barriers to trade and investment, consistent with GATT principles (APEC 1991).

It is an agenda that built on and reflected the major shift in Australian policy outlined above, in which Australia was quite deliberately opened up to competitive, international market forces and the Asian region more generally. For a comparatively small economy like Australia's, still heavily reliant on the export of rural and resource products, it made good sense to try and encourage a similar process of economic opening amongst crucial regional trading partners. And yet the crisis has presented two major challenges for APEC in particular, revolving around its own future role on the one hand, and the potential persistence of protectionism on the other.

It is becoming increasingly apparent that the process of economic liberalisation is fraught with difficulty, even for its most enthusiastic advocates. Given the close alignment between APEC's own agenda of trade and investment liberalisation, and the sorts of policies that are being more forcefully encouraged throughout the region by the IMF, the crisis might seem likely to consolidate APEC's position. But even if the question of APEC's irrelevance in such circumstances when compared with the IMF is set aside, it is not clear whether the crisis will be of unambiguous benefit to APEC's reform agenda. While there are clearly far too many imponderables to hazard a guess about longer term implications, it should be stressed that

APEC's ambitious trade liberalisation timetable was under stress even *before* the crisis (Beeson 1996), a problem that only seems likely to be exacerbated.

Meeting in mid 1998, trade ministers from the APEC economies were unable to reach agreement on a plan to 'fast-track' a number of sectoral liberalisation programmes (Yeoh 1998: 28). Predictably, given the continuing influence of its politically powerful agricultural lobby, Japan was the principal hold-out against rapid reform. Of potentially greater long-term significance, however, was Japan's claim that it represented a view which was widely supported by other nations in East Asia who were reluctant to speak out for fear of US retaliation. In other words, at a time of economic crisis, and despite being dependent on IMF assistance and the good opinion of the United States, smaller East Asian nations were still reluctant to engage in further APEC-inspired reform.

As APEC contains both the East Asians and the United States – the latter having played such a prominent role in the aftermath of the crisis – it might be supposed that APEC is ideally placed to play a crisis management role. Significantly, however, APEC has been conspicuous by its absence. This invisibility is largely explained by APEC's broad membership and consequent institutional evolution. What might have been a strength in the context of the crisis – APEC's diverse, transregional membership – has proved a weakness. The necessity of accommodating countries with such disparate political traditions and contrasting economic circumstances has meant that from the outset, APEC members, especially those from East Asia, have been hostile to the promotion of institutional consolidation along European Community lines (Beeson and Jayasuriya 1998). Simply put, there was little enthusiasm amongst APEC's East Asian members about creating an institution which might have the power to enforce specific reforms. Consequently, all APEC agreements are consensual and voluntary, intentionally giving APEC very little leverage over members. Indeed, the IMF's ability to *impose* an agenda of neo-liberal-oriented reform on the region stands in stark contrast to APEC's reliance on moral suasion and the voluntary compliance of member states to implement its ambitious timetable of trade and investment liberalisation.

Given their balance of payments difficulties, this lack of enthusiasm about encouraging greater imports through trade liberalisation on the part of some APEC members is, perhaps, understandable. In the long term, however, they would seem to have little choice but to liberalise their trade regimes further. East Asian countries' structural dependency on access to North American markets means that they are especially vulnerable to retaliatory measures by the United States, a country which has shown an increasing willingness to pursue bilateral, results-oriented strategies when dealing with the rest of the world in general and Asia in particular (Bhagwati 1990). At a time when the United States is no longer constrained by the perceived need to underwrite the region's strategic integrity as a bulwark against communist expansion, it has demonstrated a willingness to pursue a narrower, exclusively national interest – even where this threatens collectively oriented institutions like APEC.

From a US perspective, the crisis represents a possibly unique opportunity not simply to break open protectionist Asian economies, but to allow US multinationals to establish a larger presence there. In this context APEC is not only viewed as largely irrelevant to US interests – the IMF and aggressive bilateralism have proved far more effective mechanisms for prising open Asian economies – but also something that can be sacrificed in the cause of the United States' larger strategic goals. The decision to allow Russia – a country with few obvious claims to regional relevance – to join APEC (which former Australian Prime Minister Paul Keating (1998) described as an 'act of economic vandalism') was a clear reflection of US priorities. It is hard to escape the conclusion that US support for Russian membership of APEC, and its inevitable dilution of APEC's already tenuous regional identity, was delivered in return for Russian acquiescence in NATO's expansion in Eastern Europe (Kelly 1997: 1).

In short, significant changes have occurred in the international strategic and economic environment within which the APEC nations operate that have potentially reconfigured national priorities and international relations. These changes are now being paralleled at the domestic level as the crisis destabilises existent political regimes with unforeseeable consequences. While Indonesia is, of course, the most dramatic example of this effect, the populations of countries like South Korea have displayed an aggrieved sense of economic nationalism about their changed circumstances which has manifested itself in a groundswell of anti-American feeling and nascent protectionist sentiment (Richardson 1998). As western companies move to pick up East Asian assets at bargain prices, they threaten to create a visible manifestation of the region's diminished position that may leave an enduring legacy of ill-will and resentment, particularly towards those countries and institutions which were associated with neo-liberal reform.

Australia has been similarly, if somewhat ambiguously, affected. True, the neo-liberal policies which have been at the centre of both Australia's and APEC's reform agendas for almost a decade have been advanced by the IMF rather than APEC itself. Such implementation has come at some cost to the overall stability of Australia's wider strategic environment (Dibb *et al.* 1998), however, and has generated complex political effects domestically. It is this latter phenomenon that is of most immediate concern in an Australian context and which continues to make the Australian government's position especially difficult. For if the crisis and its management demonstrate one thing with great clarity, it is that major economic reform is inescapably a deeply political process with potentially highly destabilising consequences. This is nowhere clearer than in the domestic response to the crisis in particular and the process of international structural adjustment more generally.

The domestic impact

In the context of the unfolding crisis the Australian case is revealing for a number of reasons. The prominence of APEC and its concomitant neo-liberal agenda in Australia's international and domestic policies is symptomatic of an approach that has proved costly to both major parties and created a political space for the emergence of reactionary domestic politics, something that has made the development of a coherent and consistent response to the crisis by Australian policy-makers more difficult. The most dramatic manifestation of Australia's shifting political landscape has been the emergence of Pauline Hanson's One Nation Party. While not a direct offshoot of the Asian crisis, central elements of One Nation's electoral platform and appeal are a direct repudiation of the sorts of policies that have become the bilaterally supported pillars of mainstream thinking on Australia's economic and political relations with the region.

A central part of the often inarticulate sense of alienation and dissatisfaction experienced by Hanson supporters seems to be a sense that economic policy in particular has only reflected elite concerns and delivers little benefit to those most marginalised by transformative social and economic processes associated with 'globalisation'. Australia's role as the principal architect and advocate of APEC meant that it was incumbent upon Australia to pursue the sorts of deep-seated domestic reforms it was keen to persuade others to adopt. Given that the former Keating government made the redefinition of Australia's relations with the region and a concomitant *domestic* transformation major goals of its period in office, a certain weariness with interminable structural adjustment and reform was perhaps inevitable.

Despite its explicit repudiation of the Keating government's style and its declared intention of concentrating on domestic issues, the Howard coalition government has found it difficult to develop a coherent and consistent approach to the region. Compounding the coalition's difficulties has been a desire to reap the erstwhile economic benefits that might accrue from closer links to the region, while simultaneously attempting to maintain the support of the so-called 'battlers', or low-income earners, whose desertion of Labor for the coalition underpinned the latter's election victory in 1996. The difficulty for the coalition is that it has concluded that the key to regional recovery lies in 'pushing ahead on domestic reform and continuing trade liberalisation' (Fischer 1998) – precisely the sorts of policies that are causing such resentment in rural Australia and weakening the coalition's electoral position.

The Howard government therefore finds itself in the problematic position of attempting to maintain social cohesion and its own electoral position while simultaneously pushing on with even more radical economic reforms than those attempted under Keating. The potential incommensurability of these aims in the face of powerful business lobbies on the one hand, and popular opposition on the other, has been revealed in the decisions to slow the pace of domestic tariff reform and privatisation (Hartcher 1997: 12). In many ways these are defining policy challenges for governments everywhere as they struggle to balance the competing pressures of international economic openness and domestic resistance (Argy 1998). If Australia is struggling to meet such a challenge with all its advantages, how much more difficult and destabilising will it prove in the rest of the region?

Even before the full impact of the crisis has been felt in Australia, it is having a direct impact on domestic policy debates. Prior to the crisis, and stung by criticism of its perceived inept handling of both international economic relations and its inability to provide domestic leadership (Gordon 1996: 19; Skulley and Dodson 1997: 1), the coalition appeared willing to experiment with a range of more 'interventionist' industry policies, even if this actually amounted to little more than stalling further tariff reduction in sensitive sectors such as cars and textiles, clothing and footwear. Revealingly, the coalition's tentative flirtation with a greater government role in promoting economic development was one of the first casualties of the crisis. As Howard put it:

> In a global environment where capital is increasingly mobile, the key to Australia's attractiveness as an investment location will continue to be the strength of our economic foundations. The recent financial turbulence in our region has highlighted this fact and the shortcomings of highly interventionist strategies.
>
> (Howard 1998: 4)

As we have seen, not only was the Australian economy in general and the currency in particular not insulated from the sort of speculative attack or contagion effects that swept through East Asia, but what Howard (1998) calls the 'strength of our [sic] economic foundations' was of little benefit. Indeed, it should be remembered that judged by the so-called economic 'fundamentals' like the trade balance, GDP growth and foreign reserves, Indonesia was actually in better shape than Australia before the crisis struck. In other words, in an era when nation-states are reduced to the status of commodities in the eyes of key market players, small economies are acutely vulnerable to changes in market sentiment that may have very little to do with the actual competence or otherwise of national economic management (Beeson 1998). As far as the coalition is concerned, therefore, the central justification for painful domestic reform – that it would 'fire-proof' Australia from the sort of speculative attacks or externally generated shocks that undid Indonesia – looks increasingly implausible, something even Howard appeared to realise when he condemned the activities of 'poorly informed, economically illiterate money-market people' (Fukui 1998: 19).

Thus, the coalition government may find itself in something of a double bind. Domestically, it has rejected the possibility of attempting to shape economic activity in Australia more actively through the sorts of Asian-style industry policies it now takes to be discredited in the wake of the crisis. At the same time, its own preference for pushing on with further reform, especially in the areas of privatisation, trade liberalisation and tax reform, looks likely to be opposed not only by an increasingly significant part of the electorate, but from within the coalition itself (Emerson 1998: 4). Importantly, the relentless drive to increase 'competitiveness', which has been at the heart of both the coalition's and the former Labor government's domestic agendas, appears to have been a central component in voter disaffection and the shift to One Nation, a factor which threatens to derail further neo-liberal reform. The apparent repudiation of the entire rationale for nearly two decades of market-oriented reform threatens to problematise Australia's entire approach to the region.

At a time when the region is being forced to adopt major market-oriented reforms in line with IMF strictures it might be supposed that Australia would be a major beneficiary of such changes. Yet the realisation that the imposition of thorough-going neo-liberal reform is not a costless, politically or socially neutral exercise has been brought home to Australian policymakers in both the domestic *and* international spheres. After initially playing a disproportionately large role in supporting the IMF bailout of Thailand and then Indonesia, the coalition significantly altered its position when the extent of the damage to Indonesia's economy and social fabric became increasingly apparent. In a revealing and relatively successful exercise of regional diplomacy, Australian Foreign Minister Alexander Downer was instrumental in having the original, stringent IMF package watered down (Hartcher 1998: 6). In essence, Australia's security imperatives took precedence over the desire to promote market-oriented reform throughout the region.

In short, the Howard government's response to both 'Asia' generally and the crisis in particular has been contradictory, *ad hoc* and uncomfortable. True, a good deal of this ambivalence may be attributed to significant divisions within key bureaucratic departments charged with providing policy advice for government. Not only are there revealing differences between the Department of Defence (which viewed the economic decline of East Asia as having a potentially beneficial effect on Australia's security environment) and the Department of Foreign Affairs and Trade (which had invested much intellectual capital in promoting engagement with the region on the basis of its dynamism), but there is an even greater gulf between them and the Treasury Department (Toohey 1998: 28–9). Differences between Treasury and key Reserve Bank of Australia officials have also emerged over the role of financial markets during the crisis, and appropriate reform packages for regional economies as a consequence (Toohey 1998a: 1 and 6). The Treasury's close links to the IMF predispose it to support similar sorts of comprehensive market-centred reform, despite any possible negative impacts in the region.

The nuances of intra-bureaucratic contestation may not be apparent to Australia's regional neighbours. As far as other regional governments are concerned, the most enduring legacy of the crisis may have been to entrench Australia in the Anglo-American camp and raise awkward questions about enduring racism (*The Nation* 1998), something which will do little to further Australia's Asian credentials, especially if the crisis ultimately generates a more insular, specifically East Asian, response.

Conclusion

While Australia has so far not been as badly affected by the crisis as its Asian neighbours have, it is an important case study for comparative purposes. Australia has already embraced the sorts of trade and investment liberalisation policies that are currently being taken up by, or forced upon, other regional governments. As we have suggested, however, not only are the merits of such policies contestable on economic grounds, but they are proving increasingly difficult to sell within a domestic electoral context. More fundamentally, they have proved an uncertain defence against more generalised regional economic turmoil. The current coalition government's claim to have insulated the Australian economy from the impact of the crisis is looking increasingly implausible as the economic downturn shows little sign of abating and may, in fact, be about to enter a second, deeper phase, which could have a more profound impact on 'real' economic activity throughout the region.

If there is one major lesson that might be drawn from the Australian experience, it is that major economic change without adequate strategies to compensate those most badly affected will ultimately create a political back-lash. Australian policy-makers now find themselves having to deal with the social impact of nearly two decades of major structural adjustment. True, the Australian experience has not been as traumatic as Indonesia's, Thailand's or South Korea's, where the process has been brutally truncated by the collapse of their economies, but the impact in Australia has been profound, nevertheless. The uneven impact of the reform process across the Australian economy – which is closely associated with rural and manufac-turing decline – is now generating unsettling political consequences that not only threaten to undermine Australia's egalitarian domestic traditions, but will further complicate its external orientation. The palpable disenchant-ment that many Australians clearly feel towards the seemingly interminable programme of structural reform and the growing cynicism about the capacity of governments to cope with processes of globalisation mean that domestic resistance to further liberalisation and privatisation may well increase. Hence, Australian policy-makers confront a profound dilemma: if they decide to slow domestic adjustment as a consequence of increasing hostility to the reform process more generally, this will inevitably complicate the process of encouraging further economic reform in the region through institutions like APEC.

The Australian experience – and now that in Asia – suggests that the process of economic reform needs to be carefully managed. The consequences of Australia's own liberalisation experience, particularly its potentially destructive impact on unskilled labour and segments of industry, were generally poorly thought through by successive governments. The former Labor government belatedly recognised the necessity of providing compensatory policies for those most badly affected by domestic reform. Even though ALP training initiatives like *Working Nation* appeared capable of ameliorating some of the more immediate impacts of opening up the domestic economy (Junankar and Kapusinski 1998), the Howard government has chosen to dispense with them. The rise of reactionary politics and the continuation of high levels of unemployment seem the all too predictable consequences of further neo-liberal reform in the absence of any compensatory social or industry policies.

While further trade liberalisation might be the consequence of the crisis throughout East Asia – barring an unlikely, but not unimaginable, regional revolt against further neo-liberal-oriented restructuring – the possibility exists for a more differentiated reform process, especially in the financial sector. Clearly, both Australia's and East Asia's experiences with financial reform suggest that wholesale, indiscriminate liberalisation with little regulatory oversight is fraught with potential danger. In this regard, Australia could draw on its own experience and expertise to assist in the much discussed re-engineering of the world's financial architecture. Stephen Grenville's suggestion that the Chilean model of short-term capital controls might prove more suitable in an East Asian context is an important example of such an initiative (Henderson 1998).

This would, of course, necessitate deviating somewhat from the 'Washington Consensus' on appropriate economic policy, to say nothing of distancing Australia from its closely allied position to the United States. However, this, too, may be no bad thing. In the longer term, it may be in Australia's interests not to identify itself too uncritically with either the market-centred liberalisation policies that were clearly implicated in the unravelling of the Asian model, or the rigorous policing of the emergent neo-liberal order that seems to be replacing it. After all, Australia's geographic relationship is clearly something that is not going to be changed by the crisis. For better or worse, Australia's future remains inextricably bound up with Asia's.

Part V

CONCLUSION
Scenarios for East Asia

17

AUTHORITARIAN LIBERALISM, GOVERNANCE AND THE EMERGENCE OF THE REGULATORY STATE IN POST-CRISIS EAST ASIA

Kanishka Jayasuriya

Introduction: the developmental state and globalisation

Globalisation has subverted the developmental state. This chapter explores one of the central issues of this volume: the extent to which global market conditions are producing deep-seated changes in the distinctive form of East Asian political economy, which is given the generic label of the developmental state. A major contention of this chapter is that different state forms are nested within different structures of global governance. From this perspective, the developmental state, and for that matter the Western European welfare state, were both products of the post-war system of global governance. It is this system of global governance that has irrevocably changed and brought with it concomitant changes in modes of domestic governance. In short, it is argued that developmental state forms are rapidly being transformed into a new form of regulatory state.

In presenting this argument we make two distinct theoretical claims: first we shift the argument about globalisation from the somewhat infertile dispute over the extent of changes in trade and financial flows to an understanding of the *way* in which changes in international governance have served to transform domestic political infrastructure. Second, this analysis moves beyond the rather limited zero-sum relationship between globalisation and the state to a relationship which is more nuanced and reciprocal; the state forms are nested within a wider set of global structures. Therefore, the question to ask is not whether the state has declined in the face of globalisation but what kind of new state is being created as a consequence of new structures of global governance (see Jayasuriya 1997). In short, it is argued that the kind of state structure and organisation in East Asia placed under the generic label of the developmental state was an artefact of a particular regime of international governance characterised by restrictions on capital mobility and a regulated domestic financial sector. The end of the Bretton Woods system and the gradual dismantling of capital controls made developmental strategies much more difficult and problematic.

The developmental state has to be understood in terms of three main features: first, an insulated and autonomous set of economic agencies with a strong capacity to implement economic policies and programmes; second, an activist industry policy that developed competitive export-oriented global industries; and third, an understanding of governance that places strong emphasis on the role of the state in securing economic development and security (Wade 1990). Globalisation of capital markets has slowly but surely eroded salient features of the developmental state, such as those forms of activist industry policy commonly associated with East Asian patterns of economic development (Weiss and Hobson 1995; Evans 1995; Wade 1990), thereby incapacitating the kind of state strategies that distinguished the developmental state. These state strategies were a product of post-war structures of international economic governance. In this respect at least a striking parallel can be established between the developmental and the Keynesian welfare state: both sets of strategies were strongly dependent on the regulation of capital markets.

In this vein Wade and Veneroso (1998) in their account of the economic crisis emphasise the difficulty of reconciling two irreconcilable elements: dismantling of capital controls and the high debt to equity ratios of East Asian capitalism. Wade and Veneroso argue that the high debt to equity structure of East Asia is the product of two key institutional features of the East Asian political economy. First, savings are much higher than in other regions. In most East Asian nations domestic savings are about one-third of GDP (World Bank 1994) and as most of savings are held in bank deposits, it follows that bank lending is geared towards borrowing by firms. Second, in order to compete in large export markets local firms need to expand considerable resources, which can only be facilitated by extensive borrowing. Put simply, the only means of financing the export industrialisation of the kind experienced by Japan, Korea and Taiwan over the last three decades is through the mobilisation of the large reserves of domestic savings by local corporations.

However, such a structure requires a high degree of collaboration between firms, banks and the state; in other words, the high debt to equity ratios of East Asian capitalism need to be underpinned by a complex institutional infrastructure of regulations. Admittedly, the system is highly vulnerable to systemic shocks that depress the flow of capital, and for this reason it must be safeguarded against such systemic shocks as well as have in place a mechanism for the constant monitoring of private firms and banks by the state. Indeed, the whole system depends on the effective monitoring of the corporate debt by the state. Furthermore, restrictions on 'the freedom of firms and banks to borrow abroad, and coordination of foreign borrowing by government, are a necessary part of this system' (Wade and Veneroso 1998: 7).

Contrary to the neo-classical explanation of the crisis, Wade and Veneroso suggest that there is a virtuous cycle between high savings, high levels of debt to equity ratios, and close and collaborative links between state, banks and firms, which in turn lead to high investment, high levels of export performance and growth rates. But this virtuous cycle was dependent upon a high level of financial regulation of external borrowing because, amongst other things, this will lead to lower levels of monitoring by the state; in essence, given an absence of credit safety nets to stabilise the system, the high-wire act of East Asian capitalism required a significant level of governmental capacity and monitoring. To put this in Kornai's (1992) terms, this means that the governmental monitoring of private firms and bank behaviour is a system of non-price signalling vital for the stability of the distinctive system of economic coordination in East Asia. Nevertheless, the ability of the state to keep financial restrictions in place proved to be the chink in the armour of the developmental state. The crisis is explained by the fact that financial deregulation undertaken by East Asian governments:

> removed or loosened controls on companies' foreign borrowing, abandoned coordination of borrowings and investments, and failed to strengthen bank supervision. By doing so, they violated one of the stability conditions of the Asian high debt model, helping to set the crisis in train.
>
> (Wade and Veneroso 1998: 9)

In short, the virtuous cycle of the East Asian political economy became in fairly short order a particularly vicious cycle plunging these economies into deep crisis. For Wade and Veneroso (1998) opening up financial markets is akin to allowing – indeed encouraging – unlimited access to the sweet cupboard.

It is worth underlining significant differences between this historically inclined institutional model and the neo-classical moral hazard model. First, it places the structure of the financial system in a broader framework which locates determinants of economic governance in systemic features of East Asian political economy. Economic governance needs to be embedded in a wider institutional framework. Second, the model highlights the importance of understanding the crisis in dynamic terms, which raises critical research questions about the conditions or circumstances that may have led to the disruption of the high-debt model of East Asian capitalism. Institutional models, unlike neo-classical models, are premised on a historical notion of economic time which leads to a fundamentally different set of research questions.

Much of what may be termed the 'decline of monitoring capacity' argument is persuasive and takes us beyond the static neo-classical models outlined above. However, this analysis is flawed in one major respect: it fails to account adequately for the removal of financial restrictions by East Asian governments. Why did East Asian governments liberalise financial markets when the results were obviously so deleterious? For Wade and Veneroso, these policy actions were irrational and the policy-makers were misled by international financial organisations. However, the difficulty with this argument is that policy mistakes were made not just in one country, but across the entire region. These facts would seem to suggest that there are deeper structural forces at work in reducing the capacity of East Asian governments to monitor the credit behaviour of firms and banks. From our perspective, a structural explanation, rather than the simple attribution of mistakes to policy-makers, is more satisfying in explaining the disruption and instability of the East Asian model of economic governance. While such an analysis is beyond the brief of this chapter it is useful to locate the dynamic of some these changes in the gradual shift of power from technocratic elites to business groups. As I have argued elsewhere, this shift is reflected in the increasingly polycentric distribution of power within the state (Jayasuriya 1995). From this viewpoint the process of democratisation in states such as Korea and Thailand reflected the increasing assertiveness of business groups *vis-à-vis* technocratic elites (Jayasuriya 1995).

Whatever the causes of this disruption of the institutional modes of regulation of the developmental state, it is clear that these strategies of economic governance were nested within certain structures of international economic governance (what Ruggie (1983) has called 'embedded liberalism'). The most important of these post-war forms of economic governance was the capacity of states to control the movement of capital. It is this particular feature that made it possible to implement Keynesian demand management and distributive policies in Western Europe and North America as well as the development state strategies in East Asia. It is interesting to note that forms of economic governance have become more problematic in the new global economy.

The emergent authoritarian liberal global order

Normative foundations

The central argument of this chapter is that just as the post-war structures of what Ruggie called 'embedded liberalism' provided a permissive environment for the emergence and consolidation of the developmental state, the shift towards an authoritarian mode of liberalism enables the emergence of the regulatory state, the prime purpose of which is to safeguard and regulate the market. Pivotal to authoritarian liberalism is the existence of a dualistic state: a strong state combined with a liberal market economy. This notion of a 'dualistic state' (a term borrowed from Fraenkel 1941) signifies the essential features of a regulatory state where markets are quarantined from political interference, but where the success of this system of market immunisation rests on the recognition that a well-functioning market order requires the presence of strong regulatory institutions. However, these institutions are aimed at securing transparent markets, not political accountability, and hence political participation in the public sphere is highly circumscribed. In fact, pivotal to the emergence of authoritarian liberalism is the contradiction between the development of a form of 'economic' constitutionalism and a 'political' constitutionalism, which is highly limited. (Fraenkel 1941).

In his work on recent changes in the international economy, Gill (1995) has perceptively drawn attention to the idea that the international economic order is increasingly moving towards a 'new constitutionalism'; that is, one where international trade and significant sections of the domestic economy are constitutionalised. Gill defines what he calls the new constitutionalism of neo-liberalism as a

> macro-political dimension of the process whereby the nature and purpose of the public sphere in the OECD has been redefined in a more privatised and commodified way, with its economic criteria defined in a more globalised and abstract frame of reference.
>
> (Gill 1995: 412)[1]

However, the notion of constitutionalism, as used in this chapter, is more specific (rather than conflating it with the more amorphous concept of neo-liberalism) because it identifies these processes with a particular notion of *authoritarian liberalism* that lays special emphasis on the affinity between contemporary conceptions of authoritarian liberalism and the German ordo-liberal tradition, and in which the concept of 'economic constitutionalism' is one of its main normative properties.[2] Economic constitutionalism refers to the attempt to treat the market as a constitutional order with its own rules, procedures and institutions operating to protect the market order from political interference. However, these forms of economic constitutionalism demand the constitution of a specific kind of state organisation and structure: a regulatory state.

Authoritarian liberalism is a form of 'economic constitutionalism' because it attempts to place certain market regulatory institutions beyond the reach of transitory political majorities or the actions of the political executive through mechanisms that provide for a high degree of autonomy for these institutions. Further, these institutions are 'constitutional' in the sense that international agreements and treaties often require a high degree of monitoring and insulation of the economy, and this is given added significance because of the increasingly blurred boundary between the domestic economy and international trade. However, it is important to note that this is not a question of freeing the market from state intervention but an attempt to institute and insulate the regulatory institutions of the market from political interference. In essence, economic constitutionalism seeks to protect the 'market' from the processes of domestic politics.

The normative silhouette for variants of economic constitutionalism has been provided by the Chicago school of law and economics, the Virginia school of public choice and the German ordo-liberal school. The German ordo-liberal school is the most interesting (as well as the earliest) of these attempts to develop a notion of economic constitutionalism. It is pertinent to focus on the writings of this school because it highlights the link between authoritarian politics and constitutional conceptions of economic order. One of its prominent exponents, Walter Eucken,[3] was closely associated with the extremely conservative Von Papen government in the early 1930s.

Central to ordo-liberalism and Eucken's thought was the notion that the construction of economic order cannot be left to the spontaneous actions of the market; it needs to be created through a consistent ordering (*ordnungspolitik*) of the state. For the ordo-liberals of the Freibug school the 'various economic, political, legal and other social processes are interrelated'. Each act of government intervention must therefore be seen in connection with the total processes and overall economic order so as to ensure the 'system conformity of measures' (Petersmann 1991: 63). For the ordo-liberal, the state should not attempt to conduct the economy but rather should provide a system of juridical institutions that would facilitate the construction of the market. In fact, in its emphasis on the role of economic institutions in creating market order it presages the new institutional economics.[4] Important for this conception of economic order is the role played by juridical processes in safeguarding the market order. Implicit in this account is, of course, a conception of a strong state providing economic order.

The ordo-liberals, unlike the new institutional economists with whom they otherwise have much in common, are clearer about the political ramifications of notions of economic constitutionalism. Eucken and others were very concerned about the anti-competitive effects of society on the economy. Eucken, for example, echoing the thought of the conservative jurist Carl Schmitt, argued that by the end of the nineteenth century the state was increasingly captured by private interest groups; this led to the politicisation of the economy which in turn weakened the state. In other words, the main purpose of economic constitutionalism was to protect the economy from these political pressures. Therefore, this understanding of economic order implied the existence of institutions to protect the politicisation of the economy; and this required that constraints be placed on parliamentary and political institutions. The implication of this reasoning was to suggest that the kind of regulatory state advocated by the ordo-liberals could only be achieved at the expense of political constitutionalism.

What is being suggested here is that these authoritarian liberal notions of market order have increasingly come to dominate the governance of the global economic order. The functioning of the global economic order, like domestic markets, requires the existence of juridical institutions that will protect international trade and capital flows. But this needs concerted policy intervention to constitutionalise the domestic economy. However – and this is where this mode of governance sharply departs from embedded liberalism – this requires the modification or changes in patterns of domestic constitutional and legal arrangements. Similarly, there are attempts to construct economic institutions such as independent central banks that are insulated from domestic social and political pressures, and are therefore able to mediate between the domestic and international economy.

To sum up briefly, the main elements of this authoritarian liberal mode of governance are:

- Unlike embedded liberalism, the regulation of the economy does not depend merely on intergovernmental agreement which enables a certain latitude for the pursuit of domestic social programmes and industrial policy; instead, the authoritarian liberalism model relies on trade and domestic policy being placed within a strongly juridical cast. For example, consider the significance attached to the institution of regulatory frameworks such as competition and anti-trust law, intellectual property law and credible financial market laws, all of which are seen to be integral to the regulation of the international economic order.
- Economic constitutionalism requires the setting up of independent economic institutions that are insulated from domestic social and economic pressures.
- The functioning of the economic regulatory institutions is detached from the structures of political accountability, and these institutions are crucial as gatekeepers between the domestic and international economy.

The net effect of these changes in global governance is to make problematic the type of developmental state strategies pursued by East Asian states. Hence, in terms of the argument outlined above, the developmental state is transformed into a regulatory state. Two important examples of this shift towards a regulatory state are examined, namely governance programmes and the emerging role of central banks as key agencies within the state. We turn to consider each of these manifestations of transformation.

Governance programmes and authoritarian liberalism

In recent years multilateral agencies have placed a great deal of emphasis on building effective systems of governance in the developing world, especially in the transitional economies. Not only is most lending tied to the effective implementation of governance programmes, but multilateral agencies have followed up on these concerns with extensive aid programmes for institutional strengthening or capacity building. The tenor of recent economic reforms in transitional economies and in Southeast Asian countries has been towards establishing credible and independent regulatory institutions. The NICs and Japan have not been immune from the spread of these programmes to re-engineer the state such that it will have a greater regulatory role, and the recent events surrounding the Asian currency crisis have only served to accelerate institutional reform programmes in these countries. Michel Camdessus, the managing director of the IMF, notes that the

> IMF's role in governance issues has been evolving over the years, and good governance has taken on increasing importance on our traditional mandate of promoting economic stability and what I call high quality growth.
>
> (Camdessus 1998a: 1)

Moreover, he argues that the Asian crisis is ample demonstration of the disastrous effects of ineffective governance and lack of market transparency. This obviously has considerable implications for the future of the developmental state. All the recent IMF bailouts of Thailand, South Korea and Indonesia require these governments to make substantial efforts to reform their governance regimes.

Governance programmes emerged out of the experience of structural adjustment programmes of the 1980s. International policy-makers, puzzled by the apparent failure of structural adjustment programmes, began to examine more closely the capacity of economic and bureaucratic institutions to implement economic reform packages. As a World Bank discussion paper on governance noted:

> The Bank's experience has also shown that when programs and projects appear technically sound but fail to deliver results, the reasons are sometimes attributable to weak institutions, lack of an adequate legal framework, damaging discretionary interventions, uncertain and variable policy frameworks and a closed decision making process which increases risks of corruption and waste.
>
> (World Bank 1991: 1)

In fact, governance programmes provide a complementary set of institution-building programmes to support economic adjustment. In a striking fashion these governance programmes parallel German ordo-liberal concerns with the need to protect the market from the corrosive effect of society and politics, and this understanding of the juridical basis of economic order is the essence of authoritarian liberalism.

Williams and Young (1994), in one of the few efforts to understand the political theory of governance programmes, argue that notions of effective governance are permeated with a liberal understanding of the need to transform society and politics in order to make the market function more efficiently. In essence, their argument proposes that the 'World Bank constructs governance, in part at least, from liberal theory. Second, this construction of governance reproduces some important ambiguities and tensions that exist in that liberal theory' (William and Young 1994: 92). However, this identification of liberalism with governance fails to distinguish between the political notions of constitutionalism, which are the normative backdrop of variants of political liberalism, and the economic constitutionalism which is at the 'normative heart' of authoritarian liberalism.

Put simply, we need to differentiate between two distinct notions of constitutionalism. One is a political notion of constitutionalism which emphasises issues of participation and accountability. The other is an economic notion of constitutionalism which places emphasis on issues of market transparency and the juridical limitations on the influence of rent-seeking coalitions or discretionary political intervention in the functioning of the economy. Governance programmes are obsessed with the need to curb the influence of vested interests and transient political majorities. Of course, it remains the case that it is easier to implement processes of economic constitutionalism in the illiberal states of East Asia than in liberal democracies, but the effect of these regulatory institutions is to limit the latitude of both the welfare and developmental state. In the rhetoric of governance, the notions of accountability and transparency relate to very different understandings of constitutionalism. Moreover, what is insufficiently understood in the literature on governance is that economic constitutionalism, as the ordo-liberals argued, often requires the presence of an authoritarian or illiberal state with the capacity to protect the market from politics. Transparency and accountability connote not only different, but also opposing, versions of constitutionalism.

Ample support for the argument that governance belongs to a specific authoritarian liberal variant of economic constitutionalism can be found in numerous policy documents as well as the specific design of various governance programmes. For example, the World Bank argues that governance is 'assessed in terms of the capacity of the state to avoid *capture* by prominent economic interests and to formulate and implement policy independently in the public interest' (World Bank 1994: xix). Camdessus points out that the 'approach is to maximise the transparency of governmental financial operations and create systems that minimise the scope for making decisions on an *ad hoc* basis and for giving preferential treatment to individuals and organisations' (Camdessus 1998a: 2). Running through these definitions of governance is a desire to insulate and quarantine the economy from the corrosive influence of political interests, and it is this aspect of economic constitutionalism that finds a more than strong echo in ordo-liberal strategies to construct economic order.

Equally important in the constitution of governance programmes is that the emphasis placed on the role of the state as a regulator – which multilateral agencies seem to have recognised – requires not a reduction in the role of the state, but rather a restructuring of its governmental functions shifting the 'boundary between the public and private sectors, thereby enlarging the latter, with the government's role changing from direct provision to regulation' (World Bank 1994: 2). One of the concerns of the governance programme has been to ensure that the process of economic deregulation and privatisation does not lead to the capturing of key markets by politically connected groups and individuals. Authoritarian liberal forms of global governance require an emphasis on the regulatory function of the state. Governance programmes of the kind detailed above contribute to the regulative capacities of the state.

For this reason, one of the major concerns of governance is the development of the 'rule of law', and to this end there has been a concerted effort to promote legal reform programmes in a number of developing states. For example, there are a number of projects in China, which seek to establish credible and functional legal institutions. The widespread adoption of foreign commercial law in China is influenced by a highly instrumentalist approach to law and institution building; law is seen as bits of technology, dislocated from its broader normative assumptions, to be employed where useful. Chen (1995) examines closely the nature of these developments in civil law, and notes that these changes must be placed in the context of the adoption of the notion of a 'socialist market economy' by the Chinese Communist Party (CCP). Acceptance of the notion of a socialist market economy had the effect of removing ideological fetters on the development of civil law. For example, he argues that there been an extensive transplantation (or harmonisation) of foreign laws in a number of commercial areas to such an extent that the language of Chinese law has become familiar to western-trained lawyers. The importance of these examples is to suggest that legal ideas and systems are seen as bits of technology (be they foreign or local) that can be used to build the regulative capacity of the state.

Chen notes that there has been extensive debate and discussion within the academic community over issues such as the fusion of public and private law, and the importance of establishing the autonomy of private law. It needs to be recognised that these debates are not simply a response to state or party directives, but have a dynamism of their own. For example, it is noted that many theorists

> have striven to establish a secure economic autonomy for individuals and economic entities free from administrative and therefore political direction and intervention, even though their theories may be shown to be incorrect (such as the theory of the two grade legal person) or their interpretations of Party and state policies and intentions may be claimed to be wrong (such as the theory of 'ownership rights of enterprise legal person').
>
> (Chen 1995: 277)

The development of these jurisprudential ideas of private law is useful because they allow the state to depoliticise the economy and quarantine the market from discretionary action. There is justifiable scepticism as to the extent to which these legal reforms can be fully implemented. However, it remains the case that these reforms are seen as mandatory if China is to gain membership of international organisations such as the World Trade Organisation (WTO). Further, it highlights how difficult it will be for the Chinese leadership to emulate the kind of economic strategies pursued by the developmental states of East Asia.

Of course it needs to be acknowledged that accountability is often given a key role in normative accounts of governance. However, the notion of accountability used in the governance literature is unclear, ambiguous and vague. In some of the literature (see e.g. World Bank 1994), the idea of accountability refers not so much to ideas of political constitutionalism as a managerial tool to reform the public sector and to organise the delivery of public services.

The recent economic crisis in East Asia has catapulted governance issues to the top of the policy agenda. 'Good governance' is no longer a set of programmes to be associated with adjustment programmes in sub-Saharan Africa or even with the problems of market transition in command economies; it is seen as an essential component for participation in the new global economy. The implementation of these programmes in East Asian countries such as South Korea points to the fundamental way in which the developmental state is being reconstituted as a regulatory state. In Korea, for example, the IMF programme requires far-reaching changes in the regulation of the banking sector, in patterns of corporate governance, and in the structure and discretionary capacity of economic agencies to provide preferential treatment to strategic industries. A statement by the Ministry of Finance in South Korea candidly points out that the new regulatory framework is 'built upon the expectation that policy loans and direct monetary control will be phased out' (Ministry of Finance and Economy 1998a: 1).

The effect of these governance proposals is to make more problematic the sustainability of a central component of the developmental state: its ability to pursue industry policy.

Central banks

One of the major features of the development of governance is the emergence of new and powerful regulatory institutions amongst which independent central banks are likely to play a pivotal role. However, what is important in this respect is not the mere fact that central banks have become powerful actors but that this has been accompanied by moves towards giving greater autonomy and independence to central banks. Central banks, like other economic institutions, it is argued, need to be protected from political interference, and therefore need legislative and even constitutional insulation. As a consequence, independent central banks are regarded as an important manifestation of the kind of economic constitutionalism that is vital to authoritarian liberalism. As with the other institutions of economic constitutionalism, the policy and management of independent central banks are disengaged from the processes and procedures of political accountability.

The point to be noted about independent central banks is that certain key industry and social groups have a clear preference for independent central banks. From a coalitional perspective, Goodman's (1991) work on the history of central bank independence points out that the financial sector tends to be highly supportive of a strongly independent central bank, although, he points out, the ability of financial sectors to mobilise support for these preferences is limited. As he puts it, to be 'politically successful, their position must have the support of, or at least not be strongly opposed by major non-financial sectors' (Goodman 1991: 333). Furthermore, the desire to have independent central banks is driven by the twin objectives of having an anti-inflationary and credible monetary policy; in fact much of the current debate about central banks has been influenced by economic ideas which have emphasised the importance of enhancing economic credibility by pre-committing a central bank to the achievement or maintenance of a given inflationary target. It has been argued that this can only be achieved through a form of economic constitutionalism that gives central banks autonomy from the political executive.

There is more scope for debate on the origins and effects of central bank independence on economic outcomes.[5] In many countries (especially those within the OECD), the pressure for strong central bank independence emanated from powerful domestic constituencies. However, the recent push towards central bank independence emanates from international organisations and regimes that often require action by domestic state institutions and agencies. This is an important point because most of the literature on the political economy of central banks focuses on the nature and dynamics of domestic constituencies for independent central banks; in contrast, what is increasingly evident in the pressure towards the instigation of independent central banks is the role played by transnational public and private actors such as international financial markets and the IMF. In sum, central banks have become key players because they provide the link between international regimes and the domestic state. It is a moot point to say that the state is being globalised. What is more important is that some domestic state institutions and agencies, more than others, are critical of the implementation of international regimes. In this context, central banks are at the interstices of the engagement between the international economic order and the domestic state. The increasingly juridical character of central banks is a key feature in the management and regulation of this international economic order.

Therefore, a major reason for the enhanced power of central banks is the growing importance of monetary policy in an era dominated by the pressure for more global financial integration. This latter trend resulted not only in a shift of policy instruments from fiscal to monetary policy, but also in a shift of power *within* the state towards agencies such as central banks. While it is a truism to say that external factors will increasingly impinge on the domestic political process, the more urgent theoretical and empirical task is to examine the specific linkages that exist between external and international forces and domestic politics. Central banks are likely to play an important role in this linkage between the external and domestic political environment as they are ideally placed to provide the mechanism through which international forces are transmitted into the domestic political economy.

Nothing is more indicative of these shifts than recent changes to the South Korean central bank, the Bank of Korea (BOK). As Maxfield (1994) has noted, the BOK has not had a great deal of legislative or policy autonomy from the executive government. In fact, in South Korea real economic policy-making power lay with the Economic Planning Board and the Finance Ministry, while the 'central bank does little more than implement credit policies in line with overall government spending plans' (Maxfield 1994: 561). However, recent changes[6] to the BOK have significantly altered this legislative regime in three main areas. First, the new BOK effectively entrenches the autonomy of the BOK from the Ministry of Finance. While mechanisms of consultation between the Ministry and the BOK have been established, the executive is unable to impose on the Monetary Board a particular course of monetary policy. In fact, the draft act was changed to reflect the IMF preference that while the Minister for Finance and the Economy has the power to request a reconsideration of the decisions of the Monetary Board he or she cannot suspend the decision, and any such request will be made public immediately (Ministry of Finance and Economy 1998a).

Second, the membership of the Monetary Board will include – apart from those nominated by the governor, the minister for finance and the chairman of the financial supervisory board – members of the private financial community nominated by the Korea Federation of Banks and the Korean Securities Dealers' Association. The membership of these groups is clearly indicative of the fact that monetary policy will have to reflect, at least in part, the preferences of the financial community which is not likely to be sympathetic to activist industry policy (Ministry of Finance and Economy 1998a).

Finally, the BOK, regardless of the membership of its board, will be asked to pursue the objective of monetary stability. In this context, it is interesting to note that the IMF stepped in to strengthen the objectives of monetary stability further by adding a clause to make it clear that the BOK will seek to harmonise its policy with macroeconomic policy, but do so only to the extent that this does not conflict with its main objective of monetary policy (Ministry of Finance and Economy 1998a). This additional clause makes it clear that the prime objective of the BOK is to pursue monetary stability.

These changes to the BOK Act are remarkable and are a clear illustration of a shift from a developmental state to a regulatory state dominated by economic constitutionalism. An independent central bank strikes at the core of the developmental state in the following ways:

1   It removes the power and capacity of central economic agencies to direct the kind of industry policies that have been a marked feature of the developmental state. In short, it shifts power from technocratic economic agencies to actors such as central banks. More importantly, it erodes the close political relationship between business and state that informed the operation of these economic agencies.
2   It becomes difficult to pursue the growth-oriented industry policy that often favoured the export industrial sector because the clearly defined objectives of the central bank are to establish monetary stability, and in general pursue an anti-inflationary strategy.
3   The use of subsidised credit as an arm of industry policy becomes highly problematic as a result of the BOK Act as well as the recently established Financial Supervisory Body.

All of these changes signal a significant transformation from the developmental to the regulatory state.

Conclusion: from the developmental to the regulatory state

The overriding argument of this chapter is that there has been a significant transformation in the nature and structure of the East Asian developmental state as a consequence of changing global structures of governance. Of particular importance was the fact that the infrastructure of control for the developmental state was nested within certain forms of capital market regulation made possible by the Bretton Woods system. The gradual dismantling of these capital controls has significantly diminished the economic steering capacity of the state. This transformation of the state has rendered problematic some of the central components of the developmental state, in particular the power as well as the relative insulation of economic agencies and the capacity of governmental authorities to pursue the kind of strategic industry policies that we have come traditionally to associate with East Asian strong states. In short, these new state forms are products of significant changes in the organisation of global governance.

The emergent authoritarian liberal international economic order is best captured by one of the guiding notions of the fashionable governance programmes: the idea of transparency. The implementation of market transparency – which is so important to the economic constitutionalism of the authoritarian liberal order – requires the juridification of key market institutions, and is seen as a vital constitutional bailiwick against the corrosive influence of vested groups. Authoritarian liberalism tries to clear the market of the muddy streams of politics. In consequence, the constitution of economic order through mechanisms of economic constitutionalism often stands in sharp contrast to the institutions and structures of political constitutionalism. Transparency and accountability – the twins of governance programmes – are mutually inconsistent.

The German ordo-liberal tradition with its emphasis on the juridical backdrop to market order exemplifies the vital role of economic order in the construction of the market. This authoritarian liberalism presupposes the existence of a strong (or better described as politically illiberal) state with a capacity to regulate the economy. In short, the emergent authoritarian liberal order requires a regulatory state. In East Asia, the developmental state is transformed into a regulatory state. Hence, we see not the decline of the state in the face of globalisation but its metamorphosis (though not always successfully) into a state with a range of regulative capacities. In the world of this regulatory state, agencies like central banks are likely to emerge as key centres of power within the state.

It is at this point that one observes some important continuities between the developmental state and the new regulatory state. The regulatory state requires a particular kind of non-liberal state – what Oakeshott would call a purposive or enterprise organisation. In this case, the purpose of the enterprise association would be the organisation of economic order and security. In short, to use Fraenkel's term, a 'dualistic state' operates where the economy is effectively organised under the 'rule of law', but where the political sphere is not bound by notions of political constitutionalism. The East Asian notion of state (or 'stateness') is precisely the kind of enterprise organisation favoured by authoritarian liberalism (Jayasuriya 1997; 1996). Therefore it is most likely that the normative tradition of the developmental state, i.e. its activist orientation towards the objective of economic security, will probably prove to be equally vital to the new regulatory state in East Asia. In short, developing neo-liberal economic reforms require a strong state and these normative traditions of East Asian states will serve to reinforce new forms of state structures and organisation, and perhaps more importantly, point to some important differences in the kinds of regulatory states on offer in the twenty-first century.

NOTES

1 Apart from Gill (1995) the work of Petersmann (1991) has been critical in drawing attention to the constitutionalisaton of the international trade. Unlike Gill, Petersmann takes a sympathetic view of this process of constitutionalisation. This makes his work particularly useful in seeking to uncover the normative foundation of economic constitutionalism.
2 This paper is part of larger project which examines the normative and historical foundations of authoritarian liberalism.
3 For a survey of some of these theorists see Peacock and Willgerodt (1989).
4 See North (1981) for the classical statement.
5 See Jayasuriya (1994) for an analysis of the political dynamics of central bank independence in OECD countries.
6 These legislative changes were passed by the Korean National Assembly in December 1997.

BIBLIOGRAPHY

Albert, M. (1993) *Capitalism Against Capitalism*, London: Whurr.

Altbach, Eric (1997) 'The Asian Monetary Fund Proposal: A Case Study in Japanese Regional Leadership', *Japan Economic Institute Report* No. 47A: 8–9.

Amin, Samir (1993) 'Replacing the International Monetary System', *Monthly Review* 45(5): 1–12.

Amsden, Alice H. (1989) *Asia's Next Giant: South Korea and Late Industrialization*, New York: Oxford University Press.

Amsden, Alice H. (1990) 'Third World Industrialisation: "Global Fordism" or a New Model', *New Left Review* 182: 5–31.

Anderson, Benedict (1990) 'Murder and Progress in Modern Siam', *New Left Review* 181: 33–48.

Anderson, Benedict (1998) 'From Miracle to Crash', *London Review of Books* 20(8): April.

Aoki, Masahiko (1995) *Keizaisystemno Shinkato Dagensei [Evolution and Diversity of Economic System]*, Tokyo: Toyokeizai Shimbosha.

APEC (1991) Third Ministerial Meeting: Joint Statement, Seoul at http://www.apecsec.org.sg/minismtg/mtgmin91.html.

Archibugi, D. and D. Held (1995) 'Editors' Introduction', in D. Archibugi and D. Held (eds), *Cosmopolitan Democracy*, Cambridge: Polity Press.

Argy, F. (1996) 'The Integration of World Capital Markets: Some Economic and Social Implications', *Economic Papers* 15(2): 1–9.

Argy, F. (1998) *Australia at the Crossroads: Radical Free Market or Progressive Liberalism?*, St Leonards: Allen and Unwin.

Ariff, Mohamed (1996) 'Effects of Financial Liberalization on Four Southeast Asian Financial Markets, 1973–94', *ASEAN Economic Bulletin* 12(3): 325–38.

Armijo, Leslie Elliott (1999) ' "Mixed Blessing": Foreign Capital Flows and Democracy in Emerging Markets', in Leslie Elliott Armijo (ed.), *Financial Globalization and Democracy in Emerging Markets*, New York: St. Martin's Press.

Arrighi, G. (1994) *The Long Twentieth Century: Money, Power, and the Origins of Our Times*, London: Verso.

Asia Society (1998) *Asia at a Crossroads*, http://www.asiasociety.org/publications/epg.html.

Asian Wall Street Journal (1997) 'Fidelity Reassigns Chief of Battered Fund', 22 October.

Asian Wall Street Journal (1997a) 'After Thailand, Where Next for Disaster?', 23 April.

Asiaweek (1998) 'Charting the Crisis', 17 July: 41.

Asiaweek (1998a) 'Special Report Essay', 18 September: 28–38.

Asiaweek (1998b) 'I've Lost My Voice', 27 March (http://www.pathfinder. com/asiaweek/98/0327/cs4.html).

Awang Adek Hussein (1994) 'Financial System', in K.S. Jomo (ed.), *Malaysia's Economy in the Nineties*, pp. 137–69, Petaling Jaya: Pelanduk.

Bachus, S. (1998) Chairman's Opening Statement, US Congress, House of Representatives, Committee on Banking and Financial Services, Subcommittee on General Oversight and Investigations, 21 April (http://commdocs.house.gov/ committees/bank/hba48110.000/hba48110_0f.htm).

Bangkok Post (1997) *Economic Review 1997*, Bangkok: Post Publishing (http://www.bangkokpost.com/ecoreview97/review9710.html).

Bangkok Post (1998) 'The Economy. A Bump Road Ahead', *Bangkok Post, 1998 Mid-Year Economic Review* 30 June (http://www.bangkokpost.com/myer98/ myer98_01.html).

Bank of International Settlements (BIS) (1998) *68th Annual Report*, Basle, 8 June.

Bank of Korea (1998) *Internal Report*, Seoul: Bank of Korea.

Bank Negara (1998) *Monthly Statistical Bulletin*, various issues.

Bardecke, Ted (1998) 'Roaring Start to Thai Fire Sale', *The Financial Times* 26 June: 17.

Bardhan, P. (1989) 'The New Institutional Economic and Development Theory: A Brief Critical Assessment', *World Development* 17(9): 1389–95.

Beams, Nick (1998) 'The Asian Meltdown: A Crisis of Global Capitalism', World Socialist website, April (www.wsws.org).

Beeson, Mark (1996) 'APEC: Nice Theory, Shame about the Practice', *Australian Quarterly* 68(2): 35–48.

Beeson, Mark (1997) 'Who Pays the Ferryman? Industry Policy and Shipbuilding in Australia', *Australian Journal of Political Science* 32(3): 437–54.

Beeson, Mark (1998) 'Indonesia, the East Asian Crisis, and the Commodification of the Nation-state', *New Political Economy* 3(3): 357–74.

Beeson, Mark (1999) 'Reshaping Regional Institutions: APEC and the IMF in East Asia', *The Pacific Review* 12(1): 1–24.

Beeson, Mark and A. Firth (1998) 'Neoliberalism as a Political Rationality: Australian Public Policy since the 1980s', *Journal of Sociology* 34(3): 215–31.

Beeson, Mark and K. Jayasuriya (1998) 'The Political Rationalities of Regionalism: APEC and the EU in Comparative Perspective', *The Pacific Review* 11(3): 311–36.

Bell, Stephen (1993) *Australian Manufacturing and the State: The Politics of Industry Policy in the Post-War Era*, Cambridge: Cambridge University Press.

Bell, Stephen (1995a) 'The Collective Capitalism of Northeast Asia and the Limits of Orthodox Economics', *Australian Journal of Political Science* 30: 264–87.

Bell, Stephen (1995b) 'The Politics of Economic Adjustment: Explaining the Transformation of Industry-State Relationships in Australia', *Political Studies* 43: 22–47.

Bell, Stephen (1997) 'Globalisation, Neoliberalism and the Transformation of the Australian State', *Australian Journal of Political Science* 32(3): 345–67.

Bell, Stephen (1997a) *Ungoverning the Economy: The Political Economy of Australian Economic Policy*, Melbourne: Oxford University Press.

Bello, Walden (1998) 'East Asia: On the Eve of the Great Transformation?', *Review of International Political Economy* 5(3).

Bello, Walden (1998a) 'From Miracle to Meltdown: Thailand, the World Bank and the IMF', *Watershed* 3(2): 17–21.

Bello, Walden (1998b) 'The Asian Financial Crisis: Causes, Dynamics, and Prospects', Unpublished.

Bello, Walden (1998c) 'The End of the Asian Miracle', *Inside Indonesia* No. 54, April–June: 7–10 (http://www.pactok.net/docs/inside/edit54/walden.htm; also at Roubini homepage, www.stern.nyu.edu).

Bello, Walden and S. Rosenfeld (1990) *Dragons in Distress. Asia's Miracle Economies in Crisis*, San Francisco: Food First.

Bello, Walden *et al.* (1982) *Development Debacle: The World Bank in the Philippines*, San Francisco: Institute for Food and Development Policy.

Berger, M. and M. Beeson (1998) 'Lineages of Liberalism and Miracles of Modernization: The World Bank, the East Asian Trajectory and the International Development Debate', *Third World Quarterly* 19(3): 487–504.

Bernard, Mitchell (1991) 'The Post-Plaza Political Economy of Taiwanese-Japanese Relations', *The Pacific Review* 4: 358–67.

Bhagwati, Jagdish (1990) 'Aggressive Unilateralism: An Overview', in J. Bhagwati and H.T. Patrick (eds.), *Aggressive Unilateralism: America's 301 Trade Policy and the World Trading System*, pp. 1–45. New York: Harvester Wheatsheaf.

Bhagwati, Jagdish (1998) 'The Capital Myth: The Difference Between Trade in Widgets and Trade in Dollars', *Foreign Affairs* 77(3).

Bhattacharya, A. and M. Pangestu (1992) 'Indonesia: Development and Transformation Since 1965 and the Role of Public Policy', Paper prepared for the World Bank Workshop on the Role of Government and East Asian Success, East–West Center, Hawaii, November.

Biers, Dan (ed.) (1998) *Crash of 97: How the Financial Crisis is Reshaping Asia*, Hong Kong: Review.

Biggart, N.W. and G.G. Hamilton (1992) 'On the Limits of a Firm-based Theory to Explain Business Networks: The Western Bias of Neoclassical Economics', in N. Nohira and R.G. Eccles (eds), *Networks and Organizations: Structure, Form, and Action*, pp. 471–90, Boston: Harvard Business School Press.

Bondoy, Rolando (1997) 'Different Fundamentals' *Business World* 4–5 April.

BoT (Bank of Thailand) (1997) 'Economic Developments in the First 9 Months of 1997', *Bank of Thailand Quarterly Bulletin* 37(3): 5–15.

BoT (Bank of Thailand) (1997a) 'Economic Performance in 1997 and Outlook for 1998', *Bank of Thailand Quarterly Bulletin* 37(4): 5–20.

Bottomore, Tom (1985) *Theories of Modern Capitalism*, London: George Allen and Unwin.

Bowie, A. (1991) *Closing the Industrial Divide*, New York: Columbia University Press.

Boyer, R. and D. Drache (eds) (1996) *The Power of Markets and Future of the Nation State*, London: Routledge.

Bremner, Brian *et al.* (1997) 'Rescuing Asia', *Business Week* 17 November: 116.

Brenner, R. (1998) 'The Economics of Global Turbulence: A Special Report on the World Economy, 1950–98', *New Left Review* 229(May/June).

Broad, Robin and J. Cavanagh (1993) *Plundering Paradise: the Struggle for the Environment in the Philippines*, Berkeley, CA: University of California Press.

Brown, C. (1998) ' "Overseas Chinese" Business in South-east Asia', in K. Sheridan (ed.), *Emerging Economic Systems in Asia*, pp. 208–27, St Leonards: Allen and Unwin.

Brown, Jason (1993) *The Role of the State in Economic Development: Theory, The East Asian Experience, and the Malaysian Case*, Manila, Asian Development Bank, Economics Staff Paper No. 52.

Brown, Vivienne (1992) 'The Emergence of the Economy', in Stuart Hall and Bram Gieben (eds), *Formations of Modernity*, Cambridge: Polity Press.

Bryan, D. (1995) *The Chase Across the Globe: International Accumulation and the Contradictions for Nation States*, Boulder, CO: Westview Press.

Buchanan, J.M. and G. Tullock (1962) *The Calculus of Consent*, Ann Arbor, MI: University of Michigan Press.

Burchell, G., C. Gordon and P Miller (eds) (1991) *The Foucault Effect: Studies in Governmentality*, London: Harvester Wheatsheaf.

Business Times (1998) 'Defending the IMF', 5 October.

Business World (1997) 'RP Market Faces Glut, Consultant Says', 2 October.

Business World (1997a) 'Local Banks "Not Cause of Turmoil" ', 10 September.

Business World (1997b) 'Three Main Challenges for the Central Bank', 9–10 May.

Business World (1997c) 'BSP Approves 20% Loan-Loss Reserves', 25 September.

Business World (1998) 'Banks Bad-Debt Level up to 9.2%', 15 September.

Business World (1998a) 'Up, Close, and Personal: An Agenda for the Estrada Administration', Special issue, July.

Calder, Kent E. (1988) *Crisis and Compensation: Public Policy and Political Stability in Japan 1949-1986*, Princeton, NJ: Princeton University Press.

Calder, Kent E. (1993) *Strategic Capitalism: Private Business and Public Purpose in Japanese Industrial Finance*, Princeton, NJ: Princeton University Press.

Camdessus, Michel (1997) 'Asia Will Survive with Realistic Economic Policies: Parts I and II', *Jakarta Post* 8–9 December.

Camdessus, Michel (1998) 'From the Asian Crisis Toward a New Global Architecture', Address to the Parliamentary Assembly of the Council of Europe, Strasbourg, 23 June (http://www.imf.org/external/np/speeches/1998/062398.htm).

Camdessus, Michel (1998a) 'The IMF and Good Governance', Address at 'Transparency International', Paris, 21 January.

Cameron, Rondo (1993) *A Concise Economic History of the World*, Oxford: Oxford University Press.

Carey, Mike (1996) 'Singapore Sling', *SBS Dateline*, Singapore Government Press Release: http://www.gov.sg/mita/pressrelease/archives/ 96110402.htm.

Castells, Manuel (1992) 'Four Asian Tigers With a Dragon Head: A Comparative Analysis of the State, Economy, and Society in the Asian Pacific Rim', in Richard P Appelbaum and Jeffrey Hendersen (eds), *States and Development in the Asian Pacific Rim*, pp. 33–70, Newbury Park, CA: Sage.

Caton, Chris (1998) 'An Economic Outlook', Paper presented to the conference on 'The Asian Crisis: Economic and Market Intelligence', University of Melbourne, 8 May.

Cerny, Philip G. (1990) *The Changing Architecture of Politics*, London: Sage.

Cerny, Philip G. (1991) 'The Limits of Deregulation: Transnational Interpenetration and Policy Change', *European Journal of Political Research* 19(2/3): 173–96.

Cerny, Philip G. (1997) 'International Finance and the Erosion of Capitalist Diversity', in Colin Crouch and Wolfgang Streeck (eds), *Political Economy of Modern Capitalism*, London: Sage.

Cerny, Philip G. (1997a) 'Paradoxes of the Competition State: The Dynamics of Political Globalization', *Government and Opposition* 32: 251–74.

Chai-Anan Samudavanija (1997) 'Old Soldiers Never Die, They Are Just Bypassed: The Military, Bureaucracy and Globalisation', in K. Hewison (ed.), *Political Change in Thailand. Democracy and Participation*, pp. 42–57, London: Routledge.

Chalongphob Sussangkarn (1997) 'Thailand: Looking Ahead to 2020 in the Light of Global and Regional Changes', *TDRI Quarterly Review* 12(2): 3–13.

Chalongphob Sussangkarn (1998) 'Thailand's Debt Crisis and Economic Outlook', Paper presented to the conference on 'The Asian Crisis: Economic and Market Intelligence', University of Melbourne, 8 May.

Chandler, Alfred D. Jr (1990) *Scale and Scope: The Dynamics of Industrial Capitalism*, Cambridge, MA: Harvard University Press.

Chandra Muzaffar (1998) 'Need for Professionalism from Private and Public Institutions', *The Star* 3 June.

Chang Ha-Joon (1994) *The Political Economy of Industrial Policy*, Basingstoke : Macmillan.

Chao, Linda and R.H. Myers (1998) *The First Chinese Democracy. Political Life in the Republic of China on Taiwan*, Baltimore, MD: Johns Hopkins University Press.

Charoen Kittikanya and Walailak Keeratipipatpong (eds) (1997) 'Insurance', *Bangkok Post* (http://www.bangkokpost.com/ecoreview97/review9710.html).

Chaudhry, Kiren Aziz (1993) 'The Myths of the Market and the Common History of Late Developers', *Politics and Society* 21(3): 245–74.

Chaudhry, Kiren Aziz (1997) *The Price of Wealth: Economies and Institutions in the Middle East*, Ithaca, NY: Cornell University Press.

Chavez-Malaluan, Jenina Joy (1996) *Shaping Philippine Economic Policy: The Role of Neoclassical Activists*, Manila: MODE.

Chen, Jianfu (1995) *From Administrative Authorisation to Private Law: A Comparative Perspective of the Developing Civil Law of the People's Republic of China*, London: Martinus Nijhoff.

Cheng Tun-Jen (1990) 'Political Regimes and Development Strategies: South Korea and Taiwan', in Gary Gereffi and Donald L. Wyman (eds), *Manufacturing Miracle*, Princeton, NJ: Princeton University Press.

Cheng-hsiung, Paul Chiu (Taiwan Finance Minister) (1998) Interview, *South China Morning Post* 6 July (http://www.scmp.com/news/special/AsiaChallenge/).

China Statistical Yearbook (1981) (overseas Chinese edition).

China-Singapore Suzhou Industrial Park Development Co. Ltd (1995) *Singapore-Suzhou Township*, Singapore.

Chittima Duriyaprapan and Mathee Supapongse (1996) 'Financial Liberalization: Case Study of Thailand', *Bank of Thailand Quarterly Bulletin* 36(3): 35–52.

Chowhury, Neel and Anthony Paul (1997) 'Where Asia Goes From Here', *Fortune* 24 November.

Christensen, S., D. Dollar, Ammar Siamwalla and Pakorn Vichyanond (1993) *The Lessons of East Asia Thailand: The Institutional and Political Underpinnings of Growth*, Washington, DC: World Bank.

Chung, Han-young (1998) *Urinara Oichae-ui Hyoyuljok Gwanribangan [On Effective Management of Korea's Foreign Debts]*, Seoul: Korea Institute of Finance.

Clad, James (1991) *Behind the Myth. Business, Money and Power in Southeast Asia*, London: Grafton.

Cohen, Benjamin J. (1986) *In Whose Interest? International Banking and American Foreign Policy*, New Haven, CT: Yale University Press.

Colebatch, T. (1998) 'World Bank Fears Global Depression', *The Age* 17 June.

Corsetti, Giancarlo, P. Pesenti and N. Roubini (1998) 'What Caused the Asian Currency and Financial Crisis?', see Roubini homepage at www.stern.nyu.edu (March).

Cotton, James (1995) 'Interpreting Singapore: Class or Power?', *The Pacific Review* 8: 558–63.

Cotton, James and K.H.A. Van Leest (1996) 'The New Rich and the New Middle Class in South Korea: The Rise and Fall of the "Golf Republic"', in Richard Robison and David S.G. Goodman (eds), *The New Rich in Asia*, pp. 185–203, London: Routledge.

Cruz, Wilfredo and R. Repetto (1992) *The Environmental Effects of Stabilization and Structural Adjustment*, Washington, DC: World Resources Institute.

Cumings, Bruce (1987) 'The Origins and Development of the Northeast Asian Political Economy', in Frederic Deyo (ed.), *The Political Economy of the New Asian Industrialism*, Ithaca, NY, and London: Cornell University Press.

Daly, M.T. and M.I. Logan (1989) *The Brittle Rim: Finance, Business and the Pacific Region*, Ringwood, Victoria, Australia: Penguin.

Davidson, K. (1992) 'The Failures of Financial Deregulation in Australia', in S. Bell. and J. Wanna (eds), *Business–Government Relations in Australia*, pp. 221–30, Sydney: Harcourt Brace Jovanovich.

Dejevsky, M. (1998) 'Summit Agrees to Disagree on Asia Crisis', *The Independent* 25 November.

Dell, S. (1982) 'Stabilization: The Political Economy of Overkill', *World Development* 10(8).

Deng, Yingtao *et al.* (1990) *Zhongguo yushuanwai zhijin fenxi [A Study of China's Extra-Budgetary Funds]*, Beijing: Zhongguo renmin daxue chubanshe.

Deyo, F. C. (ed.) (1987) *The Political Economy of the New Asian Industrialism*, Ithaca, NY: Cornell University Press.

Dhonte, Pierre and I. Kapur (1996) 'Toward a Market Economy: Structures of Governance', IMF Working Paper 97/11.

Dibb, P. *et al.* (1998) 'The Strategic Implication's of Asia's Economic Crisis', *Survival* 40(2): 5–26.

Dicken, P. (1992) *Global Shift: The Internationalization of Economic Activity*, London: Paul Chapman.

Dolven, Ben (1998) 'Who Said Bailout?', *Far Eastern Economic Review* 11 June: 62.

Dolven, Ben (1998a) 'Pay Before You Play', *Far Eastern Economic Review* 6 August: 16.

Doner, Richard (1992) 'Limits of State Strength: Toward an Institutionalist View of Economic Development', *World Politics* 44(3): 398–431.

Doner, Richard F. and D. Unger (1993) 'The Politics of Finance in Thai Economic Development', in S. Haggard and S.B. Webb (eds), *Democracy, Political Liberalization and Economic Adjustment*, Ithaca, NY: Cornell University Press.

Dore, Ronald (1986) *Flexible Rigidities: Industrial Policy and Structural Adjustment in the Japanese Economy, 1970–1980*, Stanford, CA: Stanford University Press.

Dornbusch, Rudiger and Y.C. Park (1995) 'Financial Integration in a Second-best World: Are We Still Sure About Our Classical Prejudices?', in R. Dornbusch and Y.C. Park (eds), *Financial Opening: Policy Lessons for Korea* Seoul: Korea Institute of Finance.

Du, Haiyan (1992) *Zhongguo nongchun gongyehua yanjiu [A Study of China's Rural Industrialization]*, Beijing: Zhongguo wujia chubanshe.

Dunham, R.S. and D. Foust (1998) 'Has Bob Rubin Cried Wolf Once Too Often?', *Business Week* 25 May.

Economic Section (1998) '1998 Investment Climate Statement for Thailand', Bangkok, Department of State, United States Embassy (http://usa.or.th/embassy/invcl98.htm).

Economic White Paper (1994–1997), Korea.

Eichengreen, B. (1996) *Globalizing Capital: A History of the International Monetary System*, Princeton, NJ: Princeton University Press.

Eichengreen, B. (1997) 'The Tyranny of the Financial Markets', *Current History* November: 377–82.

Elliott, Dorinda (1998) 'The Rebel Son', *Newsweek* 14 September: 13–17.

Elliott, Dorinda (1998a) 'Here's Mud in Your Face', *Newsweek* 5 October: 24–5.

Emmerson, S. (1998) 'Nationals Embrace Policies of One Nation', *The Australian* 18 June.

Esguerra, Jude (1997) 'Devaluation – An Accident Waiting to Happen', *IDP Political Brief* 5(4): August.

Evans, Eric J. (1997) *Thatcher and Thatcherism*, London: Routledge.

Evans, Peter (1995) *Embedded Autonomy: States and Industrial Transformation*, Princeton, NJ: Princeton University Press.

Evans, Peter (1997) 'The Eclipse of the State? Reflection on Stateness in an Era of Globalization', *World Politics* 50(1).

Fair Trade Commission (various years) *The Yearbook of Fair Trade*, Seoul: EPB.

Falkus, M. (1998) 'The Historical Roots of the Thai Economic Crisis', Paper presented at the International Conference on the Asian Crisis, Chung-Ang University, Seoul, 6–7 November.

Fallows, J. (1993) *Looking at the Sun: The Rise of the New East Asian Economic and Political Systems*, New York: Pantheon.

Feldstein, Martin (1998) 'Refocusing the IMF', *Foreign Affairs* 77(2): 20–33.

Feulner, E.J. (1998) Testimony, U.S. Congress, House of Representatives, Committee on Banking and Financial Services, Sub-Committee on General Oversight and Investigations, 21 April (http://www.house.gov/banking/42198her.htm).

Fischer, S. (1998) 'In Defence of the IMF: Specialized Tools for a Specialized Task', *Foreign Affairs* July–August.

Fischer, S. (1998a) 'The Asian Crisis: A View From the IMF', Address delivered at the Midwinter Conference of the Bankers' Association for Foreign Trade, 22 January 1998 (http://www.imf.org/external/np/speeches/1998/112298.htm).

Fischer, Tim (1998) 'The Trade Imperative: Challenges and Future Directions', Speech to the Australia Summit, 16 June.

Fisher, Stanley (1998) 'The Asian Crisis, the IMF, and Japanese Economy', Tokyo Address, 8 April (http://www.imf.org).

Fitch IBCA (1998) 'After Asia: Some Lessons of the Crisis', *Fitch IBCA Sovereign Comment* 13: January.

FitzGerald, E.V.K. (1997) 'Series Editor's Introduction', in Karel Jansen, *External Finance in Thailand's Development. An Interpretation of Thailand's Growth Boom*, pp. xi–xv, Basingstoke: Macmillan.

FitzGerald, Stephen (1997) *Is Australia an Asian Country? Can Australia Survive in an East Asian Future?*, Sydney: Allen and Unwin.

Fox, Justin (1998) 'The Great Emerging Markets Rip-Off', *Fortune* 11 May (http://www.pathfinder.com/fortune/1998/980511/gre.html).

Fraenkel, Ernest (1941) *The Dual State*, transl. from the German by E.A Shils in collaboration with Edith Lowenstein and Klaus Knorr, London: Oxford University Press.

Francisco, Rosemarie (1997) 'One Foot on the Door', *The Next Step: The Philippines into the 21st Century*, Manila: Business World.

Frankel, J.A. (1998) 'The Asian Model, The Miracle, The Crisis and the Fund', Paper delivered at US International Trade Commission, April (http://www.stern.nyu.edu/~nroubini/asia/AsiaHomepage.html) (8 February 1999).

Franke-Ruta, G. (1998) 'The IMF Gets a Left and a Right', *The National Journal* 30(3).

Freedom from Debt Coalition: Philippines (1997) *Primer on Philippine Debt*, Quezon City: Freedom from Debt Coalition.

Frieden, J.A. (1991) 'Invested Interests: the Politics of National Economic Policies in a World of Global Finance', *International Organization* 45(4): 425–51.

Friedman, David (1988) *The Misunderstood Miracle: Industrial Development and Political Change in Japan*, Ithaca, NY, and London: Cornell University Press.

Friedman, T.L. (1997) 'Quit the Whining! Globalization Isn't a Choice', *International Herald Tribune* 30 September.

Frischtak, Leila (1994) 'Governance Capacity and Economic Reform in Developing Countries', World Bank Technical Paper No. 254.

Frischtak, Leila and I. Atiyas (eds) (1996) *Governance, Leadership, and Communication*, Washington, DC: World Bank.

Frobel, F. *et al.* (1978) 'The New International Division of Labour', *Social Science Information* 17(1): 123–42.

Fruin, W. Mark (1994) *The Japanese Enterprise System: Competitive Strategies and Cooperative Structures*, New York: Oxford University Press.

Fujii, Yoshihiro (1997) 'Can "Mutual Trust" Work? It's Unclear So Far', *The Nikkei Weekly* 8 December.

Fujii, Yoshihiro (1998) 'European Example Provides Boost to Backers of Single Currency in Asia', *The Nikkei Weekly* 25 May: 23.

Fukui, M. (1998) 'Currency Woes Spread South', *The Nikkei Weekly* 15 June.

Fukuyama, Francis (1995) *Trust: The Social Virtues and the Creation of Prosperity*, New York: Free Press.

Funabashi, Yoichi (1993) 'Japan and the New World Order', *Foreign Affairs* November/December.

Funabashi, Yoichi (1995) *Asia Pacific Fusion: Japan's Role in APEC*, Washington, DC: Institute for International Economics.

Gao, Xian (1997) 'China's "Balloon Economy" in Market Transition', *Zhongguo Guoqingguoli* No. 9: 17–19.

Garcia, Elisha (1997) 'IMF Suspects Bank Loans to Property Sector Higher', *Business World* 23 September.

Garnaut, Ross (1989) *Australia and the Northeast Asian Ascendancy*, Canberra: AGPS.

Garnaut, Ross (1998) 'The Financial Crisis: A Watershed in Economic Thought about East Asia', *Asian-Pacific Economic Literature* 12(1): 1–11.

Gerlach, Michael L. (1992) *Alliance Capitalism: The Social Organization of Japanese Business*, Berkeley, CA: University of California Press.

Gill, Ranjit (1998) *Asia Under Siege. How the Asian Miracle Went Wrong*, Singapore: Epic Management.

Gill, S. (1995) 'Globalization, Market Civilization and Disciplinary Neoliberalism', *Millennium* 24(3): 399–423.

Gill, S. and D. Law (1988) *The Global Political Economy: Perspectives, Problems and Policies*, London: Harvester Wheatsheaf.

Gill, T. (1998) 'Tipping the Scales', *The WorldPaper Online* March (http://www.worldpaper.com/March98/gill.html).

Gilpin, R. (1987) *The Political Economy of International Relations*, Princeton, NJ: Princeton University Press.

Godement, Francois (1998) 'The Politics of a Crisis', *Far Eastern Economic Review* 8 January: 28.

Gold, Thomas B. (1986) *State and Society in the Taiwan Miracle*, Armonk, NY: M.E. Sharpe.

Goldsmith, Arthur A. (1995) 'The State, the Market and Economic Development: A Second Look at Adam Smith in Theory and Practice', *Development and Change* 26: 633–50.

Goldstein, J.S. (1988) *Long Cycles: Prosperity and War in the Modern Age*, New Haven, CT: Yale University Press.

Gomez, Edmund Terence and K.S. Jomo (1997) *Malaysia's Political Economy: Politics, Patronage and Profits*, Cambridge: Cambridge University Press.

Goodman, J. (1991) 'The Politics of Central Bank Independence', *Comparative Politics* 23(3): 329–50.

Gordon, D. (1994) 'Twixt Cup and the Lip: Mainstream Economics and the Formation of Economic Policy', *Social Research* 61(1): 1–29.

Gordon, M. (1996) 'John Howard's Defensive Diplomacy', *The Weekend Australian* 21–22 September.

Gordon, M.R. and D.E. Sanger (1998) 'Rescuing Russia', *New York Times* 17 July.

Gore, Lance L.P. (1998) *Market Communism: The Institutional Foundation of China's Post-Mao Hypergrowth*, Hong Kong: Oxford University Press.

Gourevitch, Peter Alexis (1984) 'Breaking with Orthodoxy: The Politics of Economic Policy Responses to the Depression of the 1930s', *International Organization* 38(1).

Gourevitch, Peter Alexis (1986) *Politics in Hard Times: Comparative Responses to International Economic Crises*, Ithaca, NY, and London: Cornell University Press.

Gower, L. (1998) 'What has become of the Japanese model?', *Agenda* 5(1): 61–72.

Granovetter, Mark (1985) 'Economic Action and Social Structure: The Problem of Embeddedness', *American Journal of Sociology* 91: 481–510.

Grattan, M. (1998) 'Rage Politics', *Australian Financial Review* 24 July.

Greenhalgh, Susan (1988) 'Families and Networks in Taiwan's Economic Development', in Edwin A Winckler and Susan Greenhalgh (eds), *Contending Approaches to the Political Economy of Taiwan*, pp. 224–45. Armonk, NY: M.E. Sharpe.

Greenspan, Alan (1998) 'Fed Chairman Greenspan Testifies on Asian Economy', *Wall Street Journal* 30 January.

Greenspan, Alan (1998a) Speech to the Annual Convention of the Independent Bankers Association of America, 3 March (http://bog.frb.fed.us/board/docs/speeches/19980303.htm).

Greenspan, Alan (1998b) Statement, US Congress, House of Representatives, Committee on Banking and Financial Services, Subcommittee on Domestic and International Monetary Policy, 22 July (http://www.bog.frb.fed.us/boarddocs/hh/).

Greider, W. (1997) *One World, Ready or Not: The Manic Logic of Global Capitalism*, New York: Simon and Schuster.

Grenville, S. (1998) 'The Asian Economic Crisis', *Reserve Bank Bulletin* April: 9–20.

Griesgraber, J.M. (1997) 'Forgive us Our Debts', *The Christian Century* 114(3).

Gurry, M. (1998) 'Whose History? The Struggle over Authorship of Australia's Asia Policies', *Australian Journal of International Affairs* 52(1): 77–88.

Haarl, Jens van (1998) 'The Financial Crisis in Asia and the Role of the Asian Development Bank', *NIASnytt* 2(June): 15–17.

Haas, Peter (1992) 'Knowledge, Power and International Policy Coordination', *International Organisation* 46(1): 1–32.

Haggard, Stephan (1990) *Pathways from the Periphery: The Politics of Growth in the Newly Industrializing Countries*, Ithaca, NY: Cornell University Press.

Haggard, Stephan (1990a) 'The Political Economy of the Philippine Debt Crisis', in Joan Nelson (ed.), *Economic Crisis and Policy Choice: the Politics of Adjustment in Developing Countries*, Princeton, NJ: Princeton University Press.

Haggard, Stephan and C.H. Lee (eds) (1995) *Financial Systems and Economic Policy in Developing Countries*, Ithaca, NY: Cornell University Press.

Haggard, Stephan and A. MacIntyre (1998) 'The Political Economy of the Asian Economic Crisis', *Review of International Political Economy* 5(3).

Haggard, Stephan and Chung-in Moon (1983) 'The South Korean State in the International Economy: Liberal, Dependent or Mercantile', in John Ruggie (ed.), *Antinomies of Interdependence*, New York: Columbia University Press.

Haley, Mary Ann (1999) 'Emerging Market Makers: The Power of Institutional Investors', in Leslie Elliott Armijo (ed.), *Financial Globalization and Democracy in Emerging Markets*, New York: St Martin's Press.

Hamilton, Gary and N.W. Biggart (1988) 'Market, Culture and Authority: A Comparative Analysis of Management and Organization in the Far East', *American Journal of Sociology* 94: 552–94.

Handley, Paul (1997) 'More of the Same? Politics and Business, 1987–96', in K. Hewison (ed.), *Political Change in Thailand. Democracy and Participation*, pp. 94–113, London: Routledge.

Hanke, Steve (1997) 'The IMF: Immune from Frequent Failure', *Asian Wall Street Journal* 25 August.

Harberger, Arnold C. *et al.* (1993) 'Economic Integration and the Future of the Nation-State', *Contemporary Policy Issues* 11(April): 1–22.

Harris, N. (1988) 'New Bourgeoisies', *The Journal of Development Studies* 24(2): 237–49.

Hartcher, P. (1997) 'A Free Trade in Words', *Australian Financial Review* 22 December.

Hartcher, P. (1998) 'Australia Shifted the World on Indonesia', *Australian Financial Review* 1 April.

Hartcher, P. (1998a) 'Greatest Threat Since the 1930s', *Australian Financial Review* 25 August.

Hart-Landsberg, Martin (1991) 'The Asian NICs at the Crossroads', *Monthly Review* 43(4): 57–63.

Hatch, Walter and K. Yamamura (1996) *Asia in Japan's Embrace: Building a Regional Production Alliance*, Cambridge: Cambridge University Press.

Hawthorn, Geoffrey (1993) 'Liberalization and Modern Liberty: Four Southern States', *World Development* 21(8): 1299–312.

Hawtrey, K. *et al.* (1991) 'The Impact of Bank Deregulation on Australian Manufacturers', *Economic Papers* 10(4): 10–29.

Heilbroner, Robert L. (1985) *The Nature and Logic of Capitalism*, New York: W.W. Norton.

Held, David (1995) 'Democracy and the New International Order', in D. Archibugi and D. Held (eds), *Cosmopolitan Democracy*, Cambridge: Polity Press.

Helleiner, Eric (1994) *States and the Re-emergence of Global Finance: From Bretton Woods to the 1990s*, Ithaca, NY: Cornell University Press.

Henderson, I. (1998) 'Regulate and Avert Financial Crises', *The Australian* 22 May.

Henwood, Doug (1997) *Wall Street: How It Works and for Whom*, London: Verso.

Hewison, Kevin (1985) 'The State and Capitalist Development in Thailand', in Richard Higgott and Richard Robison (eds), *Southeast Asia: Essays in the Political Economy of Structural Change*, pp. 266–94, London: Routledge & Kegan Paul.

Hewison, Kevin (1987) 'National Interests and Economic Downturn: Thailand', in Richard Robison, Kevin Hewison and Richard Higgott (eds), *Southeast Asia in the 1980s: The Politics of Economic Crisis*, pp. 52–79, Sydney: Allen and Unwin.

Hewison, Kevin (1989) *Bankers and Bureaucrats: Capital and the Role of the State in Thailand*, Yale University Southeast Asian Monographs, No. 34, New Haven, CT: Yale Center for International and Area Studies.

Hewison, Kevin (1993) 'Of Regimes, State and Pluralities: Thai Politics Enters the 1990s', in K. Hewison, R. Robison and G. Rodan (eds), *Southeast Asia in the 1990s: Authoritarianism, Capitalism and Democracy*, pp. 159–90, St Leonards: Allen and Unwin.

Hewison, Kevin (ed.) (1997) *Political Change in Thailand. Democracy and Participation*, London: Routledge.

Hiebert, Murray (1998) 'Tactical Victory', *Far Eastern Economic Review* 2 July: 10–14.

Hiebert, Murray and S. Jayasankaran (1997) 'What Next?', *Far Eastern Economic Review* 18 September: 62–4.

Hiebert, Murray and A. Sherry (1998) 'After the Fall', *Far Eastern Economic Review* 17 September: 13.

Higgott, Richard (1998) 'The International Relations of the Asian Economic Crisis: A Study in the Politics of Resentment', Paper presented at the Conference 'From Miracle to Meltdown: The End of Asian Capitalism?', Fremantle, 20–22 August 1998.

Higgott, Richard (1999) 'ASEM: Towards the Institutionalisation of the East Asia–Europe Relationship?', in Donald Barry and Ron Keith (eds), *Asia, Europe and North America: Cooperation or Conflict?*, Vancouver: University of British Columbia Press.

Higgott, Richard and S. Reich (1998) 'Globalisation and Sites of Conflict: Towards Definition and Taxonomy', Working Paper 01/98, Warwick University: Centre for the Study of Globalisation and Regionalisation.

Higgott, Richard and R. Stubbs (1995) 'Competing Conceptions of Economic Regionalism: APEC versus the EAEC in the Asia Pacific', *The Review of International Political Economy* 2(3).

Hill, C.P. (1985) *British Economic and Social History 1700–1982*, 5th edn, London: Hodder and Stoughton.

Hill, Christine (1998) 'Can Mahathir Walk the Talk?', *Institutional Investor* May: 68–79.

Hill, Hal (1996) *The Indonesian Economy Since 1966: Southeast Asia's Emerging Giant*, Cambridge: Cambridge University Press.

Hirano, K. (1998) 'Miyazawa Flexible about Fiscal Structural Reform', *Japan Economic Newswire* 31 July.

Hirch, J. (1995) 'Regulation Theory and its Applicability to Studies on Globalization and Social Change', Working Paper 49, Department of Development and Planning, Aalborg University.

Hiroaki, Furuno (1987) 'Distaste for Power-Broking Could Cost Miyazawa Dear', *Japan Economic Newswire* 8 October.

Hirst, Paul Q. and G. Thompson (1996) *Globalization in Question: The International Economy and the Possibility of Governance*, Cambridge: Polity Press.

Hobson, John M. (1997) *The Wealth of States*, Cambridge: Cambridge University Press.

Hollerman, Leon (1998) 'Japan's Recession Is No Accident', *Asian Wall Street Journal* 27 July.

Hollingsworth, J. Roger and L. Lindberg (1994) *Governing Capitalist Economies: Performance and Control of Economic Sectors*, New York: Oxford University Press.

Hollingsworth, J. Roger and R. Boyer (eds) (1997) *Contemporary Capitalism: The Embeddedness of Institutions*, Cambridge: Cambridge University Press.

Hong, Tang Liang (1998) Tang Liang Hong homepage (http://www.ozemail.com. au/~tangtalk/).

Hopkins, N. (1998) 'Dollar Crisis Forecast', *The Australian* 3 June.

Horsley, N. (1997) 'Asia Needs a New Model', *AWSJ* 9 December: 8.

Howard, John (1998) Address to the World Economic Forum Dinner, Melbourne, 17 March.

Huang, Weiting (1996) *Zhongguo de yingxing jingji* [*China's Invisible Economy*], 2nd edn, Beijing: Zhongguo shangye chubanshe.

Hughes, H. (1998) 'IMF is Right on Indonesia', *AFR* 12 March: 18.

Hunt, E. (1979) *History of Economic Thought: A Critical Perspective*, California: Wadsworth.

Huntington, Samuel (1991) *The Third Wave: Democratization in the Late Twentieth Century*, Norman, OK: University of Oklahoma Press.

Hutchcroft, P. (1994) 'Booty Capitalism: Business–Government Relations in the Philippines', in A. MacIntyre (ed.), *Business and Government in Industrialising Asia*, pp. 216–43, Sydney: Allen and Unwin.

Hutton, Will (1997) *The State to Come*, London: Vintage.

Ibrahim, Anwar (1998) 'A Wave of Creative Destruction is Sweeping Asia', *International Herald Tribune* 2 June.

Ikenberry, G. John (1986) 'The Irony of State Strength: Comparative Responses to the Oil Shocks in the 1970s', *International Organization* 40(1): 105–37.

Ikenberry, G. John and C.A. Kupchan (1990) 'Socialisation and Hegemonic Power', *International Organization* 44(3): 283–315.

Imai, Ken-Ichi and H. Itami (1984) 'Interpenetration of Organization and Market', *International Journal of Industrial Organization* 2: 285–310.

Institute for International Finance (IIF) (1998) 'Capital Flows to Emerging Market Economies', 30 April (http://www.iif.com/about.htm).

Inter Press Service (1998) 'U.S. Lawmakers Assail IMF's Plea of Poverty', 26 July.

International Herald Tribune (1997) 'A Costly Dream: Home Ownership', in 'Fast Track 1997: Asia Business Outlook' (sponsored section), September.

International Monetary Fund (IMF) (1997) *World Economic Outlook, Interim Assessment*, Washington DC: IMF.

International Monetary Fund (IMF) (1998) 'Malaysia: Recent Economic Developments', Staff Country Report No. 98/9, January.

International Monetary Fund (IMF) (1998a) *World Economic Outlook*, Washington, DC : IMF.

Io, Jun (1995) 'Seizideki Kanryo to Gyoseideki Seizika' ['Political Bureaucrat and Administrative Politician'], *Japanese Political Science Review* Tokyo: Iwanamishoten.

Ipsen, Erik (1997) 'Asian Storm Soaks Ratings Firms', *International Herald Tribune* 22 November: 1.

Ishizuka, Masahiko (1997) 'Japan's Economy Must Be Model for Region', *The Nikkei Weekly* 29 September.

Jansen, Karel (1990) *Finance, Growth and Stability. Financing Economic Development in Thailand, 1960–86*, Avebury: Gower.

Jansen, Karel (1997) *External Finance in Thailand's Development. An Interpretation of Thailand's Growth Boom*, Basingstoke: Macmillan.

Jayasankaran, S. (1998) 'Art of the Bail', *Far Eastern Economic Review* 30 April: 62–3.

Jayasankaran, S. and M. Hiebert (1998) 'Calling for Daim', *Far Eastern Economic Review* 19 February: 14–17.

Jayasuriya, Kanishka (1994) 'The Political Economy of Central Banks', *Australian Journal of Political Science* 29(1): 115–34.

Jayasuriya, Kanishka (1995) 'Political Economy of Democratisation in East Asia', *Asian Perspective* 18(2) (Fall–Winter): 141–80.

Jayasuriya, Kanishka (1996) 'Rule of Law and Capitalism in East Asia', *Pacific Review* 9(3): 367–88.

Jayasuriya, Kanishka (1997) 'State, Market and the Rule of Law', Paper, International Studies Association Conference, Toronto.

Jayasuriya, Kanishka (1999) 'See Through a Glass, Darkly: Models of the Asian Currency Crisis of 1997–98' in Holger Henke and Ian Boxill (eds), *The End of the East Asian Model: a Reader in Comparative Development*, New York: Gruyter Books.

Jeong, Kap-young (1993) *The Industrial Organization of South Korea* [*Han'gukui sanop chojik*], Seoul: Pakyongsa.

Jessop, B. (1993) 'Towards a Schumpeterian Workfare State? Preliminary Remarks on Post Fordist Political Economy', *Studies in Political Economy* 40: 7–39.

Jesudason, James V. (1989) *Ethnicity and the Economy: The State, Chinese Business, and Multinationals in Malaysia*, Singapore: Oxford University Press.

Johnson, Chalmers (1982) *MITI and the Japanese Miracle: The Growth of Industrial Policy, 1925–1975*, Stanford, CA: Stanford University Press.

Johnson, Chalmers (1987) 'Political Institutions and Economic Performance: A Comparative Analysis of the Government–Business Relationship in Japan, South Korea, and Taiwan', in F. Deyo (ed.), *The Political Economy of the New Asian Industrialism*, Ithaca, NY: Cornell University Press.

Johnson, Chalmers (1998) 'Cold War Economics Melt Asia: A True "Asian model" Could Be the Cure, Not the Cause, of Crisis', *The Nation* 23 February.

Johnson, Chalmers (1998a) 'Enter the Dragon', *US News and World Report*, 30 March.

Johnson, Chalmers (1998b) 'Economic Crisis in East Asia: The Clash of Capitalisms', *Cambridge Journal of Economics* 22(6): 653–61.

Johnson, Ian (1998) 'Political Conflict Cleaves Malaysia's Old Power Pair', *Asian Wall Street Journal* 2 November.

Jomo, K.S. (1986) *A Question of Class: Capital, the State, and Uneven Development in Malaya*, Singapore: Oxford University Press.

Jomo, K.S. (1998) 'Malaysia: From Miracle to Debacle', in K.S. Jomo (ed.), *Tigers in Trouble: Financial Governance, Liberalisation and Crises in East Asia*, pp. 181–98, London: Zed Books.

Jomo, K.S. (ed.) (1998a) *Tigers in Trouble: Financial Governance, Liberalisation and Crises in East Asia*, London: Zed Books.

Jomo, K.S., Khoo Boo Teik and Chang Yii Tan (1996) 'Vision, Policy, and Governance in Malaysia', in L. Frischtak and I. Atiyas (eds), *Governance, Leadership, and Communication: Building Constituencies for Economic Reform*, pp. 65–89, Washington, DC: World Bank.

Jomo, K.S. *et al.* (1997) *Southeast Asia's Misunderstood Miracle*, Boulder, CO: Westview Press.

Jones, L. P. and Il Sakong (1980) *Government, Business and Entrepreneurship in Economic Development: The Korean Case*, Boston: Harvard University Press.

Jones, S. (1998) 'Indonesia: The Post-Soeharto Crisis', Testimony, US Congress, House of Representatives, Committee on International Relations, Subcommittee on Asia and the Pacific, 4 June (http://www.hrw.org/press98/june/testim.htm).

Junankar, P.N. and C.A. Kapusinski (1998) 'Was Working Nation Working?', *Journal of Industrial Relations* 40(1): 24–41.

Kahler, Miles (1990) 'The United States and the International Monetary Fund: Declining Influence or Declining Interest', in Margaret P. Karns and Karen A. Mingst (eds), *The United States and Multilateral Institutions*, Boston: Unwin Hyman.

Kane, Solomon and L. Passicousset (1998) 'Comment le general Suharto a été contraint à la demission', *Le Monde Diplomatique* Juin: 8–9.

Kang, David C. (1996) 'South Korean and Taiwanese Development and the New Institutional Economics', *International Organization* 49: 555–87.

Kaptein, E. (1993) 'Neoliberalism and the Dismantling of Corporatism in Australia', in H. Overbeek (ed.), *Restructuring Hegemony in the Global Political Economy: The Rise of Transnational Neo-liberalism in the 1980s*, pp. 79–109, London: Routledge.

Kato, Junko (1994) *The Problem of Bureaucratic Rationality: Tax Politics in Japan*, Princeton, NY: Princeton University Press.

Katzenstein, Peter J. (1978) *Between Power and Plenty: Foreign Economic Policies of Advanced Industrial States*, Madison, WI: University of Wisconsin Press.

Keating, Paul (1998) 'The Perilous Moment: Indonesia, Australia and the Asian Crisis', Public Lecture at the University of New South Wales, 25 March.

Keenan, Faith *et al.* (1998) 'Desperate Measures', *Far Eastern Economic Review* 10 September: 12.

Kelly, P. (1997) 'US Imperatives Rule in Maturing APEC', *The Australian* 27 November.

Kelly, Paul (1992) *The End of Certainty: The Story of the 1980s*, Sydney: Allen and Unwin.

Khan, Mushtaq (1996) 'An Input–Output Framework for the Analysis of Rent-seeking', Paper presented at the international workshop on Rent-Seeking in Southeast Asia, University of Malaya, Kuala Lumpur, August.

Khoo Boo Teik (1995) *Paradoxes of Mahathirism: An Intellectual Biography of Mahathir Mohamad*, Kuala Lumpur: Oxford University Press.

Khoo Boo Teik (1997) 'Economic Vision and Political Opposition in Malaysia Since 1981: The Politics of the Mahathir Era', in Peter Wad (ed.), *Transforming*

Malaysia, Special issue of *The Copenhagen Journal of Asian Studies* 12(December): 3–34.

Khoo Boo Teik (1998) 'All Over? Or All Over Again', *Aliran Monthly* 18(8): 6–8.

Khoo Boo Teik (1998a) 'Reflections on the UMNO General Assembly', *Aliran Monthly* 18(2): 2–7.

Khor, Martin (1997) 'Led Astray by Blind Faith in IMF Policies', *Sunday Star* 14 December.

Khor, Martin (1998) 'A Poor Grade for the IMF', *The Far Eastern Economic Review* 15 January: 29.

Kim Dae-jung (1985) *Mass-Participatory Economy. A Democratic Alternative for Korea*, Boston: University Press of America.

Kim Dae-Jung (1986) *Mass Participatory Economy: A Democratic Alternative for Korea*, Lanham, MD: University Press of America.

Kim Dae-Jung (1997) *Daejung Chanyeo Kyungjaeron* [*Mass Participatory Economy: A Democratic Alternative for Korea*], Seoul: Sanha.

Kim Dae-jung (1998) 'Economic Reform in Korea: Establishment of a Democratic Market Economy', Address at Stanford University, 12 June, *Korea and World Affairs* 22(2): 279–83.

Kim Hyuk-Rae (1993) 'Divergent Organizational Paths of Industrialization in East Asia', *Asian Perspective* 17: 105–35.

Kim Hyuk-Rae (1994) 'The State and Economic Organization in a Comparative Perspective: The Organizing Mode of the East Asian Political Economy', *Korean Social Science Journal* 20: 91–120.

Kim Hyuk-Rae (1998) 'Korean Economic Governance: Its Development and Future Prospect', Paper presented at the 10th Annual International Conference on Socio-Economics at the Vienna International Centre in Vienna, Austria, 13–16 July.

Kim Hyuk-Rae (1998a) 'Family Capitalism and Corporate Structure in South Korea', *Korea Focus* 6: 55–67.

Kim Hyuk-Rae (1998b) 'The Evolution of the Korean Business System', *Sangnam Forum* 1: 81–109.

Kindleberger, Charles P. (1996) *Manias, Panics and Crashes: A History of Financial Crises*, 3rd edn, New York: John Wiley.

Kitamura, Kayoko and T. Tanaka (eds) (1997) *Examining Asia's Tigers: Nine Economies Challenging Common Structural Problems*, Tokyo, Institute of Developing Economies.

Kohler, A. (1998) 'The Risk of Recession', *Australian Financial Review* 18–19 July.

Kohn, Meir (1994) *Financial Institutions and Markets*, New York: McGraw-Hill..

Korean Commerce Chamber (1993) *Sinkyungzae Ogaenyunkaehyok Bogoseo* [*Report on New Economy Five-Year Plan*], Seoul: Korean Commerce Chamber.

Kornai, J. (1992) *The Socialist System: The Political Economy of Communism*, Princeton, NJ: Princeton University Press.

Krasner, S. (1983) *International Regimes*, Ithaca, NY: Cornell University Press.

Krasner, Stephen D. (1978) *Defending the National Interest*, Princeton, NJ: Princeton University Press.

Krause, Lawrence (1998) 'The Economy and Politics of the Asian Financial Crisis of 1997-1998', Council on Foreign Relations Corporate Conference.

Krauss, E. (1992) 'Political Economy: Policymaking and Industrial Policy in Japan', *Political Science and Politics* 25(March): 44–57.

Krirkkiat Pipatseritham (1983) *Wikhro laksana kan pen chaohong thurakit khanat yai nai prathet thai*, Bangkok: Thai Khadi Research Institute.

Krueger, A.O. (1974) 'The Political-Economy of the Rent-Seeking Society', *American Economic Review* 64(June): 291–30.

Krugman, Paul (1994) 'The Myth of Asia's Miracle' (http://web.mit.edu/krugman/www/myth.html), Originally published in *Foreign Affairs* 73(6): 62–78.

Krugman, Paul (1998) 'What Happened to Asia?' (http://web.mit.edu/krugman/www/DISINTER.html).

Krugman, Paul (1998a) 'Malaysia's Opportunity', *Far Eastern Economic Review* 17 September: 32.

Krugman, Paul (1998b) 'Setting Sun Japan: What Went Wrong?' (http://web.mit.edu/krugman), June.

Krugman, Paul (1998c) 'Japan's Trap' (http://web.mit.edu/krugman), May.

Krugman, Paul (1998d) 'Will Asia Bounce Back?', Speech to Credit Suisse First Boston, Hong Kong, March (http://web.mit.edu/krugman/www/suisse.html).

Kumar, Anjali (1994) 'Economic Reform and the Internal Division of Labour in China: Production, Trade and Markets', in David Goodman and Gerald Segal (eds), *China Deconstructs: Politics, Trade and Regionalism*, p. 105, New York and London: Routledge.

Kwon, Heok-Tae (1998) *Ilbonkyongjaeui Yikiwa Sisajeom* [*The Crisis and Implications of Japanese Economy*], Seoul: Samsung Economic Research Institute.

Lee, C.H. and S. Naya (1988) 'Trade in East Asian Development with Comparative Reference to Southeast Asian Experiences', *Economic Development and Cultural Change* 36: 123–52.

Lee, Su-Hoon (1993) 'Transitional Politics of Korea, 1987–1992: Activation of Civil Society', *Pacific Affairs* 66: 351–67.

Lee, Yeon-ho (1996) 'Political Aspects of South Korean State Autonomy: Regulating the Chaebol 1980–1993', *The Pacific Review* 9(2): 149–79.

Lee, Yeon-ho (1997) *The State, Society and Big Business in South Korea*, London: Routledge.

Lee, Yeon-ho (1997a) 'The Limits of Economic Globalization in East Asian Developmental States', *The Pacific Review* 10(2): 366–90.

Lee, Yeon-ho (1998) 'Development, Capitalism and the State in Southeast and Northeast Asia', *Korea Observer* 29: Summer.

Leech, Dennis (1998) 'Power Relations in the IMF: A Study of the Political Economy of A Priori Voting Power Using the Theory of Simple Games', Working Paper 06/98, Warwick University: Centre for the Study of Globalisation and Regionalisation.

Leftwich, A. (1994) 'Governance, the State and the Politics of Development', *Development and Change* 25(2): 363–86.

Leyshon, A. (1994) 'Under Pressure: Finance, Geo-Economic Competition and the Rise and Fall of Japan's Postwar Growth Economy', in S. Corbridge *et al.* (eds), *Money, Power and Space*, pp. 116–45, Oxford: Blackwell.

Li, Junbo (1997) 'The Four Major Difficulties of Our Country's Textile Industry', *Zhongguo guoqinguoli* No. 8: 28–9.

Liddle, R. (1991) 'The Relative Autonomy of the Third World Politician: Suharto and Indonesia's Economic Development in Comparative Perspective', *International Studies Quarterly* 35: 403–25.

Lietaer, B. (1997) 'Global Currency Speculation and Its Implications', *Third World Resurgence*, 87/88: 15–17.

Lim Kit Siang (1998) *Economic and Financial Crisis*, Petaling Jaya: Democratic Action Party Economic Committee.

Lim, Linda (1998) *The Political Economy of a City-State. Government-made Singapore*, Singapore: Oxford University Press.

Lim, Linda (1998a) 'Crisis and Conspiracy', *The Far Eastern Economic Review* 19 March: 31.

Lin, Shenmu (ed.) (1993) *Zhongguo guding zican touzi touxi* [*An Analysis of China's Fixed-asset Investment*], Beijing: Zhongguo fazhan chubanshe.

Lindblom, Charles E. (1982) 'The Market as Prison', *Journal of Politics* 44: 324–36.

Lindsey, Charles (1992) 'The Political Economy of Economic Policy Reform in the Philippines: Continuity and Restoration', in Andrew MacIntyre and Kanishka Jayasuriya (eds), *The Dynamics of Economic Policy Reform in Southeast Asia and the Southwest Pacific*, Singapore: Oxford University Press.

Ling, Tom (1998) *The British State since 1945*, Cambridge: Polity Press.

Lissakers, K. (1998) Hearing to Review the Operations of the International Monetary Fund (IMF), US Congress, House of Representatives, Committee on Banking and Financial Services, General Oversight Subcommittee, Hearing Transcript, 21 April (http://commdocs.house.gov/committees/bank/hba48110.000/hba48110_0f.htm).

Longman, P.J. and S. Ahmad (1998) 'The Bailout Backlash', *US News and World Report* 2 February.

Lucas, Robert E. (1993) 'Making a Miracle', *Econometrica* 61(2).

Luttwak, E. (1990) 'From Geopolitics to Geo-Economics', *The National Interest* Summer: 17–23.

Ma, Hong (ed.) (1998) *The Economic White Book 1997–98*, Beijing: Zhonguo fazhan chubanshe.

Mabuchi, Masaru (1994) *Okurashotouseino Seijikeizaigaku* [*Political Economy of MOF's Control*], Tokyo: Chouo Koronsha.

Mabuchi, Masaru (1997) *Okurashowa Naze Oitsumeraretanoka* [*Why Has the MOF Been Bashed?*], Tokyo: Chouo Koronsha.

Machado, Kit (1989–90) 'Japanese Transnational Corporations in Malaysia's State Sponsored Heavy Industrialization Drive: The HICOM Automobile and Steel Projects', *Pacific Affairs* 62: 504–31.

Machado, Kit (1994) 'Proton and Malaysia's Motor Vehicle Industry: National Industrial Policies and Japanese Regional Production Strategies', in K.S. Jomo (ed.), *Japan and Malaysian Development: In the Shadow of the Rising Sun*, pp. 291–325, London, Routledge.

Macfarlane, I. (1998) 'Some Thoughts on Australia's Position in Light of Recent Events in Asia', *Reserve Bank Bulletin* April: 1–8.

MacIntyre, A. (1992) 'Politics and the Reorientation of Economic Policy in Indonesia', in A. MacIntyre and K. Jayasuriya (eds), *The Dynamics of Economic*

Policy Reform in South-east Asia and the South-west Pacific, pp. 138–57, Singapore: Oxford University Press.

MacIntyre, A. (1994) 'Business, Government and Development: Northeast and Southeast Asian Comparisons', in A. MacIntyre (ed.), *Business and Government in Industrialising Asia*, pp. 1–28, St Leonards: Allen and Unwin.

MacIntyre, Andrew J. (1993) 'The Politics of Finance in Indonesia: Command, Confusion, and Competition', in S. Haggard, C.H. Lee and S. Maxfield (eds), *The Politics of Finance in Developing Countries*, Ithaca, NY: Cornell University Press.

Mack, Andrew and J. Ravenhill (eds) (1994) *Pacific Cooperation: Building Economic and Security Regimes in the Asia-Pacific Region*, St Leonards: Allen and Unwin.

Mahathir, Mohamad (1986) *The Challenge*, Petaling Jaya: Pelanduk.

Mahathir, Mohamad (1986a) Speech at the Seminar on Primary Commodities, *Foreign Affairs Malaysia* 19(2): 6–10.

Mahathir, Mohamad (1991) 'Malaysia: The Way Forward', Paper presented at the Inaugural Meeting of the Malaysian Business Council, Kuala Lumpur, 28 February. Reprinted in *New Straits Times* 2 March.

Mahathir, Mohamad (1997) Speech at the Annual Seminar of the World Bank, Hong Kong, 20 September. Reprinted as 'Asian Economies: Challenges and Opportunities', *Foreign Affairs Malaysia* 30 (3): 61–9.

Mahathir, Mohamad (1998) 'Call Me a Heretic', *Time* 14 September: 21.

Mahathir, Mohamad (1998a) Speech at the 52nd UMNO General Assembly, Kuala Lumpur, 19 June. Reprinted as 'All Malaysians Should Defend our Sovereignty', *New Straits Times* 20 June.

Malaysia. National Economic Action Council (1998) *National Economic Recovery Plan: Agenda For Action*, Kuala Lumpur.

Mann, Michael (1988) *States, War and Capitalism*, Oxford: Basil Blackwell.

Marshall, J. (1998) 'Credit Risk: Active Managing Pays Off', *US Banker* March.

Marx, Karl (1969) The Eighteenth Brumaire of Louis Bonaparte', from excerpts in L.S. Feuer (ed.), *Marx and Engels: Basic Writings on Politics and Philosophy*, London: Fontana.

Marx, Karl (1978) *Capital*, Vol. 2, Harmondsworth: Pelican.

Marx, Karl (1978a) *Capital*, Vol. 3, Harmondsworth: Pelican.

Mathews, John (1998) 'Fashioning a New Korean Model out of the Crisis: the Rebuilding of Institutional Capabilities', *Cambridge Journal of Economics* 22(6): 747–59.

Maull, H.W. (1990–1) 'Germany and Japan: The New Civilian Powers', *Foreign Affairs* 69(5).

Maurice, M., A. Sorge and M. Warner (1980) 'Societal Differences in Organizing Manufacturing Units', *Organization Studies* 1: 59–86.

Mauro, Paolo (1997) 'Why Worry About Corruption?', *IMF Economic Issues* 6.

Masahiko Ishizuka (1997) 'Japan's Economy Must Be Model for Region', *The Nikkei Weekly* 29 September.

Maxfield, S. (1994) 'Financial Incentives and Central Bank Authority in Industrialising Nations', *World Politics* 46: 556–88.

McDermott, Darren (1996) 'Singapore Swing: Krugman Was Right. Stung by a Professor, the Island Starts an Efficiency Drive', *The Wall Street Journal* 23 October (http://www.stern.nyu.edu/~nroubini/asia/AsiaHomepage,html).

Mehmet, Ozay (1986) *Development in Malaysia: Poverty, Wealth and Trusteeship*, London: Croom Helm.

Mehta, H. (1998) 'Thailand Calling the Shots in IMF Talks, Say Analysts', *The Business Times* 7 August.

Miller, W.H. (1998) 'Uphill Battle for IMF Funding', *Industry Week* 16 March.

Milner, H.V. and R.O. Keohane (1996) 'Internationalization and Domestic Politics: An Introduction', in H.V. Milner and R.O. Keohane (eds), *Internationalization and Domestic Politics*, pp. 3–24, Cambridge: Cambridge University Press.

Milward, A. (1992) *The European Rescue of the Nation State*, London: Routledge.

Mingsarn Kaosa-ard (1998) 'Economic Development and Institutional Failures in Thailand', *TDRI Quarterly Review* 13(1): 3–11.

Ministry of Finance (1998) 'Joint Statement by the Ministry of Finance and the Bank of Thailand. Financial Sector Restructuring for Economic Recovery', Bangkok: Ministry of Finance and Bank of Thailand, 14 August.

Ministry of Finance and Economy (1998) *Inside Report*, Seoul: MOFE.

Ministry of Finance and Economy (1998a) Press statement on 'Outline of new legislation to reform the central banking and financial supervisory systems' (http://kiep.go.kr/imf/hot-2–2l.htm), 1 December.

Miwa, Yoshira (1993) *Ginnyu Gyousei Kaikaku* [*Financial and Administrative Reform*], Tokyo: Nihhon Keizai Shimbunsha.

Mo, Jongryn (1996) 'Political Learning and Democratic Consolidation: Korean Industrial Relations, 1987–1992', *Comparative Political Studies* 29: 290–311.

Mo, Jongryn and Chung-in Moon (1998) 'Democracy and the Korean Economic Crisis', *NAPSNet Forum* #15 (http://www.nautilus.org/napsnet/fora/15A_MoandMoon.html).

Moon, Chung-in (1998) 'Democratization and Globalization as Ideological and Political Foundations of Economic Policy', in Jongryn Mo and Chung-in Moon (ed.), *Democracy and the Korean Economy*, Stanford, CA: Hoover Institution Press.

Moon, Chung-in and S. Haggard (1983) 'The South Korean State in the International Economy: Liberal, Dependent or Mercantile', in John Ruggie (ed.), *Antinomies of Interdependence*, New York: Columbia University Press.

Moon, Chung-in and R. Prasad (1994) 'Beyond the Developmental State: Networks, Politics, and Institutions', *Governance* 7(4).

Moore M. (1987) 'From Statism to Pluralism: Government and Agriculture in Taiwan and South Korea', in G. White (ed.), *Developmental States in East Asia*, London: Macmillan.

Muehring, K. (1997) 'It's Summers' Time', *Institutional Investor* December.

Mussa, M. and G. Hache (1998) 'Take the IMF Medicine and You Will Soon Mend', *International Herald Tribune* 17–18 January: 6.

Nader, R. (1998) Testimony, US Congress, House of Representatives, Committee on Banking and Financial Services, Sub-Committee on General Oversight and Investigations, 21 April (http://www.house.gov/banking/42198nad.htm).

Nakatani, Iwao (1996) *Nippon Keizaino Rekisiteki Tenkan* [*Historical Transformation of the Japanese Economy*], Tokyo: Toyokeizai Shimbosha.

Nation (1998) Editorial, 18 June.

Nee, Victor (1992) 'Organizational Dynamics of Market Transition: Hybrid Forms, Property Rights, and Mixed Economy in China', *Administrative Quarterly* 37: 1–27.

Neher, Clark D. and R. Marlay (1995) *Democracy and Development in Southeast Asia: The Winds of Change*, Boulder, CO: Westview Press.

New Straits Times (1998) 'Moves Are Intended to Insulate Malaysia from Further Instability', 2 September.

New Straits Times (1998a) 'Move Will Revive Investor and Consumer Confidence', 2 September.

New Straits Times (1998b) 'Dr M: The Ringgit's Stability Is Crucial', 2 September.

New Straits Times (1998c) 'PM: "New Capitalists" May Dominate Asian Economies', 5 June.

Niskanen, W.A. (1998) Statement, US Congress, Joint Economic Committee, Hearing into The IMF and International Monetary Policy, 5 May (http://www.house.gov/jec/hearings/imf2/niskanen.htm).

Noguchi, Yukio (1995) *Senkyuhyakuyonjunen Taisei* [*The Japanese 1940 Year System*], Tokyo: Toyokeizai Shimbosha.

Noland, Marcus (1998) 'The Financial Crisis in Asia', Statement to the House of Representatives International Relations Committee, Subcommittees on Asian and Pacific Affairs, and International Economics and Trade, Institute for International Economics (http://www.ipe.com/jmn2–3.htm).

North, Douglass C. (1981) *Structure and Change in Economic History*, New York: Norton.

North, Douglass C. (1990) *Institutions, Institutional Change and Economic Performance*, Cambridge: Cambridge University Press.

North, Douglass C. (1994) 'Economic Performance through Time', *American Economic Review* 84(3): 359–68.

North, Douglass C. (1995) 'The New Institutional Economics and Third World Development', in J. Harris, J. Hunter and C.M. Lewis (eds), *The New Institutional Economics and Third World Development*, London: Routledge.

Nuntawan Polkwamdee (1997) 'Banking and Finance. Lesson on Greed and Laxity', in Bangkok Post (eds), *Economic Review 1997*, Bangkok: Post Publishing (http://www.bangkokpost.com/ecoreview97/review9709.html).

Oakeshott, M. (1975) *On Human Conduct*, Oxford: Clarendon Press.

Observer (1998) 21 June: B.4.

O'Connor, James (1984) *Accumulation Crisis*, Oxford: Basil Blackwell.

OECD (1998) *OECD Economic Surveys: 1997–1998, KOREA*, Paris: OECD.

Ohmae, Kenichi (1990) *The Borderless World*, New York: Harper Business.

Ohmae, Kenichi (1995) *The End of the Nation State: The Rise of Regional Economies*, London: Harper Collins.

Oi, Jean (1992) 'Fiscal Reform and the Economic Foundations of Local State Corporatism in China', *World Politics* 45(October): 99–126.

Oi, Jean (1995) 'The Role of the Local State in China's Transitional Economy', *China Quarterly* No. 145.

Okimoto, Daniel I. (1989) *Between MITI and the Market: Japanese Industrial Policy for High Technology*, Stanford, CA: Stanford University Press.

Oksenberg, Michel and K. Lieberthal (1986) 'Bureaucratic Politics and Chinese Energy Development', US Department of Commerce, International Trade Administration.

Olson, Mancur (1982) *The Rise and Decline of Nations: Economic Growth, Stagflation and Social Rigidities*, New Haven, CT: Yale University Press.

Otake, Hideo (1997) *Gyoukakuno Hassou* [*Initiative for the Administrative Reform*], Tokyo: TBS Britannica.

Ouattara, Alassane D. (1998) 'The Asian Crisis: Origins and Lessons', Address to the Royal Academy of Morocco Seminar on 'Why Have the Asian Dragons Caught Fire?', Fez, 4 May (http://www.imf.org/external/np/speeches/1998/050498A.HTM).

Oviedo, Sheila and H.F. Oviedo (1997) 'Will Real Estate Go Bust?', *International Herald Tribune* 6 May.

Pandiyan, M.V. (1998) 'Globalisation "a Means, not an End"', *The Star* 29 July (http://www.jaring.my/~star/current/29vpgl.html).

Pangestu, M. (1996) *Economic Reform, Deregulation and Privatization: The Indonesian Experience*, Jakarta: Centre for Strategic and International Studies.

Pangestu, M. (1998) 'More Misery Ahead', *Far Eastern Economic Review* 19 February: 52–3.

Panitch, L. (1994) 'Globalization and the State', in R. Miliband and L. Panitch (eds), *Socialist Register*, Toronto: University of Toronto Press.

Pasuk Phongpaichit (1995) *Thailand. Economy and Politics*, Kuala Lumpur: Oxford University Press.

Pasuk Phongpaichit and C. Baker (1996) *Thailand's Boom!*, Chiangmai: Silkworm Books.

Pasuk Phongpaichit and C. Baker (1997) 'Power in Transition: Thailand in the 1990s', in Kevin Hewison (ed.), *Political Change in Thailand. Democracy and Participation*, pp. 21–41, London: Routledge.

Pasuk Phongpaichit and C. Baker (1998) 'We Need a Crisis to Rethink Issues like Participation and Sustainable Development', *Watershed* 3(2): 22–3.

Pauly, Louis. W. (1988) *Opening Financial Markets: Banking Politics on the Pacific Rim*, Ithaca, NY: Cornell University Press.

Pauly, Louis W. (1997) *Who Elected the Bankers? Surveillance and Control in the World Economy*, Ithaca, NY: Cornell University Press.

Peacock A. and H. Willgerodt (1989) *German Neoliberals and the Social Market Economy*, London: Macmillan.

Pempel, T.J. and K. Tsunekawa (1979) 'Corporatism without Labor? The Japanese Anomaly', in G. Lehmbruch and P.C. Schmitter (eds), *Trends Toward Corporatist Intermediation*, Beverly Hills, CA: Sage.

Perraton, J. *et al.* (1997) 'The Globalization of Economic Activity', *New Political Economy* 2(2): 257–79.

Petersmann, E. (1991) *Constitutional Functions and Constitutional Problems in International Economic Law*, Boulder, CO: Westview Press.

Philippine Daily Inquirer (1997) 'DMG Advises Caution on RP Banks', Reuters, 13 September.

Philippine Daily Inquirer (1997a) 'Market-determined Exchange Rate Here to Stay', 11 July.

Philippine Daily Inquirer (1997b) 'Banks Make Killing over the Counter', 15 July.

Polanyi, Karl (1944) *The Great Transformation*, Boston: Beacon.

Pollack, Norman (1962) *The Populist Response to Industrial America*, Cambridge, MA: Harvard University Press.

Radelet, Steven and J. Sachs (1997) 'Asia's Reemergence', *Foreign Affairs* 76(6): 44–59.

Radelet, Steven and J. Sachs (1998) 'The Onset of the East Asian Financial Crisis', Cambridge, MA: Harvard Institute for International Development, 30 March (http://www.stern.nyu.edu/~nroubini/asia/AsiaHomepage.html).

RAM (1997) 'Malaysia Inc. Falters', *Aliran Monthly* 17(7): 2–7.

RAM (1997a) 'Dismal Reaction', *Aliran Monthly* 17(9): 2–6.

RAM (1998) 'The NEAC: Accountability Subverted', *Aliran Monthly* 18(2): 2–5.

Ramirez, M.D. (1991) 'The Impact of Austerity in Latin America, 1983–89: A Critical Assessment', *Comparative Economic Studies* 33(1).

Ramseyer, Mark and Frances M. Rosenbluth (1997) *Japan's Political Marketplace*, Boston: Harvard University Press.

Rapkin, D.P., J.U. Elston and J.R. Strand (1997) 'Institutional Adjustment to Changed Power Distributions: Japan and the United States in the IMF', *Global Governance* 3(2).

Rasiah, Rajah (1995) *Foreign Capital and Industrialisation in Malaysia*, London: Macmillan.

Redding, S.G. (1990) *The Spirit of Chinese Capitalism*, Berlin: Walter de Gruyter.

Richardson, M. (1998) 'Uncle Sam Risks Virulent Nationalist Backlash', *The Australian* 13 January.

Rix, Alan (1993) 'Japan and the Region: Leading from Behind', in R. Higgott, R. Leaver and J. Ravenhill (eds), *Pacific Economic Relations in the 1990s: Cooperation or Conflict?*, Boulder, CO: Lynne Rienner.

Roberts, P.C. (1997) 'Asian Crisis Proves That Industrial Policy Doesn't Pay', *Australian Financial Review* 20–21 December: 47.

Robison, Richard (1986) *Indonesia: the Rise of Capital*, Sydney: Allen and Unwin.

Robison, Richard (1987) 'After the Gold Rush: The Politics of Economic Restructuring in Indonesia in the 1980s', in R. Robison, K. Hewison and R. Higgott (eds), *Southeast Asia in the 1980s: The Politics of Economic Crisis*, pp 16–49, Sydney: Allen and Unwin.

Robison, Richard (1988) 'Authoritarian States, Capital Owning Classes, and the Politics of Newly Industrializing Countries: The Case of Indonesia', *World Politics* XLI(1): 52–74.

Robison, Richard (1996) 'Looking North: Myths and Strategies', in R. Robison (ed.), *Pathways to Asia: The Politics of Engagement*, Sydney: Allen and Unwin.

Robison, Richard (1997) 'Politics and Markets in Indonesia's Post-Oil Era', in G. Rodan *et al.* (eds), *The Political Economy of South-East Asia: An Introduction*, pp. 29–63, Melbourne: Oxford University Press.

Robison, Richard and D. Goodman (eds) (1996) *The New Rich in Asia: Mobile Phones, McDonalds and Middle Class Revolution*, pp. 2–3, London: Routledge.

Robison, Richard, K. Hewison and R. Higgott (eds) (1987) *Southeast Asia in the 1980s: The Politics of Economic Crisis*, Sydney: Allen and Unwin.

Rodan, Garry (1989) *The Political Economy of Singapore's Industrialization: National State and International Capital*, London: Macmillan.

Rodan, Garry (1996) 'Theorizing Political Opposition in East and Southeast Asia', in Garry Rodan (ed.), *Political Oppositions in Industrializing Asia*, London: Routledge.

Rodan, Garry, K. Hewison and R. Robison (1997) *The Political Economy of South-East Asia: An Introduction*, Melbourne: Oxford University Press.

ROK Government (1993) *The Five-year New Economy Plan, 1993–97*, Seoul: ROK Government.

Rose, Michael (1985) 'Universalism, Culturalism, and the Aix Group', *European Sociological Review* 1: 650–83.

Rose, N. (1993) 'Government, Authority and Expertise in Advanced Liberalism', *Economy and Society* 22 (3): 283–99.

Rosecrance, Richard (1986) *The Rise of the Trading State. Commerce and Conquest in the Modern World*, New York: Basic Books.

Roubini, N., G. Corsetti, and P. Pesenti (1998) 'What Caused the Asian Currency and Financial Crisis?', Unpublished paper (http://www.stern.nyu.edu/~nroubini/asia/AsiaHomepage.html), 8 February 1999.

Rowley, A. (1998) 'Yen Set to Renew Drift in Absence of G-7 Pledge', *The Business Times* 22 June.

Rubin, R. (1998) Remarks to Students and Faculty of Georgetown University, *Federal News Service* 21 January.

Rubinstein, Murray A. (ed.) (1994) *The Other Taiwan. 1945 to the Present*, Armonk, NY: M.E. Sharpe.

Ruey-Long Chen, Steve (Director General, Board of Foreign Trade, Taipei) (1998) 'Taiwan and the Asian Financial Crisis', Seminar, Australian National University, 11 May.

Ruggie, J. (1983) 'International Regimes, Transactions, and Change: Embedded Liberalism in the Postwar Economic Order', in S. Krasner (ed.), *International Regimes*, Ithaca, NY: Cornell University Press.

Sachs, Jeffrey (1997) 'IMF Orthodoxy Isn't What Southeast Asia Needs', *International Herald Tribune* 4 November: 8.

Sachs, Jeffrey (1997a) 'The Limits of Convergence. Nature, Nurture and Growth', *The Economist* 14 June: 19–22.

Sachs, Jeffrey (1998) 'International Economics: Unlocking the Mysteries of Globalization', *Foreign Policy* 110: 97–111.

Sachs, Jeffrey (1998a) 'Voting Against the American Way', *The WorldPaper Online* January (http://www.worldpaper.com/Jan98/sachs.html).

Sachs, Jeffrey (1998b) 'Tipping the Scales', *The WorldPaper Online* March (http://www.worldpaper.com/March98/sachs.html).

Sachs, Jeffrey (1998c) 'Global Capitalism', *Economist* 12 September: 19–23.

Sachs, Jeffrey (1998d) 'The IMF and the Asian Flu', *The American Prospect* No. 37 (http://epn.org/prospect/37/37sachfs.html).

Sakakibara, Eisuke (1995) *Nitsibeouno Keizai Shakai System* [*Socio-Economic System among Japan, US and Europe*], Tokyo: Toyokeizai Shinmbosha.

Sakakibara, Eisuke (1997) *Shinseikieno Kouzoukaikaku* [*Structural Reform for New Century from Progress to Symbiosis*], Tokyo: The Yomiuri Shimbun Sha.

Saludo, Richard and A. Shameen (1997) 'A Question of Openess', *Asiaweek* 3 October: 62–3.

Saludo, Richard and A. Shameen (1998) 'How Much Longer?', *Asiaweek* 17 July: 36–44.

Samonte, Sheila and E. Garcia (1997) 'Risky Business', *Business World* 2 April.

Samonte, Sheila and E. Garcia (1997a) 'The Next Crisis?', *Business World* 31 March.

Samsung Economic Research Institute (1995) 'Keumyungkikwan Bushilhwa Shitaewa Kwajae' ['Reality and Policy in Deteriorated Banking Sector'], November.

Samsung Economic Research Institute (1998) 'Six Months after the IMF Bailout: A Review of Social and Economic Changes in Korea', July.

Samuels, Richard (1987) *The Business of the Japanese State: Energy Markets in Comparative and Historical Perspective*, Ithaca, NY: Cornell University Press.

Samuels, Richard (1996) *Rich Nation, Strong Army*, Ithaca, NY, and London: Cornell University Press.

Sanger, D.E. (1998) 'I.M.F. Loans to Rights Violators Are Attacked in Congress', *New York Times* 22 April.

Sassen, S. (1997) 'Territory and Territoriality in the Global Economy', Paper presented at the conference on 'Non-State Actors in the Global System', University of Warwick.

Saunders, D. (1998) 'Trade Flows Trickle to Halt Amid Bleak Recovery Hopes', *South China Morning Post* 23 July.

Screpanti, Ernesto and S. Zamagni (1993) *An Outline of the History of Economic Thought*, Oxford: Oxford University Press.

Searle, Peter (1998) *The Riddle of Malaysian Capitalism. Rent-seekers or Real Capitalists?*, St Leonards: Allen and Unwin.

Seelye, K.Q. (1998) 'G.O.P. in Switch, Backs More Funds to Shore up I.M.F', *New York Times* 15 July.

Seow, Francis T. (1994) *To Catch a Tartar. A Dissident in Lee Kuan Yew's Prison*, Southeast Asia Studies Monograph No. 42, New Haven, CT: Yale University Press.

Shameen, Assif (1998) 'The Bailout Business', *Asiaweek* 27 March: 30–1.

Sheard, Paul (1997) *Mainbank Shihonshugino Kiki* [*The Crisis of Main Bank Capitalism*], Tokyo: Toyo Keizai Shimbo Sha.

Shenon, P. (1998) 'Wrangling over I.M.F. Bill at Fever Pitch', *New York Times* 8 October.

Shin, Y. (1989) 'Demystifying the Capitalist State: Political Patronage, Bureaucratic Interests and Capitalists in Formation in Soeharto's Indonesia', Ph.D. Dissertation, Yale University.

Shirazi, Javad K. (1998) 'The East Asian Crisis: Origins, Policy Challenges and Prospects' (http://www.worldbank.org/html/offrep/eap/jkssp061098.htm).

Siew, Vincent C. (1998) 'Taiwan Weathers the Asian Financial Crisis', *Industry of Free China* 88(6): 65–9.

Sjahrir (1992) *Refleksi Pembangunan: Ekonomi Indonesia 1968–1992*, Jakarta: Gramedia Pustaka Utama.

Sjahrir (1988) 'Ekonomi Politik Deregulas', *Prisma* (9): 29–38.

Sklar, Martin J. (1988) *The Corporate Reconstruction of American Capitalism 1890–1916: The Market, the Laws and Politics*, Cambridge: Cambridge University Press.

Skocpol, T. (1979) *States and Social Revolutions: A Comparative Analysis of France, Russia and China*, Cambridge: Cambridge University Press.

Skocpol, T. (1985) 'Bringing the State Back in: Strategies of Analysis in Current Research', in B. Evans, D. Rueschemeyer and T. Skocpol (eds), *Bringing the State Back in*, New York: State University Press.

Skulley, M. and L. Dodson (1997) 'Big Business Blasts Coalition', *Financial Review* 16 May.

Smith, Adam (1993) *Wealth of Nations*, Oxford: Oxford University Press.

So, A.Y and S.W.K. Chiu (1995) *East Asia and the World Economy*, London: Sage.

Soros, Georg (1997) 'The Capitalist Threat', *The Atlantic Monthly* February.

Spaeth, Andrew (1998) 'He's the Boss', *Time* 14 September: 16–20.

Spaeth, Andrew (1998a) 'Broken Dreams', *Time* 15 June: 24–8.

Srisuwan Kuankachorn (1998) 'The Roots of the Thai Crisis: A Failure of Development', *Watershed* 3(3): 37–40.

Stallings, B. (ed.) (1995) *Global Change, Regional Response*, Cambridge: Cambridge University Press.

The Star (1988) 'High Interest Rates not for Us', 1 July.

State Statistical Bureau of China (SSB) (1997) 'Economic Situation of 1996 and Prospectus for 1997', *Renminribao* 23 January.

State Statistical Bureau of China (SSB) (1998) *A Statistical Survey of China 1998*, Beijing: Zhongguo tongji chubanshe.

Stewart, F. (1987) 'Back to Keynesianism: Reforming the IMF', *World Policy Journal* 4(3).

Stigler, George J. (1975) *The Citizen and the State: Essays on Regulation*, Chicago: University of Chicago Press.

Stiglitz, Joseph (1998) 'The Role of International Financial Institutions in the Current Global Economy', Address to the Chicago Council on Foreign Relations, Chicago, 27 February.

Stiglitz, Joseph (1998a) 'Macroeconomic Dimensions of the East Asian Crisis', *Financial Crises in Asia*, Centre for Economic Policy Research, Conference Report No. 6: 54–61.

Stiglitz, Joseph (1998b) 'More Instruments and Broader Goals: Moving Toward the Post-Washington Consensus', The 1998 WIDER Annual Lecture, Helsinki, 7 January.

Stiglitz, Joseph (1998c) Second WIDER Annual Lecture, United Nations University, Helsinki, January.

Stockwin, J.A. (ed.) (1988) *Dynamic and Immobilist Aspects of Japanese Politics*, London: Macmillan.

Stokes, B. (1998) 'A Conversation with Camdessus', *The National Journal* 30(7).

Stone J. (1997) 'Of Course Corrupt Asian Markets Will Crash', *Australian Financial Review* 30 October: 21.

Strange, Susan (1996) *The Retreat of the State: The Diffusion of Power in the World Economy*, Cambridge: Cambridge University Press.

Strange, Susan (1997) 'The Future of Global Capitalism; or Will Divergence Persist Forever?', in Colin Crouch and W. Streeck (eds), *Political Economy of Modern Capitalism*, London: Sage.

Streeck, W. (1997) 'German Capitalism: Does it Exist? Can it Survive?' *New Political Economy* 2(2): 237–56.

Stubbs, Richard (1994) 'The Asia Pacific', in R. Stubbs and G. Underhill (eds), *Political Economy and the International System: Global Issues, Regional Dynamics and Political Conflict*, London: Macmillan.

Subcommittee on Asian Financial and Capital Markets of MOF (1998) 'Lesson from the Asian Currency Crises: Risks Related to Short-Term Capital Movement and the "21st Century-Type" Currency Crisis', Tokyo.

Subramaniam Pillay (1998) 'Bailout Blues', *Aliran Monthly* 18(3): 2–5.

Subramaniam Pillay (1998a) 'The Asian Financial Crisis: The Malaysian Experience', Seminar presented at the International College, Penang, 8 July.

Suehiro Akira (1989) *Capital Accumulation in Thailand: 1855–1985*, Tokyo: The Centre for East Asian Cultural Studies.

Sunday Times (1997) 'Why One Park is Better than Two in Suzhou', 14 December: 18–19.

Swedberg, R. (1986) 'The Doctrine of Economic Neutrality of the IMF and the World Bank', *Journal of Peace Research* 23(4).

Sykes, T. (1994) *The Bold Riders: Behind Australia's Corporate Collapses*, Sydney: Allen and Unwin.

Tabb, W.K. (1995) *The Postwar Japanese System: Cultural Economy and Economic Transformation*, New York: Oxford University Press.

Tabb, William K. (1998) 'The East Asian Financial Crisis', *Monthly Review* 50(2): 24–38.

Tam, Pui-Wing (1997) 'Fund Flows to Asia Shrink', *Asian Wall Street Journal Weekly* 1 September: 18.

Tanaka, Naoto (1998) 'Aziadekitouchikarano Datugakuwa Kanouka' ['Escape from Asian Model of Governance'], *Ronsou Toyokeizai* [*Monthly Debate*], May.

Tang, Min and J. Villafuerte (1995) *Capital Flows to Asian and Pacific Developing Countries: Recent Trends and Future Prospects*, Manila: Asian Development Bank.

Thailand Development Research Institute (TDRI) (1995) *Thailand Economic Information Kit*, Bangkok: TDRI.

Thailand, Government of (1997) 'Letter of Intent' (to the IMF, addressed to M. Camdessus), 25 November (http://www.imf.org/external/loi/112597.htm).

Thailand, Government of (1998) 'Letter of Intent' (to the IMF, addressed to M. Camdessus), 24 February (http://www.imf.org/external/loi/022498.htm).

Thailand, Government of (1998a), 'Letter of Intent' (to the IMF, addressed to M. Camdessus), 26 May (http://www.imf.org/external/loi/052698.htm).

Thailand, Government of (1998b) 'Letter of Intent' (to the IMF, addressed to M. Camdessus), 25 August (http://www.imf.org/external/loi/082598.htm).

The Economist (1997) 'The Asian Crash: Beggars and Choosers', 6 December.

The Economist (1997a) 'Mahathir's Roasting', 27 September: 29.

The Economist (1997b) 'An Asian IMF?', 27 September: 84.

The Economist (1997c) 'Mahathir, Soros and the Currency Markets', 27 September: 93.

The Economist (1998) 'Tigers Adrift', 7 March: 5–22.

The Economist (1998a) 'Time to Turn Off the Tap?', 12 September: 91–3.

The Economist (1998b) 'Dead Ostrich Bounce', 12 September: 92.

The Economist (1998c) 'Frozen Miracle' (Supplement), 7 March.

Thomson, William R. (1998) 'The Asian Economic Crisis: Causes and Current Status', Paper presented to the conference on 'The Asian Crisis: Economic and Market Intelligence', University of Melbourne, 8 May.

Thurow, L.C. (1998) 'Asia: The Collapse and the Cure', *The New York Review of Books* 5 February: 22–6.

Tobin, J. and G. Ranis (1998) 'Flawed Fund: The IMF's Misplaced Priorities', *The New Republic* 218(10): 9 March.

Toohey, B. (1998) 'The Experts Divide over Asia', *Financial Review* 13–14 December.

Toohey, B. (1998a) 'Treasury, RBA Split on Indonesia', *Financial Review* 14–15 March.

Tremewan, Christopher (1994) *The Political Economy of Social Control in Singapore*, London: Macmillan.

Tripathi, Salil (1998) 'Savings at Risk', *Far Eastern Economic Review* 30 April: 60–1.

Tripathi, Salil and T. Saywell (1998) 'Out of Controls', *Far Eastern Economic Review* 17 September: 52.

Tsebelis, G. (1990) *Nested Games: Rational Choice in Comparative Politics*, Berkeley, CA: University of California Press.

Tun-jen, Cheng (1990) 'Political Regimes and Development Strategies: South Korea and Taiwan', in G. Gereffi and D. Wyman (eds), *Manufacturing Miracles: Paths of Industrialization in Latin America and East Asia*, pp. 139–78, Princeton, NJ: Princeton University Press.

Unger, Irwin (ed.) (1964) *Populism: Nostalgic or Progressive?*, Skokie, IL: Rand McNally.

United Nations Conference on Trade and Development (UNCTAD) (1998) 'UNCTAD Assesses Effects of Asia Crisis on Developing Countries' Trade', Press Release TAD/INF/2751, 8 May (http://www.unicc.org/unctad/en/press/pr2751en.htm).

US Embassy (1998) 'Thailand – Economic Trends and Forecast for 1998', Bangkok (http://usa.or.th/embassy/eco.htm).

Vasquez, I. (1998) 'The International Monetary Fund', Testimony, US Congress, House of Representatives, Committee on Banking and Financial Services, Sub-Committee on General Oversight and Investigations, 21 April (http://www.house.gov/banking/42198cat.htm).

Velloor, Ravi (1998) '$2b Boost for Economy', *The Straits Times* 30 June.

Vennewald, W. (1994) 'Technocrats in the State Enterprise System of Singapore', Working Paper No. 32, Asia Research Centre, Murdoch University.

Vivat Prateepchaikul (1997) 'Telecommunications. More Competition on Line', in Bangkok Post (eds) (http://www.bangkokpost.com/ecoreview97/review9717.html).

Vogel, Ezra F. (1991) *The Four Little Dragons: The Spread of Industrialization in East Asia*, Cambridge, MA: Harvard University Press.

Vogel, Steven K. (1996) *Freer Markets, More Rules: Regulatory Reform in Advanced Industrial Countries*, Ithaca, NY: Cornell University Press.

Wade, Robert (1990) *Governing the Market. Economic Theory and the Role of Government in East Asian Industrialization*, Princeton, NJ: Princeton University Press.

Wade, Robert and F. Veneroso (1998) 'The Asian Crisis: The High Debt Model Versus the Wall Street–Treasury–IMF Complex', *New Left Review* 228(1): 24; (3): 23.

Wade, Robert and F. Veneroso (1998a) 'The Asian Financial Crisis: The Unrecognised Risk of the IMF's Asia Package', Russell Sage Foundation, mimeo, pp. 1–4.

Wain, Barry (1998) 'Why Doesn't Mahathir Bow Out?', *Asian Wall Street Journal* 12–13 June.

Walder, Andrew (1992) 'Local Bargaining Relationships and Urban Industrial Finance', in Kenneth Lieberthal and David Lampton (eds), *Bureaucracy, Politics and Decision-Making in Post-Mao China*, Berkeley, CA: University of California Press.

Walder, Andrew (1994) 'Evolving Property Rights and their Political Consequences', in D. Goodman and B. Hooper (eds), *China's Quiet Revolution*, New York: St Martin's Press.

Wallerstein, I. (1974) *The Modern World-System: Capitalist Agriculture and the Origins of the European World-Economy in the Sixteenth Century*, New York: Academic Press.

Walsh, M. (1998) 'History Might Not Repeat, But Remember 1928', *The Age* 10 June.

Warr, Peter G. and Bhanuphong Nidhiprabha (1996) *Thailand's Macroeconomic Miracle. Stable Adjustment and Sustained Growth*, World Bank Comparative Macroeconomic Studies, Kuala Lumpur: Oxford University Press.

Weekly Toyo Keizai (1996) 'Jusen, the National Tragedy', 11 May.

Weekly Toyo Keizai (1996a) 'Okurashono Inbou' ['The MOF's Conspiracy'], 30 March.

Wei, Ho-Ching and C. Christodoulou (1998) 'The Changing Relationship Between the Taiwanese Government and Small and Medium-sized Enterprises', *Asian Studies Review* 22: 239–60.

Weiss, Linda (1997) 'Globalization and the Myth of the Powerless State', *New Left Review* 225: 3–27.

Weiss, Linda (1998) *The Myth of the Powerless State*, Cambridge and Ithaca, NY: Polity Press and Cornell University Press.

Weiss, Linda (1999) 'State Power and the Asian Crisis' *New Political Economy* November.

Weiss, Linda (1999a) 'The Transformation of Developmental States: Adapting, Unravelling, Recomposing, not "Normalizing" ', *Pacific Review* October.

Weiss, Linda and J.M. Hobson (1995) *States and Economic Development: A Comparative Historical Analysis*, Cambridge: Polity Press.

Wessel, D. and B. Davis (1998) 'Global Crisis Is a Match for Crack U.S. Economists', *Asian Wall Street Journal* 25–26 September.

Wessel, David (1998) 'Greenspan, Cabinet Aides Urge Congress to Approve IMF Funds', *Wall Street Journal* 2 February: 6.

Whitehead, Laurence (1993) 'Introduction: Some Insights from Western Social Theory', *World Development* 21(8): 1245–61.

Whitley, Richard (1992) *Business Systems in East Asia: Firms, Markets and Societies*, Newbury Park, CA: Sage.

Wilks, Stephen (1996) 'Regulatory Compliance and Capitalist Diversity in Europe', *Journal of European Public Policy* 3(4): 536–69.

Wilks, Stephen (1997) 'Conservative Governments and the Economy, 1979–97', *Political Studies* XLV: 689–703.

Williams, D. and T. Young (1994) 'Governance, the World Bank and Liberal Theory', *Political Studies* XLII: 84–100.

Williams, P. (1997) *The Victory: The Inside Story of the Takeover of Australia*, St Leonards: Allen and Unwin.

Williamson, J. (1994) 'In Search of a Manual for Technopols', in J. Williamson (ed.),*The Political Economy of Policy Reform*. pp. 11–28, Washington, DC: Institute for International Economics.

Williamson, Oliver (1996) *The Mechanisms of Governance*, New York: Oxford University Press.

Wing, Lim Kok *et al.* (1998) *Hidden Agenda*, Petaling Jaya: Limkokwing Integrated.

Winters, Jeffrey A. (1996) *Power in Motion: Capital Mobility and the Indonesian State*, Ithaca, NY: Cornell University Press.

Winters, Jeffrey A. (1997) 'The Dark Side of the Tigers', *Asian Wall Street Journal* 12–13 December: 10.

Winters, Jeffrey A. (1998) 'Indonesia: On the Mostly Negative Role of Transnational Capital in Democratization Investors', in L. E. Armijo (ed.), *Financial Globalization and Democracy in Emerging Markets*, New York: St Martin's Press.

Wolf, C. (1998) 'Blame Government for the Asian Meltdown', *Asian Wall Street Journal* 5 February: 14.

Wolf, Martin (1998) 'Global Capital Flows and Emerging Economies: Lessons from the Asian Crisis', Trilateral Commission Annual Meeting 21–23 March, Berlin (mimeo), pp. 1–10.

Wolferen, Karel Van (1990) *The Enigma of Japanese Power*, New York: Vintage Books.

Wolferen, Karel Van (1998) 'The Asian Financial Crisis and the Conceptual Muddle Surrounding it', Conference on 'Regionalism and Global Affairs in the Post Cold War Era: The European Union, APEC and the New International Political Economy', Brussels, 26–27 March.

Wong, Christine (1997) *Financing Local Government in the PRC*, Hong Kong: Oxford University Press.

Wong, John (1997) 'Will China Be the Next Financial Domino?', The East Asia Institute Background Brief No. 4, National University of Singapore.

Wong, S.L. (1985) 'The Chinese Family Firm: A Model', *British Journal of Sociology* 36: 58–72.

Woo, Jung-en (1991) (now Meredith Woo-Cumings) *Race to the Swift*, New York: Columbia University Press.

Woo-Cumings, Meredith (1998) 'Industrial Policy and Corporate Governance in East Asia', Asia Development Forum, 12 March, sponsored by the World Bank, Manila.

Wood, A. (1998) 'US Puts Asia at Crossroads', *The Australian* 20–21 June.

Woodall, B. (1996) *Japan under Construction: Corruption, Politics, and Public Works*, Los Angeles: University of California Press.

World Bank (1983) *World Development Report*, New York: Oxford University Press.

World Bank (1991) *Managing Development: The Governance Dimension*, Washington, DC: World Bank.

World Bank (1992) *Governance and Development*, Washington, DC: World Bank.

World Bank (1993) *The East Asian Miracle: Economic Growth and Public Policy*, Oxford: Oxford University Press.

World Bank (1994) *Governance: The World Bank's Experience*, Washington, DC: World Bank.

World Bank (1995) *Indonesia: Improving Efficiency and Equity – Changes in the Public Sector's Role*, Country Department III, East Asia and Pacific, World Bank, Washington, DC.

World Bank (1996) *Indonesia: Dimensions of Growth*, Country Department III, East Asia and Pacific, World Bank, Washington, DC.

World Bank (1997) *World Development Report 1997: The State in a Changing World*, New York: Oxford University Press.

World Bank (1997a) *Global Development Finance: Country Tables*, Washington, DC: World Bank.

World Bank (1997b) *Indonesia: Sustaining High Growth and Equity*, Country Department III, East Asia and Pacific, World Bank, Washington, DC.

World Bank (1998) *Indonesia in Crisis: A Macroeconomic Update*, Washington, DC: World Bank.

WuDunn, S. and N.D. Kristoff (1997) 'Japan, Economic Power Aside, Seems Paralyzed by Asia Crisis', *New York Times* 17 December.

Xing, Junfang (1997) *Zhongguo ershiyi shiji jingji zhouxiang* [*China's Economic Trends in the 21st Century: Interviews with Leading Cadres at the Provincial-Ministerial Level*], Beijing: Zhongyang dangxiao chubanshe.

Yamaguchi, Jirou (1995) 'Gendai Nipponno Seikankankei' ['Politics–Bureaucracy Relations in Modern Japan'], *Japanese Political Science Review*, Tokyo: Iwanamishoten.

Yeoh, O. (1998) 'APEC Ministers Fail to Reach Deal on Trade Liberalization', *The Nikkei Weekly* 29 June.

Yoshihara, Kunio (1988) *The Rise of Ersatz Capitalism in South-east Asia*, Singapore: Oxford University Press.

Yoshihiro Fujii (1997) 'Can "Mutual Trust" Work? It's Unclear So Far', *The Nikkei Weekly* 8 December.

Yoshiko Kojo (1992) 'Burden-sharing Under U.S. Leadership: The Case of Quota Increases of the IMF Since the 1970s', in H. Bienen (ed.), *Power, Economics and Security*, Boulder, CO: Westview Press.

Zhao Yining and Han Binjie (1997) 'The Warning Siren of High Debt Ratios of State-Owned Enterprises', *Liaowang* 9: 26–7.

Zuckerman, M. (1998) 'A Second American Century', *Foreign Affairs* 77(3): 18–31.

Zysman, J. (1983) *Governments, Markets, and Growth: Financial Systems and the Politics of Industrial Change*, Ithaca, NY: Cornell University Press.

Zysman, J. (1994) 'How Institutions Create Historically Rooted Trajectories of Growth', *Industrial and Corporate Change* 3 (1): 243–83.

INDEX

Where the page number is followed by a 't' or an 'f' these locations indicate a table or figure respectively. Items in the end notes are only indexed when there is substantial discussion on the subject. In this case the page number is followed by the relevant note number, e.g. 51n9 refers to note 9 on page 51.

Abeng, Tanri 182
Act on Merchant Banks (South Korea) 122
adjustment 267
aggregate demand, China 141–2
agriculture, and populism in Thailand 209
Ahmad, Datuk 46
Ahmad Don 234
Albright, Madeleine 48
alliance capitalism, Japan 99
Amin, Samir 212, 231
Amsden, Alice H.: managed markets 21
Anderson, Benedict 159, 230
Anwar Ibrahim 225, 233–5
Apkindo 180
Aquino, Corazon 240
Armey, Dick 292, 294
ASEAN 270–1
Asean Free Trade Area (AFTA) 245
Asia–Europe Meeting Process (ASEM) 271
Asia–Pacific Economic Cooperation (APEC) 36, 270, 279, 281; and Australia 305–7, 308
Asian Development Bank: Indonesia 181; Thailand 207

Asian Monetary Fund (AMF) 289, 290, 291; role of USA 268–73
Asri, Chandra 178
austerity measures, Malaysia 225–6, 228
Australia: and APEC 305–7, 308; current account deficit 303; effect of Asian crisis 297–312; exports 302–4; GDP 303, 304; impact of international integration 13; liberalization 312
authoritarian liberalism, and governance 315–30

Baker, C. 198
Bambang Trihatmodjo 46–7
Bangko Sentral ng Philpinas (BSP) 246, 249
Bangkok Bank of Commerce (BBC) 202, 203
Bangkok International Banking Facility 28
Bank Andromeda 179–80
Bank Central Asia 185
Bank Dagang Nasional Indonesia 187
Bank of International Settlements, Thailand crisis 193–4
Bank of Japan 85, 93
Bank of Korea (BOK) 87, 91, 327–8
Bank Negara 224, 226, 231–2, 233–4
Bank of Thailand (BoT) 207; attempt to protect Baht 201, 202
Bank Umum Nasional 187
bank-mediated credit 6
bankruptcies: Japan 80, 102; South Korea 83, 102; Thailand 202–5
banks 52n10; accumulation of loans 45; China 143–4, 145f; Indonesia 28, 71,

363